FAMILY, KINSHIP AND MARRIAGE AMONG MUSLIMS IN INDIA

CONTRIBUTORS TO

FAMILY, KINSHIP AND MARRIAGE AMONG MUSLIMS IN INDIA

Partap C. Aggarwal, *Shri Ram Centre for Industrial Relations and Human Resources, New Delhi, India.*

Imtiaz Ahmad, *Jawaharlal Nehru University, New Delhi, India.*

A.N.M. Irshad Ali, *Panjab University, Chandigarh, India.*

George H. Conklin, *Sweet Briar College, Sweet Briar, USA.*

Victor S. D'Souza, *Panjab University, Chandigarh, India.*

Doranne Jacobson, *Columbia University, New York, USA.*

R.P. Khatana, *Government College, Gurgaon, India.*

Mattison Mines, *University of California, Santa Barbara, USA.*

Ismail A. Lambat, *Batley Community Project, Batley, UK.*

S.M. Akram Rizvi, *University of Delhi, Delhi, India.*

A.R. Saiyed, *Jamia Milia Islamia, New Delhi, India.*

Theodore P. Wright, Jr., *State University of New York, Albany, USA.*

Family, Kinship and Marriage among Muslims in India

Edited by
IMTIAZ AHMAD

MANOHAR
2026

First published 1976
Reprinted 1985
First paperback edition 2020
Reprinted 2026

ISBN 978-93-88540-76-6

Published by
Ajay Kumar Jain *for*
Manohar Publishers & Distributors
4753/23 Ansari Road, Daryaganj
New Delhi 110 002

Printed and bound in India

For Zuni

Contents

Preface

In 1973 I edited a collection of papers entitled *Caste and Social Stratification among the Muslims*. The object of that book was to bring together the contributions of social anthropologists and sociologists who had worked on caste and social stratification among Muslims in different parts of the country. The reception accorded to that book showed that it fulfilled an existing need for detailed and systematic accounts of Muslim communities in the country. Encouraged by the success of that book, I decided to follow up with a series of similar volumes dealing with other aspects of social life of the Muslims. This book is the second of this projected series of four volumes on the social life of the Muslims in India and deals with the institutions of family, kinship and marriage. The remaining two volumes will be devoted to a consideration of ritual and religion and modernization and social change among the Muslims.

My chief justification for undertaking to edit *Caste and Social Stratification among the Muslims* was that little empirical information was available on the subject and I felt that by bringing together a collection of studies by scholars who had researched into the matter in particular communities it would be possible to fill a gap in our existing sociological knowledge about the Muslims. The same thinking has led me to produce this volume. For, if the information on the structure and functioning of caste among the Muslims is scanty and inadequate, there is absolutely no empirical information at all on family, kinship and marriage among them. I hope that this volume will also fill a gap in our knowledge about the Muslims and will contribute towards a better understanding of their social institutions.

There are probably several reasons why sociologists and social anthropologists were not particularly interested in studying family, kinship and marriage among the Muslims. The first and most obvious reason seems to be that the study of kinship and marriage, though long recognized to be fields of special interest among sociologists and social anthropologists elsewhere in the world, has been a relatively neglected area of research in India. It is only recently that there has been some renewal of interest in this field. Secondly, the family, kinship and marriage systems of the Muslims do not present any dimensions that may be regarded as curious and, therefore, as worthy of detailed scrutiny. For example, unlike caste among the Muslims, which is directly antithetical to the institutionalized egalitarian ethos of the Islamic faith, there are no such apparent contradictions between kinship and marriage among the Muslims that can be said to call for special investigation. Lastly, the study of family, kinship and marriage is a comparatively more complex subject, and it is likely that students of Muslim social institutions have been reluctant to deal with the complexities of this aspect of social life of Muslims.

One of the consequences of this absence of scholarly interest in the empirical study of family, kinship and marriage among the Muslims has been that the structure of Muslim kinship and marriage has traditionally been analysed within the framework ordained by the Koran, and the scriptural picture of these social institutions has commonly been taken to be essentially valid even today. Islam does explicitly postulate certain specific prescriptions about the structure of family life, kinship and marriage, and it is possible that the prescribed religious rules serve as fundamental determinants for the structure and functioning of these institutions. However, the essence of Muslim family, kinship and marriage would seem to lie not so much in the presence of a prescribed body of religious norms governing them as in the peculiar social conditions within which these absolute Islamic tenents are translated into practice. It is this apparent diversity of social conditions and the impact they have had on the working of these institutions that the essays in this volume actually seek to explore.

The procedure followed in bringing together this collection of essays is the same as the one pursued for *Caste and Social*

Stratification among the Muslims. We approached all those scholars who had carried out research on the subject and requested them to report their data on family, kinship and marriage among the group or groups they had studied empirically. The contributors were not given any specific theoretical framework nor were they asked to cast their data into any uniform pattern. Each contributor was requested to exercise complete freedom in delimiting the scope of his or her contribution and to deal with that aspect on which he or she had data. We believe that the merit of these contributions lies as much in their particular orientations and theoretical styles as in their focus upon a common theme.

The essays included in this volume are presented essentially as separate and individual contributions. Ten of these contributions were written specifically for this volume and are being published for the first time. Professor D'Souza's paper was originally published in *The Anthropos* and is being reprinted here. I am grateful to Professor D'Souza and the editors of the *The Anthropos* for allowing me to reproduce the paper here. Partap C. Aggarwal's paper was originally published in *Caste and Social Stratification among the Muslims*. On account of its contents and its thematic unity with the other contributions it has been decided to include it in this collection. It will consequently be dropped from the revised edition of *Caste and Social Stratification among the Muslims* now under preparation.

Like its predecessor, this volume too owes its existence largely to the willing cooperation of the contributors and to their belief that their collective efforts will be ultimately worthwhile. It is true that the unpleasant task of sending out reminders fell on me and my repeated insistence upon their submitting their essays might have at times proved annoying, but they were throughout helpful and obliging. I am, therefore, grateful to all of them for their willing acceptance of the invitation to contribute a paper to this volume as well as for the cooperation and help they extended to me from time to time. I am alone to blame for the deficiencies that may still remain.

Jawaharlal Nehru University
New Delhi

Imtiaz Ahmad

The Contributors

PARTAP C. AGGARWAL received his training in anthropology at Cornell University where he obtained his Ph.D. in 1966. He taught for four years at Colgate University at Hamilton, New York, and is currently Head of the Sociology Division at the Shri Ram Centre for Industrial Relations and Human Resources, New Delhi. His major research interest has been in the areas of social and cultural change, social stratification, economic development and applied social science. He has contributed several papers to anthropological journals and is also the author of *Caste, Religion and Power* and *Landless Labour and Green Revolution.* He is currently engaged in the study of the impact of the special privileges granted to the Scheduled Castes under the Indian Constitution in Haryana and plans to do research on management sub-culture in India in the near future, Dr. Aggarwal will be a visiting Professor at Colgate University during 1975-76.

IMTIAZ AHMAD received his training in anthropology and sociology at the Universities of Lucknow and Delhi respectively. He was a Fulbright Fellow at the Department of Anthropology, University of Chicago, during 1967-68 and was Assistant Professor in Social Anthropology at the University of Missouri, Columbia, during 1968-70. He was a Fellow of the Indian Council of Social Science Research during 1970-72 and is currently Associate Professor in Sociology at the Centre for Political Studies of the Jawaharlal Nehru University, New Delhi. He has published articles in academic journals and symposia volumes and has edited *Caste and Social Stratification among the Muslims.* His book, *Muslim Political Behaviour*, is due for publication shortly.

A.N.M. IRSHAD ALI received his training in anthropology at the University of Gauhati where he obtained his Ph. D in

1974. He worked earlier as a Senior Research Investigator in the Agro-Economic Research Centre at Jorhat, Assam, and is currently a Lecturer in Social Anthropology at Panjab University, Chandigarh. Dr. Ali has contributed several papers to academic journals and also writes popular articles in Assamese. His research interests are focussed on the nature and content of Muslim social life and institutions in Assam.

GEORGE H. CONKLIN received his training in sociology at Colgate University and the University of Pennsylvania where he earned his Ph. D in 1971. He was Assistant Professor in Sociology at Syracuse University from 1969 to 1974, and is currently Associate Professor in Anthropology and Sociology at Sweet Briar College, Sweet Briar, USA. Dr. Conklin carried out research in India as a Fulbright Grantee in 1963-64 and as a Fellow of the American Institute of Indian Studies in 1968-69. Dr. Conklin has contributed over a dozen academic papers to international sociological journals and conferences. His research interests are centered on the ways in which the family adopts to urbanization and in turn influences the path of urbanization.

VICTOR S. D'SOUZA received his early training in sociology under Professor G. S. Ghurye at the Department of Sociology, University of Bombay, and is currently Professor of Sociology at the Panjab University, Chandigarh. Professor D'Souza has done research among the Moplah Muslims on the South-West Coast of India and on the relationship between caste and occupation in the Punjab. Professor D'Souza has published articles in several leading anthropological journals.

DORANNE JACOBSON received her traing in anthropology at Columbia University where she is currently Assistant Professor in Anthropology. She has carried out extensive fieldwork in the Bhopal region of Madhya Pradesh and has contributed a number of articles to academic journals and symposia volumes. Her main research interests are women, *purdah* and family life.

R.P. KHATANA is Lecturer in Geography at the Government College, Gurgaon, Haryana. He is simultaneously engaged in doctoral research at the Centre for the Study of

Regional Development of the Jawaharlal Nehru University, New Delhi. His research interest is centred on the socio-economic aspects of transhumance. He is the author of *Gujar, Gujari and Gujardesh* (in Urdu).

ISMAIL A. LAMBAT received his training in Sociology at the Department of Sociology, University of Bombay, and at the Institute of Social Sciences, The Hague. He currently works for the Batley Community Project at Batley, Yorkshire, UK. He has carried out extensive fieldwork among the Sunni Surati Vohras of South Gujrat and contributed several papers to academic journals and symposia volumes. His research interests include social customs and behaviour and modernization and social change among the Muslims of Gujarat.

MATTISON MINES received his training in anthropology at Cornell University where he obtained his Ph.D. in 1969. He carried out intensive fieldwork among the Tamil Muslim merchants in a commercial township of Tamilnadu during 1967-69, when he held a Foreign Area Research Fellowship of the Department of State, Government of the United States. Dr. Mines has contributed papers to several leading anthropological journals and is the author of *The Muslim Merchants of Pallavaram, Tamilnadu.* He is currently working on religious change among the Tamil Muslims. Dr. Mines' research interests include social stratification, social and religious change and economic development.

S.M. AKRAM RIZVI is a Research Scholar in Sociology at the Delhi School of Economics, University of Delhi, where he obtained his M.Phil. in 1974. His research interests are social stratification, family and kinship and the impact of urbanization and industrialization on social life. Mr. Rizvi is presently engaged in a larger study of family and industrialization among the Multani Lohars of urban Delhi.

A. R. SAIYED received his training in Sociology at the Department of Sociology, University of Bombay, and at the University of Kentucky, where he took his Ph.D. in 1967. He was Lecturer in Sociology and Social Work at the Jamia School of Social Work during 1959-1965, and Assistant Professor in Sociology at Long Island University during 1968-1970. He is currently Reader in Sociology at the Jamia Milia

Islamia, New Delhi. Dr. Saiyed has contributed papers to several leading academic journals and symposia volumes. He is currently preparing a volume based on research among the Maharashtrian Muslims for publication.

THEODORE P. WRIGHT, Jr. took his Ph. D. in international relations from Yale University in 1957, but teaches comparative politics with emphasis on South Asia. He is currently Professor of Political Science at the State University of New York at Albany. For the past fourteen years, Professor Wright has focussed his research on the politics of the Muslim minority in India since Independence. He has spent two periods of field research in India, primarily in Hyderabad and Bombay, which were made possible by grants from the Fulbright Foundation and the American Institute of Indian Studies. Professor Wright has contributed a number of articles to international academic journals and symposia volumes.

Introduction

Imtiaz Ahmad

'The theory of Islam', writes Levy, '. . . regards the empire of Islam as a theocracy, in which Allah as supreme ruler is also the only true law-giver. Muhammed the prophet was the agent through whom believers were made aware of the divine laws which were explicitly or implicitly embodied in the Koran and his (the Prophet's) *sunna*, the sum total of his ordinary doings and sayings. Upon them in turn the *shar* or *shari'a* is, by hypothesis, founded' (Levy, 1962:242). Muslims throughout the Islamic world accept the *shari'a* to be the guiding principle of their religious and social life and seek to abide by it.

There is a widespread impression that Muslims in India adhere strictly to the basic tenets of Islam as embodied in the *shari'a*. This impression has, indeed, been so widespread that even sociologists and social anthropologists, who are committed to the empirical investigation of social life, have been prone to accept it. Either they have tended to disregard the possibility of a chasm dividing the stated ideals of Islam and social practices altogether or they ignore the deviations from the stated norms, wherever they occur, and accept the normative position as a sufficiently valid basis for describing the religious beliefs as well as the social institutions and behaviour patterns of the community. The recent remarks of a sociologist illustrate this tendency. 'The Shari'at Law derived from the Koran, *sunna* and *ijma*', she writes, 'still controls most aspects of Muslim marriage, divorce and inheritance *in India* (Davis, 1976:28 italics added). Subsequently, comparing the status of Hindu and Muslim women in India, she concedes that it would be misleading to use the law as an index of difference between Hindu and Muslim behaviour, but goes on to assert, '. . . provided this caveat is respected the difference in personal law is a valid illustration of the different position of women in the two communities' (Davis, 1976:30fn).

Perhaps, sociological research focussing specifically on Muslim communities in different parts of the country would have provided a corrective to the tendency to describe Muslim social institutions in terms of stated Islamic ideals or to accept the ideal position as a statement of fact without bothering to look at the empirical reality. But while a considerable body of empirical research by sociologists and social anthropologists has appeared on social institutions in India during the last two decades,[1] both the quantum and range of sociological information on Muslims in India continue to remain scanty.[2] It is, indeed, so scanty that writers of entirely opposed persuasions have found it possible to argue their conflicting positions without much difficulty. Furthermore, the relative paucity of dependable sociological data about the social institutions, religious beliefs and attitudes and values of Muslims has allowed a wide variety of popular stereotypes about them to persist and to be argued out.

The current debate on the reform of Muslim personal law provides an excellent example of how the general paucity of factual data on Muslim social institutions and behaviour has allowed conflicting opinions or points of view to be argued out with equal fervour and zeal and for a stereotyped conception of Muslims in India as a whole to persist. Opinions on the question have ranged from total opposition to reforms to its complete overhaul or abrogation. Unfortunately, this debate has become so highly emotional and politicised that an academic discussion on it is ruled out for the present. However, it is quite clear from a general perusal of the debate that the

1. For a detailed critical survey of the literature an family, kinship and marriage in India, see Dube (1976).
2. The three detailed studies dealing with kinship and marriage among Muslims (see Dube, 1969; Kutty, 1972; and Ittman, 1976) are concerned with the Moplahs of Lakshdweep who differ from the large majority of Muslims in India in respect both of their social organisations and religious persuasion. Unlike the large majority of Muslims in the country, who follow the system of patrilineal descent and subscribe to the Hanafiite religious persuasion, the Moplah Muslims follow the system of matrilineal descent and are Shafiites.

antagonists as well as the protagonists of reform have based their arguments on false premises. They have asserted their arguments on the assumption that the law conforms rigidly to actual social practices and neglected to see the discrepancies that exist between the legal-formal principles and social practices. Neither side has tried to examine the question of how far the written Islamic laws are observed, which, if they are not practised widely, would seem to make the debate over the introduction of reform redundant and futile.

The protagonists of reform have tended to justify their position on the ground that Muslim personal law in its present form is iniquitous. Thus a sociologist states:

> A Muslim man can have up to four wives at a time, with no legal protection to the woman against the exercise of the privilege. The law does not admit polygamy as a cause for seeking divorce by a Muslim woman. Of course, the corresponding right of a woman to have more than one husband in any circumstances is inconceivable, much less granted under law. . . . A man can divorce at will just by uttering the word 'I divorce you' three times, anywhere, any time without any witnesses. He is also not required by law to give any maintenance to the wife beyond the period of iddat, which is three months and a few days. If a man divorces his wife, he is obliged to pay *mahr*, a sum of money agreed upon at the time of marriage. This provision is also taken as a security for Muslim women against easy divorce. But as long as the right to have four wives continues to be enjoyed by a man, he need not divorce his wife; if he does not wish to pay *mahr*, he can simply discard her or ill-treat her, while still taking another wife . . . So at every stage Muslim law is fettered with inequalities, with the woman in every case being less equal (Bhatty, 1976:102-104).

She concludes, therefore, that the question of equality of rights in personal law should be given immediate expression through suitable legal enactment (Bhatty, 1976:112). She shows little awareness of the possibility that the dismal picture she draws of Muslim women may not conform to existing reality and the iniquities she draws attention to may not be so severe in practice.

Clearly, those who argue along the lines implied in the statement just cited base their formulations on a rather unimaginative reading of the formal legal code without any awareness, which we expect from sociologists and social anthropologists, of the existing social realities. But if we disregard the political dimensions of the question of reform (and the debate on the question is largely political, as we have noted earlier), the sociological question still worth asking would be whether the dismal picture normally painted of Muslim women conforms to existing social realities and whether the iniquities are indeed so severe in practice. Or, if the iniquities are indeed as severe as described, can they be explained entirely in terms of the legal codes or even the religious ethos? Are they not a part of a wider socio-cultural complex which makes not only the position of Muslim women but of women in India generally somewhat iniqutous?

If the iniquities characterising Muslim women are a direct expression of their religious laws, then their would exist no possibility of any change in their position unless the code itself is changed. Yet, there is evidence to suggest that changes in this sphere have been occurring and are occurring. Surprisingly, Bhatty herself concedes, in sharp contrast to her characterisation of Muslims as a changeless and static community, that the 'broad crust of static attitudes dominating the Muslim society has cracked . . . and stirrings of progress are clearly visible *in response to certain general social forces*' (Bhatty, 1976:111; italics added). 'What is true beyond doubt', she concludes, 'is that once exposed to modern education, Muslim women not only change themselves, but become ardent advocates of change' (Bhatty, 1976:112). Surely, if this is indeed the case, it would be erroneous for anyone to assume that the *shari'a* has shaped the social life of Muslims in India or that the formal religious code to which the members of the community claim to adhere offers a representative picture of reality. It suggests, on the contrary, that Muslims in India display an enormous variety in their social organisation, religious beliefs and attitudes and values, and that sociological enquiries should be directed towards exploring this bewildering variety as well as to assessing the relative influence of the religious code and the wider socio-cultural complexes upon their social institutions and behaviour.

This collection of papers on family, kinship and marriage among Muslims in India was undertaken with a view to bringing together a body of empirical data on the actual patterns of these institutions among different Muslim communities in different parts of India and to exploring the relative impact of the *shari'a* and the local environment upon their structure and functioning. Each paper presented here is based on data collected by the authors themselves through direct personal observations. Further, each contribution seeks to describe those social institutions as they function in reality rather than on the basis of the written laws of Islam. Some authors no doubt refer during the course of their discussions to Islamic ideals and try to examine the correspondence between religious principles and social practices. For example, Saiyed treats the absence of *purdah* among the Jamaati women against an ideal—the type of *purdah* as, he thinks, it is practised among Muslims in other parts of the country. Again, Jacobson refers repeatedly to the provisions of the Shari'at, and finally offers an explanation for the observance of *purdah* among the women of the Bhopal region in terms of the Islamic rules of inheritance. Even so, Islamic laws as embodied in the Shari'at are not their principal concern. Their primary concern is to provide factual accounts of kinship and marriage among the Muslim communities studied by them.

The papers presented here range from simple ethnographic descriptions to detailed analytical discussions. Furthermore, they cover a wide range of themes, especially because each contributor has written about a theme on which he or she had data or thought was worth discussing. Therefore, the picture which emerges from these papers on family, kinship and marriage among Muslims in India is too varied and diffused to allow brief summarisation. Even so, the data provided by them suggests some tentative formulations, and in this Introduction I shall try to set them out briefly.

One anticipation arising from the general belief that the Muslim family ethos is a product of Shari'at laws would be that Muslim family and kinship norms should differ strikingly from those of other religious communities. The evidence presented in these contributions does not appear to bear out this anticipation. On the contrary, it shows that Muslim family norms in India correspond closely to those held among Hindus. Thus, Rizvi, Ahmad and Conklin explicitly state that the norms favouring joint family living—a feature so characteristic of the Hindus on account of the support provided for it in Hindu scriptural literature—are equally widely held among Muslims. The feeling for the norm is indeed so strong that, as Rizvi notes, even while several Karkhanedar families live severally in a common house, each family unit owning its own hearth and keeping its purse separately, their members continue to convey an impression of great solidarity among the different persons living in the same building (p. 32). Even Ali, who presents detailed statistics on kinship composition of households in three different social settings which show that people live preponderantly in nuclear families, concedes that the people consider the joint family arrangement to be an ideal one. It is another matter that those living in joint households are 'almost uniformly of the opinion that each nuclear family should have an independent household' (p. 11). Such disaffection arising from having to submit to the authority of a single household head is quite common among those living in joint families and has been noted by several observers.

Norms are a poor guide to social practice. People may say that they subscribe to the norm of joint living, but when they are old enough to give practical shape to their volitions they may still prefer to stay in nuclear households. The evidence presented in these contributions is unmistakingly clear that, while the large majority of the Muslims live in simple or nuclear households, the incidence of joint families among them either compares with the average incidence for the country as a whole or, in fact, shows a higher tendency. Conklin summarises the situation in this respect precisely: 'In terms of joint households, ideals of joint living, and in having sons actually stay home until the death of the father, the Muslims seem to be, in fact as well as in theory, identical to or more conservative than the non-Muslims . . .' (p. 133).

The similarity between Muslims and non-Muslims is not restricted to the incidence of joint households or to the tendency of having sons stay at home until the death of the father. It extends to patterns of family interaction among the different members of the household and to the family power structure. Thus, Rizvi and Ali equally underscore the dominant position of the household head within the family as well as the respect shown by other members of the household towards him; and Conklin highlights the tendency of households to de-emphasise the conjugal role pattern within Muslim households, resulting in a strong emphasis on the mother-son tie. Even here, Conklin concludes, 'Muslims are not statistically different from Hindus . . .' (p. 135).

Family norms and role expectations do not exist in isolation but represent a response to certain existential conditions and both Khatana and Saiyed draw attention to them. Khatana suggests that, while large households are not entirely unknown among the Gujar Bakarwals studied by him, the prevalent norms favour separation of a son from the household of his father immediately or very soon after his marriage. He attributes this to the conditions imposed upon the Gujar Bakarwals by their peculiar mode of existence and the severities of their habitat. Saiyed, on the other hand, attributes the operation of the conjugal role pattern to the truncated character of the Jamaati households and to the fact that the large majority of the Jamaati men stay away from home for long periods. Rizvi too focuses attention on the same theme when he shows that the ownership of karkhanas by most Karkhanedar households has eroded both the internal authority structure as well as the pattern of interaction among household members.

The family is the smallest and most basic sociological unit based on descent and filiation. Extending outward from this basic unit, people operate in a number of larger kin groupings which too have descent and affinity as their constituent bases. The extent of elaborateness and longitudinal depth of these groupings varies widely from society to society. Thus, kinship relations in western societies are largely closest within the family but tend to become diffuse and attenuated beyond. On the contrary, the web of extra-familial kinship groupings in African and Asian societies remains elaborate. Among Hindus, the web of extra-familial groupings tends to be quite elaborate, and the same pattern replicates itself among Muslims.

Not all papers included here focus on the web of extra-familial kinship groupings, but those of them that do reveal a picture of striking similarity to the Hindu pattern. Ali discerns three groupings—*chauba*, a patrilineal kin grouping functioning more or less as a sub-lineage, *bangsha*, a lineage, and *khel*, a grouping of descendants tracing descent from a common ancestor—as the principal kin groupings among the Assamese Muslims and suggests that in their structure they are quite similar to the same groupings among Hindus. D'Souza refers to *tharavads* and *kulams* as the principal extra-familial kin groups among the Moplahs, and Khatana notes the presence of the *dada potre* as an important extra-familial kin grouping among the Gujar Bakarwals. Likewise, Aggarwal and Mines describe an elaborate and ramifying structure of extended kinship groups which resemble those found among the general population in the areas they have studied. These wider kinship groupings are not a motley accretions of kin but perform critical functions in ordering property relations, distribution of inheritance and regulating marriage regulations as they do among other religious communities, particularly Hindus, in India.

Of course, the similarities in the structure and function of these groupings is not the same among Hindus and Muslims, nor do they enjoy equal significance among both. Khatana notes that though the *gotra* is recognised as an extra-familial kin grouping among the Gujar Bakarwals it does not any more fulfill its function of regulating marriage as it does among Hindus. Again, Mines shows that most Tamil Muslims, as indeed Tamil Hindus, recognise *pangali* to be an important kin grouping, but its significance is greatly modified among the former. 'Among Muslims the unit has no ritual significance and death pollution is not theoretically recognized' (p. 304). These differences serve to underscore religious differences, but the presence of identical social groupings equally highlights the fact that, in terms of the structure of family and kinship groupings, the Muslims in India are not necessarily distinguishable from their non-Muslim neighbours. They seem to be a part of a wider cultural complex shared equally by all those who reside in the region as a whole.

The imprint of the regional cultural environment on Muslim kinship and marriage patterns is not restricted to family norms and role relationships alone. It extends to marriage customs and practices as well as to the distribution of inheritance. The contributors to this volume concur that the *nikah* ceremony, prescribed by Islam for sealing a marital union between two persons, is uniformly observed by Muslim groups studied by them. However, several contributors note that this ceremony occurs side by side with a series of other social ceremonies which serve to underscore its social and religious significance. Lambat provides an elaborate description of these ceremonies among the Sunni Surati Vohras, but others too note that the ceremonies centring around the *nikah* are elaborate and are often viewed as of greater singificance than the *nikah* itself in sealing a marital union. For instance, D'Souza points out that *kalyanam* is by far a more important ceremony than the *nikah* for sealing a marital union among the Moplahs studied by him. 'Although the central and most important ceremony of a Muslim marriage is the ceremony of marriage contract called *nikah*, for Moplahs', writes D'Souza, 'this ceremony is not sufficient to enable the bridal couple to live as man and wife. The consummation of marriage can take place only after holding another function. This latter function is called *kalyanam* . . .' (p. 157). The Moplah word for marriage is used for the *kalyanam* rather than the *nikah*.

Furthermore, there is evidence in these contributions to suggest that the customs and rituals observed by Muslim communities at the time of marriage are adaptations of the customs and rituals observed generally within the region. Thus, Ali notes that the customs of presentation *(joran)*, of singing of songs by women (*bainam*) and of the ritual purificatory baths given to the bride and the groom (*noani*) are easily comparable to similar customs observed by the Hindus of that area. Lambat notes a similar pattern among the Sunni Surati Vohras of South Gujarat. He admits that while fundamentalist opinion disapproves of the continued observance of typically Hindu customs and ritual observances, they continue to prevail among the Sunni Surati Vohras despite these objections.

The practice of preferential cousin marriages has been recorded as a characteristic feature of Muslims, though Hindu groups too are found to practice certain forms of preferential cousin marriages in some parts of the country. The evidence presented in these papers does not support the contention that preferential cousin marriage is either practised universally among Muslim communities in India or that this preference is always adhered to while arranging marriages. Khatana observes that, though different types of cousin marriages do occasionally occur among the Gujar Bakarwals and are accorded the status of legitimate unions, they are generally disapproved of socially. Others too note that the endogamous unit traditionally tends to be so large as to rule out the possibility of such marriages. On the other hand, Aggarwal finds that the Meos are clearly opposed to such marriages, which they consider incestous, and attempts by fundamentalist groups to encourage such unions on the ground that they are sanctified by religion have so far proved abortive.

Like preferential cousin marriages, the practices of polygamy and divorce too are closely associated with Muslims in India, though, again both of them are fairly widespread among other religious communities. The practice of polygamy, in particular, is so strongly associated with Muslims that its continued provision in legal codes has tended to send some writers into an uproar (see, for example, Ahmadullah, 1969; Dalwai, 1970; Davis, 1976; and Bhatty, 1976). There is no doubt that the Shari'at law permits polygamy, subject to certain provisions, and as a vestigial survival of a feudal order cases of polygamous unions are often found among Muslims, as well as non-Muslims, in India. However, the evidence presented in these contributions does not lend much support to the suggestion often made that this practice is either widespread among Muslims or that its provision makes the Muslim woman absolutely defenceless against the possibility of her husband taking on a second or a third wife. Even though the sanction offered for polygamy would seem to make her position weak in theory, the Muslim woman is not entirely defenceless in practice. Lambat's observation regarding poligamous marriages bears this out. 'Usually, as soon as a man takes a second wife, or even contemplates a second marriage, his first wife will ask for a divorce' (p. 54).

Islam does not grant a woman the right to divorce her husband. She can secure a divorce only if she can persuade her husband to agree to a divorce. 'Clearly', writes Bhatty, 'the law aims at making it as easy as possible for men to give divorce and as difficult as possible for women to secure it' (1976:102). While the law is clearly iniquitous in this respect the situation is not altogether as dismal in practice as it appears to be in theory. First, the evidence provided by the contributions in this book indicates that divorce is disapproved socially among most groups and results in the loss of social prestige not only for the parties involved but for their families as well and is consequently an occurrence of considerable rarity. Second, social practice admits certain organisational channels whereby a woman can force a divorce upon her husband. Thus, Khatana observes that 'elopement is often resorted to by Gujar Bakarwal women to force a divorce so that they can be free to marry someone else' (p. 102). Thus, while Islamic law clearly makes a woman's position weak in respect of both polygamy and divorce, social practice in both these respects varies and differs widely from the provisions of the law.

Closely bound up with the questions of marriage and divorce is the question of inheritance. The Shari'at law allows women the right of inheritance, though their right is not equal to men, and detailed instructions are given in the Koran for the disposal of the property of a person dying intestate. 'God instructs you', the Koran says, 'concerning your children: for a male the like of the portion of the two females, and if there be women (i.e., daughters) above two, then let them have two-thirds of what (the deceased) leaves. If there be one, then let her have a half' (Koran, v, 12; quoted in Levy, 1962:97).

Opinions differ as to the fairness of the Koranic prescriptions regarding the distribution of inheritance. Some writers have tended to view the Koranic prescriptions as a marked improvement over those prevailing in other religious communities, which deny women the right of inheritance altogether. Others, particularly those who are committed to an ideology of absolute equality of sexes in all respects, have been prone to dismiss the Koranic prescriptions as largely iniquitous, rendering women inferior to men in respect of inheritance rights. These opinions are based on entirely different value premises and, hence, cannot be reconciled. But a point which requires discussion from the sociological perspective is the extent to which the Koranic rules of inheritance are actually observed in reality. This question is often ignored completely in discussions on Muslims, and the two opinions cited above themselves clearly rest on the assumption that there is total correspondence between Koranic injunctions and social practice in this regard.

Among the contributors to this volume, Jacobson alone suggests that the Koranic rules of inheritance are observed by Muslims. 'The Muslims of Nimkhera, particularly the Pathans', she writes, 'attempt to follow Islamic rules of inheritance. Both daughters and widows inherit shares of wealth, including land and houses, from their parents and husbands. Some women receive their property shares from their parents at the time of marriage' (p. 186). Still, the fact that she qualifies her statement by adding 'particularly the Pathans' suggests that the Koranic rules of inheritance are not observed universally. Perhaps, among other groups in Nimkhera the distribution of inheritance is in accordance with customary rules, and women are excluded from inheritance except what their fathers set aside as a marriage portion.

This seems to be the general practice among all the other communities on whom we have data. Among the Gujar Bakarwals described by Khatana, 'the daughters who are admitted in theory to be eligible to receive one fourth of all property belonging to their father, actually receive a share of moveable property only. Thus, they are given animals when they are married and this is supposed to terminate their rights in the estate of their fathers. Even if she is unmarried, a daughter does not enjoy any claim to pasture lands. She is entitled to receive dowry from her brothers when she is married. Even the wife of a man has no rights of ownership over pasture lands. If she has small children, she can use the pasture lands to the benefit of the family, but as soon as the children grow up she has to allow the estate to be divided among her sons. All that she receives are the animals she brought as part of her dowry' (p. 110).

A similar situaton is noted for the Jamaati women by Saiyed and for the Meo women by Aggarwal. '. . . the Jamaati women', writes Saiyed, 'do not enjoy the right of inheritance as daughters, even though this privilege has been granted to them by their religion. The reason for this anomaly is that in several cases (due to the absence of their husbands) the parents continue to look after their daughters even after they have been married. As a compensation for this prolonged support, daughters are denied a share in parental property' (p. 260). Thus, it would seem that in respect of the rules of inheritance Muslim communities in India have been influenced by customary rules which are indistinguishable from those of neighbouring non-Muslim communities.

Perhaps we would need a large number of individual studies of particular Muslim communities and some comparative research before we can hope to arrive anywhere close to a truly definite picture of family, kinship and marriage among Muslims in India. Even so, the studies presented here clearly indicate that the Islamic laws governing these social institutions among Muslims in India are heavily overridden by traditional usages and, as Levy notes: 'Where family life is concerned, in marriage, divorce and the distribution of inheritance, the provisions of the *shar'* would appear to be very widely neglected' (Levy, 1962:244).

Several contributors refer to social changes taking place in the customs and values of the communities studied by them. Thus, Lambat observes that the practice of singing folk songs by Sunni Surati Vohra women at the time of marriage is dying out and the programme of *qawali* at the girl's house on the eve of a wedding is being replaced by religious discourse. Jacobson similarly notes that, while *burka* is gradually taking on slightly negative connotations among high status Muslims, it is increasing in popularity among the less prestigious socio-economic groups. 'Because of its previous association with the leisured and prosperous classes, the observance of *purdah*—or at least some of its obvious features—adds to the prestige of many low and middle status Muslims in their own circles' (p. 209). Aggarwal too points out that the Meo women living in Mewat have adopted *purdah* and that the old custom of dowry, typical of Hindu high castes of the region, is being replaced by the custom of bride-price which is, suggests Aggarwal, 'facilitated by the fact that they are becoming more Islamized and are relatively less concerned about their status in the Hindu caste hierarchy' (p. 287). These changes, the contributors to this volume suggest, are stimulated by the desire of the members of the various communities studied to project an image of themselves as Muslims and are resulting in the displacement of customary usuages by elements of *shar'*.

It has been customary in the writings on Muslim communities to refer to these and similar social changes as Islamization. The etymological meaning of the term Islamization is quite clear, but its sociological usage has been clouded by a certain amount of confusion. First, the term has been used to denote both a process of social mobility within the system of social stratification among Muslims whereby lower social groups seek to move up the social ladder by adopting the customs and characteristics of higher social strata[3] as well as through the spread of Islamic *shar'*. Second, the process has been conceptualised as a one-way transformation of social customs and practices along the lines indicated by the scriptural literature. Clifford Geertz, a perceptive student of Islam, was probably among the first to express this conceptualisation of Islamization. 'The typical mode of Islamization', he writes,

> has thus been, like all educational processes, painfully gradual. First comes the Confession of Faith, then the other Pillars, then a certain degree of observance of law, and finally, perhaps, especially as a scholarly tradition develops and takes hold, a certain amount of learning in the law and the Koran and *Hadith* upon which it rests. The intricate norms, doctrines, explications, and annotations that make up Islam, or at least Sunni Islam, can be apprehended only step by step, as one comes to control to a greater or lesser degree the scriptural sources

3. These two processes are distinguishable and the distinction between them should be clearly recognised. For a detailed discussion of the differences, see Ahmad (forthcoming).

> upon which it rests. For most people, such control never goes beyond accepting, at second hand, the interpretations of those who control those sources directly. But that learning, however crude, and access to scholarship, however shabby, are central to becoming a Muslim in anything more than a formal sense, is apparent everywhere in the Islamic world. . . . Islamic conversion is not, as a rule, a sudden total overwhelming illumination but a slow turning toward a new light (1965:96-97).

The conception of Islamization as a unilinear or one-way process of social and cultural change has been very widespread in writings on Muslim communities in India (see Ahmad, 1969; Misra, 1964).[4] Those who have written on the subject have been prone to argue that the changes subsumed under this process are likely to result in an increasingly rigid adherence to basic Islamic principles or elements of the *shar'*. Further, they have argued that this process would produce a growing tendency among the members of different Muslim communities to see the entire Muslim population in the country as a unified social category sharing and abiding by a common religious ethos and orientation (see Singh, 1974). The evidence presented in these contributions shows that Islamization is neither the only process of social change taking place among Muslim communities in India nor is its transformative impact as unilineal and straight as has been commonly assumed. Firstly, Islamization, as Wright's paper ably demonstrates, is competing with processes like modernisation and westernisation, which owe themselves to wider social forces. Second, Islamization does not always result, as is implied in its unilinear conception, in the widespread acceptance of elements of the *shari'a*. Quite often, it results in the displacement of one set of hetrodox practices by another set of practices which are equally heterodox. Furthermore, several customs and practices are able to successfully survive the transformative effects of Islamization and continue to persist either in their old or a slightly modified form.

4. Of course, Misra seems to have changed his ideas on the subject in a recent paper (see Misra, 1973).

Lambat's paper provides an excellent example of this pattern. 'For sometime', Lambat writes, 'the Surati Vohras have been experiencing a struggle between custom and religion and in recent years this struggle has picked up great momentum because of the increase in religious education among the members of this group. However, the customary rites and ceremonies continue to enjoy a very strong hold on the group and have not been replaced by alternate religious practices. The religious leaders who raise a hue and cry over un-Islamic customs have not been able to provide Islamic substitutes for them. For example, they have vehemently opposed the singing of *geet* by women, but they have not been able to raise their voices as strongly against the loudspeakers that blare out the latest film hits. No doubt, some customs and ceremonies are being dropped because of greater Islamization as well as an increase in secular education, but many others are still practised widely and are likely to remain popular in the future' (p. 80). Aggarwal makes a more or less similar observation: '. . . the non-Meo Muslims, particularly the religious practitioners, wish that the Meos should accept the custom of cousin marriage. But the Meos have strongly resisted it thus far. Their relative isolation from the wider Muslim community, and close contact with local Hindus, account for this resistance. The Meos are also under pressure to adopt *purdah*, i.e., seclusion of women. This they resist because Meo women have to work in the fields. Also, since women in modern society are struggling to improve their status *vis-a-vis* men, it is unlikely that the Meo women will accept *purdah*' (p. 295).

The conclusion suggested by these observations is obvious. Far from promoting strict adherence to elements of the *sharia*, Islamization has allowed the different Muslim communities in India to either legitimize local customs and practices or to reconcile them with the *sharia*. It has, in other words, allowed the Muslim communities to have, and to project, a truly Islamic image of themselves and yet continue to remain an integral part of the cultural complex within which they are embedded.

Bibliography

Ahmad, Aziz (1969), An *Intellectual History of Islam in India*, Edinburgh, University of Edinburgh Press.

Ahmad, Imtiaz (forthcoming) 'Exclusion and Assimilation in Indian Islam', in Attar Singh (ed.), *Islamic Impact on Northern India*, Chandigarh, Panjab University.

Ahmadullah, Deena (1969), 'A Comparative Note on the Special Marriage Act 1954 and Muslim Personal Law', *The Secularist*, 5.

Bhatty, Z, (1976), 'Status of Muslim Women and Social Change', in B.R. Nanda (ed.), *Indian Women: From Purdah to Modernity*, New Delhi, Vikas Publishing House.

Dalwai, Hamid, (1970), Muslim Opposition to Secular Integration', *The Secularist*, 7.

Davis, Christie (1976), 'The Relative Fertility of Hindus and Muslims', *Quest*, 99, pp. 19-32.

Dube, Leela (1969), *Matriliny and Islam*, University of Saugar Monographs in Sociology and Social Anthropology, No. 1, Delhi, National Publishing House.

———(1976), 'Sociology of Kinship', in ICSSR, *Survey of Research in Sociology and Social Anthropology*, New Delhi, Orient Longman.

Geertz, Clifford (1965), 'Modernization in a Muslim Society: The Indonesian Case', in R.N. Bellah (ed.), *Religion and Progress in Modern Asia*. New York, The Free Press.

Ittman, K.P. (1976), *Amini Islanders: Social Structure and Social Change*, New Delhi, Abhinav Publications.

Kutty, A.R. (1972), *Marriage and Kinship in an Island Society*, University of Saugar Monographs in Sociology and Social Anthropology No. 2, Delhi, National Publishing House.

Levy, Reuben (1962), *The Social Structure of Islam*, Cambridge, Cambridge University Press.

Misra, S.C. (1964), *Muslim Communities in Gujarat*, Bombay, Asia Publishing House.

———(1973), 'Indigenization and Islamization in Indian History', Paper presented at the ICSSR Colloquium on Problems of Muslims in India, Hyderabad.

Singh, Yogendra (1974), *The Modernization of Indian Tradition*, New Delhi, Thomson Press.

Kinship and Marriage among the Assamese Muslims[1]

A.N.M. Irshad Ali

The character and quality of social relations based on kinship have always been regarded as a major foci of interest by social anthropologists in their study of small-scale rural communities (see, for instance, Radcliffe-Brown and Fortes, 1905; Goody, 1958; and Fortes, 1973). The principal reason for this is that kinship in such communities, whether tribal or peasant, plays a dominant role in social organization. 'Social anthropologists', writes Beattie,

> are sometimes accused of concerning themselves over much with the refinements and complexities of kinship terminologies, of indulging in what Malinowski calls "kinship algebra". But there are good reasons for this concern. Very few of the interpersonal relationships which make up a Western European's social world are kinship ones. Kinship plays little or no part in his relationship with his friends, his employers, his teachers, his colleagues, or in the complex network of political, economic and religious associations in which he is involved. But in many small-scale societies

1. This paper is based on data which I collected as a research student of the Department of Anthropology of Gauhati University between 1969-71. I am deeply indebted to my research supervisor, Dr. A.C. Bhagabati, for his constant encouragement and guidance during all phases of my research.

kinship's social importance is paramount. Where a person lives, his group and community membership, whom he should obey and by whom be obeyed, who are his friends and who his enemies, whom he may and may not marry, from whom he may hope to inherit and to whom pass on his own status and property—all these matters and many more may be determined by his status in a kinship system (1964:93).

It is, indeed, a well established fact that as societies progress from a folk stage to an urban and complex 'civilization' stage, kinship loses its central position in the organization of inter-individual relations (see, for instance, Nimkoff, 1965; Goode, 1963; and Wolf, 1966). The study of kinship and marriage thus constitutes a significant area for social anthropological research in the developing countries both because such research can indicate the direction of change in their kinship and marriage systems as well as allow us to understand the factors that shape the character and tenor of kinship and marriage relations in them.

This paper deals with kinship and marriage among the Muslims of Assam in eastern India. Several social anthropological and sociological studies focussing on Muslim social life have suggested that Muslim familial life exhibits a peculiar synthesis of Islam and Hindu traditions (Hashim, 1970), that the kinship terminology of the Muslims is comparable to that of the Hindus (Vreede-de-Steurs, 1968) and that the marriage customs of the Muslims are often characterized by a curious mixture of Hindu and Muslim rituals (Uddin, 1972). A study of a group of convert Muslims shows that Islam, which is essentially patrilineal in orientation, co-exists along with a matrilineal kinship system (Dube, 1969; Kutty, 1972). This paper attempts to portray the ways in which kinship plays a part in the general socio-economic life of the Assamese Muslims and examines the extent to which Islamic principles and indigenous folk traditions determine the character and tenor of kinship and marriage relations amongst them. The extent to which the social organization of the Assamese Muslims is determined by kinship factors is also examined.

The Assamese Muslims

Assam came into contact with Islam for the first time in

A.D. 1203 when the Turkish Army led by Muhammad bin Bakhtiyar made an expedition to Tibet through this region. Following Bakhtiyar, several other expeditions were made by a number of other Muslim invaders in the subsequent centuries (Bhuyan, 1949; Gait, 1963). Later, in A.D. 1532, a Muslim army commanded by Turbak invaded Assam. The Muslims were defeated in a battle and those who were captured and taken prisoners by the Ahom king were sent to different parts of Assam.

The history of Assam's contact with the Muslims clearly suggests that they never really gained enough of a foothold in the region. However, these early encounters contributed towards the propagation and strengthening of the Islamic faith in Assam (Neog, 1965:74) and some traits of Islamic culture were assimilated by the indigenous population.[2] Furthermore, the prolonged wars between the Muslim rulers and the Assamese kings led to the growth of a Muslim population in Assam.

The Muslims taken prisoners by the Ahom King in A.D. 1532 were the earliest Muslim settlers in the Assam valley. They came to be known as Maria. The traditional occupation of the Marias is brass-working which is practised by many Marias even to this day. Gait (1893:153) mentions that the descendants of the Muslim prisoners who had chosen to marry Assamese women behaved exactly as the Assamese and there was nothing Islamic about them except their names. It is quite clear from Gait's observation that these early Muslim settlers in Assam had adapted themselves to the indigenous culture and had lost whatever Islamic moorings they had earlier.[3]

2. It has been suggested that the first signs of Islam appeared after the invasion made by the ruler of Gauda in A.D. 1257. The ruler is said to have erected a mosque to celebrate his victory and is also reported to have initiated the Friday congregational prayers. For details of the social history of the Assamese Muslims, see Allen (1905-7), Bhuyan (1926,1947,1949, & 1956), Bora (1936), Driberg (1883), Gait (1893, 1963), Hamilton (1940), Hunter (1897), Lloyd (1923), Malik (1958), McSwiney (1912), Mullah (1932), Neog (1965), Ramgopal (1959), Robinson (1841), Saikia (1967), Sarkar (1915) and Sarma (1969).
3. It seems that in the early years the Marias adhered to the Islamic faith only in a marginal way. The first Census enumeration (1872) included the Marias under the list of aboriginal tribes. Also see Robinson (1841:244) and Hunter (1897:39).

The consolidation of Islam in the Assam valley dates from the early part of the seventeenth century. A Muslim saint named Shah Milan, popularly known as Azan Faquir, was the chief source of this consolidation. He is said to have come to Assam during the 1630s and to have promoted and stabilized Assamese Islam which had deviated considerably from the salient principles and practices of the faith as practised in northern India (Malik, 1958). Through his preachings, as well as through those of the other preachers who followed him, a large section of the indigenous population was converted to Islam. Presumably, these preachers were encouraged by the Ahom rulers to engage in missionary work and to propagate the Islamic faith. Gait (1893) believes that the majority of the people who were converted to Islam in Assam were drawn from lower Hindu castes and aboriginal tribes as was the case in eastern parts of Bengal.[4]

The present-day Assemese Muslims would thus appear to be the descendants of three different groups of people: (a) the Muslim soldiers captured by the Ahom ruler during the first Muslim invasion of Assam; (b) the Muslim artisan families brought by the Ahom rulers and appointed to the various departments of the state (Bhuyan, 1949:4); and (c) converts to Islam. These Muslims are distributed throughout the Brahmaputra valley districts of the state and Assamese is their mother tongue. Furthermore, they share many other points of cultural similarity with the Assemese Hindus of the Brahmaputra valley amongst whom they live.

The Assamese Muslims[5] are divided into three ranked social

4. Gait also maintains that the process of conversion to Islam occurred in Assam later (1893:39).
5. It is difficult to estimate the numerical strength of the Assamese Muslims since language is not the criteria on which Hindus and Muslims are classified in the Census. According to the 1961 Census, the total population of Assam is 11,872,772. The total number of Muslims enumerated in the districts of the Brahmaputra valley was 2,199,330. It would be safe to assume that a significant majority of these Muslims belong to the Assamese Muslim category. There is a sizeable population of recent immigrants from east Bengal, but they are not regarded as Assamese Muslims. Even this group of Muslims is undergoing a process of Assamization. However, this discussion does not cover this category of Muslims.

classes; Syed, Garia and Maria. The Syeds claim to be descendants of Arab immigrants. Till recently, they were also regarded as a priestly class and occupied a dominant position in the social structure of the Assamese Muslims. The Garias claim to have come originally from Gaur, the ancient Muhammedan capital of Bengal, and are generally placed after the Syeds. The Marias[6] are, as we noted earlier, the descendants of the Muslim soldiers who were taken prisoner by the Ahom king during the first Muslim invasion of Assam and occupy the lowest social standing The Syeds and the Garias usually maintain a certain degree of social distance from the Marias. Each of these three groups maintains a considerable degree of autonomy on the social plane, and social relations, including marriage, are confined within the group. However, the spread of religious knowledge, the expansion of education and the levelling influences of contemporary economic forces are gradually breaking down the social barriers among these groups.

The Setting

This discussion of kinship and marriage among the Assamese Muslims is based on research in three different socio-economic settings: a village named Singimari in the Darrang District, a peri-urban community called Uttar Jalukbari in the vicinity of Gauhati, and Gauhati city proper. Following intensive field research in these socio-economic settings, a rapid month-long field tour was also undertaken of some of the villages and towns of Lakhimpur, Dibrugarh and Sibsagar districts of Upper Assam[7] in order to obtain some idea of Muslim social life in that region of the Brahmaputra valley. Let us present a brief description of the three social settings before turning to a consi-

6. Hunter (1897:39) suggests that the names Garia and Maria actually originated from the particular occupation which the early Muslim settlers in Assam adopted. Those who took to tailoring came to be known as Garias and those who took up brass-work were called Marias.
7. The eastern and western parts of the Brahmputra plains are known as Upper and Lower Assam respectively. The villages and the city described in this paper are situated in the Lower Assam region. It is pertinent to note here that the socio-cultural life of the Assamese Muslims of Upper and Lower Assam shows many points of difference.

deration of the kinship and marriage patterns of the Assamese Muslims.

Singimari is situated some thirty-two kilometers north-east of Gauhati city on the Gauhati-Tezpur Road. It is essentially a peasant village as almost all its inhabitants depend upon rice cultivation. There are fifty-four Muslim and sixty Hindu households in the village. The Muslims of Singimari, like the Assamese Muslims in general, belong to the Sunni sect. Their total population in the village is 404. They live in a well-defined sector of the village, which comprises three separate clusters of houses (*chuba*). Each of these clusters of houses is referred to by a distinct name such as *uttar chuba* (northern hamlet), *maj chuba* (middle hamlet), and *dakhin chuba* (southern hamlet). The *chuba* is an aggregate of patrilineally related kins. The Hindu population of Singimari is 449. It is divided into three castes. There are forty-five households of the Koch caste, thirteen households of the Hira caste and two households of the Ganak caste. Singimari's population, both the Muslims and Hindus, constitutes a corporate unit in many ways.[8] Nonetheless, the different Hindu castes and the Muslims maintain their distinct social boundaries through their separate religious institutions. These institutions are the independent *namghars* (community prayer houses) of the Hindu hamlets and the common mosque of the Muslims.

Uttar Jalukbari is situated on the western outskirts of Gauhati at a distance of about nine kilometers from the centre of the city. Its population comprises those who moved to this locality from two adjacent villages. This shift was necessitated by the government's acquisition of land for the construction of the North-east Frontier Railway Headquarters and Gauhati University Campus. The village contains 337 Muslims distributed through forty-eight households.

The people of Uttar Jalukbari have retained their ancestral village identities in their new location, and this is reflected in the settlement pattern of the village. The houses on the southern and northern sides of the highway, which runs through the village, belong to the members of two ancestral villages. Each

8. For a detailed discussion of the content and quality of social relations between the Hindus and Muslims in Singimari, see Ali and Bhagabati (1972).

of these halves, which are now called *khel*,[9] possesses a mosque and the members of the *khel* offer prayers in their own mosque. The relation of the *khel* to the mosque exhibits the same pattern as the Hindu *khels* of Assamese villages where each *khel*, usually made up of people belonging to the same caste, has a *namghar* (community prayer house) of its own.

Like other villages in the plains of Assam, agriculture is the traditional occupation of the people of Uttar Jalukbari. However, a gradual change in the economy of the village was evinced following the migration of the villagers to the present site. The occupational pattern of Uttar Jalukbari Muslims has undergone a shift from a rural agriculture-based economy to an urban wage occupation-based economy. They lost much of their cultivable land and gradually started taking up other means of livelihood. For the villagers, the process of losing land has continued over the years due to the expansion of urban frontiers all around the village. Urban growth has also resulted in the establishment of factories, offices, workshops and market places within easy reach of villagers. Many villagers have found employment in these establishments.

Gauhati city has a total population of 100,707. This population comprises members of a number of different religious faiths. There are 11,522 Muslims in Gauhati. Besides the Assamese Muslims, this population includes the Muslims who have come from Bangladesh, Bihar and Rajasthan. These immigrant Muslims are mostly engaged in petty business. Some of them are day labourers and rickshaw pullers. An analysis of the occupations of the city's population reveals that the local Assamese' participation in trade and commerce is negligible. Many Assamese Muslims of Gauhati are, however, engaged in petty business. There are also Muslims who are employed in various categories of jobs in administrative offices, educational institutions and privately-owned firms. There is a business as well as a professional section among the Assamese Muslims of Gauhati.

9. '. . . a body of Hindus who eat and drink together and associate with each other . . . ' (Gait, 1893:202). During the Ahom reign, the adult population of Assam was divided into *khels* having to render specific service to the State. Sometimes *khels* were also composed on a territorial basis (Bhuyan 1949:10).

The concentration of the Muslims in certain parts of the city has led to the formation of a number of Muslim neighbourhoods. Each neighbourhood normally possesses a mosque in which the residents offer prayers and also look after the management of the mosque. There are as many as twelve Muslim neighbourhoods within the city boundary and one outside of it situated towards the south of the city. The Muslim neighbourhoods of Gauhati have emerged at different dates. The neighbourhoods situated in the central part of the city are relatively older than those in the outlying sections. The old Muslim neighbourhoods are mainly occupied by city-born Muslims, while the recently established neighbourhoods are occupied by the people who have come to the city over the last two or three decades from various parts of the state. The factors leading to migration to Gauhati have been many. However, unfavourable economic circumstances and lack of employment in their original places of residence are mentioned by most immigrants as the reasons for their migration to Gauhati. Gauhati city offers substantial scope for employment and this automatically encourages immigration.

The Household

Like in most other Indian communities, the basic unit of the kinship system among the Assamese Muslims is the household. It is called *ghar* in the vernacular, and refers essentially to a residential and domestic unit comprising the person or persons living together under the same roof and eating food cooked in a common kitchen (Shah, 1974:8).

Size of Households

Households vary widely in their numerical composition. Table 1 shows the distribution of Muslim households in Singimari, Uttar Jalukbari and Gauhati according to numerical size. There is a considerable range from one to nineteen or more members per household, but the average size of the households—seven in Singimari and Uttar Jalukbari and six in Gauhati—tends to be much smaller. The majority of the households have between four to nine persons. These figures clearly indicate that most of the Assamese Muslims live in small and medium households as is the case in India as a whole (Shah, 1974:13).

TABLE 1 : Numerical Size of Muslim Households in Singimari, Uttar Jalukbari and Gauhati

No. of persons per Household	*Singimari: No. of House-holds*	*Singimari: Per Cent*	*Uttar Jalukbari: No. of House-holds*	*Uttar Jalukbari: Per Cent*	*Gauhati: No. of House-holds*	*Gauhati: Per Cent*
1—3	6	10.5	7	14.6	20	17.2
4—6	22	38.6	19	39.6	50	43.1
7—9	22	38.6	14	29.1	30	25.9
10—12	4	7.0	5	10.4	10	8.6
13—15	2	3.5	—	—	6	5.2
16—18	1	1.8	1	2.1	—	—
19 and above	—	—	2	4.2	—	—
Total	57	100.0	48	100.0	116	100.0

Composition of Households

The range in kinship composition is much wider than the range in numerical composition, but here again a broad pattern is clearly discernible. Most of the households are either typical nuclear units consisting of a man, his wife and unmarried children, or constitute variations of this type of family organization. For instance, 138 out of the 221 households in the three field areas are nuclear or simple households composed of the whole or a part of a parental family. The remaining eighty-three households are joint or complex households comprising members of two or more patrilineally related households. Table 2 sets out the distribution of households in Singimari, Uttar Jalukbari and Gauhati according to their kinship composition.

The majority of the complex or joint households are based on the principle of residential unity of patrikin and their wives. For example, nine out of the ten joint or complex households in Singimari, five out of the sixteen complex households in Uttar Jalukbari, and thirty-five out of the forty-seven complex households in Gauhati are either lineal or collateral joint households. The remaining complex or joint households are based on the reversal of the principle of residential unity of patrikin and their wives through accretions of kin. Such accretions are temporary in some cases while in others they are of a more permanent nature. There are instances where married women have returned to

TABLE 2 : Kinship Composition of Singimari, Uttar Jalukbari and Gauhati Muslim Households*

Composition	*Singimari*		*Uttar Jalukbari*		*Gauhati*	
	No. of House-hold	*Per Cent*	*No. of House-hold*	*Per Cent*	*No. of House-hold*	*Per Cent*
Ego (E) (Widow/ Wido-wer)	—	—	4	8.3	1	0.9
E, Wife (W)	1	1.8	—	—	3	2.6
E(Widow), children(c)**	2	3.5	3	6.3	—	—
E, W, C	32	56.1	25	52.1	61	52.5
E, W, Widowed mother	1	1.8	—	—	—	—
E, two Ws, c	4	7.0	—	—	1	0.9
E, W, c married sons (s), sw, sc	7	12.3	4	8.3	7	6.0
E, w,c, married brothers (bObw, bc, unmarried brother, sisters	1	1.8	1	2.1	24	20.6
E(Widow/widower), c,s, sw,sc,	7	12.2	—	—	3	2.6
E(widow/widower,) c,s,sw, sc, married daughter (md),c	—	—	9	18.7	—	—
E(widow), c,s,sw,sc, divor-ced daughter (d). dc	—	—	1	2.1	3	2.6
E,w,c,md,md's husband	—	—	1	2.1	1	0.9
E,w,c, daughter-in-law, c	1	1.8	—	—	—	—
Widowed co-wives, c	1	1.8	—	—	—	—
Widowed,d'sc	—	—	—	—	3	2.6
Widow, c, widow's h's brother	—	—	—	—	1	0.9
Widow, c. unmarried brothers, unmarried sisters	—	—	—	—	5	4.2
E,W,cE'sB's (widow), sc	—	—	—	—	1	0.9
E, brothers, sisters	—	—	—	—	1	0.9
E(unmarried famale) Sister, E's sister's daughter	—	—	—	—	1	0.9
Total :	57	100.0	48	100.0	116	100.0

*With the head of the household as Ego(E) always a male, unless otherwise indicated.

**Unmarried children.

their parental homes along with their children and stay with their parents or close kins after being divorced by their husbands or following widowhood. In such situations they find their parental homes a place of economic and social security. There are also instances where married women have come back to their parental homes with their husbands or have brought some of their paternal kin to their conjugal households. Kin accretions in Assamese Muslim households underscore the functional importance of kinship quite clearly.

The people of Singimari who live as members of joint households are almost uniformly of the opinion that each nuclear family should have an independent household. They say that though the joint family is an ideal type, in practice it is better to live separately from parents or brothers following one's marriage. This, according to them, saves a lot of unpleasantness which often results from a prolonged common sharing of the same economic and domestic arrangements. Among the Singimari Muslims it is common for married sons to establish separate households within a year or two of marriage. Among the Singimari Muslims one often encounters a single domestic area or compound which includes as many as three or four different households belonging to the primary or familial kin circle. Thus, recent years have witnessed a clear shift from the joint family to the elementary family-centered household system even among people who depend primarily on agriculture.

Like the Singimari people, the Muslims of Uttar Jalukbari also say that each nuclear family should have a separate house and establish an independent household. But it is not possible for many of them to fulfil this goal due to the lack of housing sites and finance. Besides, most of the village land-holdings have already become too small or fragmented so that separation for married brothers or parents and married sons is often not economically viable. In this way the physical setting has a distinct impact on the composition of many Uttar Jalukbari households.

In the case of the Gauhati Muslims, in some instances houses are clustered together to form a compact settlement. Such clustering is the result of the lack of additional space to build houses with compounds. This pattern is more particularly noticeable in the old Muslim neighbourhoods. The gradual breakdown of joint families into independent elementary family-centered households has also furthered the emergence of clusters of houses. It is found that following a family separation, say between parents and married sons, each elementary family lives in the ancestral house for a while. Such an arrangement is regarded as temporary. When the elementary family increases in size or disputes arise between the families, additional houses may be built by those who can afford to do so. Some move out to other neighbourhoods.

Kinship and Community

Among the Singimari Muslims the *chubas* are not merely geographical divisions—they constitute kin groups as well. The heads of all households in any *chuba* are patrilineally related to one another. Thus, each *chuba* is a patrilineal kin group functioning more or less as a sub-lineage. This has resulted from the lack of physical mobility outside one's own hamlet following marriage. The residents of a *chuba* feel that they are like one big family which is demonstrated by frequent inter-household interaction and economic cooperation in agriculture or at times of crises. This feeling of kinship is quite strong and is brought into play whenever necessary. The sense of patrilineal kinship unity, however, does not end at the *chuba* level. As a matter of fact, the entire Muslim community of Singimari corresponds to a wider patri-kin unit.

Within the Muslim community of Singimari, certain standards of interpersonal relations and behaviour have to be maintained including the practice of village exogamy. Even when no demonstrable kin links exist between any two persons they address one another using kinship terms.[10] Inter-individual relations and standards of behaviour among the villagers operate within a framework of kinship structure. The corporate lineage-like organization of the Muslim community of Singimari is largely responsible for maintaining village level solidarity. When conflicts arise between individuals they are quickly settled on the plea that it is wrong for relatives to fight.

Authority, communication and social control within the

10. The kinship terminology of the Assamese Muslims of the Lower Assam region is comparable to that of the Assamese Hindus of the same region. For an account of the kinship terminology of the Assamese Hindus of Lower Assam region see Mahanta (1973:27-34).

Singimari Muslim community are maintained by a system of leadership evolved on the basis of kinship. For instance, the elderly men of each *chuba* are regarded as informal leaders of the *chuba*. These leaders are called *menas*, and their verdicts are obeyed by the people of the *chuba*. The *menas* from different *chubas* together comprise an informal council of elders which functions both as a kin as well as a community council. The factor of kinship helps the Singimari Muslims to maintain harmony and solidarity and also makes it possible for them to take up various community level activities.

Each *khel* in Uttar Jalukbari forms a loose patrilineal kin group. However, the identity of a *khel* as a descent group or a clear-cut kin group is rather weak at Uttar Jalukbari. Most of the villagers do not seem to emphasize the point that each *khel* is, by and large, also a patrikin unit. Strictly speaking, a *khel* does not function as a corporate kin group.

Since there are many ties of kinship among the Muslim inhabitants of Uttar Jalukbari, any dispute between members of the two *khels* more often than not involves people who are related to one another. However, in such cases one's *khel* identity takes precedence over the kinship factor. At times, disputes might arise among closely related persons of the same *khel*. Even in such cases, the issue is frequently settled at the level of the *khel* and not merely as a dispute between two kinsmen. Thus kinship plays a less important role than *khel* identity in village social life.

Some elderly men are regarded by the Uttar Jalukbari villagers as informal leaders of the two *khels*. They are usually referred to as *murrabbis*, an Arabic word which means headmen.[11] All the matters relating to the *khel* are usually discussed by the people under the general guidance of the *murrabbis*. The *murrabbis* exercise their powers within their respective *khels*. However, when a marriage proposal between a boy and a girl belonging to two different *khels* of the village is negotiated, the *murrabbis* of the two *khels* are invited by the families of the boy and the girl to take active part in the negotiations. Disputes

11. Usually the Assamese Muslims also refer to the head of the household as a *murrabbi*.

between persons across the *khel* boundaries are also taken up for settlement by the *murrabbis* of both the *khels*. However, the leadership pattern at Uttar Jalukbari is not well-defined. Individually, a *murrabbi* is insignificant in the village. It is only when the *murrabbis* of both the *khels* meet as a common body that they tend to carry some weight in the village society.

The Muslim neighbourhoods of Gauhati are spatially separated from one another. The distance between some neighbourhoods is more than three miles. However, the neighbourhoods in the central part of the city are relatively close to one another. In such a situation, it is not possible for the residents to know one another intimately or behave as members of one local community. On the other hand, in the case of Singimari and Uttar Jalukbari, the compact settlement pattern has led the Muslims to constitute distinct local communities in which everybody knows everybody else. This 'knowing' also determines the quality and content of the social relations among the villagers. In the case of Gauhati, social intimacy is usually confined to the residents of a neighbourhood. It may be extended when the neighbourhoods are situated close to one another or when kinship ties link the residents of different neighbourhoods.

The residents of the old Muslim neighbourhoods, who are in most cases city-born persons, tend to maintain close social contacts among themselves. The city-born Muslims trace their descent from the earliest Muslim settlers in Gauhati. Besides, marriage relations involving the city-born Muslims have linked up various households situated in different neighbourhoods of the city. This way kinship ties have frequently cut across the boundaries of various neighbourhoods. But, even then, effective interaction in day-to-day situations takes place largely between kinsfolk who reside close to one another.

The intimacy and active interaction which one observes among the residents of the old Muslim neighourhoods are partly due to ties of kinship. But, except among the Marias, kinship ties have not been able to evolve a strong sense of unity at the neighbourhood level among the other city-born Muslims. This is mainly because most of the old Muslim neighbourhoods of the city are gradually becoming heterogenous in nature following the emergence of business establishments and the increase in the number of non-Muslim residents in these areas.

As in the case of Singimari Muslims, the factor of kinship also helps the Marias of Gauhati to maintain harmony and solidarity. Authority, communication and social control among the Marias are maintained by a system of leadership. The mosque managing committee of the Marias is referred to as a *panchayat*, and the elderly members of the *panchayat* are regarded by the Marias as being their leaders (*murrabbis* or *motowallis*).

The socio-political situations obtaining among the Marias are unique among the Muslims of Gauhati. Two forces appear to have been at work simultaneously which have given rise to this situation. First, the social distance which the other Muslims maintain towards this community has led the Marias to re-inforce their own identity. This consolidation has, in turn, helped them to maintain unity among themselves. Secondly, the socio-economic background and the network of kinship have helped to create a sense of solidarity within the Maria neighbourhood. The social situation obtaining among the Marias approximates to the social life of those Muslims who have concentrated in the *bustees* (slums) of Calcutta. Among these slum-dwellers one comes across a sense of unity and solidarity based on common background and kinship. There is also a fairly strong leadership system in the *bustees* which acts as an agency of social control over the residents of the *bustees* (Siddiqui 1969:1919).

Extra-local Kin

The practice of village level exogamy by the Singimari Muslims has led to a proliferation of affinal kinship. In contrast to Singimari, marriage between a boy and a girl belonging to Uttar Jalukbari is permitted by the village folk. However, some Uttar Jalukbari people now feel that the villagers have come to be so closely related to one another through descent and marriage that it is no longer desirable to establish marital ties between village households. Recently a clear trend has emerged among the Uttar Jalukbari people to marry outside the village. Both the Singimari and Uttar Jalukbari Muslims select girls from the vicinity of their villages for marriage. In the same manner, their girls are married mostly to men from nearby villages. Among the Muslims of Gauhati, marriages are frequently contracted between persons residing in the city itself. But the Gauhati Muslims seem to differ from both Singimari and Uttar Jalukbari Muslims when they have to choose brides from outside Gauhati. In that case the Gauhati Muslims will tend to go further afield than the vicinity of the city.

Table 3 shows the number of women from the villages and the city married to men from other localities and women brought to the villages and the city through marriage.

TABLE 3: Singimari (S), Uttar Jalukbari (UJ), and Gauhati (G) Women Married to Men from Other Localities and Women Brought Through Marriage to S, UJ* and G

Distance from S, UJ, and G (in miles)	*Number of Women Married Away From:*			*Number of Women Brought From other Localities to:*		
	S	*UJ*	*G*	*S*	*UJ*	*G*
1-5	45	34	—	64	38	—
6-10	8	3	2	10	2	1
11-15	1	2	—	1	—	—
16-20	2	—	9	2	1	1
21+	1	2	26	3	1	20
Total	57	41	37	80	42	22

*It was found at the time of field investigation that as many as 28 marriages were contracted between persons belonging to the two *khels*.

When questioned, the people of both the villages say that they prefer to establish marital ties in the neighbouring villages because that way it is possible to keep in close and frequent touch with their relations.

To a Singimari Muslim his *chuba* people are his 'effective kin'[12] in most day-to-day situations. Corporate kin groups outside the range of immediate familial kin are absent as effective units both among the Uttar Jalukbari and Gauhati Muslims. The strength of the ties which are maintained with extra-local kin varies according to the nature of the situation and from person to person. There is a fair amount of choice with regard

12. 'Those with whom siginificant contacts are maintained . . . (Piddington, 1961:15; also see Firth, 1956:41).

to interactions with extra-local kin excepting for 'priority kin'[13] such as wife's parents, wife's brothers or mother's brothers.

Among the rural Muslims, contact with extra-local kin can be easily maintained and there is a great deal of visiting between such kin, especially in the free days following harvesting. This is due to the fact that most of the extra-local kin live in close proximity. In Singimari most households related by marriage frequently cooperate in agricultural activities, such as share-cropping, ploughing, transplantation and harvesting.

Marriage

There is a broad sense of kinship involving all the Muslim households of Singimari. We have already stated that each Muslim *chuba* at Singimari is an aggregate of patrilineally related kinsfolk. Again, all the heads of the Muslim households of the village regard themselves as descendants of six different ancestors who happened to be patrilineally related to one another. On inquiry it was, however, not possible to place all the Muslim households in a single genealogical table, nor was it possible to trace exact kin links between the different Muslim households of the village. Nonetheless, among the Singimari Muslims the fiction of 'everyone being related to everyone else' within the village is quite strong. They say that they all belong to the same *bangsha* (lineage).[14] The Muslim community is thus organized like a lineage. This is reflected by the existence of

13. 'Members of the individual family and kinsfolk closely related to it, particularly parents of the spouses' (Piddington, 1961:15).
14. The term *bangsha* covers the kin, living or dead, close or remote, with whom relationship is assumed to be traceable on the paternal side. Besides *bangsha*, certain other terms are also used by the Singimari villagers, both Hindus and Muslims, for different circles of kin—for example, the term *bhagi* is used to denote the members of village households with whom a villager can actually trace kin link on the father's side. The *bangsha* appears to be a wider unit than the *bhagi*, since the former term is generally used by the villagers to refer to the kinsfolk belonging to their village and elsewhere, while the later term is invariably used to refer to village households only. Another term, *kurma*, is used to denote the affinal kinsfolk only. A social visit to the home of an affine is *kurma khowa* (literally, 'dining with affines'), while establishing relations with others through marriage is *kurma pata*.

strong feelings against marriage involving village households which belong to the same *bangsha*, such a marriage being regarded as incestuous. The Singimari Muslims therefore constitute an exogamous community. The practice of village-level and patri-kin exogamy is an interesting phenomenon among the Singimari Muslims in as much as there is no stigma attached to such alliances in Muhammedan law except, of course, to marriages involving one's primary kin. The Muslim communities surrounding Singimari, however, do not observe village-level exogamy. Nevertheless, marriage among patrilineally related kin are avoided even in the surrounding villages, though marriage within the village is common.

Each of the two *khels* at Uttar Jalukbari forms a loose patrilineal kin-group in the sense that the heads of most of the male households trace their descent from a common ancestor. Unlike Singimari, marriage relations within the village are a common occurrence in Uttar Jalukbari. Moreover, marriages between members of the same *khel* are also permitted and have in fact taken place with the exceptions of certain restricted categories of kin. Thus, intra-*khel* and intra-village marriages have linked up most of the village households in a kinship network.

Among the Muslims of Gauhati, marriages are frequently contracted between persons residing in the city itself. An analysis of the data collected from 116 Muslim households shows that in sixty-five households the wives are Gauhati-born women. Again, as many as thirty-six girls from the sample households have been married in different neighbourhoods of the city. In this regard the Gauhati Muslims approximate the Uttar Jalukbari Muslims who also contract marriages within the village. City-born Muslims usually confine their social relations among themselves. There are few ties of marriage with village people. Only the Marias regularly establish marital ties with people of their own community who still live in villages.

The Gauhati Muslims contract marriages even between kin, but they observe the restricted degrees dictated by Islam. In the course of my investigation, I encountered a number of cases where a man had married his parallel cousins (father's brother's daughter). Kin marriages are frequently contracted among the Marias of Gauhati. This is due primarily to the social distance which the other Muslims maintain towards them. The Marias have become a sort of 'kin-community' (Murdock, 1949: 88)within which ties of kinship and marriage link one household with many others.

It may be pointed out that among certain other Muslim communities of India, i.e., among the Muslims of Gujarat, kin marriages are performed with a view to retain family wealth within the wider family since the daughter is an important beneficiary under Muslim law (Misra, 1964:153). Again, kin marriages are preferred by certain other Muslim communities (i.e. Punjabi Muslims) with a view to renewing and strengthening an already existing connection. It is also viewed as a means whereby the shortcomings of a family may not be exposed to outsiders (Eglar, 1960:93). Punjabi Muslims also consider it an index of social prestige (Alavi 1972:6).

The Ceremony

A wedding consists of two formal ceremonies: the ring ceremony (*magni* or *angathi pindhua*) which is followed by the actual wedding ceremony (*nikah*). After the finalization of the negotiations between the families of the future bride and the groom, a party consisting of the close kinsfolk and the parents of the groom-to-be visits the future bride's home. The party carries a gold ring, silk clothes and sweets as presents. The negotiations are sealed with the presentation of the engagement ring to the future bride.

Among the Gauhati Muslims, the groom reaches the bride's home by late evening on the day of the marriage ceremony. The party which accompanies the groom consists of kinsfolk, neighbours and personal friends. One of the intimate friends of the groom remains very close to him on this day. He is known as *dara dhara* or *tamuli*. This custom is very common among the Assamese Hindus as well. The *nikah* is usually performed after dinner has been served to the groom's party. Following this the groom's party returns along with the bride. Among the Singimari and Uttar Jalukbari Muslims the groom reaches the bride's home by midnight and the *nikah* is performed early in the morning. Again, among the rural and urban Assamese Muslims of Upper Assam, the groom reaches the bride's home usually between noon and late evening and the *nikah* is performed before dinner is served to the groom's party.

To perform a *nikah*, the parents of the bride and the groom fix the *mahr* (bride's financial security). When either the bride or the groom belongs to a place outside Gauhati, the *mahr* is usually fixed on the day of the ring ceremony. It may also be pointed out here that among the rural Muslims of Lower Assam the *mahr* is fixed on the day of the *nikah* while among the Muslims of Upper Assam it is fixed on the day of the ring ceremony. At the time of the *nikah*, the proposal and acceptance is made in the presence and hearing of two adult male witnesses. Another person, known as *ukil*, asks the bride and the groom for their consent to the marriage. As soon as the consent is obtained the Imam recites verses from the Koran. Following this, the Imam leads a supplication in which all the persons present also join.

In some parts of Assam, the custom of presentation (*joran*) is also prevalent. This is a custom observed by the Assamese Hindus. The groom's mother and a close kin bless the bride by putting vermillion on her forehead and present her with clothes, ornaments, a comb and a mirror. Among the Assamese Muslims, however, only clothes, ornaments, the comb and the mirror are presented to the bride during *joran*.

The practice of signing a legal document (*nikahnama*) to solemnize a marriage is becoming obsolete among the Assamese Muslims.[15] By and large, the Assamese Muslims belong to the Sunni sect and they follow the practices of Sunni marriage.

As noted earlier, the Assamese Muslims have adopted some of the marriage customs of the Assamese Hindus.[16] For example, the Muslims also fix the date of marriage in consultation with a *panjika*. In some parts of Upper Assam, the bride and the groom take a ceremonial bath (*noani*) on the day of the marriage and they also exchange betelnuts and *pan*. *Bianam* (songs sung by females during the marriage) is also prevalent among the

15. Ali (1969:8) observes that the practice of signing a legal document was prevalent among the Assamese Muslims of a part of the Lower Assam region.
16. For an account of the marriage customs of the Assamese Hindus, see Kar (1972:53-62).

Assamese Muslims. The custom of *ath mongola* is also observed by the Assamese Muslims. The bride and the groom are invited by the bride's parents on the eighth day following the marriage and they are entertained with a feast. The Assamese Muslims, like the Assamese Hindus, arrange marriages generally in all the months except *puh* (December/January), *chait* (March/April), *bhado* (August/September) and *kati* (October/November). It should be mentioned that the Assamese Muslims usually do not arrange marriages during the month of *Ramzan* also because during this month they observe *roza*. Both the Assamese Hindus and the Assamese Muslims prefer the months of *phagun* (February/March) and *bohag* (April/May) to celebrate marriages. During the days of February and March, the rural people are not engaged in agriculture and they have enough leisure to celebrate the occasion.

Conclusion

This paper has dealt with kinship and marriage among the Assamese Muslims and the discussion has been based on a study of three communities, representing three socio-economic contexts. This discussion suggests a number of conclusions and they may be briefly summarized here.

The Muslim households in all the three communities show an overall similarity in size and composition. In the urban, peri-urban as well the rural settings, the elementary family-centered household is the predominant unit. Although the household is a discrete socio-economic unit, it often forms a part of a wider kin group. As among Singimari Muslims, the effective kin group often includes a number of households among whom mutual assistance is a recognized ideal and practice.

Kinship is an important dimension of social relationships among the Assamese Muslims, although its role is rather diffused among the urbanized Assamese Muslims. The urbanized Muslims have an element of choice with regard to the kinsfolk they will interact with more closely than others. Thus, the rural and urban situations differ somewhat with regard to their patterns of kin relationship.

It appears that the persistent functional importance of corporate kin groups among the rural Muslims is to a large measure due to the common pattern of livelihood which is based entirely on agriculture. The various stages of agricultural operations call for the active cooperation of a number of individuals. But not many households have more than a few working persons At the same time, Singimari Muslims are not prosperous enough to hire labourers. Hence, mutual assistance among the villagers on a kinship basis is an eminently suitable device to tide over the problem of labour at critical points. In the social life also, there are many occasions when people need help and assistance. Within the limited horizon of the rural society, it is the kinsfolk upon whom an individual can rely for such help and assistance. Thus, the imperatives of economic and social life explain the continuing functional importance of kin groups in the rural society.

As one moves to peri-urban and urban settings, it is observed that new avenues, other than those based on kinship, of co-operation and reciprocal help and assistance are opened for individuals. The occupational pattern is highly diversified and the economic condition of the households is no longer homogenous. Even closely related households often pursue different occupations. Such kinsfolk sometimes belong to different social classes. Thus, factors other than those of kinship become operative in the field of social and economic relations. New avenues of relationships—such as those based on personal friendship, neighbourhood clubs, various committees and organizations and professional associations and unions—have tended to minimize the importance of kinship among the urbanized Muslims. At the same time, one also comes across, in the case of the Maria residents of Gauhati, a pattern resembling the rural situation in an urban milieu.

The marriage customs of the Assamese Muslims vary in detail not merely in the rural-urban context but also on a regional basis. The indigenous folk traditions also have an appreciable impact on the marriage customs of the Assamese Muslims.

The role of kinship among the Singimari Muslims is unique in some ways in the context of Muslim social norms. They have harmonized their social relations according to the dictates of indigenous folk traditions by totally excluding patrillineal marriages. This pattern approximates to Hindu rather than Islamic principles among the Assamese Muslims.

The indigenous folk cultural elements have been blended with Islamic doctrine among the Assamese Muslims. Elements from both these sources co-exist within the same social framework. The presence of folk elements in the social life of the Assamese Muslims is to some extent explicable in terms of the proselytization of local populations into Islam at some earlier dates.

Bibliography

Alavi, Hamza A. (1972), 'Kinship in West Punjab Villages', *Contributions to Indian Sociology*, New Series, 6, pp. 1-27.

Ali, Abu Nishar Md. Irshad, and Bhagabati, Ananda Charan (1972), 'Hindus-Muslim Relations in an Assamese Village', *Bulletin of the Department of Anthropology*, Gauhati University, 1, pp. 69-80.

Ali, Nazar (1969), *Mor Jibanar Kichu Katha*, M. Ibrahim Ali (ed.), Mangaldai, Kachijon Sampadana.

Allen, B.C. (1905-7), *Assam District Gazetteers*, Shillong, Government Printing.

Beattie, J.B. (1964), *Other Cultures*, London, Oxford University Press.

Bhuyan, S.K. (1926), 'Mirjumla and Ram Singha in Assam', *Journal of Indian History*, 5, pp. 138-142.

———, (1957), *Annals of Delhi Badshahate*, Gauhati, Department of Historical and Antiquarian Studies.

———, (1949), *Anglo-Assamese Relations*, Gauhati, Department of Historical and Antiquarian Studies.

———, (1956), *Mir Jumlar Asam Akraman*, Gauhati, Lawyers Book Stall.

Bora, M.I. (1936), *Baharistan-i-Ghaybi*, 2 Vols., Gauhati. Department of Historical and Antiquarian Studies.

Driberg (1883), *Report on the Census of Assam, 1881*, Calcutta. Government Printing.

Dube, L. (1969), *Matriliny and Islam: Religion and Society in Laccadives*, University of Saugar Monographs in Anthropology and Sociology No. 1, Delhi, National Publishing House.

Eglar, Zekiye (1960), *A Punjabi Village in Pakistan*, New York, Columbia University Press.

Firth, Raymond, (ed.) (1956), *Two Studies of Kinship in London,* London, The Athlone Press.

Fortes, M. (1959), *The Web of Kinship among the Tallensi,* Oxford, Oxford University Press.

Gait, E. (1893), *Report on the Census of Assam, 1891, Vol. III, Part—I,* Shillong, Government Printing.

———, (1963), *History of Assam,* (third revised edition), Calcutta, Thacker Spink and Co.

Goode, William J. (1963), *World Revolution and Family Patterns,* New York, The Free Press.

Goody, J. (ed.) (1958), *The Developmental Cycle in Domestic Groups,* Cambridge, Cambridge University Press.

Hamilton, Francis (1940), *An Account of Assam,* Gauhati, Department of Historical and Antiquarian Studies.

Hashim, Amir-Ali (1970), *The Meos of Mewat,* New Delhi, Oxford and IBH Publishing Company.

Hunter, W.W. (1897), *Statistical Accounts of Assam,* 2 vols., London, Trubner & Co.

Kar, R.K. (1972), 'Rites and Customs Associated with the Marriage of the Assamese Hindus', *The Bulletin of the Department of Anthropology,* Dibrugarh University, I, pp. 53-62.

Kutty, A.R. (1972), *Marriage and Kinship in an Island Society,* University of Saugar Monographs in Anthropology and Sociology No. 2, Delhi, National Publishing House.

Lloyd (1923), *Report on the Census of Assam, 1921,* Shillong, Government Printing.

Mahanta, K.C. (1973) 'Features of Kaiborta Kinship System,' *The Bulletin of the Department of Anthropology,* Dibrugarh University, II, pp. 27-34.

Malik, Syed Abdul, (ed.) (1958), *Ashamiya Zikir Aru Jari,* Gauhati, Gauhati University.

McSwiney, J. (1912), *Census of India, 1911, Assam, Vol. III, Part—I,* Calcutta, Government Printing.

Misra, S.C. (1964), *Muslim Communities in Gujarat,* Bombay, Asia Publishing House.

Mullah, S.C. (1932), *Census of India, 1931, Assam, Vol. III, Part—I,* Shillong, Government Printing.

Murdock, G.P. (1949), *Social Structure,* New York, The Macmillan Co.

Neog, Maheswar (1965), *Sankardeva and His Times*, Gauhati, Gauhati University.

Nimkoff, M.F., (ed.) (1965), *Comparative Family Systems*, Boston, Houghton Mufflin.

Piddinston, Ralph, (1961), 'A Study of French Canadian Kinship', *International Journal of Comparative Sociology*, 2, pp. 3-22.

Radcliffe-Brown, A.R., and P.M. Fortes (ed.), (1950), *African Systems of Kinship and Marriage*, London, Oxford University Press.

Ramgopal (1959), *Indian Muslims: A Political History*, Bombay, Asia Publishing House.

Robinson, William (1841), *A Descriptive Account of Assam*, Calcutta, Government Printing.

Saikia, Mohini (1967), *Assam-Muslim Relations and its Cultural Significance*, Ph.D. Thesis, Gauhati, Gauhati University.

Sarkar, Jadunath (1915), 'Assam and the Ahoms in 1660', *Journal of Bihar and Orissa Research Society*, I. pp. 28-41.

Sarma, Benudhar, (1969), *Phul Sandan*, Gauhati, Asom Jyoti.

Siddiqui, M.K.A. (1969), 'Life in the Slums of Calcutta: Some Aspects', *Economic and Political Weekly*, 4, pp. 1917-1921.

Shah, A.M. (1964) *Household Dimension of the Family in India*, Delhi, Orient Longman.

Uddin, Qamar (1972), 'Marriage Customs among Muslims of Western U.P.', *Indian Journal of Social Work*, 33, pp. 215-216.

Vreede-de-Steurs, Cora (1968), *Parda: A Study of Muslim Women's Life in Northern India*, Essen, Van Gorkum & Co.

Wolf, E.R. (1966), 'Kinship, Friendship, and Partron—Client Relations in Complex Societies', in M. Banton (ed.), *The Social Anthropology of Complex Societies*, New York, Praeger.

2

Kinship and Industry among the Muslim Karkhanedars in Delhi[1]

S.M. Akram Rizvi

Several sociologists and social anthropologists have commented upon the inadequacy of sociological studies on Muslim communities in India (see Ansari, 1959; Misra, 1964; and Ahmad, 1972). For instance, Ahmad recently argued that 'Indian society comprises not only Hindus, who constitute the dominant majority, but also Muslims, Christians, Parsees, Jews and the adherents of the three major off-shoots of Hinduism, namely, Buddhism, Jainism, and Sikhism. Each of these groups claims inheritance from a distinctive socio-cultural and religious tradition. Ideally, a sociology of India should encompass all these groups and their traditions. It is, however, one of the characteristics of the discipline today that it has tended to emphasise the study of Hindus and their religious tradition; the study of non-Hindus and of their traditions has been sadly neglected by both Indians and foreigners' (1972:172).

1. This paper is based on field work carried out among Muslim Karkhanedars in the locality called Pandit Kuchan in Old Delhi between September 1971 and July 1972. I wish to take this opportunity to thank Dr. Anand Chakravarti under whom this work was done. An earlier version of this paper was presented at a Seminar of the Department of Sociology, University of Delhi. I am thankful to the members of the Seminar for their criticisms and comments on the paper. I am also grateful to Professor Andre Beteille for his detailed comments and criticism on an earlier draft of this paper.

Ahmad goes on further to suggest that studies focussing specifically on these communities should be undertaken to bridge the gap in our sociological knowledge about them.

The present study is an attempt in this direction. It deals with a Muslim *biradari* (community) called the Multani Lohars. The name indicates the place of origin (Multan) and the ancestral occupation of the group. Living deep inside the narrow lanes of the old city of Delhi, the Multani Lohars are popularly known as the Karkhanedars. We shall therefore refer to them in this paper as the Karkhanedars.

The Karkhanedars

Karkhanedar is a vernacular term used for a person engaged in the business of manufacturing of which he is generally the owner. A karkhana may be defined as a workshop for manufacturing machinery or spare parts of machinery in which not less than two and not more than thirty-five persons may be employed. The karkhanas under study operate in domestic conditions and, therefore, have certain pervasive effects on the life of the karkhanedars who work in them. Particularly when such industries initiate changes in the day-to-day life, the institutional behaviour of the people tends to be adaptive. But this does not mean that such industries are themselves not affected by the social forces operating in a society. Industry and society are, in fact, highly interrelated and interdependent and this interdependence is not simple, direct, and uniform. This paper explores this interrelationship and interdependence between social structure and industry by focussing upon how the economic forces generated by the growth of karkhanas have affected the kinship structure of the Karkhanedars. More specifically, it examines the changes that have come about in the structure and composition of households, the range of kin ties and the marriage preferences of the Karkhanedars as a result of their improved economic conditions.

There are no authentic accounts covering the period before the arrival of the Karkhanedars in Multan, nor for the period during which they stayed there. They are said to have come to Multan from Uzbekistan some time during the sixteenth century. They were blacksmiths in Uzbekistan, manufacturing agricultural tools and implements, and were known as *temorchi* (blacksmith), a term which is still in use in Turkey (Aqil, n.d.:14). From Uzbekistan they migrated to Multan towards the beginning of the sixteenth century, where they continued their traditional occupation. The Karkhanedars are said to have occupied the fourth position in the economic hierarchy of Multan, the landowners being at the top and the *bhangis* (scavengers) at the bottom.

In the wake of Akbar's invasion of Sind there followed a large-scale migration of people from Multan to various princely States for safety and survival. They chose these states because they offered good conditions for trade and employment. Among those who moved out were the Karkhanedars, who ultimately settled in princely states such as Rewari, Bhopal Jaipur, Bharatpur and Hyderabad (Deccan). They were employed by these states as manufacturers of war weapons and armour. This was a very important development in their history as it meant that their manufacturing skills were utilized and patronized. The unsettled political conditions that then prevailed kept up the demand for war materials, and as a consequence the business of the Karkhanedars flourished.

When the British took over from the Mughals political life became less fluid. The British assumed control over the external relations of the princely states, and the incidence of internecine warfare was greatly reduced. Consequently, the services of the Karkhanedars gradually became redundant.

Having lost their jobs in the princely states, the Karkhanedars were forced to move out in search of alternative employment. Many of them came to Delhi towards the end of the nineteenth century. Around this time various factories and engineering workshops were being established in Delhi. The Karkhanedars got employment in these as foremen, mechanics, turners and fitters. Some of them were also employed by the Public Works Department and the Delhi Municipal Committee as roadroller drivers. In this way almost all the members of the community who migrated to Delhi were able to secure employment.

The Karkhanedars did not initially possess the skills for the jobs for which they had been employed. But their long tradition of manufacturing enabled them to adapt themselves rapidly to their new jobs. With the passage of time a fair number of Karkhanedars were able to display their talents. Their proficiency enabled them to occupy important positions in various factories.

The knowledge and the experience that the Karkhanedars thus acquired prompted some of them to set up their own karkhanas. In 1918, one Haji Abdul Shakoor, a foreman in Ganesh Flour Mills, established his own karkhana. He kept his job in the Flour Mills and devoted his spare time to his karkhana.[2] He steadily expanded his establishment, and by 1925 he was in a position to employ over a hundred of his *biradari*-fellows in his karkhana. Shakoor also helped some members of the *biradari* to open their own karkhanas by providing them financial assistance and technical guidance. By 1947 there were three karkhanas owned by the Karkhanedars.[3]

The partition of the country in 1947 forced the Karkhanedars to choose their domicile. A large number of them,[4] including owners of two karkhanas, migrated to Pakistan. This trend persisted till about 1955, by which time the Karkhanedars appear to have recovered from the shock of partition and set out to strengthen themselves in the country of their choice.

The expansion of entrepreneurial opportunities arising out of the rapid industrialization of Delhi in the post-Independence period and a ban on the import of certain machines

2. Haji Abdul Shakoor's monthly wage at the time was eighty rupees only. Shakoor had managed to save enough money for making the initial investment, a fact which testifies to the frugality and protestant ethic of these Karkhanedars. For an elaboration of the relationship between the Protestant ethic and capitalist development, see Weber (1964).
3. In the pre-Independence period, a total of seven karkhanas were established by the members of various Karkhanedar households. Not all of them could survive, however. Generally speaking, the prevailing conditions were not conducive to these enterprises since there was insufficient demand for their products.
4. Shakoor chose to remain in India. His karkhana continued to run for some time, till a family quarrel led to its closure. Thus, within a few years of partition, there was not a single karkhana owned by the Karkhanedars. The karkhanas observed in the course of field work were all set up after 1947.

created a congenial climate for indigenous production. The Karkhanedars exploited this opportunity by starting their own karkhanas and manufacturing the items which were banned. There was a rapid growth of karkhanas[5] so much so that a large majority of the Karkhanedars started their own karkhanas. Thus, of the eighty-eight Karkhanedar households covered, seventy (79.5 per cent) own their own karkhanas, while the members of sixteen households (18.2 per cent) depend on employment in karkhanas. The remaining two households (2.3 per cent) have mixed sources of income; some members of a household are employed in karkhanas as *karigars*, while some own their own karkhanas. In the pre-Independence period only three households had karkhanas of their own. This suggests that the community, after independence, has achieved a position where the majority of the members own their own means of production.

Household Composition

The Karkhanedars are a patrilineal community, and the mode of residence at marriage is patrilocal. For analytical purposes I have divided their households into two broad categories: simple and complex. For this categorization I have followed Shah's distinction of simple and complex households (1974). A simple household is one which comprises either a nuclear family (a married couple with unmarried children) or an incomplete one, such as, husband and wife. A complex household, on the other hand, includes kinsmen other than those forming a nuclear family, such as, married brothers with their wives and children. According to this classification, of the eighty-eight Karkhanedar households covered, thirty-nine are simple and forty-nine are complex.

The living space in a house (building) is shared by a

5. Karkhanas fall into two main types according to the place of work—house-based and shop-based karkhanas. A house-based karkhana is installed in the house where the Karkhanedar lives. A shop-based karkhana is installed in a shop outside the owner's residence. When a Karkhanedar wishes to set up a karkhana, he usually begins by establishing one in his own house because it requires less investment than a shop-based karkhana.

number of households. Every household has its own separate *choolah* (hearth). In other words, a *choolah* determines the separateness of a household. To an external observer, however, all the members of a house may appear to form one large household. The Karkhanedars themselves try to convey this impression as a way of displaying a high degree of solidarity among the different persons living in the building. This is because joint living, especially among married brothers, has long been valued in the Karkhanedar community. Among the Karkhanedars married brothers normally pool their income from a karkhana, which they may have started jointly, and household expenses are met from a common fund. They generally try to be as frugal as possible in meeting their domestic requirements in order to invest as much as possible in their karkhana. When a man no longer pools his income in a common purse, it signifies his desire to separate himself and his immediate family members from the larger unit.

In this classification of simple and complex households, therefore, two factors are important: separation of *choolahs* and separation of income.

There are studies which suggest that the joint family has not broken down in the wake of industrialization. Singer's study (1968), for instance, maintains that the joint family continues to be the norm among entrepreneurs despite changes in their material conditions. Singer concludes:

> . . . while there have been striking changes within three generations in residential, occupational, educational and social mobility, as well as in patterns of ritual observances, these changes have not transformed the traditional joint family structure into isolated nuclear families. On the contrary, the urban and industrial members of the family maintain numerous ties and obligations with the members of the family who have remained in the ancestral village or town or have moved elsewhere. And within the urban and industrial setting a modified joint family organization is emerging. The metropolitan industrial centre has simply become a new arena for the working of the joint family system (1968:444).

Our own data, however, tend to suggest that changes in the composition of households are indeed taking place as a result of the improved material conditions of the Karkhanedars though there are factors which also tend to keep complex households together. Let us first examine the factors tending to keep complex households intact despite changes in material conditions. These are mainly two.

Social Insurance Against the Collapse of Infant Karkhanas

Starting a karkhana requires a nucleus of capital. The main sources of capital available to the Karkhanedar who wishes to set up a karkhana are usually: savings from wages; earlier savings; borrowed money (*qarz*) from friends or agnatic relations; loans (*qarza*)[6] from a bank or a government agency; and help from affines. Savings from wages has been the most preponderant source of capital among the Karkhanedars. For instance, 46 (65.8 per cent) of the karkhanas studied had been set up with savings from wages, 12 (17.1 per cent) with previous savings and the remaining 12 (16.9 per cent) with other sources.

Savings from wages are slow to accumulate. If several brothers live jointly they can also save enough for starting a venture. The following case illustrates this observation.

□ Sultan,[7] aged forty years, owns a shop-based karkhana with his three younger brothers. It was started in 1959 in the house where all the brothers now live. Sultan was employed in a factory as a foreman and was proficient in his craft. At that time two of his younger brothers were also employed in different factories. They were together earning between 900 and 1,000 rupees a month. They were living in a complex household of which Sultan was the head. He was the only married brother. One day he suggested that if all of them made a joint effort, they could have their own karkhana. One of the brothers asked, 'How can we when we do not have

6. A distinction is made between *qarz* and *qarza* in Urdu. The former means an interest-free loan obtained from a friend or relative, while the latter is a loan obtained from a bank or some government agency usually with interest payable on it.

7. All names used in the cases are fictitious.

money for investment.' Sultan replied, 'We shall not give up our present jobs. Instead, we shall try to save as much as possible from our wages and thereby manufacture our own machines as we accumulate money.'

It took two years for the brothers to manufacture one lathe, one drill, and one grinding machine. They made a total investment of Rs. 2,600. Throughout this period they remained employed, and they continued to be so for another two years after the establishment of a karkhana in their house. Initially, they manufactured pistons, which fetched a good price. Five years after the installation of the karkhana in the house they shifted it to a shop which they rented after paying Rs. 10,000 as *pagri*.[8] □

Infant karkhanas also need constant attention in the early stages of development. If a karkhana is jointly started by several brothers living together, they can also give their collective attention to the karkhana as well as plough back their meagre profits into their business.

Dominant Role of Father or Elder Brother

The father, or, in his absence, an elder brother, is the head of a complex household. The head of the household is held in great esteem by his sons or brothers, and, therefore, enjoys a dominant position. At the same time, an elder brother as the head of a household does not enjoy the same dominance as a father does. The head of the household shoulders the responsibility of running the house. The successful carrying out of his functions depends on the degree of respect accorded to him by other members of the house. As head of the household, he is also supposed to resolve the conflicts between the wives of his brothers and his sons. If his own wife is involved in a conflict with his brother or brother's wife, the situation tends to become complex and may ultimately lead to a great deal of tension in the household. An elder brother as the head of a household has a more difficult task, therefore, than a father. Among the Karkhanedars the members of a complex household abide by the wishes of the head. This conforms

8. *Pagri* is a lump sum which one is often required to pay at the time of renting accommodation and is in addition to the monthly rent.

to the traditional means of tension management through which disputes among members are resolved. The following case illustrates this.

□ Qamar, aged sixty-five years, lives with his five sons, two of them married, in a complex household. He owns a shop-based karkhana in which his sons are partners, and they work with him in the karkhana. One of the married sons has three children, while the other has four. Conflicts between the wives of Qamar's sons is a daily feature. Sometimes they quarrel over minor things, such as the use of utensils and the playing of their children in the house. These conflicts are usually quickly resolved and the tension lasts only for a short time. But there are occasions when these minor disputes take a serious turn. One day Qamar came back from the karkhana for lunch and found his sons' wives quarrelling among themselves. The point of dispute was that a child had been beaten by his aunt on the ground that he had snatched food from his cousin. The mother of the beaten child took a very serious stand and threatened to live separately. Qamar realized the gravity of the situation and told the lady who had beaten the child that it was bad on her part to beat the child so severely, though she had every right to beat him. He then said that he would not take his lunch unless the incident was forgotten and the concerned women promised not to convey it to their husbands.□

However, the improved material conditions of the Karkhanedars have resulted in new sources of tension in their households which cannot be resolved through the traditional means of tension management. Let us now examine the sources of these tensions which have tended to influence the composition of complex households.

New Sources of Tensions in Karkhanedar Households

An important source of tension in Karkhanedar households has been generated by the new entrepreneurial opportunities arising from the growth of industries in Delhi. Their tradition of craftsmanship made it possible for the Karkhanedars to exploit the new economic opportunities. As shown earlier, from a community of craftsmen who depended on others for employment, they had emerged as a community of self-employed, small manufacturers owning their own means of production. The ownership of the means of production became a means of enhancing one's prestige in the eyes of the community. Being an employee in a factory, on the other hand, began to be looked down upon by its members.

The improved material conditions of the Karkhanedars, resulting from the establishment of their own karkhanas, influenced the composition of their households. The desire to set up independent karkhanas was the driving force which affected the ties in complex households. The members of several complex households decided to have separate *choolahs* in the same house. Let me illustrate this point by a case.

☐ Yousuf, aged fifty-five years, an employee in a karkhana, was the head of a complex household of five brothers, three of whom were married. They occupied a double-storeyed building. Of the five brothers, four were employed in various karkhanas. Yousuf, as the eldest brother, had the responsibility of running the house and meeting the expenses from the common purse in which all his brothers pooled their monthly wages. In 1955, they decided to start a karkhana from their savings. They hired a shop and jointly launched a karkhana. They manufactured motor parts till July 1959. During this period the fourth brother also got married and the fifth, who was till then working in another karkhana, joined the family enterprise. In July 1959, they successfuly fabricated a replica of a type of compressor valve which had been imported from Germany till 1956. Owing to the ban on its import the indigenous production of this item fetched a good price. By 1962 they were manufacturing compressor valves and three kinds of motor parts in three different shops. At this stage, the three youngest brothers were tempted to separately own the means of production in order to reap the profits individually. This move was initially opposed by Yousuf and his immediate younger brother. The conflict went on for some time, and finally it was decided that the two brothers who were opposed to separation would own their karkhana jointly, while the others might have separate karkhanas. The three shops were then divided among four brothers, and the fifth was given finance for hiring a shop to start another karkhana. This had an immediate effect on their household.

All the brothers, except the two who jointly shared a karkhana decided to have separate *choolahs* in the same house because, they argued, they had separate sources of income.□

The establishment of a karkhana within a house also influences the composition of the household. This happens because a portion of the house is used for housing the karkhana. If there is already a shortage of living space, some of the members may be required to vacate the house in order to provide space for the proposed karkhana. The solution, therefore, is to allow some of the members of the household to set up independent households. But the process of moving out is not simple and is liable to create friction among the members. For instance, there is the problem of who should move out. However, those who agree to move out get financial assistance for hiring another place. Sometimes it turns out to be of benefit to both parties as both establish separate karkhanas. The following case illustrates this.

□ Mahmood, aged forty years, was living with his two younger brothers, one of whom was married. He had three children and was the head of the complex household. All the three brothers were employed in various karkhanas and factories as skilled workers. Mahmood successfully fabricated a replica of a motor part the import of which had been banned. This greatly encouraged him to start his own karkhana. His employer Malik tried to persuade him to continue in the job, but he said, 'Let me discuss it with my brothers.' Later it was decided that two karkhanas should be set up to manufacture the motor part. One was to be owned by the two elder brothers, and the other by the youngest, provided he set up a separate household. In this way the youngest brother, Rasheed, set up an independent household, consisting of his wife and unmarried children. Therefore, one complex household, comprising three married brothers, gave birth to a simple household as a result of new entrepreneurial opportunities.□

Another development leading to change is when married sons seek permission from their parents to set up separate households. In such cases permission is sometimes accorded by the parents themselves because they want to avoid the conflicts which may arise from living jointly. If their financial condition permits, they give some money to the married couple for meeting the expenses of getting a place for residential purposes and setting up a karkhana. There were also cases where the parents themselves encouraged their sons to move out. Among the Karkhanedars in Pandit Kucha five simple households were set up in this way during the course of my field work. The following two cases illustrate this.

☐ Saghir, aged twenty-six years, was a partner in his father's karkhana. He had three brothers, two of whom were working in the same karkhana and shared the partnership equally. He was married to the daughter of another Karkhanedar. Saghir's father, Rifaqat, who had a well-established business, was manufacturing compressor valves, a profitable item. Rifaqat, in consultation with his wife, suggested to Saghir that he should acquire a place for himself in order to set up an independent household. The latter did not like the idea and requested his mother to plead his case with his father. His mother politely told him that Rifaqat did not have any ill-will towards him. She pointed out that, '*Yei tumahari behtri ke liye kiya ja raha hai; tum zada mehnat se kaam kar sako ge, aur hum main mohabbat bhee bareh gi; sath rahe to ho sakta hai ke dilon mein farq ajahe, woo bohat boora hoga.*' (This is being done for your own good; you will be able to work harder, and the love and affection between us would grow; if we live together, this may possibly divide our hearts, and that would be very bad).

In this way Saghir's parents tried to persuade him to live separately and set up an independent karkhana, the initial expenses of which were to be borne by them.☐

☐ Sajid, aged twenty-four years, was granted permission to set up an independent household and a karkhana. Majid, his father, owned a shop-based karkhana. Sajid had two brothers and two sisters. When Sajid got married, he made a proposal to his mother that, if his father permitted him, he would set up a separate household for his family. He told her that he was scared of his father because he might take it ill. He added, however, that if he had his own karkhana he would work diligently and in two years his karkhana would be a flourishing enterprise. He tried to persuade his mother to influence his father to endorse his plans. When Majid was approached for advice he said that he was quite doubtful about the success of his son's plans. However, he obtained the full details of the latter's plans and gave him some suggestions. Subsequently, Sajid set up a simple household and established a new karkhana. □

It is important to note that in all the four cases of branching off that I have discussed, the fathers owned their own karkhanas and were in a financially sound condition. Because of this their sons were able to set up separate households and karkhanas.

Differences in the degree of proficiency among a group of brothers may sometimes generate friction among them. Thus, a proficient member of a complex household may find that his efforts to succeed in business are frustrated by the other members. He, then, thinks of having a separate karkhana so that he can display his talents as he has full control over the management of the karkhana.

Old Sources of Tension in the New Setting

The traditional means of tension management cannot resolve the conflicts arising from the growth of karkhanas and the changed material conditions of households. Conflicts over the share of income drived from the karkhana, for example, have influenced the composition of complex households. It is true that conflicts over the use of money have always been a source of tension and existed even before the emergence of the Karkhanedars as owners of karkhanas. But it has become disruptive under the changed material conditions of complex households.

The responsibility of running a household, though primarily that of the father or elder brother, is shared by all the adult members who are required to behave in a manner conducive to the solidarity of the household. Here women, in their role as wives, become important in determining whether a complex household will continue as one unit. We find that more often than not trouble starts from quarrels among the women over the use of money. There tends to be friction over the share of income and the manner in which it is consumed by various members of the household. This is illustrated by two cases.

□ Seven brothers, five of whom were married, lived in a complex household along with their wives and children. They had an equal share in the karkhana, which was under the supervision of the eldest brother who was also the head of the household. The karkhana was prospering, but there was a conflict over the use of the income derived from it. This was mainly because two of the five married brothers each had five children, while two had four and two children respectively, and the fifth had one child. The wives of those who had fewer children complained that more money was being spent on the children of the other brothers.

The climax came on the occasion of *Id* in 1967 when purchases were being made for the festival. The two wives who had the least number of children complained that they wanted better clothes and other things for their families. The two unmarried brothers unsuccessfully tried to pacify them. The conciliatory efforts of their menfolk, including those of the head of the household, were also in vain. It was finally decided that each nuclear family should have its own *choolah*, and for this purpose a fixed amount would be divided equally among them from the income of the karkhana. In this way five *choolahs* came into being. The two unmarried brothers joined their eldest brother's household. Three years later, on the occasion of the sixth brother's marriage, the assets of the karkhana were also divided among the brothers. The value of the eight lathes installed in it was assessed and was divided equally among all the brothers.□

□ Shaboo, aged forty years, had three brothers. All of them were married and they were living together in a complex household of which he was the head. All the brothers together owned a shop-based karkhana. One day Shaboo was having his lunch at home when his younger brother Zahoor told him that he would like to have a household of his own. Shaboo became disturbed on hearing this, and asked his brother to explain why he wanted to do so. Zahoor told him that he had overheard the wife of another brother accusing him of consuming a major portion of the income derived from the karkhana. She had been complaining to a visitor that he was extravagant, and that the other members of the household had to tighten their belts for his sake. Shaboo called the lady concerned and asked her what was the matter. She denied Zahoor's charges, and a big quarrel ensued among the members of the household. They hurled accusations at one another. Finally, it was decided that it was high time for all the brothers to set up independent households in order to avoid friction in future. The assets were calculated and the money was divided among them. Those who stayed in the same building were given less money, while those who moved out were compensated for renting accommodation. Likewise, the value of the machines in the karkhana was assessed and divided among the brothers. Shaboo and his youngest brother Naeem got four of the five machines, and the two other brothers were given a machine and money for hiring a building on payment of *pagri.*□

Another source of tension has been the shortage of living space. In pre-Independence India, when the Karkhanedars were not well-to-do, it was very difficult for them to set up independent households even if there was a conflict in the house. The members of a complex household had to live jointly and pool their resources for their economic survival. But with the Karkhanedars emerging as owners of the means of production, they can afford to set up independent households in the event of quarrels among members of a household. The natural growth of a household by marriage or birth brings about changes in its composition and creates shortage of living space.

The death of either parent also influences the composition of complex households. The parents are generally a great source of unity and solidarity in a complex household. They regulate and govern the behaviour of their married children and their wives. They always try to maintain the unity of the house by emphasizing certain norms and values. Since the Karkhanedars are experiencing an economic transition, the death of either parent normally leads to a loosening of unity and the household is often subjected to daily tensions, especially in matters pertaining to financial management. If a household breaks up, the next step is the setting up of separate *choolahs* by each nuclear unit. This ultimately leads to the division of the karkhana.

Extra-Familial Kin Ties

Extra-familial kin ties enter the lives of the Karkhanedars in a variety of ways. For one thing, close kinsmen can often be tapped for loans for starting new ventures or for expanding them. Relatives normally give loans on comparatively easier terms. While one is obliged to repay loans taken from a kinsman, there are not the same compulsions to do so as with the debts incurred from friends. Furthermore, the help rendered by affines may also enable a person to start a karkhana. The wife's brother or some other affinal relative may extend monetary help for establishing a karkhana without expecting the money to be returned. A girl's family generally knows the financial position of the boy before marriage, and if they can afford to make a contribution towards the setting up of an enterprise, they do so. From the boy's side it is taken for granted that financial help for this purpose would be forthcoming after marriage. The ownership of a karkhana brings prestige and honour to the owner, whereas being an employee is looked down upon. In a way, the prestige that a Karkhanedar attaches to the ownerhip of a karkhana parallels that derived from the ownership of land in village India (see Srinivas, 1966; Bailey, 1958; Dube, 1955). This explains the keenness of the girl's side that the prospective bridegroom should be well-placed. The following is a case in point.

□ Chaman is now aged thirty-five and owns a shop-based karkhana. He was originally employed in Bhaiji's karkhana as a *karigar* on a wage of 150 rupees a month. Bhaiji had two unmarried daughters and he was very anxious to get them married as they had attained puberty. He tried to look for a good match but was unsuccessful. Ultimately, he approached Chaman's father, Rasheed, and made an offer that if he married his son to his eldest daughter, he would provide all the money needed to start a karkhana. A week after the proposal Rasheed went to Bhaiji's house and conveyed his approval. After the marriage, Bhaiji approached Rasheed and discussed with him the plan for the proposed karkhana. He ultimately spent about 10,000 rupees for the installation of the karkhana.□

Kinship also plays an important role in the recruitment of *karigars* (workers) in the karkhana. There are two categories of *karigars* in a karkhana: kinsmen of the master-craftman and non-kinsmen. Of the 521 *karigars* working in the karkhanas surveyed, as many as 415 were found to be the kinsmen of the owners. This provides clear testimony to the fact that preference in the matter of recruitment is given to kinsmen.[9] *Karigars* who are kinsmen also receive better treatment than those who are non-kinsmen. This is manifested in higher wages, more holidays, and preferential treatment in various matters. The following case illustrates the favourable treatment of *karigars* who are also kinsmen.

□ Shoukat and Noor work in Reyasat's shop-based karkhana. The former is a cousin of the owner while the latter belongs to U.P. Shoukat got the job in the karkhana by virtue of his relationship with Reyasat. Noor was employed through his father's friend who knew Reyasat. At the time of hiring both had more or less the same experience and skill, but they were not paid the same wage. Noor was offered Rs. 300 a month while Shoukat was employed on a piece-work basis which gave him a monthly income of between 350 and 500 rupees. Further, Reyasat has always been helpful to his cousin. He is very friendly with him and even advances him money, which is denied to Noor. He also tries to encourage Shoukat to set up his own karkhana, assuring him of all possible help.□

However, relations between kinsmen have tended to become selective in recent years. Meetings between brothers who live separately take place very rarely. Even brothers who share the same building have few contacts. A Karkhanedar's life has become so busy that he does not find time to maintain kin ties, especially extra-familial ones. A kin-group has therefore shrunk into a much smaller group. Let me illustrate this by a case.

□ Jamil and Basir are two married brothers living with their wives and children in the same building. Both own separate karkhanas. They were separated in 1968 when there was a conflict between their wives over the sharing of the income derived from a karkhana, then jointly owned by them. With the division of the karkhana, the two brothers separated and set up independent *choolahs*. Since they now own separate karkhanas, the amount of work has increased considerably. Contacts

9. There are several reasons, mostly related to the organization of the karkhanas and the short supply of *karigars*, which are responsible for this. I have omitted a detailed discussion of the reasons as they do not concern us here.

between the two brothers have been reduced considerably and they do not spend as much time together as they used to. They say that, '*Zimmedari barh gaee hai*' (Responsibilities have increased).□

A Karkhanedar, after working to the point of exhaustion in his karkhana, enjoys nothing better than sitting in the company of his immediate family members. According to one of my informants, '*Din bhar ke thake huye aadmi ke liye ghar jannat hai*' (Home is heaven for a person who is exhausted after the day's work). Besides this, the business is such that no business secret- is leaked out to any member of the community. This attitude is often taken to an extreme when one brother avoids meeting another if he runs a separate karkhana. This point is illustrated by the following case.

□ Jamil and Basir, the two brothers in the case cited above, avoid meeting each other because they do not want their business secrets to leak out. They manufacture ball-bearings, and they do not want their clients, and the agreements with them, to be known to each other. They fear that if they meet each other frequently they may give away their business secrets. According to them, '*business to bhai se bhee chhopaya jata hai*' (business is kept secret even from brothers).□

Regular contacts are maintained only with those with whom there are common business interests. The basis of such relations is, therefore, business rather than consanguinity. These relations are generally of short duration, depending upon the period during which business is transacted. The following cases illustrate this observation.

□ Waseem, aged thirty-two years owns a shop-based karkhana in partnership with three brothers. He manufactures oil engine parts. One day he got an order for 5,000 pieces of spare parts for oil engines Since this was a large order, he knew it would be difficult for him to complete the delivery within a month, which was the time stipulated in the order. He immediately contacted Baboo, who manfactured the same item but whose economic condition was not good. The latter, therefore, demanded an advance. An agreement was reached and it was decided that Baboo would manufacture 2,000 pieces in a month's time. In this way a sub-contract was given to a manufacturer of inferior standing.

□ Shahid, who owns a shop-based karkhana, got an order for the manufacture of compressor valves. The order was large, and delivery had to be made within three months. This was Shahid's biggest ever order, and he was greatly worried about making the delivery in time. Although he knew that Tasneem, unrelated to him, manufactured the same item, he was not sure that he would be able to produce quality goods, as required by his customer. He contacted Tasneem and discussed the matter. He made it very clear that unless the latter's work came up to the required standard he could not give him a sub-contract. Tasneem prepared a sample and got it approved by Shahid, who finally agreed to give him a sub-contract.□

Marriage Preferences

In pre-Independence India, most Karkhanedars, as mentioned earlier, lived in complex households. Marriages between parallel cousins and cross cousins were preferred due to their weak economic conditions. Marriages of this kind, occurring within the kin group, involved limited rights and responsibilities, and did not involve any major expenditure on dowry, feasts, and exchange of articles. They did not necessitate any major reshuffling of units. The only thing which resulted from such marriages was that the relationship that had existed between the parents of the marrying couple was further cemented. This situation corresponds to the one described by Uberoi, where kin marriages are preferred to non-kin marriage (1971). Similarly, Dass, discussing the structure of marriage preferences based on a study of Pakistani fiction, states that 'the system defines a circle of kin in terms of a khandan and then postulates the rule that the nearest female kin of ego's own generation is the preferred spouse, subject to the operation of the incest taboo on full siblings and the ban on inter-generational marriage' (1973:42).

The marriage preferences of Karkhanedars have changed since Independence because of their changed economic circumstances. The fact that some of them are more well-to-do than others has led to a sense of status consciousness among them. The term status is used here in the Weberian sense to mean style of life (see Weber, 1964). With regard to the Karkhanedars, this includes the scale of the karkhana, educational qualifications, mode of living, and political standing in the community. The financial position of a household is reflected in the scale of the karkhana owned, if any. By educational qualifications we mean the formal education of a person. If a person has obtained formal education it is appreciated by the members of his community. The mode of living refers to the observable characteristics of a person, such as the quality of his clothes, the interior decoration of the building he lives in, and the extent of conspicuous consumption. By political standing we mean that a person has contacts both with his own people and those who matter, such as municipal councillors and police officials. A person who has at least some of these attributes is well placed in the community in terms of the respect shown to him.

The consciousness of these attributes has increased considerably over the past twenty-five years and is expressed in the marriage preferences of the Karkhanedars. During the course of my field work three marriages took place. In all of them consciousness of status played a decisive role in determining the choice of partners. The following case illustrates this observation.

☐ Amin is an entrepreneur who manufactures automobile parts in a karkhana in which ten persons are employed as *karigars*. There are eight lathes installed in the karkhana. He sells his finished products on cash to dealers. His reputation for manufacturing items such as compressor valves and bushes is fairly good. Two parties, neither of whom were members of his kinship group, were interested in obtaining the hand of his daughter for their sons. One of them was Majid who enjoys the same status as Amin. But the other, Farekh, occupies an inferior position. A tug-of-war ensued between Majid's and Farekh's households. At one stage Amin came near to accepting Farekh's proposal because his son was both handsome and modest. When Amin's cousin, Shahid, came to know this, he immediately intervened and pleaded on behalf of Majid's son on the ground that he belonged to the same status group. He pointed out that it would be a disgrace if Farekh's proposal was accepted. Shahid brought in some more relatives to further convince Amin. Finally, Farekh's proposal was rejected. Amin, who would have married his daughter to his wife's sister's son, Pappu, did not do so because Pappu's status is inferior to his.□

Conclusion

This paper has been concerned with a discussion of the impact of the economic forces generated by the growth of karkhanas on the domestic life of the Karkhanedars. It has been argued that the improved material conditions of the Karkhanedars has been accompanied by the growth of economic individualism among them. This has resulted in new sources of tension in their households which cannot be resolved through the traditional means of tension management. Certain factors, such as the death of either parent or conflicts over the share of income in a complex household, which operated even in the past, have become disruptive in the changed economic conditions of the Karkhanedars. We tend to find that large households, comprising several brothers and their children, are getting partitioned into smaller units. The economic advancement of the community has thus influenced the composition of households.

This conclusion is in contrast to that of Singer (1968), for instance, who maintains that the joint family continues to be the norm of entrepreneurs in Madras. The point to be noted in his study is that the industrialists come from well-to-do families and go in for joint ventures. This they do in order to maintain possession of, and control over, a large establishment. Further, an enterprise owned by a joint family can secure certain concessions, such as a rebate on income tax. Among the Karkhanedars, however, joint ownership may not be of much benefit since they own small karkhanas. Moreover, since the establishment of a karkhana does not involve much capital investment, the members of a complex household are tempted to start karkhanas independently of each other. This is both a sign of economic individualism and a factor that contributes to its growth. Consequently, complex households are tending to diminish in size. This has its own implications on the stability of wider kin ties, which are becoming weaker.

Finally, the marriage preferences of the Karkhanedars have also undergone a change and we find that there tends to be a greater emphasis on status considerations as against marriage within the kin groups as in the past. In pre-Independence India parallel and cross-cousin marriages were preferred, but today this no longer seems to be the case. There is an emphasis on the similarity of status of the parties involved.

BIBLIOGRAPHY

Ahmad, Imtiaz (1972), 'For a Sociology of India', *Contributions to Indian Sociology*, New Series, 4, pp. 172-178.

Aqil, M.A.H. (n.d.), *Paijham-i-Baidari* (in Urdu), Meerut, All India Mughalia Sudhar Committee.

Ansari, G., (1959), *Muslim Castes in Uttar Pradesh*, Lucknow, Ethnographic and Folk Culture Society.

Bailey, F.G. (1958), *Caste and the Economic Frontier*, Bombay, Oxford University Press.

Beteille, Andre (1964), 'Family and Social Change in India and Other South Asian Countries', *Economic Weekly*, 16, pp. 237-244.

Dass, Veena (1973), 'The Structure of Marriage Preferences: An Account from Pakistani Fiction', *Man*, 8, pp. 30-45.

Dube, S.C. (1955), *Indian Village*, London, Routledge and Kegan Paul.

Misra, S.C. (1964), *Muslim Communities in Gujarat*, Bombay, Asia Publishing House.

Shah, A.M. (1974), *The Household Dimension of the Family in India*, Delhi, Orient Longman.

Singer, M. (1968), 'The Indian Joint Family in Modern India', in Milton Singer and B.S. Cohn (eds.), *Structure and Change in Indian Society*, Chicago, Aldine Publishing Company.

Srinivas, M.N. (1966), *Social Change in Modern India*, Berkeley, University of California Press.

Uberoi, J.P.S. (1971), 'Men, Women and Property in Northern Afghanistan', in S.T. Lokhandwalla (ed.), *India and Contemporary Islam*, Simla, Indian Institute of Advanced Study.

Weber, Max (1964), *Max Weber: Essays in Sociology* (H.H. Gerth and C.W. Mills eds. and trans.), London, Routledge and Kegan Paul.

Marriage among the Sunni Surati Vohras of South Gujarat[1]

Ismail A. Lambat

The aim of this paper is threefold. First, it tries to present a detailed account of the rites and ceremonies associated with marriage among the Sunni Surati Vohras of South Gujarat. The conception of Muslim marriage as a civil contract has tended to create the impression that marriage among Muslim groups in India is a relatively simple affair (Ansari, 1962:1). I hope to show through this detailed description of marriage customs and ceremonies among the Surati Vohras

1. I began my study of the Muslim communities of South Gujarat as a member of the Indo-Dutch research project on the modernization process in Bulsar district of Gujarat. Fieldwork was conducted during 1971-72 in twenty villages of which seventeen are in Bulsar District and three in Surat District. Seventeen of the twenty villages covered were Sunni Surati Vohra villages. I am thankful to the sponsors of the research project, the Netherlands Foundation for Tropical Research, The Hague, for providing funds for fieldwork and to the other members of the research team for their help and cooperation. I am particularly grateful to Dr. S. Devadas Pillai who started me on the study of the Muslims of Gujarat and discussed some parts of the paper with me, and to Professor Imtiaz Ahmad who persuaded me to write for this volume despite my shortcomings and offered useful advice and suggestions at every stage of the preparation of this paper. I am alone responsible for the numerous deficiencies that still remain.

that the relatively simple ceremony of *nikah* among the Muslims is actually punctuated by elaborate rites and ceremonies which serve to underscore the social significance of the event both for the individual and his group. Second, it examines the place of marriage in the kinship system. Muslim marriage practices are supposed to recognize few restrictions regarding whom one may marry beyond those explicitly prescribed by the Koran. Even so, restrictions based on considerations of kinship, caste and village do exist in practice. Kinship also enters the numerous rites and ceremonies that are traditionally associated with the celebration of marriage. Lastly, this paper proposes to outline the impact of recent social changes—such as the spread of education, economic prosperity and Islamization—on the marriage customs and ceremonies as well as the structure of marriage preferences among the Surati Vohras.

The discussion presented in this paper is based on data drawn from a detailed investigation of a Sunni Surati Vohra village, though information gathered from other villages has been frequently utilized in the interpretation and elaboration of the principles and rules relating to marriage. The village was selected randomly, but the knowledge of the area indicated that it was representative of Sunni Vohra villages in general. The data were gathered by being both a participant and an observer. Besides, a number of knowledgeable persons were also interviewed. These included elderly men and women as well as young men with Islamic learning and those with secular education. In addition, the village marriage register was also consulted. It provided information on who had married whom. It also provided information on girls who had married outside the village, i.e., in other villages, or when they had been married by proxy to someone living in a foreign country. It did not provide the same kind of information on the men who had married a girl from another village or when a man living abroad married a girl from another village by proxy. The marriage register also provided a clue to the age at marriage of the registered spouses, though the dates recorded often tended to be arbitrary and were not always reliable. Besides, the marriage register also showed whether those who got married had had some schooling, i.e., whether they were able to write their names in the register or not.

The Sunni Surati Vohras

The state of Gujarat is well-known for its Bohra and/or Vohra community. Explaining the origin of the community, S.C. Misra writes,

> The name Vohra can be said to stand not for any single community but for several whose broad similarity is that they are mainly of indigenous origin. Undoubtedly, a number of other communities are also indigenous, but their special character, for instance, of recruitment from a particular Hindu caste or community has given them an individuality. Such, for instance, are the Girasias, Maleks and other Rajput and semi-Rajput communities. The word Vohra, however, embraces a more general category of primarily agrarian communities which were converted to Islam probably during the reign of the Sultans of Gujarat (1964: 121)

The Vohras are divided into two major groups on the basis of their sectarian affiliations. The first group comprises the Shi'a Ismaili community called the Daudi Bohras and its offshoots which have also formed into distinct communities (Misra, 1964:121). The second group consists of the Sunni Vohras who again do not constitute a single community but are formed of a number of distinct regional units which are separate from one another. However, there are also other differences between these two groups besides religious or sectarian differences. The Bohras are mainly an urban community and live predominantly in cities and towns where they are mostly engaged in trade as dealers in paint and hardware. On the other hand, the Vohras are a predominantly rural community and are petty landowners and agriculturists.

The Vohras are divided into a number of sub-groups, each one of whom is separate and bears a distinct name. 'The tendency of people,' writes Misra, 'to marry in small units and again to keep marriage connexions localized and intimate has further led to the splintering of this broad mass into different units. Broadly, therefore, it is possible to distinguish several regional sections or independent communities: (1) Patani Vohras, (2) Kadiwal Vohras, (3) Charotar Vohras, (4) Sunni Surati

Vohras, (Misra, 1964:125).

The Sunni Surati Vohras are found mainly in the districts of Surat and Bulsar in South Gujarat. The term Surati derives from Surat and continues to be attached to this group of the Vohras because they were concentrated entirely in the Surat District before the separation of Bulsar District in 1954 These Vohras live in approximately 114 villages, usually located between 5 to 15 miles inland from the sea-coast. These villages are dominated by them socially and economically and also, to some extent, politically. However, there are some more villages in the area which are inhabited both by Surati Vohras and caste Hindus. Moreover, the Surati Vohra villages do not form a cluster of their own. They are interspersed by villages dominated by one or the other Hindu castes. Among them, the Pattidar dominated villages are the most numerous.

A typical Surati Vohra village is usually inhabited by the Surati Vohras, two or more Muslim service castes or occupational groups as well as a number of Scheduled Tribes and Scheduled Castes.[2] The Surati Vohras usually serve as the nucleus of a caste-like arrangement with the other endogamous Muslim castes in the village.[3] This caste-like arrangement has been in existence for centuries, but it has never incorporated any of the Hindu castes or Scheduled Tribes and Castes. This feature of the Surati Vohra villages distinguishes them from the Muslim Meos described by Aggarwal (1971 & 1973). The linkages of the Muslim Meos extend to a number of Hindu castes

2. For a detailed description of the caste composition and social structure of Vohra and non-Vohra villages see Lambat (forthcoming).

3. These 'castes' include the Mulla, Hajjam (barber) and Devan (village messenger). This caste-like arrangement has undergone a partial change in recent years as a result of the introduction of Islamic religious education. Prior to 1947, when Islamic religious education first penetrated into the Sunni Surati Vohra villages, the religious needs of the Vohras were met by the Mullas. This is no longer the case. The Mullas have been replaced by other functionaries. However, other service castes, such as the Hajjam and Devan, continue to perform their duties much as their forebears did earlier. Moreover, the mode of payment for their services continues to be traditional; it continues to be made in kind rather than being changed to cash transactions.

resident in the village. The Surati Vohras do not have any linkages with the Hindu castes. The situation of the Surati Vohras appears to be even more striking in this respect as they do not form linkages even with the Hindu service castes, like carpenters, blacksmiths, etc., on whom they have to depend constantly for repairs to their agricultural implements.

The traditional occupation of the Surati Vohras was cultivation and even today most of them are engaged in agriculture.[4] At the turn of the century, a number of Surati Vohras migrated to South Africa. Later on they also migrated to a number of East African countries and, from the 1950s onwards, they have been migrating to Great Britain. Called Safaris, these Surati Vohras are usually engaged in trade, commerce and service.[5] More recently, 'an increasing number of young men in urban areas are taking to the professions and their number is rising in schools and colleges' (Misra, 1964:125). These developments have naturally led to changes in the Surati Vohras social institutions, including marriage customs and ceremonies.

Types of Marriages

Like in most Indian communities, marriage among the Surati Vohras is looked upon as essential for both males and females. Parents are said to be 'not free' unless they see their daughters and sons happily married. Marriage is also looked upon as a *sunna* and therefore it is regarded as an obligation which must be fulfilled. Furthermore, all daughters are said to be *par gaheri*, literally meaning 'for someone else's house'. This belief compels parents to get their daughters married as soon as they reach marriageable age and a suitable match can be found for them.

Formerly, the age at marriage was extremely low. Many old people still speak of themselves, and of others whom they

4. In my study of seventeen Surati Vohra villages I did not come across a single Vohra who did not own some land.
5. Most of the money earned in Africa and other foreign countries is remitted to the village and invested in land and construction of large houses. The lands purchased through such remittances are usually passed on to relations for cultivation. This has meant that some Surati Vohra villagers have a higher acreage of land under cultivation than they actually own.

know, as coming to know that they were married only when someone told them after they were old enough to understand. This shows that formerly people were married at a very early age. However, today practically no one below the age of sixteen gets married and for boys the marriageable age is usually eighteen teen. Even this age is looked upon us being quite early by most people, but sometimes early marriages are arranged to please elderly grandparents who insist on seeing their grandchildren married before their death.

Polygamous Marriages

The accepted pattern of marital arrangement among the Surati Vohras is monogamy. Of course, as a Muslim, a Surati Vohra man can enter into a polygamous union and one occasionally comes across stray cases of persons with two wives. However, such cases are usually rare and are normally the outcome of the first wife being unable to bear children or the uncooperative behaviour of the wife which forces the husband to take a second wife without dissolving the first marriage. Sometimes a love affair too may end up in a second marriage. There are only two cases of men with two wives in the village studied out of a total population of 700. One of them had married for the second time because of a love affair and he had both of his wives living together. The other man was frequently commuting between South Africa and India and took a second wife in India so that she could take care of his assets there. The first wife lives in South Africa. Usually, as soon as a man takes a second wife or even contemplates a second marriage, his first wife will ask for a divorce. Only under exceptional circumstances, such as when she has grown up children or she has no one to turn to, will she tolerate her husband's second marriage.

Uxorilocal Marriages

Again, the accepted mode of residence at marriage among the Surati Vohras is verilocal, but uxorilocal marriages do sometimes occur. Such marriages usually take place under two circumstances. Sometimes the man takes up residence at his wife's parental home if she is the only child of her parents, or, she may be having sisters who are married and so her parents may want a *ghar jamai* for her.[6] This usually happens where the kinship bond between the husband and the girl's family is quite close. Thus, many a time a man getting married to his paternal or maternal uncle's daughter will go and take up residence there. The other situation in which a uxorilocal marriage takes place is when the girl's parents are relatively well-to-do and do not have a son. Parents who do not have a son do need someone to look after them in their old age and the *ghar jamai* is about the best alternative to having their own son.

Previously, poverty used to drive some young men to seek an uxorilocal (*ghar jamai*) marital arrangement. Nowadays it is not greatly favoured. As a matter of fact, there has been, and still is, a stigma attached to it. It is said that a man who cannot find a wife for himself will enter into this type of a union. For this reason, young men nowadays do not like this type of marital arrangement. They prefer that their wife should come to live with them but they will help their parents-in-law, particularly if they do not have their own son, and cultivate their lands while still residing in their own homes.

Widow Remarriage

No stigma is attached among the Surati Vohras to the marriage of widows. Widow remarriages are quite common and take place easily. It is only when a widowed woman has children that she may prefer to remain a widow. Usually, those with very young children are reluctant to remarry for fear that her children may suffer if she takes them to her new husband's house, where they will be looked upon as step-children, or if she leaves them with her deceased husband's parents or brothers they may not get proper treatment and the maternal love that she would be able to give them. On the other hand, those with grown up children are reluctant to get remarried because they think that they already have the necessary economic and social security and there is no need to

6. '*Ghar jamai*' literally means a 'son-in-law in the house'. For a detailed discussion see Van der Veen (1972).

go to a 'stranger's house'. These considerations are almost always taken into account before a widow remarries. However, remarriage of widows can, and often does, take place.

Divorcee Marriages

So does the marriage of divorced women. Of course, a divorced woman usually finds it hard to get an unmarried man for a husband, but she can always find a divorced man or a widower to get married to. Like the widow who remarries, a divorced woman nevertheless faces two distinct disadvantages in the event of her wanting to remarry. Firstly, she may not be able to get an entirely suitable match. If she is looking for a match of her own age, the chances usually are that he would be quite poor. On the other hand, if she looks for a rich or well-to-do husband, there would usually be a wide disparity between her and her husband's age. Second, even if she has no children from her previous marriage, her husband may have children from an earlier marriage. This can often lead to complications, particularly if she has children subsequently. Consequently, many divorced women prefer not to remarry. This is more generally the case if they have well-to-do parents or brothers with whom they can afford to spend their days in comfort without having to look for a second husband.

Levirate

The Surati Vohras allow levirate. There is no objection to a levirate marriage if the parties concerned agree upon it. Usually the practice is for a levirate marriage to take place between the woman and her deceased husband's younger brother. Marriage to the deceased husband's elder brother is not against Islam, but this type of marriage is not generally practised. Such marriages take place rarely.[7] The primary

7. I recorded two instances of such levirate marriages in the village. One concerned a woman of eighty. The other was a case of a woman whose husband had left for England and refused to have anything to do with his wife who was a distant cousin. The man's father intervened in this case, forced his son to divorce her and later persuaded her to get married to an elder son who had also divorced his first wife.

consideration in such marriages is the consent of the parties concerned. Sometimes the woman's deceased husband's brother may not like the idea of such a marriage and may refuse. Or, the widow too may refuse to marry her deceased husband's brother. Her objection tends to be stronger, and also carries greater weight, if she is asked to become the second wife. If she has children, she sometimes decides to stay on with her affines without marrying her deceased husband's brother. Or, she may decide to return to her natal home whether she has children or not.

Sororate

Marriage under the sororate system is not objected to either and in some cases the deceased woman's parents are actually persuaded to give their second daughter in marriage to their deceased daughter's husband. This is especially the case where the deceased leaves behind small children. It is usually argued that only a sister can give the true maternal love and affection to her deceased sister's children. However, there are no hard and fast rules governing this type of marriage. Such marriages are not obligatory and do not follow a set pattern. Whether they take place or not depends largely upon the inclination of the parties and the willingness of the girl's parents.

Exchange Marriages

Since there is a strong tendency among the Surati Vohras to arrange marriages within related circles, some marriages tend to become marriages by exchange. Such exchange marriages do not take place at the same time. Generally, as children grow up and get married, the exchange is completed. However aside from such exchange marriages, there is often also a more direct exchange of brothers and sisters. When there is a scarcity of eligible boys or girls, the parents who have a son and a daughter of marriageable age tend to look for an exchange marriage rather than try to settle their marriages separately.

Marriage by exchange also becomes necessary when a girl from a good or respectable family loses her reputation or is not particularly good-looking. Under those situations her brother is made to take for a wife a girl from a relatively poor background so that his sister can be accommodated. Money usually plays a prominent part in all marriages of this type as the boy who marries the girl must be compensated. Such marriages do mean less expenditure on the actual wedding, since two marriages can be held for the expense of one, but the other reasons far outweigh the consideration of expenditure. In fact, except for the outlay on a dinner and a few other minor items of expenditure, the saving effected through an exchange marriage is not considerable.

Structure of Preferences

The Surati Vohras are an endogamous group and they practise endogamy strictly. However, among the Surati Vohras there are no restrictions relating to *sapinda*, *gotra* and village exogamy as have been widely reported for most Hindus (see Kapadia, 1958; Van der Veen, 1972; and Pocock, 1972) and some Muslim groups (see Aggarwal, 1971). This would seem to suggest that they have a very wide choice when it comes to selecting a spouse in the sense that anyone belonging to the group, except those close relatives who are prohibited by custom and religion, are eligible as marriage partners. However, this is not the case in practice and the range of choice open to a Surati Vohra in the selection of his spouse is actually much narrower. It is indeed narrowed down to such an extent that when we speak of the group as being endogamous what is actually implied is that there are many small endogamous units within the endogamous framework of the entire group. Furthermore, the preferences for spouses belonging to each one of these units are systematically structured.

Since marriages are arranged by parents among the Surati Vohras and they take place according to customary rules, it is absolutely necessary to understand the structure of endogamous units within the group and the basis upon which they are founded. It is possible to identify three endogamous units or marriage circles among the Surati Vohras. These marriage circles are those of kins or relatives, those of *khandans* and those of inter-marrying villages. These circles are not mutually exclusive, but do sometimes overlap. Furthermore, they need not be adhered to with equal rigidity. Except for the circle of villages, marriages outside the circle do often take place and no stigma attaches to them.

Circle of Kins

When a man starts looking for a partner for himself, his first choice is from among his father's brother's daughters, or his father's sister's daughters, or his mother's brother's daughters, or his mother's sister's daughters.[8] If he cannot find an eligible partner within this circle of cousins, his choice is next extended to his second cousins. He can marry either his father's cousin brother's daughter, or his father's cousin sister's daughter or his mother's cousin brother's daughter, or his mother's cousin sister's daughter. If he still cannot find a partner, he will next bring more distant relatives into the orbit of eligible marriage partners.

The principal reasons for considering relatives as eligible marriage partners are two: the family wealth will remain within close kins; and the belief that relationships 'fade away' unless they are renewed by marriages among offsprings of related families. However, this preference for marriage among close kins is not always strictly adhered to. Sometimes other factors influence the choice of marriage partners and a shift in the preferred arrangement takes place. For example, there were eight cases between 1965-75 when cousins did not get married. In three of these cases the marriage did not take place due to family quarrels; in three cases there were no

8. These kin preferences need not necessarily be followed in the order presented here. Usually, both parallel and cross-cousins are thought to be most eligible partners and hence they are expected to get married. They do get married in most cases, but not always. The tendency to strengthen existing relationships is quite strong among the Surati Vohras and this checks a great deal of deviation from established preference patterns.

eligible partners; and in the remaining two cases the boys preferred to marry girls whose parents could sponsor them to migrate to England and the fathers of the girls were already in England.

Circle of Khandans

Besides the circle of kins or relatives, there is the circle of families bearing the same or similar surnames. These families, usually referred to as *khandans*, are favoured as in-laws above *khandans* bearing other names. These families or *khandans* are often ranked and differ as to their status and prestige though the precise basis of their ranking is not quite clear. Most villages have some families bearing certain surnames whose members dominate village life. All the members of these families are not wealthy, but at the same time, more often than not, they had more land than others some time in the recent past. Another indication of their wealth is that their houses are situated in prominent places in the village. Hence, to the average person in the village, these families represent the 'big people'. Some of these families also have a longer tradition of Islamic education. It seems that the principal bases of *khandan* rank are wealth and Islamic education and the possession of these elements elevate some *khandans* above the others.

Originally, landholding used to be the principal criterion for arranging marriages outside the circle of kins. Sometimes the parents of girls ignored the sons of close relatives to give their daughters in marriage to the sons of families owning large amounts of land. However, this usually happened only with families from villages with which effective marital relations existed already. A father would not think of giving his daughter in marriage to a total stranger, irrespective of the size of his landholding.

Around the turn of the century, the importance attached to land as the only asset came to be gradually replaced by the possibilities of emigrating to Africa. From the 1930s onwards[9] especially, more and more value came to be placed on persons who had either emigrated or had the opportunities of emigrating. This sudden change was the outcome of the prospects of making money which Africa offered. Parents of girls started thinking that those boys who had been to Africa usually had wealth and that such persons would make better husbands for their daughters than those owning land.[10]

The sudden affluence generated by the handsome earnings of those who had emigrated to Africa helped many *khandans* to improve their social ranking. In many cases, boys from lower *khandans* proposed and managed to get brides from higher *khandans*, and, in others, parents of girls of lower *khandans* who had emigrated and earned quite well in Africa were able to find matches for their daughters among boys from higher *khandans*.[11]

After 1947, England became another focal point for emigration among the Surati Vohras, as indeed among several other Gujarati groups. Those who were unable to emigrate to Africa or could not benefit from emigration to Africa took the opportunity to go to England. This shift again brought about a reshuffling in the choice of marriage partners. Parents of boys from higher *khandans* started looking for girls whose fathers were in England and were willing to sponsor their sons.

9. Emigration to Africa had started in 1902, but the possibilities of making good money were greatly restricted in the initial stages. It was only around the 1930s that they brightened up and picked up great momentum during the Second World War.

10. However, emigration to Africa and the growth of economic prosperity does not result in the enlargement or expansion of marriage circles in all cases. Even after a family emigrates to Africa, and since 1947 to England, it continues to adhere to the traditional marriage circles. For example, five girls from one village, whose parents were settled in Malawi in East Africa, went over to England when it was time for them to get married and sponsored their relatives from India who were eligible mates. Thus, the marriages of all five girls were arranged according to customs and within the traditionally preferred marriage circles.

11. This should not be taken to mean that the conventional adherence to marriage circles has completely broken down. Usually, the new

Parents of boys from lower *khandans* who had emigrated to England looked for brides from higher *khandans* for their sons.

It is difficult to characterize marriages between higher and lower *khandans* as either hypergamous or hypogamous. Firstly, these marriages are still regarded as falling within the endogamous circle. Second, they do not involve either dowry or bride price or an unnecessary increase in the bride's trousseau. Such marriages are arranged because parents of girls of higher *khandans* think that marrying their daughters to boys of lower *khandans* who are economically well-to-do would offer greater security for their daughters. On the other hand, those who belong to lower *khandans* and have been able to improve their material prospects, tend to arrange the marriage of their daughters in good or higher *khandans*, especially if they are able to help their prospective sons-in-law to emigrate. The tendency among the parents of girls of higher *khandans* these days is also to look out for such an arrangement, and it works out to the economic and social advantage of both parties.[12] Under these circumstances, the question of dowry or bride-price does not usually arise.[13] The whole arrangement is usually justified by the parents of girls from higher *khandans* by saying, 'we would like our daughter to be happily married', and by the parents of boys of lower *khandans* on the ground that,

pattern exists side by side with the old. Generally, one or two children are married according to the new pattern, but the rest are married according to the old pattern.

12. Some old women who were married into *khandans* possessing large landholdings which suffered an economic decline subsequently, regretfully told me that their parents had declined proposals from some young men who had emigrated to Africa. The explanation offered for such refusal was that the boys had belonged to lower *khandans* even though they were rich. Consciousness of *khandan* rank has not entirely disappeared. However, there are powerful economic forces operating against it. Even the women whom I interviewed on the subject regretted the decision of their parents as they had to work quite hard to work the land and the economic condition of their families had undergone a decline.
13. Around 1946 there was a dearth of girls among the Surati Vohras and at that time the practice of bride-price had crept in among

'after all, those who get married should be able to lead a good life financially'.

Circle of Villages

Aside from the kins and the *khandan*, the village constitutes the third circle of marriage. People do not usually like to leave their village and go to another village in their search for eligible partners. Only when no eligible match can be found in one's own village would one decide to look for a match in a village with which marriage ties already exist. It is only when an eligible match cannot be found either in one's own village or in villages with which marriage ties already exist that people would consider the possibility of arranging a marriage in a village with which no prior marriage ties exist. Such an eventuality is extremely unlikely and rarely do people contract marriages outside the circle of those villages amongst whom prior marital links exist. However, under no circumstances can a person look for a marriage partner beyond the circle defined by custom as the outer circle of endogamy.

Among some of the Hindu castes in Gujarat, a formal arrangement exists to contract marriages amongst a set of villages (see Pocock, 1972). This arrangement is called *ekada*. There is no such formal arrangement among the Surati Vohras, but still marriage ties exist by custom and tradition within a set of villages. For example, though there are approximately a total of 135 Surati Vohra villages in the Bulsar and Surat districts, the effective marriage ties of the studied village were found to exist only within a set of seven villages, and the outer-

them. However, this practice did not become institutionalized and faded away as soon as the ratio of males and females was restored to normal. The bride-price was known as '*khavana paisa*', literally, 'money for consumption'. It was usually demanded by parents of girls who were poor and who belonged to low ranking *khandans*. Nowadays, poor parents may ask for a few hundred rupees from the boy's parents for spending on their daughter's marriage, but no bride-price is actually demanded or paid.

most circle from which one could select a spouse was limited to twenty-four villages. Furthermore, there is a strong tendency to limit marriages to the circle of villages amongst whom effective marital links already exist. Thus, anyone trying to get married in a village outside the circle of villages amongst whom prior marital links exist will be discouraged from doing so by his own kinsmen as well as by the people of the village from which he wishes to seek a bride. Fellow villagers in such cases usually ask why the person should wish to change the established pattern, while the girl's people suspect that the suitor is unable to get a bride in his own circle of villages due to his reputation. Usually such proposals are rejected.[14]

There were a total of 123 marriages in the village studied between 1948 and 1971. This figure includes only those marriages which took place in the village and were recorded in the village marriage register. It does not include those marriages where the men of the village married in other villages or followed their fiances to foreign countries and got married there. These 123 marriages were distributed as follows: seventy-one were intra-village marriages, twenty-eight were proxy marriages of local girls to men living in foreign countries who were either from their own village or some other villages, and twenty-four were marriages of girls who married men belonging to other villages. These figures suggest quite clearly that preference for marriage within the village is quite strong.

All the twenty-four marriages of local girls to men from other villages were restricted to a set of seven villages which constitute the effective circle of marriage of the village studied. There are several cases in which inter-marriages between two villages have taken place for several successive generations.

14. Some poor Surati Vohras do sometimes bring wives from non-Vohra groups living outside the circle of effective marriage ties. Such marriages are, however, not celebrated in any way whatsoever. The word *shadi* (marriage) is also not used to describe such unions. People talk of such unions as 'so and so has brought a woman'. Persons entering such unions are not ex-communicated, but they nevertheless become marginal to the group. They have also to arrange the marriages of their children in similar marginal families.

For example, in one case a man's mother and his grandmother had both belonged to the studied village, and he was again trying to settle the marriage of his two sons in his wife's village. The compulsion for a person to limit his search for a bride within the circle of these seven villages is so great that people rarely dare go beyond it in search of a suitable match for their sons or daughters. The common argument advanced for sticking to these villages in the arrangement of marriages is that the customs and habits of the people in them are the same and there is little risk attached to matches arranged among them.

Even where a match has to be arranged outside the circle of villages amongst whom effective marriage ties exist, an effort is subsequently made to remedy this departure from the customary practice. Thus, in one case a man could not find a suitable match within his own village or in the villages with whom effective marriage ties existed. He came from a good *khandan*, but his parents were poor and they did not own much land. Nor could they offer the opportunity of emigration to Africa or England to their son. Consequently, no one was willing to give his daughter to him in marriage. This state of affairs left the man and his parents with no other alternative except to look for a bride outside the circle of villages with whom effective marital ties existed. He eventually managed to marry a divorced woman after paying a bride price. In course of time the man became the father of three sons and two daughters and also grew a little prosperous financially. When the time came to arrange the marriages of his children, he tried to find connections within the circle of marriage as defined by custom. He married his eldest son to the daughter of a close relative on his father's side who was considered exceptionally prosperous by local standards, his eldest daughter to his sister's son, his second son to a girl from a lower *khandan* whose parents were willing to sponsor him to emigrate to England and his second daughter into another lower *khandan* which had become prosperous lately. For his fifth child, a son, he is again looking for a bride whose parents can sponsor the boy's migration to England.

Marriage Negotiations

Since Surati Vohra marriages usually take place within related circles, we may be tempted to think that formal negotiations are dispensed with and the settlement of marriages is a relatively simple affair. There are cases where the parents of the boy and the girl agree to the marriage of their children when they are quite young. Furthermore, the strong tendency towards marriage within known social or kinship circles often implies that the families have already given their consent. Yet, marriage negotiations are always formally conducted—a formal proposal is nearly always made and the details of the marriage are worked out between the families concerned according to customary rules before a marriage is taken as settled.

The Marriage Proposal

The most important part of marriage negotiations is making a formal proposal. Marriage negotiations can be initiated either by the boy's or the girl's family, but the formal proposal can be made only by the boy's family. Usually, the parents of the boy start the negotiations and send word to the girl's parents asking for their daughter's hand in marriage for their son. This is usually done through a professional matchmaker, or a close relative or friend of the family. The person acting as the go-between goes to the girl's family, either alone or with two or three other persons, and talks to the father or both parents of the girl. If the girl has any elder brothers, they too are made to listen to the proposal. Usually, an outright answer is not given at this time, nor is one really expected. The girl's side instead promises to give an answer to the proposal within a few days. The period usually ranges between two to twenty days, depending upon the number of relatives that the parents have to consult and where they live.

Before the day fixed for giving an answer to the proposal, the girl's parents consult their close relatives as well as their daughters and the girl's attitude towards the proposal is ascertained. Sometimes, the girl does not agree to the match which her parents may find suitable. Such objection or disagreement is over-ruled in some cases, but not normally.

Often pressure is brought to bear upon the girl through relatives and friends of the girl to persuade her to agree to the proposal.

If the relatives approve of the match and the girl is agreeable to the marriage, the acceptance of the proposal is a mere formality. On the appointed day, the boy's go-between again visits the girl's family to obtain an answer to the proposal and their decision is conveyed to the boy's parents. If the answer is in the affirmative, another day is usually fixed when the boy's parents will visit the girl's family to finalize details regarding *mahr*,[15] the jewellery and clothing to be bought for the girl, the number of guests to be brought to the wedding, and to fix the date of marriage.

Sometimes the girl's parents are themselves interested in arranging the marriage of their daughter to a particular boy. In such situations, the girl's side sends a go-between who pretends that he is making the suggestion on his own initiative and the fact that the girl's family has sent him is kept a closely guarded secret. If he finds that the boy's family is agreeable to the proposal, he tells them that he will approach the girl's family and try to ascertain their reactions. From

15. *Mahr* is a sum of money which is payable to the bride by her husband at the time of marriage. This word is usually translated as 'bride-price', but this is quite erroneous. Ordinarily, bride-price goes to the parents of the girl, but the *mahr*, according to Islam, does not go to her parents. It remains the property of the girl. There are many Islamic explanations for the payment of this sum to the bride, but the one most commonly used is that this amount is a compensation paid by the husband for causing her physical injury by deflowveration if she is a virgin and for using her sexually if she is not a virgin.

The *mahr* is a must and it has to be given by every male when he gets married. It should be handed over to the girl when the *nikah* is performed, but this is usually not done. If a marriage is dissolved, the *mahr* is supposed to be paid before the dissolution. What normally happens in practice is that the wife exonerates her husband of the *mahr* in the presence of two male witnesses. If the husband dies without paying the *mahr* to his wife, she exonerates him in the presence of two witnesses after his death. The amount of *mahr* varies widely, but the commonly accepted amount is Rs. 127.50. It is not known how this amount came to be fixed. When a marriage takes place in a foreign country, the amount of the *mahr* is the equivalent of this fixed sum in foreign currency.

thereon the marriage negotiations take place as if the proposal was sent by the boy's side and the same procedures are followed as described above.

The Role of Matchmakers

Parents of boys and girls of marriageable age do not like to approach the other side directly with a marriage proposal. This means that someone else has to act as a go-between. Matchmakers normally perform this function and they are an indispensable feature of all marriage negotiations.

Sometimes the matchmakers act only when they are asked by one of the parties to negotiate a marriage. Generally, however, they approach the parents of boys and girls on their own. Matchmakers seem to derive a great deal of pleasure out of bringing about a marriage between eligible matches and often go to extremes to try to convince the respective parents of the suitability of particular matches.

The matchmakers are not always able to successfully conclude all marriage proposals that they initiate, but it is widely recognized that they have considerable expertise in conducting marriage negotiations and in bargaining with the boy's family about the jewellery and clothing, etc. A matchmaker can quote cases of marriages that he has personally brought about and he can thus persuade the parties to accept his views regarding what is the best thing to do in marriages. The matchmakers do not merely negotiate marriages but are relied upon for marriage preparations as well. They are supposed to be adept at buying gold and ornaments and getting them designed and fashioned. They are also supposed to know what types of clothing are in fashion[16] and generally accompany the families to Surat city when their members go on a clothes buying trip. The matchmakers enjoy a reputation as good 'hagglers' and it is commonly believed by those whom they serve that they can strike good bargains if the matchmaker goes with them.

The matchmaker is normally involved at all stages of a

16. Fashions change quite a lot. Sometimes women's fashions are influenced by fashion changes in South Africa.

marriage—from the time the marriage negotiations are first initiated right up to after the marriage takes place and the bride goes to her husband's house. Consequently, most matchmakers tend to be well off or have grown up sons who look after the agricultural work. Sometimes the matchmakers are widows or widowers who have a relatively steady and stable income.[17]

Matchmakers do not expect any payment for their services, but usually receive some gifts. They are given a piece of cloth by the shopkeeper from whose shop the cloth is bought and a set of clothes by the boy's or the girl's parents. They can also expect some help during planting or harvesting time, and can get a bullock for ploughing or transport purposes from their client's family. Sometimes food is sent for the matchmakers and during the mango season they get a share of the produce. These gifts are usually made whilst the matchmaking is in progress and for some time after the marriage has taken place.

Marriage Gifts

When the boy's parents visit the girl's house after the marriage proposal has been accepted, the most important subject discussed is that of the gifts to be bought by the boy's side for the girl. The girl's parents demand as much jewellery and clothing as possible and the boy's side tries to bargain for as little as possible. This haggling usually takes place behind a facade of mutual accommodation and with the girl's side claiming not to put any pressure upon the boy's family. Usually, the girl's father and relatives will say: 'We don't want the jewellery; after all, our daughter will be taking it with her to her in-laws place.'[18] To this the boy's representatives reply: 'What do you

17. Even in those foreign countries where the community has become established there are some who play the role of a matchmaker. For example, in England a 43 year old man from the studied village is approached every now and then by young Surati Vohras not only for arranging marriages between boys and girls who are residing there but also for arranging marriages when one of the partners is living in India or some African country.

18. One reason why the girl's parents demand more jewellery and gifts is that they can have the satisfaction that their daughter has been worth much.

prefer more for your daughter—a couple of more *tolas* of jewellery or a good husband and very good in-laws who have a lot of money and land?' A promise is also made that, in future, if she needs more jewellery they will have it made for her. In short, an amicable solution is reached. It sometimes happens that a solution cannot be reached, in which case the intended marriage is dropped.

The jewellery is given to the bride but remains the property of her husband and his family. If the marriage is dissolved, the woman does not receive it. In some cases, however, the jewellery is given to the bride as a 'gift' (*bakshish*) and if a marriage gets dissolved the woman has a right over it. When the jewellery is given as gift it is usually put in writing in the marriage agreement so that the husband or his family cannot go back on their promise.

Sometimes a cash amount is also stipulated as a gift. This amount varies between Rs. 500 and Rs. 5000. Usually, such gifts are made because the girl's parents may foresee some risk in their son-in-law. He may be socially deviant, may have had a love affair with someone else, or may have divorced his first wife. It is believed in such cases that, if the son-in-law and his family are made to sign an agreement regarding jewellery or cash, the son-in-law will try his level best to make the marriage work.

After the details of the gifts to be presented by the boy's family to the girl have been agreed upon, the date of the marriage is discussed. No exact date is fixed at this time but a tentative agreement is reached as to the possible timing of the marriage. This is followed by a discussion regarding the number of guests to be invited. Usually the boy's as well as the girl's parents are supposed to provide food for all the guests both from their own village as well as those invited from outside. When the boy and the girl are from different villages, the girl's parents will in some cases stipulate the number of guests that may accompany the marriage party. In most cases no limit is set and, therefore, the groom's party consists of as many people as are ready to go.

Marriage Ceremonies

A Surati Vohra marriage is usually marked by a number of ceremonies and rites. As soon as a marriage is settled, the cycle of these ceremonies starts and continues until the actual performance of the marriage itself. However, these ceremonies are not held in the case of persons who have been married before. This section will describe some of these ceremonies briefly.

Engagement

The first ceremony to be held after a marriage has been agreed to is the *mangni*, literally meaning 'asking'. If the engagement ceremony is of persons from the same village, the boy's parents usually ask the village Devan to invite all the members—males as well as females—of the Surati Vohra families in the village, or, occasionally, all the Muslim families of the village, to the *mangni*. The *mangni* ceremony usually takes place in the evening or the late evening. The girl's parents too send their invitations through the Devan, but they normally call only their relatives. Usually more people converge at the boy's than at the girl's place. From the boy's place the invitees move in a body to the girl's place for the *mangni*. The males walk in front, and the women at the rear singing songs. Three women carry trays containing a set of clothes for the girl, sugar which is fed to the girl, and candies or dates which are distributed to those gathered there. Besides this, the boy's mother will carry some ornaments of silver with which she is supposed to deck her future daughter-in-law.

On reaching the girl's residence the boy's party is welcomed with a shower of rice thrown by the girl's mother, or her paternal aunt, or any other elderly relative. The women folk enter the house and are seated on the floor which is usually covered with big sheets of coarse cloth used at other times for threshing of agricultural produce or for covering foodgrains. The males are seated outside on big bunks borrowed from neighbours which have been arranged there for this purpose.

The bride to be is seated in a somewhat isolated corner of the house, dressed in reasonably good attire. The boy's mother and sisters, or in their absence some other close relatives who are not widows, approach the girl and help her put on the clothes which they have brought for her. After this they place the silver ornaments on her and then the boy's mother and three other married women in turn feed her with sugar and throw a shower of rice over her. They also make her hold her scarf in front of her and place in it one coconut, a sum of one rupee and twenty-five paise, one betelnut and one dried date (*kharch*). After this, every woman who is present gives the girl a rupee. The girl's mother presents the boy's mother with a scarf (*odhni*).

As soon as these rites are over, the message is conveyed to the males seated outside. Thereupon, the Imam of the mosque, or someone else, reads the *fatiha* and the dates or candies brought by the boy's people are distributed to all those gathered there. This completes the *mangni* ceremony and the boy's party returns home. It is not customary for the boy's family to go again tc the girl's house and very few really do so.

If the *mangni* is of two persons from different villages, only some men and women travel to the girl's village taking with them the set of clothes, the silver ornaments, as well as sugar and candies. They do not put up at the girl's place but at someone else's house. Some people from the village join them for the ceremony and the girl's parents gather as many people as possible. The rites and ceremonies are the same as described above.

Fixing the Date of Marriage

The period between the engagement and the marriage is usually a short one. It normally varies between a month to about three months. On a pre-determined day sometime after the engagement, about four persons from the boy's side, sometimes including the boy's father, go to the girl's house to fix the actual date and time of the marriage. The girl's people will also invite a couple of their relatives and in most cases dinner is also served.

The Muslims in general adhere to the lunar calendar and therefore the marriage date is usually fixed according to it. The lunar dates of 16, 17 and 18 are avoided because these dates are not supposed to be good for marriage. Sunday is also avoided, but if the lunar date is alright then there is no objection to holding a marriage on a Sunday. There is no religious significance attached to the avoidance of marriage on these days. The avoidance of Sundays most probably stems from the Surati Vohras' involvement with agriculture. They usually avoid planting some types of vegetables on Sundays because, they claim, that the vegetables borne by plants planted on Sundays are bitter. Thus they believe that a marriage held on a Sunday will be a bitter instead of a happy affair.

The Surati Vohras usually do not hold marriages in one particular month. This is the eleventh month of the Islamic calendar called *zil kadd.* It is termed *khali,* meaning 'empty', in the local vernacular. Islam does not forbid marriage in this month, but it has come to be avoided by custom and tradition. It is considered inauspicious for celebration of marriages.

As soon as the date of marriage is fixed, invitations are sent to the people to be invited to the wedding through the village Devan. Usually the boy's and the girl's families send out joint invitations, especially if they are from the same village, but sometimes they invite their friends and relatives separately. Since there is always some existing kinship relationship between the families of the boy and the girl, most invitations tend to be common.

The period between fixing the date of marriage and the actual wedding usually ranges between a week to two weeks. During this period, finishing touches are put to the preparations for the wedding. The womenfolk, both relatives and others, are kept busy with cleaning rice and pulses. Others plaster the house with mud, if it does not have a stone floor. There is usually a great deal of singing of songs (*geet*) while these tasks are being performed. Eight days before the wedding, the singing begins in real earnest and songs are sung late into the evening and from early morning. Through greater Islamization in recent years, much of the singing has been abandoned but the practice has not been totally discontinued.

Turmeric Smearing Ceremony

Four days before the wedding, a ceremony called *pithi* is held. On this day some young female relatives of the boy visit the girl's house and smear the girl with turmeric powder (*pithi*) mixed with some herbs and oil. After this they present her with two coconuts and two rupees. The girl's parents return to the boy's house double the number of coconuts and the amount of money, but not the turmeric powder.

Pithi is also applied to the boy as well as the girl by their respective sister's-in-law as well as three other married women. The maternal aunt is one of them. The girl has to undergo nine applications and the boy seven. The turmeric smearing ceremony traditionally took place four days before the wedding date, but this is no longer always the case. In some families it has been reduced to a mere formality and is therefore held either a day before the wedding or on the wedding day itself. The spread of Islamic religious learning and Islamization have led to an abandonment of the ceremony, but it has not completely died out.

The day of the marriage begins early both at the boy's and the girl's house. The boy and the girl are usually given a bath. The Hajjam (barber) helps the boy with his bath after giving him a hair-cut and a shave. Formerly, the barber's wife used to help the girl with her bath but of late this practice has been totally discontinued in most villages. Even when the barber's wife used to help the girl with her bath, she (the bride) was aided by her younger sister or her equivalent and four other married women. The younger sister would hold a coconut over her sister's head and the other four women put a little curd one after the other on the coconut so that it fell off on to the girl's head. After this they would all help her rub her body and help her with her bath. The clothes that both the boy and girl take off at the time of the bath are given to the barber and his wife.

After the bath the boy as well as the girl are dressed in good clothes and accompanied by their friends they go about the village to meet their elderly relatives. These relatives usually give them a rupee each as well as their good wishes. They spend about two hours in meeting their respective relatives and then return home, where a number of brief ceremonies take place.

The Mehndi

About two hours before the *nikah*, if the marriage is to be held within the village, or earlier if the marriage party has to proceed to another village, the *aughar* and *mehndi* ceremony is held at the boy's house. *Aughar* literally means grapes, but no grapes are actually involved in this ceremony. It refers to a sweet dish prepared out of crushed wheat. Young girls from the girl's house bring the *aughar* to the boy's house, feed him with it and apply some *mehndi* (henna paste) on the palm of his right hand. They also present to the boy's mother seven betelnuts (*sopari*), four betel leaves (*pan*) and seven bouquets of flowers (*kalghit*). The boy's mother gives two rupees to the girls for the *aughar* and Rs. 1.25 for the *mehndi*. After receiving their customary gift the girls return to the bride's house.

Mosalu and Paheramni

These two ceremonies, strictly speaking, do not concern the groom and bride so much as their parents. *Mosalu* refers to the gifts that the grooms and the bride's mother's brother bring for their respective sisters and sisters' husbands. These gifts usually consist of clothing. However, the bride's and the groom's mother's brother also brings some gifts—usually clothes or utensils—which are presented to them at the same time.

Paheramni refers to the gifts which other relatives bring for the groom or the bride. These presents usually consist of clothing or small utensils. Usually, close relatives of the groom or the bride bring gifts of clothing and the term *paheramni* is applied to them alone. The other relatives and friends prefer giving small utensils and a few rupees. These are commonly referred to as *bakshish*.

There is also a custom, called *vadhao*, of giving about a kilo of wheat and the same amount of sugar to the families of the groom and the bride by their respective relatives. This custom must be a symbolic hangover of the help that must have been given in earlier days. However, it is no longer thought of in those terms.

The Wedding Party

If the marriage is between persons of different villages then the wedding ceremony is usually held in the afternoon so that those who attend the wedding can return home in good time. But sometimes such marriages too take place in the late evening. In such cases, an entertainment programme or a religious discourse is arranged.

Qawalli

Qawalli was formerly a programme held at the girl's place. Of late this practice is fading away. In some cases a religious discourse is held instead for which purpose a well-known *alim* is invited. This programme takes place only if the *nikah* is held late in the evening. If the *nikah* is performed during the day then no *qawalli* or discourse is arranged. The main reason why such a programme is arranged is that it is pretty difficult to find adequate sleeping space for all the guests. Hence a *qawalli* programme or a religious discourse is organised so that the guests can pass their time listening to it.

If the marriage is to take place in another village, the *baraat* (*jan*) leaves the boy's village for the girl's village in the early morning by bullock carts. When it reaches the outskirts of the village, it is met by some young men in a bullock cart who block the way and demand money. They are given a coconut and five rupees before they allow the *baraat* to continue. When the *baraat* comes from another village, special arrangements have to be made to accommodate the party. Because of the the extensive web of kin relationships, the boy's party puts up in most cases at one of their relative's house and his in-laws are not required to provide an *utrao* (the place where the *baraat* puts up).

The Nikah

The essential element of the wedding ceremony among the Surati Vohras is the *nikah*. Formerly the *nikah* used to be performed at the bride's house but due to greater Islamization it is now-a-days conducted in a mosque. Before the *nikah*, two men approach the girl and ask her for her consent to the marriage. She is seated in a corner of the house, dressed in her best attire, surrounded by her friends. Her father or elder brother usually tells her to give her consent. As soon as the bride gives her consent to the wedding, the men leave the house for the mosque where the *nikah* ceremony is to be performed.

As the boy proceeds to the mosque with the male members of his party, the womenfolk go directly to the bride's house. There they are welcomed by a shower of rice. The groom's mother immediately goes to the bride and helps her put on one of the sets of clothes brought by her and decks her with the jewellery. She then feeds her with a little sugar, showers some rice on her, and places two rupees in her lap. The groom's mother is followed by three other women who too feed her rice and place a rupee each in her hand. Other women also give the bride small sums of money ranging from a fraction of a rupee to a rupee. In some cases a rite called '*okanni*' is also performed—small denomination coins are circled around the girl's head and given to the poor women who are standing around. Among the recipients would be the barber's wife, the Devan's wife, or other poor women who may be standing around.

The groom's mother receives a dress from the bride's mother. Some of the other close female relatives of the boy are also given clothes and an *odhni.*

The *nikah* ceremony at the mosque is a brief affair. The Imam of the mosque who officiates at the ceremony asks those who had approached the girl if she gave her consent. When they say that the girl has, he asks the two witnesses to the ceremony if they were listening to what was being said. After this there is a short recital in Arabic and Urdu which is followed by a little prayer (*dua*). The boy is made to sign the marriage register which is kept by all the villages and which the girl has signed already after giving her consent. Four more persons —those who asked the girl whether she consented and those who witnessed the ceremony—also sign the register. Three village seniors who witness the *nikah* ceremony are also asked to sign the register.

As soon as the signing ends, the bride's younger brother offers the groom a glass of sweetened, coloured milk. The Imam is also given a glass of milk. After offering the milk, the bride's brother presents a muffler to his sister's husband. As soon as this exchange is over, the groom stands and shakes hands with a good number of relatives and friends and the whole retinue leaves for the bride's place.

On reaching the bride's house the groom enters accompanied by one of his friends. First he is met by his mother-in-law who presents him with a gold ring. Then the bride's sisters greet him and give him some money. These are followed by other female relatives of the bride who are all eager to see the son-in-law and give him some money.

If the marriage takes place in the afternoon then the groom's whole retinue is served dinner before they leave with the bride. In case the *nikah* is held at night, then no dinner is served but some food is provided the following morning. The meal served by the Surati Vohras is quite simple. It always consists of fried rice and *dal* (lentils) cooked with mutton. Only in some cases is a sweet dish added to the meal.

Bidai

While leaving for her husband's house, the bride usually indulges in a lot of weeping and wailing and leaves her parental home with great reluctance. Finally, when she leaves, she is accompanied by a few of her relatives and friends. When the marriage party returns home, the front door of the house is closed by the groom's younger brother and the bride and the groom are not allowed to enter. He opens the door and allows them to enter the house only when he is paid Rs. 5.

Once the bride and the groom enter the house, a few brief ceremonies take place. These include the showering of rice and the seating of the bride and the groom together when they are given gifts of money by their relatives.

The bride comes to her husband's house with all her belongings, such as her clothing as well as the utensils given to her by her relatives and friends. She does not stay at her husband's place overnight but returns to her parental home with her relatives and friends. Early next morning the groom's sister or some other young relative goes and fetches her, and this time she stays at her husband's place for four days before she returns to her parent's home again.

Anna

The girl stays with her parents from two to four days. If the bride is from another village, the groom also sometimes accompanies his bride and stays with his in-laws until his wife returns. Even if the husband accompanies the bride, she does not return on her own. Usually, the groom's people come especially to fetch her. This ceremony of fetching the bride is called *anna*, and it is the last ceremony directly associated with the wedding. After this ceremony, the bride visits her parental home but no ceremonial importance is attached to such visits. It is only when she starts expecting and reaches the seventh month of her pregnancy that she is formally fetched by her people for her first delivery.

Conclusion

This somewhat patchy account has tried to present a discription of a typical marriage among the Sunni Surati Vohras of South Gujarat. We saw that marriages in this group generally take place within closed marriage circles, and that economic considerations play a very important part in marriage decisions. The male members do not expect a dowry, but the wife can bring a relatively large trousseau. Besides, there are other advantages. A bride from a prosperous family can enable a person to get financial support whenever it is needed or she brings many items as gifts from her parents and brothers, or she can come into an inheritance upon the death of her parents. Furthermore, there is also the psychological satisfaction that some derive by getting married to a rich man's daughter.

The search for an affluent bride has in many cases led to the distortion of the preferred types of marriages. It is noticeable that in many cases there is a deliberate effort on the part of a 'new rich' Vohra to try his level best to get the daughter of another rich Vohra as a bride for his son. However, it should not be surmised from this that the traditional marriage preferences have ceased to operate. Deviations are known but do not take place as a rule nor has the preference for *khandans* been discarded completely. An effort is usually made to remedy some of the deviations and departures from conventional practice.

The marriages are arranged by parents, but those getting married have a say. Very rarely is a decision regarding marriage taken either against the boy's or the girl's wish. Sometimes the boy or the girl agrees to a marriage just in order to please their respective parents.

Since marriages take place between close kins, there is relatively little chance of a feeling of inferiority or inequality developing between the families of the boy and the girl. Furthermore, the absence of dowry and bride-price also creates fewer occasions for bargaining and argument between the families. This also tends to minimise the feeling of indebtedness. Although it is relatively easy to obtain a divorce and the parents of the girls concede that the son-in-law has an upper hand in a marriage, he is not shown any undue respect. He is not looked down upon nor is he pampered.

A marriage among the Surati Vohras is the occasion for a number of rites and ceremonies involving showering of rice, application of turmeric powder and giving of coconuts, betel-nuts and *pan*. Some of these rites and ceremonies are analogous to the customs and rites practised by the lower-middle Hindu castes in the area. For sometime, the Surati Vohras have been experiencing a struggle between custom and religion and in recent years this struggle has picked up great momentum because of the increase in religious education among the members of this group. However, the customary rites and ceremonies continue to enjoy a very strong hold on the group and have not been replaced by alternate religious practices. The religious leaders who raise a hue and cry over un-Islamic customs have not been able to provide Islamic substitutes for them. For example, they have vehemently opposed the singing of *geet* by women but they have not been able to raise their voices as strongly against the loud-speakers that blare out the latest film hits. No doubt, some customs and ceremonies are being dropped because of greater Islamization as well as an increase in secular education, but many others are still practised widely and are likely to remain popular in the future.

Bibliography

Aggarwal, P.C. (1971), *Caste, Religion and Power: An Indian Case Study*, New Delhi, Sri Ram Centre for Industrial Relations.

——— (1973), 'The Meos of Rajasthan and Haryana', in Imtiaz Ahmad (ed.), *Caste and Social Stratification Among the Muslims*, Delhi, Manohar Book Service.

Kapadia, K.M. (1958), *Marriage and Family in India*, Bombay, Oxford University Press.

Lambat, I.A. (forthcoming), 'Rural Muslims', in S.D. Pillai (ed.), *Changing India*, Bombay, Popular Parkashan.

Misra, S.C. (1964), *Muslim Communities in Gujarat*, Bombay, Asia Publishing House.

Pocock, D.F. (1972), *Kanbi and Patidar*, London, Oxford University Press.

Van der Veen, K.W. (1972), *I Give Thee my Daughter: A Study of Marriage and Hierarchy Among the Anavil Brahmins of South Gujarat*, Essen, Von Gorkum & Co.

4

Marriage and Kinship among the Gujar Bakarwals of Jammu and Kashmir[1]

R. P. Khatana

In this paper I shall discuss some aspects of marriage and kinship among the Gujar Bakarwal Muslims of Jammu and Kashmir. The Gujar Bakarwals are a community of pastoral nomads who transhume within the territorial limits of the state, according to set schedules, in search of suitable pastures for their animals. Their repeated oscillation within a specific space-time continuum has exercised a decisive influence in shaping the structure of their marriage patterns and kinship groupings, so much so that even Islamic norms relating to these institutions, to which they formally adhere, have been adapted to suit the limits imposed by their peculiar mode of existence and physical environment.

The discussion that follows is based on data collected through fieldwork among the Gujar Bakarwals during 1973-74. My contacts with the Gujar Bakarwals and other Gujar

1. I wish to thank Professor Moonis Raza, Professor of Geography in the Centre for Regional Studies at the Jawaharlal Nehru University, for his constant encouragement and advice during the course of research on which this paper is based. I am also grateful to Miss Sarojni Bisaria for her help and advice in the preparation of this paper. I am, however, alone responsible for the many weaknesses which still remain in this discussion.

groups in the state of Jammu and Kashmir began several years earlier. As a Hindu Gujar from Haryana, I became interested in the history and spatial distribution of the Gujars and periodically visited the areas inhabited by the Gujar Bakarwals. However, those early contacts were sporadic and the observations I made then were largely unstructured. Therefore, I decided to undertake a more systematic study of this community. Although the detailed data presented here relate only to the two *kafilas* with whom I lived and spent most of my time, I travelled with forty-four *kafilas* (Appendix Table 1 lists these forty-four *kafilas*) and the observations I made amongst them have been utilized in this account of their marriage and kinship.

Professional social anthropologists and sociologists may find this discussion lacking in both richness of detail and analytical rigour. This deficiency owes itself largely to my academic training. As a geographer, I became interested in the Gujar Bakarwals with a view to studying the nature of transhumance, and most of the data I gathered related to aspects directly relevant to my central concern (see Khatana, 1976). I collected data on the Gujar Bakarwals' social organization, including their marriage and kinship patterns, only peripherally. Furthermore, the Gujar Bakarwals' reticence to divulge information about themselves is also partly responsible for this deficiency. The reader will, I hope, bear these limitations in mind while perusing this paper.

The Gujar Bakarwals

The state of Jammu and Kashmir has a sizeable Gujar population.[2] There is no written history of these people. Therefore, it is very difficult to fix the precise date of their migration to this part of the country or to trace the circum-

2. The last population figures available for the Gujars in Jammu and Kashmir are those of 1931. At that time their population was 3,81,457 (see India, 1931:13). Estimates based on linguistic identity indicate that, today, the Gujars account for approximately ten per cent of the total population of the state.

stances of their conversion to Islam.[3] The Gujars themselves tell several stories of their migration to this area. Some old Gujars said that their ancestors had entered the territory of Kashmir at the time the Sultan 'ordered that the tenth month should be repeated after every two years and nine months, thus raising the number of months in the year to thirteen'. This event occurred during the reign of Sultan Shamsuddin of the Shahmir family (A.D. 1339-42). Others reported that their ancestors had entered Kashmir when Vijay Singh was the ruler of the area beyond Pir Panjal. King Vijay Singh, to whom this story apparently refers, was the ruler between A.D. 1127 and 1157. Clearly, therefore, the accounts given by the Gujars themselves do not help us to date precisely their entry into Kashmir.

The myth of *ban budhi* is of considerable importance to the Gujars in fixing the probable period of their migration to Kashmir. Old Gujars claim that, while coming to the area, they were constantly troubled by short statured women living in the higher altitudes. These women were corrupt and lured all the men of the house. This probably refers to the old polyandrous system of Ladakh, which lies in the neighbourhood of the Gujar Bakarwals' summer pastures; but this myth, again, is unhelpful in determining the date of the Gujars' entry to the Kashmir region.

Historians are of the view that the Gujars of Jammu and Kashmir are the descendants of the great Gujar tribe which gave its name to the Gujarat district and Gujranwala of West Punjab (Pakistan), the peninsula of Gujarat and the tract known as Gujargarh in Gwalior,[4] and who migrated to

3. Unlike the Gujars in other parts of the country who are all Hindus, the Jammu and Kashmir Gujars are Muslims and follow the basic tenets of the Islamic faith. Their sectarian affiliation is a matter of some controversy, though some are inclined to regard the Gujars as Shia's.

4. The racial origin of the Gujars is a matter of some controversy among historians. Some scholars are of the opinion that the Gujars are of foreign racial stock, representing those pastoral nomads from the steppes of Central Asia who entered India either with the Huns or a little latter. Others are of the view that they are of indigenous origin. This controversy still remains unresolved.

Kashmir for political and economic reasons as well as in search of fresh pastures. According to the 1941 Census, a part of the tribe migrated towards the state of Jammu and Kashmir after the outbreak of a serious famine in the regions (now known as Rajasthan and Gujarat) inhabited by the tribe. This migration is supposed to have taken place at the time of the *Satahsiya* famine. However, it seems more reasonable to assume that the Gujars now living in the state are the descendants of two separate migrations—one directly from Rajasthan and Gujarat, and the other from the plains of Punjab. This view is partially supported by the fact that many Gujar families now living in Jammu and Kashmir claim that they originally belonged to the Gujarat district of West Punjab (Pakistan).

The Gujars were a powerful group during Mughal rule. The centre of their power was Lohorkot or Loherene, now known as Loran, in Poonch district, and many Gujars served in high capacities at the Poonch court for many centuries. At the end of the eighteenth century, Wazir Rahulla Khan Sangu, a Gujar of village Khaneter in Poonch district, convincingly defeated Maharaja Ranjit Singh and established his power at Poonch. However, when the Sikhs re-established themselves in the region, the Gujars split up and migrated in small sections to different parts of the state. Some probably moved along the old Mughal route through Bhimbar, Rajouri, Shopiyan and Srinagar, while others crossed the hills and settled in the districts of Baramula and Muzafarabad. Today, the Gujars are found in practically all the districts of the state.

The Gujars in Jammu and Kashmir can be divided into three principal groups according to their mode of existence and occupational pattern. The first group comprises the sedentary or settled Gujars who have taken to the cultivation of land as their primary occupation and live in permanent villages in the plains bordering the foothills. The second group consists of the semi-settled or sedentary-transhumant Gujars. These Gujars combine the cultivation of land with pastoralism in varying degrees. They are settled permanently in the lower mountain areas where they engage in cultivation, but move during the summer season to the middle mountains and Pir Panjal pastures. The third group comprises the transhumant Gujars who are wholly pastoral nomads and oscillate between winter and summer pastures.

The transhumant Gujars can be further divided into two distinct groups. Members of the first groups are called Dodhis or Baniharas. They earned their name as they specialise in tending buffaloes and selling milk (*dudh*) and milk products and because they live in dense forests (*ban*). Those belonging to the other groups are referred to as Bakarwals as they are skilful goat (*bakri*) and sheep (*bher*) breeders. It is worthwhile noting here that the terms Dodhi and Bakarwal were not coined by the Gujars themselves but were employed by non-Gujars to distinguish these two groups along occupational lines. Today, however, these terms are widely accepted and are used by the Gujars as well.

The Gujar Bakarwals divide themselves into two sub-groups called the Kunhari Gujar Bakarwals and the Illahiwal Gujar Bakarwals. These terms reflect the areas which members of the sub-group claim they originally belonged to and thus indicate the history of their migration. Those who describe themselves as Kunhari Gujar Bakarwals claim that their ancestors belonged to the valley of Kunhar while the other subgroup contends that their ancestors belonged to the valley of Illahiwal, Kohistan and Swat in the Pakhtoon-speaking areas of Pakistan. The Illahiwal Gujar Bakarwals speak Gujari with an accent which seems to have been influenced by Pushto speech and follow the traditions of the Pusto-speaking people in their customs, dress and personal names. However, the Kunhari-Illahiwal division among the Gujar Bakarwals does not have any direct functional relevance today, except that of identifying their places of origin.

Pattern of Transhumance

As mentioned above, the Gujar Bakarwals are skilful sheep breeders and raise goats and sheep as their main source of income. Consequently their economy is dependant upon the availability of extensive pastures. While the area they inhabit is fertile and pastures are plenty, the Gujar Bakarwals are at the mercy of the seasons. During winter the higher mountains are covered with snow and adequate pasturage is available only on the lower hills and in the plains. As summer approaches, the pastures in the plains and lower reaches dry up, but those higher up begin to thaw. As a result, the Gujar Bakarwals move back and forth from the plains and lower mountain regions, where they live in mud-stone houses (*kothas*), to summer pastures in the upper mountains at altitudes ranging between 14,000 to 15,000 feet above sea level. Over the years the Gujar Bakarwals have beaten out well-defined tracks from one area to the other and drive large herds through precipitous mountain passes and along rivers. Figure 1 shows the traditional route of migration known as the Pir Panjal Pass route or Mughal Road in Jammu and Kashmir and Figure 2 sets out the routes and flow pattern of seasonal migration of the forty-four *kafilas* of the Pir Panjal Pass route upon an observation of whom this paper is based.

The Gujar Bakarwal's annual cycle of migration, which corresponds roughly to the three principal seasons of the year, starts in the month of April when they leave the winter pastures of the middle mountain zone, south of the Pir Panjal range. While their winter pasture zone does not experience snow-fall it is severely cold nevertheless. Consequently, from December until April the Gujar Bakarwals are preoccupied with protecting their animals from the cold and in searching for food.

From about the middle of April, they start moving towards summer pastures. This is the time when the rise in temperature begins to deplete the pasturage lower down, while various types of grasses start springing up at higher altitudes with the melting of the snows. The migration is slow to start but swells as the heat increases. As this journey is an arduous one through difficult terrain, large caravans (*kafilas*) consisting of members of different households (*deras*) join together for the purpose. The Gujar Bakarwals halt sparingly *en route*, and their daily activities are confined to meeting the exigencies created by constant travelling and the needs of their animals.

From July until the first week of October, the Gujar Bakarwals stay in the summer pasture zone. This zone does not

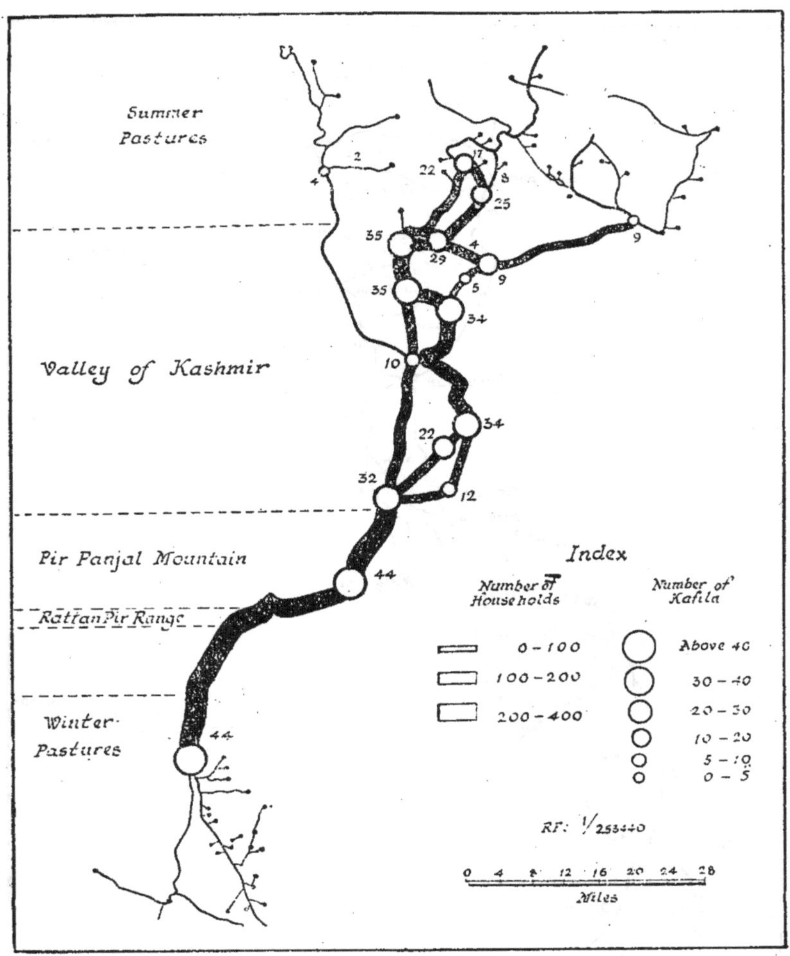

Chart : Migration Route of Gujar Bakarwal Kafila (Pir Panjal Pass)

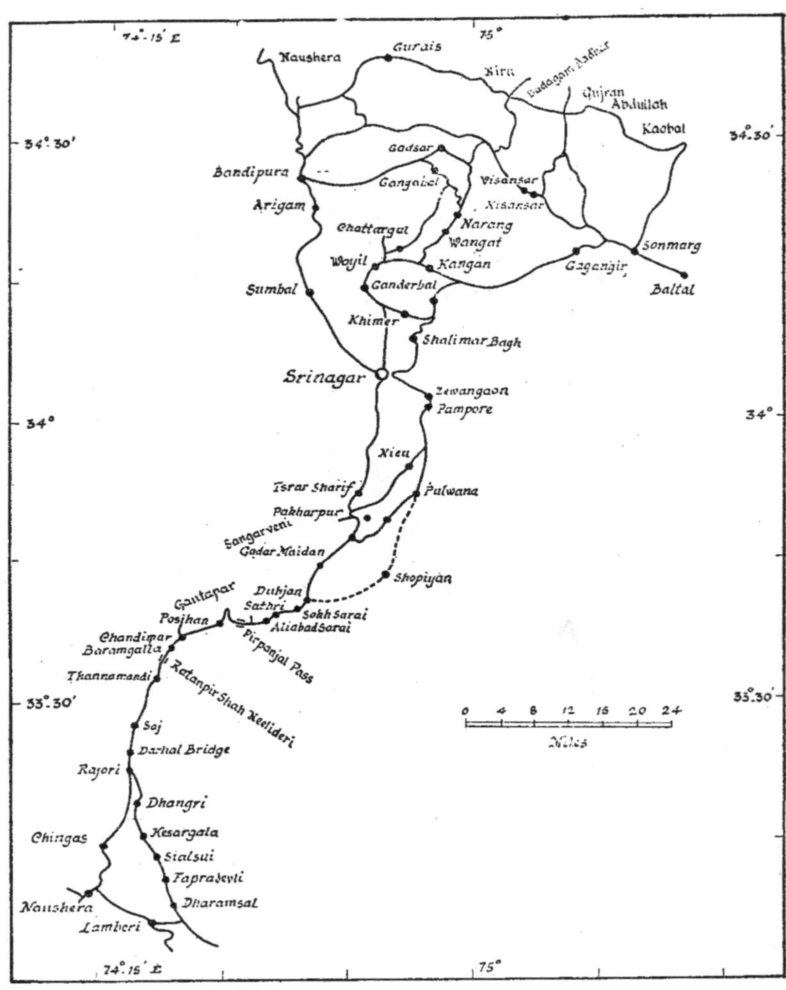

Chart 2 : Flow Map – Gujar Bakarwal Migration

experience the monsoon and the melting snow provides greenery all around. Life during this period is leisurely and comfortable and allows considerable scope for other activities. Thus, the animals are sheared during this period and the proceeds from the sale of wool are utilized for various ceremonies.

As winter starts approaching, the Gujar Bakarwals begin moving towards the winter pastures again. Unlike the movement upwards, the return journey is comparatively fast and takes a shorter time. The fear that an untimely snowfall or sudden rain may block up the passes resulting in heavy loss of animal and human life spurs the Gujar Bakarwals to hurry on down. Back to their winter pastures, the Gujar Bakarwals settle down in their *kothas* and start attending to their animals. Fig. 3 shows the annual migratory cycle of the Gujar Bakarwals and the activities characteristic of each phase. This seasonal cycle is repeated almost uniformly every year and constitutes the basic framework of the Gujar Bakarwal's social and economic life. Therefore, this background must be constantly borne in mind while looking at and interpreting the data about their marriage patterns and kinship organization.

Marriage Patterns

Marriage constitutes an important basis out of which kinship relations grow and are sustained. I shall, therefore, begin this discussion of marriage and kinship among the Gujar Bakarwals with a consideration of their marriage patterns and then go on to analyze the structure of their kinship groups. My discussion of these aspects is limited to a consideration of two related questions: What are the norms governing marriage in the context of their ecology and physical setting? And, how do marriages take place and what are the ceremonies associated with their performance?

The first thing which must be noted with regard to marriage among the Gujar Bakarwals is that there is a wide disparity in the proportion of males to females. As they are not ennumerated separately by the Census we do not have the latest figures on the sex-ratio of this community, but the figures

Yearly Cycle of Gujar Bakarwals
Dec
Jan
Feb
Mar.
Apr
May
Jun
July
Aug
Sept
Oct
Nov
Camps in winter pastures
Stay at winter abodes grazing around neighbouring hills, house-hold industry, labour, breeding of lambs, selling of wool, little agriculture, repair of equipments, purchase of house-hold goods.
Spring migration
Slow daily movements along with grazing, crossing of long stay at Rattan Pir Range, crossing vale of Kashmir Pir Panjal Mts., with fast and long journeys, visit to way side shrines, sale and purchase of goods.
Camps in summer pastures
Leisure time activities, grazing, shearing of wool, marriages, games and sports, hunting, selling of wool, zriga sessions, religious activities.
Autumn migration
Fast daily movements along with grazing, crossing of vale of Kashmir, crossing of Pir Panjal mountains, short stay at Rattan Pir range

Chart 3.

provided by the 1931 Census serve to indicate the extent of this disparity. There were approximately 856 females per every 1,000 males among the Gujar Bakarwals at that time, and there is no reason to suppose that this disparity has been reduced. Given the arduous life that they lead, it is not surprising that there is a shortage of women among the Gujar Bakarwals.

The Gujar Bakarwals look upon marriage as a desirable and normal institution but the demographic imbalance mentioned above has a direct bearing upon their marriage patterns. Firstly, there is the possibility that some males may be unable to find a wife for themselves and thus be forced to remain unmarried. The figures I collected for the two *kafilas* with whom I travelled and spent a good deal of time indicate that there were eight unmarried males among the seventy-five adults in the *kafilas*. Secondly, it places women in an exceptionally advantageous position. Our survey revealed that there were several women who had been married more than once, whereas there were very few cases of polygynous unions. Lastly, the disproportionate sex-ratio also results in a relaxation of norms relating to the arrangement of marriages within specified social boundaries and in the attitudes towards elopement and divorce. We shall return to these presently after discussing the method and the proscriptions and prohibitions relating to the selection of spouses.

Selection of Spouses

The Gujar Bakarwal ideal holds that the marriage of an individual should be arranged by his parents, or by his senior relatives in case his or her parents are not alive. Table 1 shows that this ideal is usually upheld. This is true both in the case of a first marriage as well as subsequent marriages.

TABLE 1: Mode of Arrangement of Marriage

Mode of arrangement	*No.*	*Per cent*
By Parents	40	81.63
By Senior Relatives	8	16.33
By the Individual Himself	1	2.04
Total	49	100.00

Even widowers do not arrange their own marriage but through senior male relatives. However, there are a fair number of exceptions to the rule and, as we shall see, elopements are not only quite frequent but usually occur with the mutual consent of and agreement between the parties concerned.

When parents start looking for a suitable match for their son, their search is governed by both proscriptions and prescriptions. The proscriptions commonly observed today are those laid down by Islam. Thus, the Gujar Bakarwals avoid marrying the children of the same mother, foster brothers and sisters and sisters' and brothers' children. Furthermore, they also try to avoid marrying their patrilineal descendants. Some informants said that in the past marriage within the boy's patrilineal *gotra* was avoided and some persons even now avoid marrying their sons into their own and their wives' *gotras*. However, such restrictions are no longer strictly adhered to and marriages within one's *gotra* as well as in one's mother's *gotra* are quite common.

The Gujar Bakarwals recognise marriage with both parallel and cross cousins to be legitimate. However, instances of such marriages are extremely rare. While such marriages are accorded the status of regular marriages whenever they occur, they are not considered desirable by the Gujar Bakarwals as a whole.

The prescriptions determining the selection of spouses are those of the group. Ideally, the Gujar Bakarwals prefer that the first marriage of their children should take place within their own community. Thus, as far as possible, they try to arrange the marriage of their children within the community. However, because of the chronic scarcity of women in this community, this is not always possible. In order to overcome the serious limitation placed in this respect, some resort to the convenient procedure of exchange marriages whereby a man exchanges another person's son and daughter for his own daughter and son. These exchanges can be both direct or indirect. In a direct exchange marriage, a person will marry his own son to another person's daughter and get his son to marry his own daughter. On the other hand, in an indirect exchange, he would marry his own son to another person's daughter and get that person's daughter for one of his close kinsmen. Sometimes, especially where a person fails even to arrange an exchange marriage, he has to resort to marriage by purchase. Such marriages by purchase whereby Gujar Bakarwals bring in girls from outside the community are recognized as genuine marriages, but they are not as widely respected as the marriages within the community.

Social status and wealth of a family do enter into a marriage. Asked to indicate the considerations which would weigh with them while arranging the marriage of their children, thirty-five out of the fifty respondents in one *kafila* indicated wealth and social status of the girl's family to be significant considerations. However, they all agreed that group loyalty would be an uppermost consideration in the selection of spouses for their children. They would consider the clan or community base of the girl's family first and would consider its wealth and social status later on. Clearly, therefore, the Gujar Bakarwals subscribe to the ideal of community endogamy, except that the chronic shortage of women in their community does necessitate their taking women from outside the group occasionally.

Care is taken at the time of arranging a marriage that there is not a wide disparity between the ages of husband and wife. Table 2 shows the difference in the ages of husbands and wives in fifty families in the three *kafilas* we surveyed. It will be seen from this table that in eight cases the husband and wife were of roughly the same age, in twenty-seven cases the husband was senior to his wife and in another fifteen cases the wives were senior to their husbands. Of the twenty-seven cases wherein the husbands were senior to their wives, there were fifteen cases where the age difference was between one and three years, seven cases where the difference was four years and only five cases where the difference was between five years and nine or more years. These last cases were of those men who had married a second time. Similarly, the wives were senior to their husbands in fifteen cases, but in twelve instances the disparity was three years or less. There were only three cases of disparities ranging between five to ten years and these involved remarried widows or second marriages. Thus, it is clear that the disparity in the ages of

TABLE 2: Age of Husband and Wife in Fifty Households in Three Kafilas

Age of Husband in Relation to Wife's Age	*No. of Cases*			
	1st Kafila	*2nd Kafila*	*3rd Kafila*	*Total*
+ 10 or more	—	—	1	1
+ 9	2	1	1	4
+ 8	—	—	—	—
+ 7	—	—	—	—
÷ 6	—	—	—	—
+ 5	—	—	—	—
+ 4	3	2	2	7
+ 3	2	1	2	5
+ 2	2	2	1	5
+ 1	1	2	2	5
Same as Wife's	2	4	2	8
— 1	1	—	1	2
— 2	2	3	1	6
— 3	2	1	1	4
— 4	—	—	—	—
— 5	1	—	—	1
— 6	—	—	—	—
— 7	—	—	—	—
— 8	1	—	—	1
— 9	—	—	—	—
— 10	—	—	—	—

husbands and wives does not usually extend beyond three or four years, except in the case of second marriages or remarried widows.

Betrothal

The process of settlement of a marriage is a relatively simple one. Usually, when the parents of a boy have decided in favour of a girl, the boy's father makes a formal offer of marriage to the girl's parents. A *Maulvi* and some elder members of the community are normally called in to attend the ceremony which is arranged at the girl's house.[5] In the

5. On this occasion, the boy generally remains away from his elders. It is considered undignified for the boy to be present at the ceremony.

presence of these witnesses, the boy's father says to the girl's father: 'I want your daughter in marriage for my son. Do you accept the offer?'[6] If the boy's father is not alive, a senior male relative or some elderly kinsman or friend usually takes the place of the father. If the offer is acceptable to the girl's family, which is usually the case as the ceremony is arranged only after the two parties have informally agreed to the arrangement, the girl's father or grandfather or some senior male relative replies: 'I accept this offer (*rishta*).'[7] This brief exchange is followed by a feast and the presentation of some gifts in the form of clothes to the girl. Thereafter, the couple are deemed to be betrothed.

The betrothal ceremony among the Gujar Bakarwals takes place fairly early, usually when the couple are seven or eight years old.[8] Once the parents of the boy and the girl have agreed to the betrothal, they start helping each other in different ways and extend cooperation in such transhumant activities as the shearing of wool and the taming of animals, etc. On important occasions and festivals, gifts for the girl and her female relatives are sent by the boy's side. If the girl's father refuses to accept these gifts it is an indication that the betrothal is being revoked.

A betrothal can be revoked by either party any time before the solemnization of the marriage. No ceremony is required for this revocation. Furthermore, in the event of elopement or death of the girl the betrothal is automatically considered revoked. However, the revocation of a betrothal results in the loss of social prestige for both the boy's and girl's side and is socially frowned upon.[9] It is usually effected

6. The boy's father asks for the girl by saying:' *Am* (naming the girls' father) *ki tee* (naming the girl) *ko apne putter* (naming the boy) *ka nal mangto. Apne paee sabb qabulai.*'
7. The girl's father accepts the offer by saying: '*Am yo rishta qabuliyo.*
8. There are, however, exceptions to the rule—girls are sometimes betrothed at the age of 15 and boys after they are 25 years old.
9. Cases of feuds have often occurred over such disputes. However, the *zirga* (council) is the final decision-making body in all such cases.

only in extreme cases, especially when there are over-riding considerations in its favour.

Marriage Ceremonies

The marriage is usually solemnized four years after the betrothal, but in some cases the period between betrothal and marriage can be as long as seven to eight years. It is never extended beyond. The parents of the contracting spouses consult each other and arrive at a mutually acceptable date after consulting their relatives, friends and the *Maulvi*. Since the Gujar Bakarwals' mode of existence requires them to attend to their animals during winter and as the periods of migration are full of tensions and worries, marriages usually take place during the summer season (*garmiyan*) when everyone has more time to spare. The elders of the community are informed about the date of the marriage and invitations (*neúta*) are extended to all relatives and friends who are supposed to attend the marriage.

The actual solemnization of a marriage among the Gujar Bakarwals is a relatively simple affair, but this is often preceded by ceremonies at both the boy's and the girl's *dera*.[10] At the boy's *dera*, the bridegroom is prepared for the occasion by the womenfolk of his family. He is shaved and given a ritual bath by the barber while his female relatives stand around him singing songs and clapping their hands. After the bath, he is dressed in new clothes by a *Maulvi*. As he is being dressed, the womenfolk fling raisins over him to protect him from the evil eye (*bad nazar*). The dress he wears is provided by his own family, except the head gear (*pagri*) which is sent by the bride's side. Once these ceremonies are over, the bridegroom (*shahwala*) and the marriage party (*janj*) start off in a procession.[11]

10. These ceremonies are held only in the event of the first marriage of the girl. Where she has been married before, these ceremonies are not held.

11. Professional musicians called *mirasis* usually accompany the procession, and horse races, stick fights and weight-lifting contests are arranged as the procession wends its way to the bride's house.

The rites performed at the bride's *dera* parallel those held at the bridegroom's. Her hair is washed, fresh butter is applied to it and it is woven into beautiful plaits. A necklace (*jeejaron ka har*), which is considered to be auspicious, is placed around her neck, and her palms and feet are coloured with henna (*mehndi*). Her female relatives also colour their palms and feet with henna. Older male relatives apply henna to their beards. She is, then, dressed in the clothes and jewellery brought to her *dera* by a messenger (*manji*) of the bridegroom's family.

The Gujar Bakarwals perform the *nikah* ceremony to solemnize the marriage and the form of this ceremony is the same as the one prescribed by Islam. The *Maulvi* sits on a slightly raised platform surrounded by all the invitees and two adult males from the boy's side go over to the girl's parents to find out if she is agreeable to her marriage. She affirms her agreement through one of her friends[12] and her affirmation is announced by the witnesses to the marriage party. Similar affirmation is then sought from the boy. Once the consent of both parties has thus been obtained, the *Maulvi* recites an offering (*fatiha*) from the Koran.[13]

As soon as the *nikah* has been read, the bridegroom's father is required to fix the dower (*mahr*). This can either be deferred or handed over immediately, and paid in cash or in kind. Usually, forty per cent of the dower is payable immediately and the rest is deferred. The negotiations over the dower are usually prolonged and a great deal of haggling takes place, the settlement usually being brought about by the *Maulvi* and the other elders present. When the boy's father accepts the sum proposed, a marriage contract (*nikah nama*) is drawn up by the *Maulvi*, a copy of which is given to the bridegroom while the original is kept by the *Maulvi*. This is usually followed by the wedding feast.

Among the Gujar Bakarwals the consummation of a marriage does not take place immediately after the wedding though

12. It is interesting to note that the girl does not reply directly, even though that is a requirement under Islamic law.

13. *Noor-Nama*, a religious poem in Gujari language, is also often recited on this occasion.

the bride comes to the bridegroom's house along with the marriage party. She is escorted to her husband's *dera* by her brother who hands her over to her mother-in-law (*sass*) along with a gift of the whitest possible lambwool and requests her to return his sister back after seven days as white as wool. For seven days, the girl remains with her mother-in-law and other senior female members of the family. She is not supposed to be seen by the menfolk of the family nor by her husband. The violation of this rule is considered to be a serious affront to the bride's family.

On the seventh day (*satma*), the girl's father, brother and other male relatives come to her father-in-law's *dera* to fetch her back. She is again dressed in her bridal dress and presented with sweet cakes of maize prepared for the occasion. She takes these cakes to her mother who distributes them among her relatives. This is supposed to indicate that she has been kept a virgin during the seven days she spent at her husband's *dera*. The female relatives of the girl present at her house enquire about what happened at her husband's house and try to confirm that she is a virgin. If the girl's virginity has been tampered with during the seven-day period, this is taken as an insult to their prestige by her family members and can lead to a serious feud between the parties concerned.

The consummation of the marriage takes place after a ceremony called the *rukhsati* has been performed. This ceremony is usually held three to four years after the *nikah*, but in some cases it takes place even after nine to eleven years thereafter.[14] The idea behind providing this gap between marriage and consummation seems to be that the consummation should take place only after a girl attains the age of twenty to twenty-two years. This age is considered by parents a fit age for their daughters to bear the strains of child-bearing in the difficult conditions of a transhumant way of life.

When the *rukhsati* takes place, the girl is given a dowry (*daaj*) by her father. This includes items for domestic use, sheep, goats and horses which would have been her share in her father's property. At her father-in-law's place, the couple are

14. There are instances where this ceremony was performed soon after the *nikah*, but the girls were quite mature in those cases.

given a separate nuptial tent (*dera*) and the bride is prepared for the consummation of marriage After the consummation of marriage when the boy declares that he is happy with his marriage his father offers a sacrifice (*qurbani*) of a goat or a chicken in the name of Allah. Sometimes sacrifice is also offered at a shrine (*mazar*) to ensure many children to the couple and for the general welfare of the family in future.

Divorce and Elopement

The normal expectation among the Gujar Bakarwals is that a marriage will remain intact so long as both the parties to it are alive, but, in keeping with Islamic law, there is a provision for divorce (*talaq*). However, this provision exists more in theory than in practice. Because of the shortage of women in the Gujar Bakarwal community, cases of men divorcing their wives are rare. Furthermore, divorce is also disapproved by the community at large and tends to lower the reputation of the family. If a divorce takes place, it is mostly at the initiative of women and assumes the form of elopement.

Elopement is generally frowned upon by the community and is supposed to bring shame to a woman, but it occurs nevertheless. Elopements are of two kinds. The first kind involves unmarried girls. This kind of elopement is considered a crime and often leads to serious feuds between the boy's and the girl's families and kinsmen. The community takes serious note of this kind of elopments and the tribal council (*zirga*) often imposes punitive sanctions against the erring persons and their families.

The second kind of elopement is that involving divorced or married women. This type of elopment is not considered to be a serious offence but it results, nevertheless, in a loss of prestige for the families involved and feuds have occurred over them as well. Indeed, there have even been cases of armed conflicts among the families, resulting in murders, over such elopements. The chances of such conflicts are greater where the elopement involves a married woman and such cases are usually taken to the tribal council (*zirga*) for adjudication.

When a married woman elopes with another man, attempts are made by her husband and the members of his as well as her family to bring her back. However, if persuasion fails, the boy's parents try to pressurise the husband to divorce his wife. Since Islamic rules do not allow a woman to divorce her husband, elopement is often resorted to by Gujar Bakarwal women to force a divorce so that they can be free to marry someone else. Of course, in cases of such elopement-divorces, the woman forfeits her claim to her dowry and *mahr*.[15] The argument of the *zirga* in allowing such elopement-divorces is that it is better to let the eloped woman, who is unwilling to return to her husband, enter into a regular marriage with another man rather than lead a life in sin and adultery.

The death of the husband is taken as the dissolution of a marriage. There is no taboo against widow remarriage among the Gujar Bakarwals. There are, of course, cases of widows leading independent lives, but such widows are either women with children or those who were widowed after they were forty-five years old. There are no young widows among them as even widows are in considerable demand as wives on account of the overall shortage of women in Gujar Bakarwal society.

When a woman becomes widowed, an attempt is made by her husband's family to keep her within the kin group. This is done through the custom of levirate. No ceremony is required in such cases, except the offering of bangles and the placing of a sheet (*chaddar*) over her by her new husband. This type of marriage solves the problems relating to children and division of property.

If the woman does not want to marry one of her deceased husband's brothers, she can claim the dowry (*daaj*) which she brought with her at the time of her marriage and settle down with another man. If she has children from her previous marriage, she can also demand their share in their father's property either immediately or when the children grow up. This is an accepted practice even if the widow marries another man. However, if the widow remarries, then the children continue to retain their rights in the patrilineal kinship group.

15. In all such divorces, the sons of the first marriage return to the father after five years. But the daughters remain in the custody of their mother till they are married.

When a girl who has been married but has not started living with her husband becomes a widow, she can do one of two things. She can remain with her deceased husband's family without undergoing the *rukhsati* ceremony afresh and start living there as the wife of one of her deceased husband's brothers. Or, alternatively, she can undergo another *nikah* ceremony with a man not related to her deceased husband. If she chooses the latter alternative, a great deal of trouble usually ensues over the return of the gifts given by her deceased husband's family. In this event, the girl's parents tend to send her in *rukhsati* to another man in consideration for a sum of money and use that amount to return the gifts given by the deceased husband's family. Usually the tribal council adjudicates those disputes which cannot be resolved through mutual agreement between the concerned families.

Kinship Groups

The preceeding section dealt with marriage patterns among the Gujar Bakarwals. The object of the discussion was to delineate the patterns and customs relating to the selection of spouses and the ceremonies and rituals associated with this event. An attempt was also made to trace the influence exerted by the Gujar Bakarwals' environment and life style on their marriage customs. Let us now turn to a consideration of the structure of kinship groups amongst them.

There are three principal kinship groups among the Gujar Bakarwals: the household (*dera*), the lineage (*dada potre*) and the clan (*gotra*). All these kinship groups are important to a Gujar Bakarwal in one context or another, and the importance enjoyed by each has tended to vary according to a series of both internal and external changes to which the Gujar Bakarwals have been exposed from time to time. I shall discuss each of these kinship groups separately and shall try to point out the importance given to them in the Gujar Bakarwals' day-to-day existence.

The Household

The *dera* (household) is the basic unit among the Gujar Bakarwals. They count their numbers and describe their grazing and *kafila* groups in terms of the number of *deras*.

A *dera* usually comes into existence when a person establishes an independent household, which happens ordinarily after his marriage. The common practice among the Gujar Bakarwals is for a young man to leave his father's hearth soon after his marriage and establish his own *dera*. Each son, thus, establishes his own *dera* as he gets married, which is usually in the order of their birth, and receives a share in the patrimony. Most fathers try to give an equal number of animals to all sons, but the number of animals which a particular son receives is quite often determined by the number of animals available in his father's flock at the time of separation. Thus, it can happen that a son who breaks away from his father's *dera* in a lean year gets a smaller number of animals in patrimony than the one who gets married and establishes his *dera* at a time of relative prosperity.

The *deras* usually tend to be small, comprising on an average four to six persons. Table 3 sets out the distribution of persons per *dera* in the two *kafilas* for whom detailed statistics are available. It would be seen that, while some

TABLE 3: Number of Persons per Dera Unit in Two Kafilas

No. of Persons in the Dera	*No. of Deras*
1—3	7
4—6	17
7—9	9
10—12	3
Total	36

deras contain as many as eleven or twelve members, *deras* comprising four to six persons predominate.

Furthermore, most *deras* tend to be nuclear in their composition, consisting of a husband, his wife and unmarried children. Extended patrilineal or complex *deras* consisting of two or more nuclear family units are usually few. Appendix Table 1 presents the details of the composition of Gujar Bakarwal *kafilas* on whom detailed data were collected.

Table 4 summarises the figures on kinsmen living within each *dera* by *dera* type.

TABLE 4 : Kinsmen within each Dera Divided by Dera Types

Type af *Deras*	*Number*
Incomplete *Deras*	
(a) Widow(er) and unmarried children	1
(b) Single person	1
(c) Unmarried brothers	1
Simple or Nuclear *Deras*	24
Simple or Nuclear *Deras* with additional relatives	
(a) Ego, wife, unmarried children and ego's mother	5
Complex or extended patrilineal *deras*	4
Total	36

TABLE 5: Distribution of Deras by Number of Sheep, Goats and Horses owned by Thirty-six Deras in one Kafila

No. of Animals Owned	*No. of Households*
Sheep	
None	11
1-25	21
26-50	3
300	1
Goats	
None	2
1-25	15
26-50	12
51-75	1
76-100	4
200	1
500	1
Horses	
None	9
1	10
2	7
3	5
	5

Each *dera* has its own hearth and owns its own property. The property consists of a tent for use during the annual migrations, sheep and goats, dogs and mules or horses. Appendix Table 3 sets out details of the property owned by thirty-six *dera* units in one *kafila* surveyed. The data in Table 5 indicate the number of sheep, goats and horses owned by the various households. The table shows that the majority of the *deras* surveyed own between one to fifteen heads of sheep, an equal number of goats and one horse. However, some rich *deras* own as many as fifty sheep, 100 goats and four horses. In most cases, the *dera* members look after the animals themselves. However, wealthy persons with large flocks of animals sometimes employ servants to look after their flocks. Some also give a part of their flock to poor shepherds (*ajris*) on annual contracts.[16] The flocks belonging to each *dera* carry distinct marks or colours for purposes of identification.

The *deras* usually have a clearly demarcated hierarchy of authority and division of labour among its members which regulates its functioning. Where the *dera* consists of a nuclear family, the head is always the husband. Where it is comprised of an incomplete family, the senior male member enjoys the status of a head. Only in cases where there is no adult male member in the *dera* is the woman considered the household head. There was one such case in one of the *kafilas* surveyed and she was represented by her male relatives (cf. Barth 1961: 14). The head of the *dera* holds all rights over the property of the *dera* and represents it in its dealings within the community as well as with outsiders. He is also responsible for taking all important decisions (cf. Barth 1961:14).

Labour is divided among the members of the *dera* by sex and age, though the tasks formally assigned to each sex or age group are not strictly adhered to always. The women and girls perform the domestic tasks of cooking, washing, the bringing of water, the rearing of children, the collection of wood and the making of woollen garments. The repair of equipment,

16. The importance of shepherds has been emphasized by several students of pastoral nomadic groups. See, for instance, Barth (1961: 20-21) and Swiddler (1972:74); also see Irons (1972).

the upkeep of tents, the twining of ropes and the tending and herding of animals are done by male adults.

An average Gujar Bakarwal *dera* is on the move for about 110 to 130 days out of the year (see Figure 3). The Gujar Bakarwal tents are struck and repitched in precisely the same manner as Barth has described for the Basseri. 'These frequent migrations consume much time and labour and strongly affect the organization of the daily round. Activity starts well before daylight when the sheep and goats, which have spent the night by the tents, depart in the care of the shepherd who is usually a boy or a man . . . . The tent is usually struck before sunrise, while the household members snatch odds and ends of left-over food . . .' (Barth, 1961:15). At the time of migration the packing and loading are done jointly by all members of the *dera* without any formal division of labour.

The Lineage

While discussing the organization of the *dera* unit, we noted that the principal function of the *dera* is economic. It is the basic unit of consumption and production which, in a transhumant group such as the Gujar Bakarwals, depends upon the raising of animals. The successful pursuit of this economic activity eventually rests upon the availability of pastures for grazing. In the state of Jammu and Kashmir the pastures are not allotted to individual families (*deras*) or to their heads. On the contrary, they are deemed to be the property of kinship groups whose ancestors had first established control over them and used them traditionally. These kinship groups are called *dada potre* and their rights over pastures and migration routes are traditionally recognized both by the community as a whole as well as by the forest department and the revenue authorities.

The *dada potre* is a group of patrilineally related kinsmen tracing their ancestry to a common ancestor. The size of this group is extremely variable and may comprise as many as 250 or more persons, depending upon the extent to which the division of pastures and migration routes has taken place. Usually, while a Gujar Bakarwal father divides his cattle wealth among his children as and when they get married, the division of pastures and migration routes is postponed until much later. This results in a situation where all his descendants continue to depend upon him for access to pastures and migration routes during his lifetime. Sometimes he may decide to divide his rights over pastures while he is alive, but this is unusual. Thus, the generation depth of a *dada potre* unit extends into several generations and includes a person's siblings, cousins and distant relative in addition to uncles.

This highly complex composition of the *dada potre* unit may be seen by referring to the genealogy of one Mian Bagga (Fig. 4). He had two sons called Mian Mulan Ali and Faquira. Mian Mulan Ali had two sons from his two wives while Faquira had four sons. The living descendants of each of these sons, who are all deceased, are today divided into separate *dada potre* units usually named after their forebears. They have their own pastures in the land which was transferred to them for this purpose by their respective ancestors. Subsequently, as their *dada potre* units expand and grow in complexity, they will, in all probability, divide into further *dada potre* units.

The critical significance of the *dada potre* unit derives from its common ownership of pasture lands which are themselves essential to the economy of the Gujar Bakarwals. Therefore, membership of a *dada potre* unit is critical to the survival of a Gujar Bakarwal in an economic sense and gives the unit a unity of interests. Even though there are no formal restrictions upon a person's pursuit of his economic activities, this freedom is greatly limited in his choice of whom he attaches himself to for the herding of animals and for the migration between winter and summer pastures by his membership of a particular *dada potre* unit.

Since pasturage rights are of critical importance to the Gujar Bakarwals, their division and transfer is regarded with considerable interest and is subject to strict control by the tribal council. The division of pasturage rights within the *dada potre* units usually follows the principle of patrilineal descent. Even though the Gujar Bakarwals are Muslims and claim to adhere to the traditional Islamic rules of inheritance, in practice this rule is ignored where the division of the joint

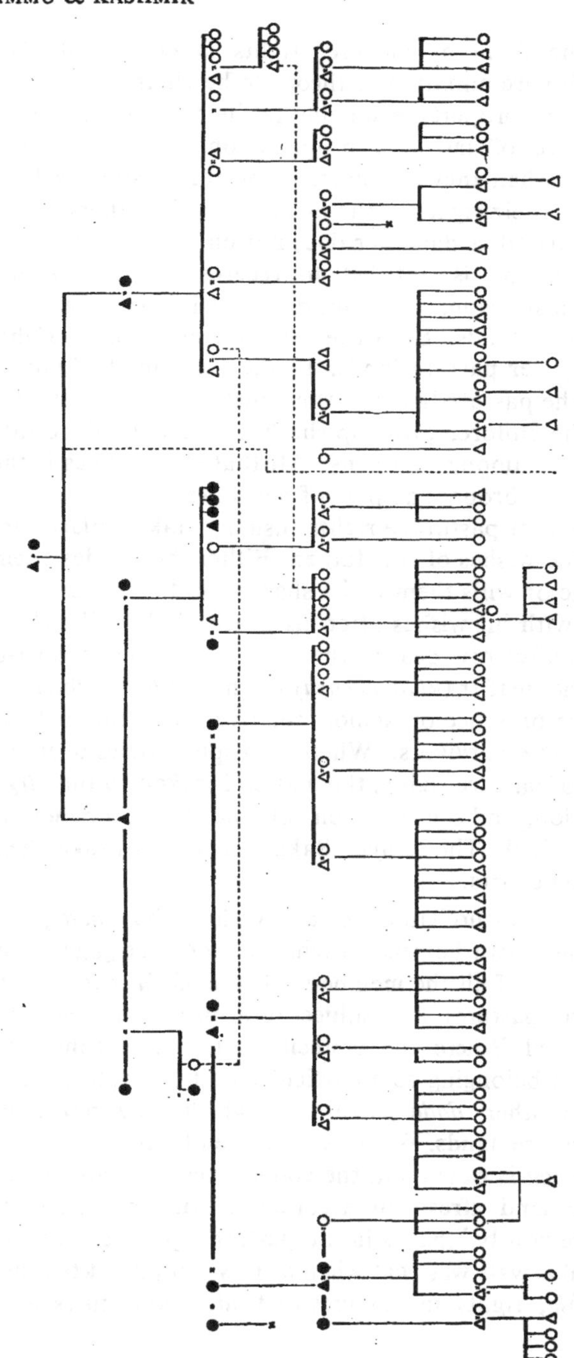

Chart 4 : Genealogy of Mian Bagga Leader of Gujar Baharwal Kalifa of Lamberi

estate in the form of pasture rights is concerned. The daughters, who are admitted in theory to be eligible to receive one-fourth of all property belonging to their father, actually receive a share of movable property only. Thus, they are given animals when they are married and this is supposed to terminate all their rights in the estate of their fathers. Even if she is unmarried, a daughter does not enjoy any claim to pasture lands. She is entitled to receive dowry from her brothers when she is married, but does not inherit the right to the pasture lands. Even the wife of a man has no rights of ownership over pasture lands. If she has small children, she can use the pasture lands to the benefit of the family, but as soon as the children grow up she has to allow the estate to be divided among her sons. All that she receives is the animals that she brought as part of her dowry.

The division of pasturage rights usually takes place according to the wishes of the father. Either he divides them in his lifetime or wills them to be shared by his children in accordance with his wishes after his death. If he wills them to be divided after his death, the will is usually recorded orally by the leader (*khar peench*) of the *kafila* to which he belongs in the presence of senior relatives and the will is executed by the survivors. Where a dispute arises over the distribution of pasture rights, the matter is taken to the *zirga* for adjudication, and the decision of the tribal council is accepted as final. The Gujar Bakarwals do not take their disputes to the courts.

The rights to pasture lands remain within the *dada potre* unit. This right can be sold, exchanged or mortgaged only with the consent of all the members of the *dada potre* unit. However, the pastures are subject to arbitrary allotment by the tribal council. Where the council leaders are convinced that the land belonging to a particular unit is surplus, it can allot it to another *dada potre* unit which may not have adequate pasture lands. Where a shortage of pastures occurs, the tribal council is called and the council headmen are asked to distribute land afresh in accordance with the needs of each unit. Previously, that is in the past, the practice among the Gujar Bakarwals was that when a new group of families joined a *kafila*, rights in pastures and migration routes were provided to them. However, this no longer happens.

The *dada potre* unit derives its importance largely from its ownership of rights over pastures, but it is also a powerful political and administrative unit. Thus, each *dada potre* unit has a head who is responsible for the socio-economic and political activities of his group and represents the group in the tribal council. The headship of the unit is based on the principle of primogeniture and passes on to the eldest son either after the death of the father or when the father chooses to retire from that position. Usually, succession to the position of headship of the *dada potre* unit is marked by the tying of a turban on the head of the eldest son in the presence of tribal leaders. This ceremony is called *dastarband.*

The Clan

The entire Gujar Bakarwal community is divided into a number of clans (*gotras*). Unlike the *dada potre* unit which is based on actual patrilineal descent, the clan is based on a fiction of common descent. The members of a clan believe that they are descendants of a common ancestor but it is not necessary for them to demonstrate their kinship links in order to justify this claim.

The presence of *gotras* among the Gujar Bakarwals seems to owe itself to their Hindu ancestry. This view receives some support from the fact that the names of Gujar Bakarwal clans (*gotras*) are generally the same as those found among the Hindu Gujars in other parts of the country. The *gotra* name is usually used by the Gujar Bakarwals as a suffix to their names.

Perhaps the traditional function of the clan division among the Gujar Bakarwals was the same as that among the Hindu Gujars, but this does not seem to be the case today. Old Gujar Bakarwals say that inter-marriages among members of the same *gotra* were avoided in the past, but this does not seem to be true nowadays and cases of inter-marriage among clan members are not unknown. It seems, therefore, that the significance of the clan group among the Gujar Bakarwals has declined gradually since their conversion to Islam and it does not perform its traditional function of regulating marriage. Nor is it today a very effective kinship grouping among the Gujar Bakarwals.

Kinship and Functional Groupings

The *dera*, the *dada potre* unit and the *gotra* are the three main kinship groups among the Gujar Bakarwals, but their transhumant mode of existence requires them to form a number of functional groups for the satisfactory pursuit of their pastoral activities. The foregoing discussion of kinship groups among the Gujar Bakarwals would be incomplete without a consideration of the role of kinship in the formation of these functional groupings. Such a discussion is also warranted by the fact that, except for the *dera*, the Gujar Bakarwals live for the most part as members of these functional groups rather than as members of kinship groups. A consideration of kinship in the formation of functional groups will show the articulation of kinship groups among them.

The Herding Unit

The primary functional group among the Gujar Bakarwals is the herding unit. This is a group comprised by *deras* who come together to form a group for the efficient grazing and care of their animals. The function of the herding unit is to provide labour for milking and shearing, and the *deras* forming a herding unit usually move together and pitch their tents in the same area during migration.

The size of herding units among the Gujar Bakarwals is variable and combines between five to ten *deras* depending upon their animal holdings and the availability of labour. Since these factors are not constant and keep changing from year to year in response to natural conditions, the membership of the herding units fluctuates and changes every year. As the size of the flock increases or decreases beyond a manageable limit, the households constituting a herding unit often break up and join other herding units. Thus, the number of animals per *dera* is critical in the formation of a herding unit.

Since the ultimate viability of the herding unit is based on the size of the flocks and the availability of labour, kinship plays little part in its formation.[17] This is not to say that kinsmen do not, or cannot, form herding units. As a matter of fact, they do occasionally choose to become members of the same herding unit but only where the considerations critical to the formation of a herding unit also converge. However, kinsmen rarely form a herding unit if other economic factors are not conducive to their functioning as a viable unit.

TABLE 6: Social Links among Households of Three Herding Units in one Kafila

Herding Unit	*No. of Deras*	*Kins*	*Distant Relations*	*Friends*	*Household* Head Lucky in Herding Operations*
1st	10	2	1	6	1
2nd	20	4	3	11	2
3rd	30	6	5	13	5

* Good luck is an important consideration in the formation of herding groups. People who enjoy a reputation as being lucky in herding operations are often sought after as members of herding groups.

17. cf. Spooner: 'The dynamics of functioning and the process of development in an herding unit in this ecological area can be explained by the size and structure of the herding groups, which influence the relationships among the individuals and their economic functionings. . . . When the size of the flock is allowed to exceed or fall below that number by more than a determinable amount not only the efficiency of the herding operation but the actual welfare of the animals suffer significantly. The individual holdings of animals increase and decrease in size unpredictably. So it is required that a group of people form one flock of nearly optimum size. The process by which the optimum size of the flock is maintained in many cases depends on the fluctuations in size of the flocks of various individuals. The fluctuations in the size of the flocks vary seasonally in this area. So the individuals are interested more in the welfare of their flocks and the composition of the herding groups as a sociological unit is not stable among these pastoral nomads' (1972:125).

Table 6 sets out the herding units in one *kafila* comprising sixty households distributed in three herding units. It will be seen from the table that close kins were members of the same herding unit in only ten cases. In the remaining cases the herding unit was comprised by distant relatives or friends. It seems, therefore, that kinship considerations are by themselves irrelevant in the formation of a herding unit and its organization is usually determined by economic considerations mixed with feelings of friendship or considerations of good luck of the persons constituting it (see Barth, 1961:22-23; Swidler, 1972:73).

The Kafila

The second important functional group among the Gujar Bakarwals is the *kafila*. A *kafila* is a group of families which move together during the annual migrations and submit themselves to the authority of the *kafila* leader practically for the period of their annual migratory cycle. It is the transhumant counterpart of the compact village settlement of sedentary groups.

A *kafila* is usually built around a leader who is an experienced old man and is supposed to be knowledgeable about migration routes, weather conditions and the habits of animals. However, the basis of the formation of *kafilas* among the Gujar Bakarwals is the need for safety and security from natural calamities like snowfall, hailstorms and occasional floods. While moving from their winter pastures to their summer pastures and back, the Gujar Bakarwals traverse precious mountain passes and cross many small rivers. Thus, they are all in constant need of assistance to enable them to cross these barriers safely. In short, the Gujar Bakarwals form themselves into *kafilas* so that the members of a *kafila* can help one another during these arduous journeys.

Unlike the situation described by Barth for the Basseri (see Barth, 1961:25-48), the *kafila* among the Gujar Bakarwals is not a permanent grouping nor does it enjoy equal importance and relevance during the entire period of the annual migratory cycle. Among the Basseri the camps are relatively permanent social units whose membership remains fixed.

Furthermore, the camp leader also enjoys considerable political significance within the Basseri political organization through his links with the tribal chieftain. This is not the case among the Gujar Bakarwals. For one thing, the membership of the *kafila* is not permanent. Second, the *kafila* is important only during the migratory periods.

When the migration begins, the households, who are members of a common herding unit, start moving towards the intervening pastures lying to the south of natural bottlenecks. Those who start earlier wait there for the other *deras* to arrive. After all the households belonging to the *kafila* have assembled, they move onwards as a group. Once they have reached the other side of the valley they again break into herding units and travel separately. Thus, while *deras* become members of a *kafila* for the whole year, they act as a *kafila* only part of the way during their migration cycle. Nonetheless, the *deras* belonging to a *kafila* are subject to the control and authority of the *kafila* leader. Disputes arising out of the order in which a *kafila* should move on a particular route or conflicts occurring over thefts of animals across *kafilas* are usually settled by the *zirga* council of *kafila* leaders (*kafila zirga*) and the *kafila* is represented at these council meetings by the *kafila* leader. Furthermore, the *kafila* leader is alone entitled to take day-to-day decisions regarding whether the *kafila* should move or stay camped at a particular place and, if they move, by what particular route they should travel. Needless to say, this places the *kafila* leader in a position of great responsibility and authority and makes his position of critical significance.

A *kafila* leader cannot expect to exercise this authority, nor can he expect unquestioned allegiance from the *kafila* members, unless he has some means available to him whereby he can control the *deras* constituting his *kafila*. Among the means available to him there are two—political power derived from the community or the government and popular support. As already noted, the Gujar Bakarwals are not organized into a well-knit community with a clear-cut internal political structure such as the one described by Barth for the Basseri. For example, there is no chief among them who may be said to confer power upon the *kafila* leaders. Nor do they enjoy any special powers from the government. Each *kafila* usually has two leaders. One is the headman (*lambardar*) who is formally recognized by the state government and the other is the informal leader who is regarded by common consent as the *kafila* leader. This distinction has broken down in the state and practically all informal *kafila* leaders are today recognized as *lambardars* by the government. Even so, this does not confer any special political strength upon the *kafila* leader and he cannot hope to lead the *kafila* upon the strength of such recognition.

A *kafila* leader can draw some political power from his economic position, especially since he is nearly always a person possessing a large flock of animals. However, economic pre-eminence is subject to fluctuations. There have been cases where *kafila* leaders have lost their animals and the members of their *kafila* have compensated their loss by voluntary donations of animals rather than form a *kafila* under the next richest man in the unit. There is, therefore, little direct correlation between wealth and *kafila* leadership and wealth or economic power, and the power of the *kafila* leader can be derived from economic resources only to a small extent.

Since the *kafila* leader neither enjoys any external political support nor is he able to use his economic position to further his influence, he is ultimately dependent upon his ability to invoke already existing solidarity links for getting his decisions accepted and for the maintenance of his authority. These links are usually those of kinship and friendship. Friendship is frequently used, but the principal link which gives the *kafila* leader his authority and influence within the *kafila* is his kinship linkage with the other members of the *kafila*.

There is among the Gujar Bakarwals a proverb which runs: 'A *kafila* is formed by the like-mindedness of those who compose it.' What this proverb implies is that the continuity and harmony of a *kafila* is maintained by the continuous reaffirmation by all its member *deras* of the authority and wisdom of the *kafila* leader. This reaffirmation is achieved through invoking both agnatic and matrilateral or affinal kinship relations.

Unfortunately, I do not have detailed data on the kinship linkages of the member *deras* in any of the *kafilas* surveyed, but the general observations I made suggest that kinship relations were a primary basis in the formation of the *kafila* grouping. So far as my observations allow me to generalize, I found that the *kafilas* tended largely to be kin groupings. First, they were dominated by members of a single *dada potre* group who were closely related through agnatic ties. Second, they consisted of affines of the member *deras*. Unrelated *deras* were sometimes incorporated into the *kafilas*. However, attempts were made subsequently to establish affinal links with such households to strengthen solidarity with them. Thus, though not primarily a kinship grouping, the *kafilas* tend by and large to be kin groups based on ties of consanguinity and affinity, and the *kafila* leader is often the individual with the largest number of kinsmen in the *kafila* (see Barth, 1961:49-70; and Swidler, 1972:69-75).

Conclusion

This essay has been concerned with a discussion of marriage and kinship among the Gujar Bakarwals of Jammu and Kashmir. The discussion was based on data I gathered primarily as a geographer for a study of Gujar Bakarwal transhumance. I have described the Gujar Bakarwal marriage and kinship and tried to indicate the relationship which exists between these aspects of their social life and the physical and ecological environment of their habitat. This environment has exercised a determining influence in shaping their social institutions and without an appreciation of its influence the understanding of those social institutions is likely to remain inadequate.

Bibliography

Barth, Fredrik (1961), *Nomads of South Persia*, London, George Allen and Unwin.

India, Government of (1931), *Census of India, Vol. XXIV*,

Part I. Jammu and Kashmir, Report, Delhi, Superintendent of Government Printing.

—— (1941), *Census of India, Vol. XX, Part I, Jammu and Kashmir*, Delhi, Superintendent of Government Printing.

Irons, William (1972), 'Variation in Economic Organization: A Comparison of the Pastoral Yomut and Basseri', in William Irons and Naville Dyson-Hudson (eds.), *Perspectives on Nomadism*, Leiden, E. J. Brill.

Khatana, R.P. (1976), *Some Aspects of Transhumance in a Mountainous Tract—A Case Study of Gujar Bakarwals of Jammu and Kashmir*, Unpublished M. Phil. Dissertation, New Delhi, Jawaharlal Nehru University.

Spooner, Brian (1972), 'The Status of Nomadism as a Cultural Phenomenon in the Middle East', in William Irons and Neville Dyson-Hudson (eds.), *Perspectives on Nomadism*, Leiden, E. J. Brill.

Swidler, W.W. (1972), 'Some Demographic Factors Regulating the Formation of Flocks and Camps among the Brahui of Balluchistan', in William Irons and Neville Dyson-Hudson (eds.), *Perspectives on Nomadism*, Leiden, E.J. Brill.

APPENDIX TABLE 1: List of Kafilas Travelling through the Pir Panjal Route

S.No.	*Name of the Kafila Leader*	*Winter Camps*	*No. of House-holds*	*Flock Size (Sheep & Goats only)*	*Summer Pastures*
1.	Haji Suleman Bajran	Androot	50	5000	Bada'ab
2.	Mehndi Haji Bokra	Androot	40	4000	Jugnei
3.	Yaqub Khatana	Swani Grati (near Androot)	30	3000	Bhuti Mali
4.	Abdul Barhwal	Androot	20	300	Jibdor, Sukhnei
5.	Abdul Aziz Khatana	Samkar	60	6000	Sonmarg
6.	Abdul Aziz Poswal	Godar	10	2000	Bisansar (Sonmarg)
7.	Haji Lala Jatla	Godar	10	2000	Jibdor
8.	Ch. Gulam Nabi Bajran	Lamberi	60	3600	Jibdor, Badagam (Tilel)
9.	Samundar Gakkar	Batera	10	2500	Las Nei
10.	Munsi Ismail Bajran	Batera	15	2900	Matayan
11.	Haji Kalam Din Bajran	Chani	20	3100	Maseet Nar
12.	Habibula Bajran	Chani	20	3200	Neelgagar
13.	Fazel Din Kandal	Kurlian	15	2800	Tilel (Bawgam)
14.	Baiduila Kalgan	Katwari	10	2200	Bhutimali Malagam
15.	Raju Swati	Sado (Saddar)	14	3000	Gurez (Chor Bani)
16.	Aziz Bajar	Kurlian	10	2000	Malat, Kadara (Towards Bandi Pura)

Appendix Table 1 (Contd.)

S. No.	*Name of the Kafila Leader*	*Winter Camps*	*No. of Households*	*Flock Size (Sheep & Goats only)*	*Summer Pastures*
17.	Malli Khatana	Kharak Panja	30	2200	Sonmarg
18.	Abdul Karim Swati	Kharak Panja	15	2000	Sari (Wangat)
19.	Kalam Din Bajran	Kharak Panja	20	2700	Nar (Wangat)
20.	Habib Khatana	Kharak Panja	10	2000	Ramal (Sonmarg)
21.	Maqadam Ismail Bajran	Dali Shahr	20	3100	Nar (Tilal) Neeru Nar
22.	Manjid Bajran	Tatta Pani	10	1800	Neeru Nar
23.	Dalli Bajran	Jigni	20	2500	Jugnei
24.	Saida Khatana	Jigni	10	2100	Bhuti Mali (Tilel)
25.	Abdul Aziz Bajran	Jata	5	1000	Maseet Nar
26.	Baba Bajran	Damal (Kalakot)	20	2300	Jibdor
27.	Yasuf Bajran	Tilhot (Kalakot)	10	2000	Nar
28.	Mehndiya	Bhatyardi (Kalakot)	10	1500	Bisansagar (Sonmarg)
29.	Kalam Din Bajran	Dharamsal	10	1500	Neelgagar
30.	Baja Bajran	Dharamsal	4	700	Jibdor
31.	Mian Bhai Bajran	Dharamsal	5	1000	Neelgagaı
32.	Khan Khatana	Dharamsal	20	2000	Sonmarg
33.	Misri Chauhan	Padat	6	800	Jugnei
34.	Kalu Bajran	Dhandki	6	800	Jibdor
35.	Habib Bajran	Bohani (Naushera)	5	600	Maseet Nar
36.	Makhmud Bajran	Bohani (Naushera)	20	2100	Trisang (Sukhnei)
37.	Gulam Nabi Kalu Khel	Androot	10	1700	Sukhnei
38.	Mustfa Awan	(Kalakot)	10	1600	Jibdor
39.	Ismail Bajran	Suma	5	800	Jibdor

Appendix Table 1 (Contd.)

40.	Buba Khatana	Pootha	6	750	Jibdor
41.	Ussba Barwal	Dlahori	20	2200	Sukhnei
42.	Dalli Abdula Khatana	Dlahori	20	2100	Surduab (Tilel)
43.	Gami Swati	Jimala	6	800	Chor Bani (Gurez)
44.	Mir Mohammad Thikariya	Pind Lalan Ki Padot (near Chamb, Jorian)	5	700	Sumali (near Sonmarg)

Note : During field work I had a strong feeling that the Gujar Bakarwals were not revealing the exact number of their animals for fear of officials of the forest department who impose a tax (*Ghass Charai* tax or *Goon*) on the basis of the number of animals in a herd.

Another reason for this reluctance was that they are very supertitious about their flocks. They do not allow outsiders into their flocks as they want to keep them away from evil eye (*bad nazar*).

APPENDIX TABLE 2: Composition of Gujar Bakarwal Deras in one Kafila

S. No.	Name of the Household Head	Dependent Members									Total
		Father	Mother	Wife	Sons	Daughters	Sons' Wife	Sons' Sons	Sons' daughters	Others	
1.	Gulam Nabi Bajran	—	—	1	2	5	1	1	—	—	11
2.	Mohamad Yaqus Bajran	—	—	1	—	2	—	—	—	—	4
3.	Abdul Gaffor	—	—	1	5	1	—	—	—	—	8
4.	Nazir Ahmad Bajran	—	1	1	1	3	—	—	—	1(*Mai*)†	8
5.	Gulam Hussain Bajran	—	—	1	5	4	—	—	—	—	11
6.	Mohamad Jawan Bajra	—	—	1	3	1	—	—	—	—	6
7.	Abdul Rasid Bajran	—	1	1	4	2	—	—	—	—	9
8.	Mahmud Yusub Bajran	—	—	1	3	1	—	—	—	—	6
9.	Master Israil Bajran	—	—	1	4	1	—	—	—	—	7
10.	Nurudin Jangal	—	—	—	3	1	2	1	—	—	9
11.	Sher Din Jangal	—	—	1	1	1	1	1	—	—	6
12.	Rehm Din Jangal	—	—	1	2	—	—	—	—	—	4
13.	Mir Mohmad Jangal	—	—	1	5	5	—	—	—	—	12
14.	Mitha Jangal	—	—	1	6	1	—	—	—	—	9
15.	Israil Jangai	—	1	1	5	1	—	—	—	—	—
16.	Suleman Jangal	—	—	1	1	2	—	—	—	—	5
17.	Sanai Jangal	—	—	1	2	—	—	—	—	—	4
18.	Chandi Jangal	—	—	1	2	1	—	—	—	—	5

19.	Abdulla Jangal	—	—	1	1	—	—	—	—	—	3
20.	Mohmad Amin Jangal	—	—	1	1	—	—	—	—	—	3
21.	Mohmad Kasim Bajran	—	1	1	—	1	—	—	—	—	4
22.	Mohmad Amin Bajran	—	—	1	2	1	—	—	—	—	5
23.	Abdul Latif Bajran	—	—	1	4	—	—	—	—	—	6
24.	Saida Bajran	—	1	1	2	1	—	—	—	—	6
25.	Latif Bajran	—	—	1	—	—	—	—	—	—	2
26.	Khateja (Widow)	—	—	—	4	—	—	—	—	—	5
27.	Israil Bajran	—	—	1	—	—	—	—	—	—	2
28.	Kalu Bajran	—	—	—	—	—	—	—	—	—	1
29.	Abdul Khan Saki	—	—	—	—	—	—	—	—	2	3‡
30.	Halim Bajran	—	—	1	—	2	—	—	—	—	4
31.	Abdul Rehman	—	—	1	—	3	—	—	—	—	5
32.	Yaqub	—	—	1	—	—	—	—	—	—	2
33.	Ismail Syal	—	—	1	2	3	—	—	—	—	7
34.	Nizam Syal	—	—	1	3	2	—	—	—	—	7
35.	Israil Awana	—	—	1	1	1	1	—	—	—	5
36.	Ismail Awana	—	—	1	—	3	—	—	—	—	5

†*Mai* is a maid servant.

‡This household comprises three brothers.

APPENDIX TABLE 3: Productive Property Owned by Deras in one Kafila

Sl. No.	*Name of the Household*	*Sheep*	*Goats*	*Horses*	*Khachhar*	*Dogs*	*Oxen*	*Buffallows*	*Cows*	*Agriculture Land*	*Service or Labour*	*Servants*	*Remarks*
1.	Gulam Nabi Bajran	300	500	4	15	5	2	—	—	130 Kanal	—	8	Ajri
2.	Mohmad Yaqus Bajran	10	50	3	2	1	—	—	—	31K	—	1	—
3.	Abdul Gaffor	10	100	3	1	2	2	—	—	28K	—	—	—
4.	Nazir Ahmad Bajran	30	200	4	3	2	2	—	—	100K	—	2	—
5.	Gulam Hussain Bajran	—	30	1	1	1	2	3	2	50K	—	—	—
6.	Mohamad Jawan Bajran	50	30	1	—	1	2	3	1	80K	—	2	All Sons are kids
7.	Abdul Rasid Bajran	10	30	2	—	1	2	—	1	50K	—	—	—
8.	Master Israil Bajran	20	20	2	2	1	—	—	1	60K	—	—	—
9.	Mahmud Yasub Bajran	5	30	1	1	1	1	—	—	40K	—	—	—
10.	Nurudin Jangal	20	80	—	2	1	2	—	1	60K	—	—	—
11.	Sher Din Jangal	10	80	—	2	1	—	—	—	3K	—	—	—
12.	Rehm Din Jangal	—	25	1	1	—	—	—	—	32K	—	—	—

13.	Mir Mohmad Jangal	10	70	—	2	2	—	—	—	35K	—	—	—
14.	Mitha Jangal	8	50	3	3	1	—	—	—	40K	—	—	—
15.	Israil Jangal	20	40	3	2	1	—	—	1	25K	—	—	—
16.	Suleman Jangal	22	90	4	1	2	—	—	—	24K	—	—	—
17.	Sanai Jangal	30	90	4	1	—	—	—	—	—	—	—	—
18.	Chandi Jangal	—	10	—	1	—	—	—	—	—	Yes	—	Work as Agriculture labour
19.	Abdulla Jangal	—	20	4	—	—	—	—	—	20K	—	—	—
20.	Mohmad Amin Jangal	—	10	2	—	—	—	—	—	—	Yes	—	Work as Agriculture labour
21.	Mohmad Kasim Bajran	10	20	2	4	—	2	—	—	30K	—	—	Agriculture labour
22.	Mohmad Amin Bajran	4	15	1	1	—	—	—	—	30K	Yes	—	Work as Agriculture labour
23.	Abdul Latif Bajran	3	10	4	—	1	—	—	—	30K	—	—	Deals in Trade of animals
24.	Said Bajran	—	20	—	—	—	2	—	8	15K	Yes	—	—
25.	Latif Bajran	5	15	1	—	—	—	—	—	—	Yes	—	—
26.	Khateja (Mrs) (Widow)	10	30	3	—	1	—	—	—	—	—	—	—

Appendix Table 3 (Contd.)

Sl. No.	Name of the Household	Sheep	Goats	Horses	khachhar	Dogs	Oxen	Buffallows	Cows	Agriculture Land	Service or Labour	Servant	Remarks
27.	Israil Bajran	2	20	1	—	—	—	—	—	—	Yes	—	Works as Ajri
28.	Kalu Bajran	10	—	—	—	—	—	—	—	—	—	—	Very old man
29.	Abdul; Khan, Saki	—	30	—	—	—	—	—	—	—	Yes	—	As Ajri (Three brothers)
30.	Halim Bajran	—	5	—	—	1	—	—	1	15K	—	—	Blind & old man
31.	Abdul Rehman	—	5	1	—	—	1	—	—	10K	—	—	—
32.	Yaqub	5	—	1	—	—	1	—	—	10K	—	—	—
33.	Ismail Syal	2	30	—	2	1	—	—	—	10K	—	—	—
34.	Nizam Syal	—	5	—	—	—	—	—	4	—	—	—	Begger
35.	Israil Awana	—	20	2	—	1	—	—	—	20K	—	—	—
36.	Israil Awana	4	30	2	—	—	—	—	—	20K	Yes	—	—

Muslim Family Life and Secularization in Dharwar, Karnataka[1]

George H. Conklin

Little has been written about most aspects of Muslim family life in India. Indeed, when Goode (1963) was summarizing the literature on family role relationships in India for his influential work on the future of the family in various parts of the world, he neglected to even mention the Muslim family in India. Even in his long discussion of the role relationships of the family in societies where Islamic family law is dominant, Goode observed, 'There are no contemporary studies of the changes in relations among the various members of the Arab family, except for a few comments here and there on the husband-wife relationship' (1963:139). The few comments seem to be limited to the observation that, as Ross (1961) and others have found in India, '. . . the mother-son relationship . . . is . . . intensely emotional, and the mother viewed the young bride to be as an interloper'. (Goode 1963:139).

In general, the authors of the few existing comments on the Muslim family in India seem struck by the assumed similarity between the family patterns of the Muslims and the Hindus. Mandelbaum comments that while 'Muslims usually differ

1. The survey discussed in this paper was undertaken while the author was a junior fellow of the American Institute of Indian Studies in 1968-69. The author would also like to thank the Demographic Research Centre, Dharwar, for their help in the field work and Dr. B.D. Kale, the Deputy Director of the Centre.

from Hindus in certain family practices, as in permitting parallel-cousin marriage. . . , in other family relations they are usually like the Hindus of their place and social level' (1970:547). However, Mandelbaum is unable to quote any firm data to support his argument. The conclusion thus seems to rest on general impression rather than on any specific studies which have carefully examined the various aspects of the question.

Kapadia (1966) has argued that the joint family in India is not an institution which is found only among the Hindus. In fact, he believes that the joint family is found commonly among all groups living in India, including most Christians. Cormack (1961:43) found that certain Muslim students, who were included in her sample of university students being asked about aspects of family life, found the questionnaire on family practices to be 'too Hindu' only in the section which asked specifics about religious practices such as attending a festival. Otherwise, it would seem, little difference in actual practices was noted by Cormack between Muslim and Hindu family attitudes.

It is unusual to find such uniformity of opinion on any one subject in social science. Elsewhere I have argued (Conklin, 1973a, 1973b) that many theories of change in India have been only partially correct, in spite of general agreement about certain points. The issue, however, remains: just how correct is the general notion that in day-to-day practice, Muslim family life is quite similar to that of Hindus in spite of religious differences and history?

To examine the effects of social change and how kinship might change in an urban setting, I conducted a survey of family and kinship practices in Dharwar, Karnataka State, in the spring of 1969. The purpose of the study was to study social change in a systematic fashion through the use of ran dom samples of residents of both rural Dharwar Taluka and the city of Dharwar itself. Information was collected on the number of sons who had set up separate households before the death of their fathers, a violation of the usual rules of solidarity between father and son in India. Information on household composition was also tabulated in detail (28 household types), as was information on roles found within the family, such as avoidance patterns between husband, wife and children. Each husband who was currently living with his wife was asked the questions on role relations, while all heads of household were asked the questions on household structure, income and other demographic measures. Households were defined as in the census: all those eating food cooked from a common hearth and living under one roof. In the 26 villages sampled, households were enumerated and then every sixth household was interviewed. In the city of Dharwar, half a random sample being collected by the Demographic Research Centre of the Institute of Economic Research was reinterviewed with the present questionnaire. A total of 766 rural household heads were interviewed, as were 382 in the city. Muslim families make up about 10 per cent of the rural population and about a quarter of the urban population (see Table 2).

How different are Muslims and Hindus as regards the ideals of father-son solidarity in maintaining a joint household? As an ideal, for example, Goode gives the case of the Arab Islamic family consisting of

> . . . a large extended family under one roof. Ideally . . . the wives would have many sons. These sons, in turn, would be married at a relatively early age to fertile women who would produce more sons. The father would continue to supervise the work of the family . . . . The brothers would live in harmony, with some authority given to the eldest son. After the father's death, the eldest brother . . . would deal equitably with all his brothers . . . . Ideally, a man became a patriarch in his elder years, full of wisdom and authority; he would be supported by his married sons (Goode, 1963:123).

Compare this ideal-type description with that given by Orenstein and Micklin for India, based upon Mitakshara Law:

> We believe that in most of present-day India, as in *shastric* times, the norm requires that Hindus accept paternal authority so long as the father remains capable. They anticipate remaining in a joint family while he is alive. Brothers believe they may, if they wish, continue to live jointly after their father dies, but while it may be thought to be the ideal to do this in some parts of India, it is not

usually the norm, and most do not (Orenstein and Micklin 1966:320).

Of course, as both Goode and Orenstein and Micklin point out, most families are not joint at any one time due to the demographic constraint upon the norm. Not all couples have sons, nor, on the average, does a man live very long after the marriage of his son. As Goode (1963:123) puts it '. . . the facts of fertility, mortality, and finances have prevented all but a few men in most major civilizations from attaining . . .' the objective of living jointly. Still, however, it is of note that the two portraits of family life are quite similar.

In Dharwar, Muslims and Hindus were asked specifically whether or not they thought living jointly was good. The question was asked: 'Which do you think is correct? Is it better that the husband and wife should stay alone after marriage, or is it better that a couple should stay with the husband's parents after marriage?' The proportion of respondents agreeing with the second statement is shown in Table 1. It is safe to say that there is an overwhelming majority in both the Muslim population and the non-Muslim families that

TABLE 1: Proportion of Muslim and Non-Muslim Respondents Agreeing that Fathers and Sons should Live Jointly

(*per cent*)

	Muslims	*Non-Muslims*	X^2	*Sig Level.*	*N*
Rural	91.7	93.7	0.4	N.S.	615
Urban	94.5	91.0	0.9	N.S.	294

believe that joint living is the ideal. Not only is the desire to have sons stay at home after marriage apparently expressed in the religious ideals of both Muslims and Hindus, it is also the expressed opinion of all the respondents in both urban and rural Dharwar.

But how does this expression of faith in the ideal of a joint household square with reality? It is, of course, possible to agree to a simple question without actually personally following a particular practice. To check on actual practice, household composition was computed for the Muslims of Dharwar

(Table 2).[2] In neither the city nor the villages is the *de facto* household composition any different comparing Hindus and Muslims. While there are some differences in the figures, especially for the city, the differences are not large enough to be statistically significant. It should also be noted that there is no significant shift in household type between the city and the village samples. Further, the patterns presented in Table 2 hold even if broken down into 28 possible household types.

TABLE 2: Household Composition of Muslim and Non-Muslim Families

(*per cent*)

	Household Type					
	Subnuclear	*nuclear*	*transitional*	*joint*	*N*	
RURAL						
Muslim	17.3	45.3	22.7	14.7	75	
Non-Muslim	13.2	44.0	24.0	18.8	287	$X^2=1.5$ *Sig.*=N.S.
URBAN						
Muslim	17.5	35.8	32.6	21.1	95	
Non-Muslim	13.8	42.0	26.1	18.0	983	$X^2=2{\cdot}7$ *Sig.*=N.S.

However, household types are only a crude measure of the norm of joint living between father and sons. Some families, for example, may not have a son at all, while others may not have a son who is old enough to be able to move away from home and thus break the rules of joint living. Additional calculations were therefore made to separate those families who had sons aged fifteen or older from those who did not. For each family which actually had one or more sons

2. The household structures presented here could be further broken down into 28 more specific groupings. The definitions are as follows: sub-nuclear, a household without a married couple; nuclear a couple and any unmarried children of that couple; transitional, nuclear household plus one or more unmarried relatives living with them; joint, two or more couples. Recently Shah (1974:186) has criticized this typology of household types as not being sufficiently exhaustive. However, breaking down the household types further does not change the results, and means that there are many empty cells when dealing with only part of the sample, i.e., Muslims as compared to non-Muslims.

over fifteen years of age, we checked to see if any of them were living away from home in violation of the norms. Table 3 presents the results for both the urban and rural samples.

TABLE 3: Proportion of Muslim and Non-Muslim Households which have One or More Sons Aged 15 or Over and Having One or More Sons Living Away. Rural and Urban Samples.

(per cent)

	No Son Living Away	*One or More Sons Living Away*	*N*	$X^2=0.0$
RURAL				
Muslim	90.0	10.0	40	
Non-Muslim	89.8	10.2		$X^2=0.0$ *Sig*=N.S.
URBAN				
Muslim	95.6	4.4	45	
Non-Muslim	85.3	14.7	150	$X^2=3.4$ *Sig*=N.S.

It would appear that while the rural Muslims are exactly identical to the non-Muslims in that both groups have ten per cent of the families with one or more sons living away in violation of the traditional rules of residence, in the city the Muslims are about ten per cent more likely to have all the sons living at home. The differences for the city, however, are not yet statistically significant at the accepted .05 level, although it would seem that Muslims are even more conservative than the Hindus when it comes to keeping their sons at home. There is no clear explanation for this observation except that, on the whole, the Muslims seem to be slightly more conservative regarding joint living than the non-Muslims even if income, education and other socio-economic variables are controlled by employing a multi-variable regression equation. This pattern was masked until demographic availability was controlled, and perhaps future research with even larger samples might come up with a statistically significant relationship.[3]

3. Only in exceptionally large samples (over 10,000) is it safe to assume demographic normality for each group in it. Increasing the size of a sample increases the chance that a difference of just ten per cent

In terms of joint households, ideals of joint living, and in having sons actually stay home until the death of the father, the Muslims seem to be, in fact as well in theory, identical to or even more conservative than the non-Muslims in Dharwar. However, an analysis of household structure does not tackle the issue of what goes on inside the household. For example, how do husbands treat their wives? What specifically are the role relationships between husbands, wives and children? To ascertain the role relationships in the family, each husband living with his wife at the time of the interview was asked a series of questions on practices within the family. The specific questions were drawn from the literature on family life in India. Principal among the problems researched was the common hypothesis that in order to keep husband, wife and married sons living together happily under one roof it is necessary to de-emphasize the conjugal role patterns, or more specifically, the husband-wife tie. Gore (1968) has put the concept most clearly, but essentially the debate has suggested that when the husband-wife tie is de-emphasized to keep peace among several generations of men, the result is a strong emphasis on the mother-son tie. While I know of no survey which tests to see if this assumption is also true for Muslims in India, Miner and De Vos argue that for the Muslim families in their survey '. . . the erotic attachment of men to their mothers and sisters is very strong . . . nor are these feelings one-sided' (quoted in Goode, 1963). Hsu (1961) and Ross (1961) have also shown that among Hindus in India the mother-son tie is in fact the most close emotional relationship within the family.

To test variations in the husband-wife role patterns, several questions were asked of each respondent currently living with his wife. First, each man was asked if he felt emotionally closer to his mother or to his wife after they got married. Secondly, the degree to which the husband-wife tie was de-emphasized in the family was gauged by finding out whether or not the husband usually took meals with his wife, or ate

between two groups would be statistically significant. Only about five per cent of households were brother-brother joint households, indicating that brothers do separate quickly (within a year) after the death of the father.

alone (or with the other men, if any). Thirdly, each husband was asked if he refrained, as a sign of respect for elders, from playing with his children when his elders were present.

Tables 4, 5, and 6 tabulate the results according to urban and rural samples. In order to reduce the number of tables presented, correlates were worked out using dummy variable regression techniques. In this way, it is possible to let a variety of variables try to predict the answers to each question. The specific socio-economic and other factors which entered each regression equation were as follows: Muslim or non-Muslims,[4] urban or rural residence,[5] education of the wife and the husband (in years), actual income in rupees, an index[6] of visible wealth to check on the declared income, per capita income,[7] and whether or not the wife was employed.[8] Since the urban-rural difference is usually the largest correlate, the data is presented in tabular form by urban and rural samples, and the correlates of each answer presented below the tables in the form of dummy variable regression analysis. Readers should keep in mind that the computer programme takes the largest single correlate, enters it into a regression equation, then selects the next most powerful variable to help explain the results, and so on, until there is no significant addition to be made by adding the other factors. In this way, it is possible to control many factors at one time without dividing the sample

4 Muslims and non-Muslims were entered into the dummy variable regression equation as follows: Muslim=1, non-Muslim=0.

5. Urban and rural residence were entered as follows: rural residence=0 urban residence=1.

6. Because of the possibility that all income might not be reported, a visible wealth scale was built into the study. A respondent received one point for each of the following items: brick house, tile or cement roof, separate tap, separate bath area, separate latrine, house ownership, aluminium or stainless steel cooking vessels, clock, radio, fan, kerosene stove, gas stove, bicycle, sewing machine, telephone, steel cupboard, table and chairs, wrist watch, motorcycle or car.

7. Per capita income was grouped, and the scores entered the equation. The groupings were as follows: Rs. 0—74=1; 75—99=2; 100—129=3; 130—159=4; 160—199=5; 200—299=6; 300—399=7; 400—499=8; 500 up=9.

8. By employment is meant gainful employment outside the household. Unpaid employment in the family farm did not count for this computation.

into numerous tables, each with a small number of cases. Thus, if the programme does not select the Muslim-non-Muslim factor, it can be concluded that Muslim and Hindus have expressed similar opinions.

The majority of both the urban and rural residents say that they feel emotionally closer to their mothers than to their wives. While there is still a decline in the proportion feeling emotionally isolated from their mothers in the city, conjugal role patterns are not yet the dominant pattern even in urban Dharwar. Muslims are not statistically different from Hindus in this matter if the usual .05 level of significance is applied. However, being a Muslim is the second most important of the variables entered into the regression equation, and is shown in Table 4. It reveals a slight positive relationship between being

TABLE 4: Were you Closer to your Wife or to your Mother after Marriage?

*(per cent)**

	Mother	*Equally Close*	*Wife*	*N*
Rural	74.4	1.0	67.4	616
Urbar	54.4	2.3	32.6	298
		$X^2=38.4$	*Sig.*=.001	

REGRESSION ANALYSIS*

Element Added	*Multiple r*	*Simple r*	*Sig. Level of Element in Final Equation*
1. Urbanization	0.19	—0.19	.001
2. Muslim	0.20	+0.02	.1
3. Other factors not significant			

* Entered as mother or equally close=1, wife=0.

a Muslim and the conservative position of feeling closer to mother than to the wife. This finding fits in with the results of the analysis on having sons living outside the household, where it was found that if Muslims are different from the average in Dharwar, they were, if anything, a little more conservative than would otherwise be expected. Apparently, the strong mother-son tie observed by Miner and De Vos in Arab Muslim countries is also true of the situation in India.

TABLE 5: Do you Dine with your Wife or Alone?

*(per cent)**

	With wife	*Alone*	*N*
Rural	9.1	90.0	616
Urban	32.3	67.7	303
		$X^2=78.7$	*Sig.*=.001

REGRESSION ANALYSIS

Element Added	*Multiple r*	*Simple r*	*Sig. Level of Element in Final Equation*
1. Education of Wife	0.29	—0.29	.001
2. Urbanization	0.33	—0.27	.001
3. Wealth Scale	0.34	—0.26	.05
4. Other factors not Significant			

*Entered as with wife=0, alone=1

As for dining with the wife, urbanization results in a sharp decline in ritual avoidance. Husbands and wives are much more likely to dine together in the city, and Muslims are very average in this practice. Not playing with one's own children in front of the elders is a custom which allows the elders added respect, at least in theory. Urban husbands are much more likely to ignore this old custom. The decline of traditional ritual avoidance patterns in the city reflects the emergence of conjugal role patterns in Dharwar City (Conklin, 1973b); and, all in all, Muslims are feeling the effects of urbanization nearly as strongly as Hindus.

Social control mechanisms, especially customs which strictly control marriage, are essential in maintaining group solidarity. Are Muslims as concerned over who their children marry as non-Muslims? Each head of household living with his wife was asked if the children should have any say in choosing their mates. Those who answered yes did not exactly come out in favour of a love marriage, but rather felt that the son should at

TABLE 6: Do you Play with your Children in Front of your Elders?

*(per cent)**

	Yes	*No*	*N*
Rural	37.4	62.6	602
Urban	70.7	29.3	300
		X^2=88.8	*Sig.*=.001

REGRESSION ANALYSIS*

Element Added	*Multiple r*	*Simple r*	*Sig. Level of Element in Final Equation*
1. Urbanization	0.31	—0.31	.001
2. Education of wife	0.24	—0.24	.001
3. Other factors not significant			

* Entered as Yes=0, No=1.

least be consulted as a marriage was being arranged (Table 7). Nearly 30 per cent of the urban residents felt that some consultation should be allowed.

TABLE 7: Should you Alone Pick the Bride, or Should the Children Have Some Say?

*(per cent)**

	No Cansultation	*Some Say*	*N*
Rural	90.0	10.0	617
Urban	72.1	27.9	293
	X^2=47.7	*Sig.*=.001	

REGRESSION ANALYSIS*

Element Added	*Oultiple r*	*Simple r*	*Sig. Level of Element in Final Regression Equation*
1. Urbanization	0.22	—0.22	.001
2. Per Capita Income	0.26	—0.18	—01
5. Muslim	0.27	+0.04	—05

* Entered as no consultation=1, some consultation=0

Those with higher income were more liberal than those with less. Even after controlling for place of residence and income, Muslims nevertheless emerge as significantly more conservative than the non-Muslims in this respect. While a zero order correlate of only .04 appears very small, regression analysis reveals that the element itself is statistically significant at the .05 level, and represents about a seven per cent difference between Muslims and non-Muslims. Again, Muslims emerge as being rather more conservative as compared to non-Muslims. The difference is not large, but the pattern is surely consistent.

While Muslims appear quite similar to Hindus in many respects in relation to family and kinship, it should not be concluded that there are no differences between Hindus and Muslims on religious issues. Elsewhere I have argued (Conklin, 1974) that the practice of going on a pilgrimage may serve as a useful indicator of secularization. Hindus in Dharwar are significantly less likely to have taken one or more pilgrimages in the past five years if they are (a) urban residents, (b) gain their income through the ownership of land which depends on the rain, and (c) are of high caste status employed in government service. As compared to Hindus, Muslims in Dharwar are much less likely to have been on a recent pilgrimage, reflecting perhaps the different role pilgrimage plays in Islam as compared to Hinduism (Table 8). From the comments recorded on the interview schedules, it would seem that Muslims are more likely to take

TABLE 8: Proportion of Muslims and Non-Muslims Who Have Been on One or More Pilgrimages in the Past Five Years

*(per cent)**

	No Pilgrimage	*Pilgrimage*	*N*
RURAL			
Muslims	71.9	28.1	57
			X^2 = 13.2
			Sig. = .001
Non Muslims	46.6	53.4	545
URBAN			
Muslims	82.2	17.8	73
			X^2 = 13.1
			Sig. = .001
Non-Muslims	48.8	41.2	221

* Only two Christian families appeared in the survey. They have not been included in the tabulations in this article.

fewer but more expensive pilgrimages than Hindus. However, the main point still remains: both Muslims and Hindus are less likely to have been on pilgrimage in the past five years if they are urban residents. Secularization is thus affecting both groups in Dharwar.

Muslims are also unique in regard to the choice of marriage partners. While Hindus in Dharwar prefer a cross-cousin marriage wherever possible (Conklin 1973a), Muslims prefer a parallel cousin. While the exact proportion of Muslims married to a cousin was not determined in the survey, examination of the data for the Hindu population showed that there were few or no social consequences involved in marriage to a close relative. In other words, role patterns are similar in all families, whether the bride is a cross-cousin or a stranger to the household when she moved in. There is no reason to expect a different pattern among the Muslims.

Conclusion

The literature about kinship and family among the Muslims is so scant that there is an almost total lack of empirical findings and theoretical formulations on the subject. In this paper I have stuck quite close to empirical findings and kept theoretical discussion to a minimum. The findings of this discussion suggest clearly that, on most points, Muslims are quite similar to Hindus and that the Muslim ideals, practices and role patterns are as conservative, or perhaps a tiny bit more conservative, as those of Hindus of a similar social status. Of course, this does not mean that Muslims are identical in all respects. Differences may very well exist on other aspects of family life not included in this survey, including, but not limited to, concepts of pollution and ties with more distant kin. Muslims in Dharwar speak a local variety of Hindustani and follow the festival days of Islam. And, of course, other specific religious practices, such as going on pilgrimages reflect differences of religion. However, in the present case it is safe to conclude that, at least in Dharwar, Muslim family practices are quite similar to those of Hindus in everyday life. This finding would seem to confirm the consensus of available literature when it suggests that family patterns are common among all elements of society in India given similar education and other social attributes. Hopefully, other researchers will continue to investigate how true this finding is in other parts of India. The reader should bear in mind that both Muslims and non-Muslims in the sample are being very much influenced by the effects of urbanization and education, especially the women. These two factors, together with industrialization, may very well continue to modify, in the future at least, the role patterns in the families of all social groups in India.

Bibliography

Conklin, George H. (1973a), 'Urbanization, Cross-Cousin Marriage and Power for Women: A sample from Dharwar', *Contributions to Indian Sociology*, New Series, 7, pp. 53-63.

——— (1973b), 'Emerging Conjugal Role Patterns in a Joint Family System: Correlates of Social Change in Dharwar, India', *Journal of Marriage and the Family*, 35, pp. 742-748.

——— (1974), 'Secularization and Economic Development in India: An Exploratory Study', *Asian Survey*, 14, pp. 418-428.

Cormack, Margaret L. (1960), *She Who Rides a Peacock: Indian Students and Social Change*, Bombay, Asia Publishing House.

Goode, William F. (1963), *World Revolution and Family Patterns*, New York, The Free Press.

Gore, M.S. (1968), *Urbanization and Family Change*, Bombay, Popular Prakashan.

Hsu, F.L.K. (1961), 'Kinship and Ways of Life: An Exploration', in F.L.K. Hsu (ed.), *Psychological Anthropology*, New York, Dorsey Press.

Kapadia, K.M. (1966), *Marriage and Family in India*, 3rd ed., Bombay, Oxford University Press.

Mandelbaum, David G. (1970), *Society in India*, Berkeley, University of California Press.

Orenstein, Henry and Michael Micklin (1966), 'The Hindu Joint Family: The Norms and the Numbers'. *Pacific Affairs*, 39, pp. 314-325.

Ross, Aileen D. (1961), *The Hindu Family in its Urban Setting*, Toronto, University of Toronto Press.

Shah, A.M. (1974), *The Household Dimension of the Family in India*, Berkeley. University of California Press.

Kinship Organization and Marriage Customs among the Moplahs on the South-West Coast of India

Victor S. D'Souza

This essay is concerned with a discussion of the kinship organization and marriage customs of the Moplah Muslims of the South-West Coast of India. Originally formed through intermarriage between maritime Arab traders and local women, the Moplahs are today a hetrogeneus community characterized by ethnic, regional and social diversities. This essay shall first focus upon their kinship organization and the related property concepts and then go on to deal with their marriage customs.

Kinship Organization and Property Concepts

The many diversities found among the Moplahs have led to different types of kinship organizations and property concepts among them. Some of the kinship organizations are matrilineal and some patrilineal and property concepts as a rule are related to these systems. There are three distinct types of kinship systems among the Moplahs: the kinship system of the Arabis which is patterned after the Arabic system; the kinship system of the father-right Moplahs which is patterned after the indigenous patrilineal kinship system; and the kinship system of the mother-right Moplahs which is patterned after the indigenous matrilineal system.

Kinship System of the Arabis

The kinship system of the Arabis is of the Arabic type. The Arabis live in nuclear family units of husband, wife and children. A woman after marriage goes to live in the house of her husband. The father in the family is the head of the household. Several families tracing descent from a common male ancestor in the male line constitute a clan or sib. These clans are called *qabilas*, or tribes, after the Arab fashion. The name of their *qabilas* are typically Arabic as, for instance, *Baduba*, *Barghaiba*, *Basqaran*, *Barami* and *Hafeef*. On the other hand, the names of the clans of other patrilineal Moplahs are of the local Malayalam type, such as, *Kurikkal*, *Koorimannin*, *Valiamannin*, *Avunhipurath*, *Kathiassam-Veedu* and *Karuthedam*. A special feature of the *qabilas* of the Arabis is that they are not exogamous and among them marriages between children of brothers are the most favoured type of unions. All the *qabilas* of the Arabis together form an endogamous group although hypergamous types of marriages do occasionally take place between the Arabis and the other groups of Moplahs. The inheritance of property is based strictly on the principle of Muslim law.

Kinship System of the Father-right Moplahs

The Moplahs following the indigenous type of patrilineal kinship system, such as that found predominantly in the interior of South Malabar and scattered everywhere in the region of the Moplahs, live in households of nuclear families like the Arabis. Among them also several families related in the male line constitute a clan or sib. But whereas the clan of the Arabis is called *qabila*, the clan of the other Moplahs is called a *tharavad*. However, what distinguishes a *tharavad* from the *qabila* is that, unlike the *qabila*, the *tharavad* is exogamous. Among these Moplahs also the father in the family is the head of the household. But on all ceremonial occasions the seniormost male member of the patrilineal *tharavad*, who is called *karanavar*, acts as the head, no matter in which household he lives. Among the Arabis there is no position in the *qabila* which is similar to the position of the *karanavar* in the *tharavad*, the father in the family being the chief authority on all occasions.

In accordance with clan exogamy, marriages cannot take place between persons who are related in the male line, such as the children of brothers, although such marriages are the favoured type of unions in Muslim countries in general and among the Arabs in particular. But there is no objection to the children of two sisters, or of a brother and a sister, marrying each other as in these cases the marriage partners would belong to different patrilineal *tharavads*. It may be pointed out that while cross-cousin marriages may take place among the father-right Hindus of the locality, parallel cousin marriages are prohibited whether between children of two brothers or of two sisters. So it would appear that the father-right Moplahs' acceptance of marriages between the children of two sisters is due to the influence of Islam. But this influence has been ineffectual where the Muslim practice of marrying the children of two brothers is incompatible with the kinship system of the Moplahs.

While marriages between members of the same patrilineal *tharavad* cannot take place, several *tharavads* form an endogamous group. In any locality of father-right Moplahs there are generally several endogamous groups.

Among the patrilineal Moplahs a married woman lives in the house of her husband. The property is divided according to the Islamic law of inheritance but by tradition the house goes to the share of the youngest son.

Kinship System of the Mother-right Moplahs

The kinship organization and property concepts of the mother-right Moplahs are much more elaborate and complex. Since mother-right is indigenous to Kerala where several of the Hindu sections, particularly the Nairs, also follow it, it would be useful to examine the mother-right traits of the Moplahs against the background of the similar traits among the Nairs.

The mother-right Nairs[1] are divided into a number of matrilineal joint families known as *tharavads*. The *tharavad* is

1. In some parts of Kerala the Nairs also follow the father-right social system.

the basic social unit recognized by custom and law. A typical *tharavad* includes a woman and all her brothers and sisters, her and her sisters' children, her and her sisters' grand-children born only of their daughters and so on—in short, the woman's and her sisters' relatives on the female side, however distant their relationship may be. The husbands of the female members of the *tharavad* and the wives and children of the male members are excluded from its membership. Only the female members have a permanent interest in the *tharavad* in the sense that it is their children and their progeny in the female line that become heirs to the rights and privileges accruing from it, while the male members take only a life-interest, for their children belong to their wives' *tharavads* which are quite separate.

Usually the members of a *tharavad* live together in the family house, have a common table, and own and enjoy all the family property in common. However, living in a common house and enjoying property jointly are not the prerequisites of the *tharavad*—the term mainly indicates kin relationship among the members. When the *tharavad* as such has no family property and the members live separately, they are still bound together by certain social ties, the chief among them being the community of pollution. The relation of such members with the *tharavad* is known as *pula-sambandham*, meaning relationship by pollution.[2] When the members enjoy common property, the relation is called *mudal-sambandham*, or community of property which also presupposes community of pollution. Thus, the *tharavad* among the mother-right Moplahs may be regarded as a matrilineal clan.

Although each and every member of the *tharavad*, either male or female, has an equal right to the *tharavad* property—and this is manifested by the fact that the property cannot be parted with or divided without the consent of all the members—the management or the direction of affairs in the *tharavad* rests

2. The members so related are considered polluted at the time of birth or death of any of the members and so have to observe certain rituals on that occasion.

only with the eldest male member who is called the *karanavar*.[3] The *karanavar*[4] is the most important member of the *tharavad*, having the power and authority to manage all property, arrange and conduct all social and religious functions, meet the economic needs of the members, etc., and by virtue of his position and authority he is the person most to be respected or feared by the other members. The right to succession to the office of the *karanavar* devolves on the next seniormost male member, be he a brother of the preceding *karanavar* or a nephew (sister's son) or any other kinsman related to him in the female line. The law regulating the succession to the office of the *karanavar* is known as *marumakkathayam*.[5]

Within the *tharavad* itself the group of members who are the descendants in the female line of any female member are collectively called the *thavazhi* and the seniormost male member of the *thavazhi* is its head and is also known as *karanavar*. The members of a *tharavad* may multiply sometimes to an unmanageable number (there are *tharavads* with membership exceeding two hundred even) and in such cases the smaller groups or *thavazhis* may live separately and enjoy different portions of the *tharavad* property apportioned to them by the *karanavar*. The *karanavars* of the separated *thavazhis* can also succeed to the office of *karanavar* of the *tharavad* by seniority.

By virtue of their common descent from the same ancestress, the members of a *tharavad* cannot intermarry. Since the sisters' children belong to the same *tharavad* they cannot marry each other. But marriages between the children of brothers and sisters can take place. In this case, although the brothers and sisters belong to the same *tharavad*, their children belong to different *tharavads*.

3. In some Sudra *tharavads* and some royal houses the females also have equal right to succeed to the office of *karanavar* in the order of seniority (see Iyer, 1883:8).
4 The term *karanavar* is the plural of *karanavan*. But since the position of the *karanavan* is highly respected by all the term is never used in its singular form.
5. *Marumakkathayam* literally means succession by nephews (sister's sons). But in this case the succession is not restricted to nephews alone. However, the term implies that in the second generation the successors to a man's office are not his sons but his sister's sons.

The *tharavads* are included in the bigger exogamous subdivisions called *kulams* which are said to correspond to the original *tharavads*. Members of the group of *tharavads* belonging to the same *kulam* cannot intermarry. The *kulams* are again grouped together to form sub-castes which are usually endogamous. These sub-castes are graded into a social hierarchy and, for the purpose of marriage, they are subject to the rule of hypergamy whereby a woman is enjoined to marry a man either from her own sub-caste or from a sub-caste which is higher in social status than her own, but never from a lower sub-caste. A man's social status and caste privileges are not altered by marrying a woman of a lower sub-caste, but a woman marrying a man of a lower sub-caste not only loses her own status and privileges in her sub-caste but also brings the same calamity upon her children.

The mother-right Nairs have a visiting type of marriage in which the husband has to visit his wife at her own *tharavad* house, but he does not stay there permanently. Should a man desire to take his wife to live with him permanently he cannot take her to his *tharavad* house but has to have a separate house.

The Moplahs of North Malabar—for instance, those residing in Cannanore, Tellicherry and Quilandy—have retained even to the present day the important features of the Nair *tharavad* system to a remarkable extent and they follow the *marumakkathayam* system of inheritance.[6] A typical *tharavad* household comprises many individuals immediately or distantly related to one another, but all tracing their ancestry in the female line to a common female ancestor. Every individual acquires rights in the *tharavad* by birth. These rights include the co-ownership of the *tharavad* property and the right to have a share if and when the property is divided by the common consent of the members of the *tharavad*.[7] The eldest male

6. The *marumakkathayam* system of inheritance is fast dying out among the Hindus themselves, but the Moplahs are holding on to it tenaciously.
7. A notable departure from the *marumakkathayam* law in this connection is that the self-acquired property of an individual does not go to the *tharavad* but is divided according to the rules of Muslim Law.

member is the *karanavar* having sole authority over the management of *tharavad* property and the affairs concerning the members of the *tharavad*. Usually, the husbands make their permanent abodes in the *tharavads* of their wives.[8] When this is not possible they can visit their wives every night or occasionally.[9] If a man can afford it he may build a separate house and live with his wife there, but under no circumstances can he compel his wife to settle with him in his *tharavad* house. The practice of the husband staying permanently in the *tharavad* of his wife is common among the Moplahs of Tellicherry and Cannanore where it is confined mainly to the higher groups.

Since the woman resides in her own *tharavad* house, she is maintained by the *karanavar* out of the *tharavad* property and her husband is not bound to maintain her.[10] As a matter of fact, in many of the rich *tharavads*, notably in the *Arakkal tharavad* or the so-called Ali Raja family of Cannanore, the women as well as their husbands are maintained out of the *tharavad* funds. However, it is becoming increasingly common for the husband to maintain his wife and family even though the wife resides in her mother's *tharavad* for purely social reasons (cf. Ali, 1938:88-89).

The *tharavad* property is either enjoyed jointly, all the members eating from a common table, or apportioned among different *thavazhis* or members who have separate apartments.[11] When a married male member resides in his wife's *tharavad* he is either given his share of the income from his own

8. Although the custom for the husband to reside in his wife's house is not peculiar to Islam, the Moplahs do not find it un-Islamic for they contend that the Prophet was himself living in the house of his wives.
9. Since marriage as a rule is matrilocal and the husband resides in his wife's *tharavad* house, the married male members of a *tharavad* do not live in the (*tharavad*) house.
10. This is quite in confirmity with the rules of the *tharavad* organization. But even on the grounds of Muslim law, a wife in such a situation cannot claim maintenance from her husband, because it is deemed obligatory on the part of a Muslim husband to maintain his wife only on condition that she resides with him.
11. If the several women, each with her dependents all living in the same *tharavad* house, have separate cooking establishments, the cooking has to be done in the common kitchen while they may eat their food in their respective apartments in the house.

tharavad or he may forego his share in favour of the other members of his own *tharavad*. In practice, the income derived from the *tharavad* properties is spent according to the discretion of the *karanavar* who is usually reluctant to give money to members residing outside the *tharavad*.[12] A man, however, spends his personal earnings on his wife and children. There are also cases in which a man gives his earnings not only to his wife and children but also to his sisters and their children.

Among the richer sections, since a man, because he stays in his wife's *tharavad*, virtually forfeits his share of income from his own *tharavad*, the wife's *tharavad* has to make ample provision for his economic well-being. This is done by a series of dowries. Dowry, as a payment made to the groom by the father or kinsman of the bride, has never been a part of the Muslim marriage. The only property transaction sanctioned by Islam on such an occasion is the payment of a contracted amount called *mahr* by the groom to the bride. The *mahr* is solely the property of the bride. But among the Moplahs, although the amount of *mahr* is mentioned in the marriage contract, it is seldom paid except among the Arabis where the *mahr* is the only payment made on the occasion of the marriage. The other Moplahs, on the contrary, lay much importance upon the payment of dowries of which one type, called *kizhipanam* (literally, 'purse money' because it is handed over in a purse) or *kashipanam*, is prevalent universally among them. While the payment of *mahr* is ignored, *kizhipanam* is paid outright to the bridegroom by the bride's father in cash on the day of the marriage function called *kalyanam*. Among the father-right Moplahs, excepting the Arabis who do not pay dowry, this is the only type of dowry that is paid. In the interior of South Malabar, the amount of *kizhipanam* varies from Rs. 35 to Rs. 1,000. But among the mother-right Moplahs, especially those residing in Tellicherry and Cannanore, in addition to *kizhipanam*, which here ranges from Rs. 2,000 among the poorer sections to about Rs. 10,000 among the richer ones, there are two other types of dowries

12. *Karanavars*, who are known for their good sense of distributing the family income even among the members staying in the *tharavad* of their wives, are spoken very highly of. This only shows that such instances are rather rare.

called *sthridhanam* (also called *pirivu*) and *kadam-vaiyippa*. *Sthridhanam* (literally, 'woman's property') consists of some property of the bride's *tharavad* made over to the bride in addition to her maintenance. The management of this property rests with the husband while, of course, he is expected to share the income with his wife and children. *Kadam-vaiyippa*, according to its literal connotation, is a loan which is given to the bridegroom in order to enable him to start a business or any other economic activity for the benefit of his wife and children. This 'loan', however, is not expected to be returned. While the *sthridhanam* type of dowry is common among all mother-right Moplahs, the so-called *kadam-vaiyippa* is paid only when the husbands stay permanently in the *tharavads* of their wives.

Marriages between members of the same *tharavad* or inter-related *tharavads* are taboo. For example, as the children of sisters belong to the same *tharavads*, marriages between their children are prohibited while there is no such restriction in the case of children of two brothers since they belong to their mother's *tharavads* which would always be different. So also marriages may take place between children of brothers and sisters. Thus, as among the indigenous father-right Moplahs, here, too, the choice of a marriage partner is rigidly limited by the kinship organization despite the influence of Islam. But whereas among the father-right Moplahs individuals related in the male line cannot marry each other, among the mother-right Moplahs those related in the female line cannot marry.

While the inter-related *tharavads* form exogamous groups, several such exogamous groups constitute a larger endogamous group. Families of an endogamous group have the same social status within the community and different endogamous groups have different social status. In any particular Moplah locality the various endogamous groups can be arranged according to a hierarchy of status differences. Thus, the different status groups may be regarded as constituting something of a caste structure among the Moplahs.

The Keyi *tharavads* of Tellicherry may serve as a good illustration. The Keyis are a prominent land-owning and business class of Moplahs in Tellicherry. All the Keyi families trace their origin to one *tharavad* called Chowackaran. In course of time the Chowackaran *tharavad* broke up into four *tharavads* called Orkateri, Keloth, Puthiyapurayil and Valiapurayil respectively. These four *tharavads* are subdivided into a large number of *thavazhis*, but every Keyi regards himself as basically belonging to one of the four *tharavads*. Since all the Keyi families are related in the female line, marriages cannot take place between members of all the Keyi *tharavads*.

While the members of the Keyi *tharavads* cannot intermarry they have to seek their mates from *tharavads* of equal social status, such as, Acharat, Kadankandi, Thailakandi, Pommanichi and Mukkathumpuram. All these *tharavads*, together with the Keyis, form an endogamous group.

Although marriages take place within the endogamous group as a rule, inter-group marriages take place in very rare cases. But such marriages are socially acceptable only if the social status of the husband's group is higher than that of the wife's group. A woman marrying a man from a lower social group will suffer social ostracism and bring the same calamity upon her children. Even the other members of her *tharavad* will come down in the estimation of the group. When a man marries someone of a lower status than himself it is largely with a woman from a group which ranks next to his own in social status and not from a group which is very much lower.

Almost all sections of Moplahs in North Malabar have the mother-right social organization and, especially among the richer sections, the husband resides in the wife's *tharavad*. Naturally, the mother-right family organization is strictly adhered to in families having ancestral property. Where there is not much family property, marriages are of the visiting type. This is especially the case among the Pusalars who are a poor people leading a hand-to-mouth existence. Among them in a few instances the husbands have even taken their wives to their own houses. However, in all such cases in the eventuality of the death of the husband the wife has to return with her children to her own mother's house. Where visiting marriage is common, as among the Pusalars, a man may sometimes have more than one wife.

In the coastal North Malabar, as one proceeds southwards to places like Quilandy and Badagara, the mother-right social organization undergoes a change. The change becomes quite distinct in the coastal region of South Malabar. The change in mother-right traits in this area may primarily be attributed to the fact that, whereas in North Malabar the ancestral property is inherited exclusively in the female line, in the south it is inherited according to the Islamic practice whereby the major share of the property is transmitted in the male line. But the social organization is essentially mother-right and the modifications are such as suit the change in the principle of inheritance.

As in North Malabar, in the coastal region of South Malabar also descent is traced in the female line and so the members belong to the family of the mother and not to that of the father. A woman does not leave her mother's house after marriage. But here, unlike in North Malabar, the husband does not permanently reside in the house of his wife but visits her at night. In North Malabar, where the husband resides permanently in the house of his wife, he has to depend mainly upon the resources of his wife's *tharavad*. Although, theoretically, he is entitled to a share of income from his own *tharavad*, in practice such payments are not made to persons residing in their wives *tharavads*. So the income is solely enjoyed by the residents of the *tharavads* who are usually the women who can very well see to the maintenance of their husbands also. But in South Malabar, where the property is divided according to Islamic law, the woman's share is not sufficient to maintain her husband. As a matter of fact, the responsibility of maintaining her and her children devolves on the husband. The husband is also in a position to do so because he secures a separate share of the ancestral property.

Even though property is divided according to Islamic law, the house is excluded from such divisions and it becomes the common property of the members of the family. Since descent is traced in the female line, it is the women of the family who have a permanent interest in the house, as it will be handed down to their children and their daughters' children and so on. The children of the male members will reside in their maternal homes. In most cases the house is the only common *tharavad* property. But there are some instances where the immovable common property of the *tharavad*, such as coconut groves, paddy fields, buildings, etc., is not divided, but enjoyed in common bythe members of the *tharavad* as in North Malabar.

If a man builds a separate house for his wife and children so that he may reside permanently with them, at the time of division of his property the house will become the joint property of the family, particularly of his daughters who will stay there permanently.

The effect of the Islamic mode of inheritance is to a still further extent nullified by giving dowries to the daughters in the shape of *sthridhanam*. The dowries in the coastal region of South Malabar are of a slightly different type. The custom of *mahr*, however, as in the case of North Malabar, is merely symbolic. The amount of *kizhipanam* is fixed at 300 *panams*.[13] Thus here also the amount which is paid outright to the birdegroom is symbolic. But the *tharavad* property made over to the bride in the form of *sthridhanam* is substantial, sometimes sufficient for the subsistence of the woman and her children. Especially so long as the mother of the woman is alive the *sthridhanam* property is managed by the *karanavar* of the *tharavad* and the woman and her children are supplied food from the common kitchen. In that case the husband needs to provide only for the sundry requirements of his family, such as clothes, cosmetics, etc. But as soon as the mother dies, the *tharavad* property is divided. The woman and her children as a rule will set up a separate cooking establishment and, instead of the *karanavar*, the husband will have to manage the *sthridhanam* property and the other properties accruing to the wife as a result of the division. Under these circumstances, the husband has to see to the entire expenses of his wife and children. Thus, whereas in North Malabar the husband's management of the *sthridhanam* property entails no strict obligation on his part to maintain his wife and children, in South Malabar such a privilege is accompanied by the duty of looking after all the needs of his family. But here the husband is also in a better position to accept this responsibility, for he can supplement the income from his wife's property with the income from the share he inherits from his own *tharavad*. Once the husband takes up the full responsibility of looking after his wife and children, he attaches himself more and more

13. A *panam* is an old local coin, now no longer in circulation. Where it is used for counting, its value is fixed at 28 paise, a paisa being the hundredth part of an Indian rupee.

to his wife's house. Whereas previously he would only take his breakfast in his wife's house, now he may take all his meals there. At the same time he will keep his connections with his own *tharavad* house, by visiting it often.

The type of dowry called *kadam-vaiyippa* which is common in North Malabar does not prevail in South Malabar, for, in South Malabar, there is no need for such a provision as the man also inherits a part of the ancestral property.

Strictly speaking, the members descended from the same female ancestor, however distant, cannot inter-marry. This rule is followed scrupulously in North Malabar. But in the coastal region of South Malabar, particularly at Ponnani, it is relaxed somewhat. Here, if persons are distantly related in the female line, they may inter-marry, provided that they do not live in the same *tharavad* house. All the same, such inter-marriages are few and far between. But they are noteworthy because such marriages are unheard of among the mother-right Moplahs of North Malabar. In the South, the favoured types of marriages are those between children of two brothers or between the children of brothers and sisters.

Of the different kinship systems discussed above the kinship organization of the Arabis unmistakably points to their Arab ancestry. But the Arabs are not known to have brought their women folk along with them to Kerala and so their descendants appear to be the progeny of Arabs and local women.[14]

However, as has already been pointed out earlier, besides the Arabis there are also many other Moplahs with Arab ancestry who have lost their Arab genealogy on account of the adoption of the mother-right kinship system in which one cannot trace the male ancestry. The kinship system of the Moplahs, as also of the other people of Kerala, are reflected in their system of names (For details, see D'Souza, 1955:28-44). The Moplahs usually have four names which, in the case of the father-right kinship system, are: the name of the patri-

14. It has never been the practice of Arabs to take their wives with them on their journeys or voyages although they were noted for travelling with slave girls. Travelling with a girl was more convenient as the man owed no responsibility towards her. She could be bought, sold or exchanged without any difficulty.

lineal *tharavad*; the name of the head of the family who is usually the father or some other senior male related in the male line; one's own personal name; and a surname which is inherited in the male line—as, for example, Kurikkal Ahmed-Kutty Hasan Kutty. The surname, Kutty, is also repeated in the name of the father out of respect. In the mother-right kinship system the four names are: the name of the matrilineal *tharavad*; the name of the *karanavar* or the head of the *tharavad* who is usually the seniormost maternal uncle or any other seniormost male related in the female line; one's own personal name; and a surname which is inherited in the female line—as in Ponmanichintakath Hasan-Koya Muhammed Koya. In this case also the surname is repeated in the personal name of the *karanavar*. Thus, the system of names provides a device for tracing the lineage of a person; however, in the father-right kinship organization the system of names does not provide any clue as to the female lineage, while in the mother-right organization the names of a person do not indicate the male lineage.

The system of names of the Arabis is patterned after the Arab practice. They usually have three names: one's own personal name; father's name; and the name of one's patrilineal tribe—as in Muhammed bin Hasan Barghaiba. The father's name is preceded by the term 'bin' meaning 'son of' in Arabic.

Because of these peculiarities of the different prevailing systems of names, so far as the father-right Moplahs are concerned, it is at once possible to know which of the father-right Moplahs have Arab ancestry, for people with Arab ancestry will bear the Arabic type of patrilineal clan or tribal names. Moreover, the order of names among them is different from that among the indigenous people. Among people with Arab descent the clan name comes last, while among the others it comes first in the series of names.

But among the mother-right Moplahs there is no way of establishing the male Arab ancestry from the system of names which does not indicate the male lineage. Only in the case of Thangals is the identity of the Arab lineage noticeable in the system of names despite the fact that, by and large, they have a mother-kinship system. But this is because of very special circumstances. The Thangals are accorded high honour and respect mainly on account of their descent from the Prophet's family. It is therefore necessary for them to establish the fact of their venerable pedigree—and the connection with the Prophet's family has to be traced in the male line. But at the same time it is essential for them to preserve the female lineage, for their mode of life is the same as that of the other mother-right Moplahs. Under the circumstances, the Thangals have adjusted themselves by combining both the Arab and local systems of names. Thus, a Thangal usually has a long list of seven names, as in Syed Muhammed bin Mustafa Hydroos Vetampokirianakam Atta-Koya Thangal. In this example, Syed is the honorific title given to all Arabs tracing their descent from the Prophet's family, Muhammed is the personal name, Mustafa is the father's name, Hydroos is the name of the patrilineal Arab tribe, Vettampolirianakam is the name of the matrilineal *tharavad*, Atta-Koya is the name of the *karanavar* of the mother's *tharavad*, and Thangal is the group name which is common to all Thangals. The matrilineal surname of Koya is suffixed to the name of the *karanavar*. A Thangal, therefore, has in his system of names the names of both his patrilineal and matrilineal clans. When the patrilineal and matrilineal clan names of the Thangals are examined, it will be invariably found that the patrilineal clan names are of the Arabic type and the matrilineal clan names of the local Malayalam type,[15] leading to the conclusion that the male ancestors of the Thangals were Arabs and the female ancestors were local Malayalam women.

However, not all Thangals keep the full set of names. People of position and importance belonging to reputed matrilineal clans make use of the full set. The others keep either to the Arabic system or to the local system, but in either case they are aware of the other system of names.

The other mother-right Moplahs of Arab ancestry have had no incentive for remembering their male Arab ancestry as in the case of the Thangals. On account of their adoption of the matrilineal kinship system of their female ancestors the identity

15. The following are some of the patrilineal clan names (*qabilas*) of the Thangals: Bafaqqih, Bahasan, Ba'lawi, Hydroos, Jifri, Maqbool, Mash-hoor, Munaffar, Shatiri. Their typical matrilineal *tharavad* names are: Waliajaram, Padinharakam, Vettampokirianakam, Malikakkal, Ussambiakam, Pazhiyakam, etc.

of their male Arab ancestry is lost to pôsterity. All the same, the anthropometric evidence is there for anyone to see.

For obvious reasons, inter-marriages among members of different kinship systems and those with different modes of inheritance of property usually do not take place. However, in very rare cases such marriages take place between mother-right sections of slightly divergent social organizations. But, unlike the broad ethnic divisions of Thangals, Arabis, Malbaris, Pusalars and Ossans, these kinship divisions do not form a system of status hierarchy and they may have to be regarded as merely segmental divisions because very often they cut across status divisions. Most of the Thangals have a mother-right social organization manifesting different degrees of regional variation, but a few of them follow the father-right system of the Arabic type. The Arabis follow only the father-right system of the Arabic type. The Malabaris follow both father-right and mother-right systems of the indigenous types. The Pusalars also have both the father-right and mother-right systems but those following the mother-right system are greater in number. The Ossans follow the father-right system of the local type.

Marriage Customs

The regional and sectional divergences in the culture of the Moplahs are also reflected in their marriage customs. The relationship between some of the practices connected with marriage, such as choice of partners, dowry, etc., on the one hand, and the type of kinship systems and property concepts on the other has already been pointed out. Here an attempt may be made to detail some of the salient features of the marriage functions. The marriages of the mother-right Moplahs, who form the dominant section, are performed with greater pomp and éclat. It is therefore proposed to detail the marriage functions with special reference to this section, particularly the Moplahs of coastal South Malabar, and to point out the regional and sectional peculiarities in appropriate places.

The Moplahs marry young. In the past, pre-puberty marriage was the rule for girls. In that case the boys were married after they were twelve years or so of age. Such marriages are now rare. But ages of twelve to fourteen for girls and fifteen to eighteen for boys are considered to be suitable ages for marriage. It may be pointed out that even if the marriage takes place before the girl has reached maturity, there is no objection to the couple's living together as husband and wife. This practice is observed and approved by Muslims all over the west coast of India.

Among the mother-right Moplahs the proposal for the match has to come from the bride's side. This is usually done with the help of an intermediary like the mosque official or a local *karanavar*. When the preliminaries are settled, a day is fixed for the formal betrothal ceremony called *vakkukodukkal* (literally, word giving) which has to take place in the house of the bridegroom. The *karanavar* of the bride's *tharavad* along with near relatives—such as the bride's father, maternal uncles, sister's husband and leading persons of the locality—go to the groom's house and are received by a similarly constituted gathering of men there. This is mainly a men's function. Invitations for women will be restricted only to the close relations of the bridegroom. The chief parties to the discussions are the *karanavars* of both sides. The fathers of the bride and groom have no formal say in the matter. As a matter of fact, in some places like Mangalore and Cannanore, the father of the bride usually does not accompany the party to the groom's house. At the function, the terms and conditions of marriage are made public to the gathering. The terms and conditions are mostly one-sided—the side that is called upon to fulfil them being the bride's party. As a symbol of the acceptance of the terms, betel is exchanged between the *karanavars* of both the sides. The functions connected with marriage are held at night.

While accepting a girl for marriage, neither the bridegroom nor any of his relatives, including the women, have any opportunity of seeing the bride, for, among Moplahs, as soon as a girl is considered to be of marriageable age she has to observe *purdah* (seclusion) not only towards men but also towards women who are not related to her.

Although the central and most important ceremony of a Muslim marriage is the ceremony of marriage contract called *nikah*, for Moplahs this ceremony alone is not sufficient to enable the bridal couple to live as man and wife. The consummation of marriage can take place only after holding another function. This latter function is called *kalyanam*, or marriage, and the ceremony of *nikah* is called *kaniyath.* They make a clear distinction between these two ceremones and sometimes, by no means rarely, the *nikah* ceremony is held months ahead of the *kalyanam* function. But the bridegroom cannot even see the face of his bride until after the *kalyanam* function. If *nikah* is not performed much in advance of the *kalyanam* function, it is held a day or two before the latter. If it is performed earlier, it takes place a few days after the betrothal in the house of the bridegroom.

A few days before the *kalyanam,* a function called *nishchayam* is held in the bridegroom's house for fixing the date of the *kalyanam.* As in the case of the betrothal function a party of men from the bride's side goes to the groom's house.

Once the date for *kolyanam* is fixed, preparations for the function have to be made. Most of the subsequent functions take place in the bride's house and it is therefore the birde's side that has to take the greater pains and spend more money. One of the important items of preparation is the decoration of the bridal chamber, called *mandakam,* in the bride's house. Two cots, each a double one, one with a canopy and the other without one, are placed in a room which is profusely decorated. Among the higher sections in North Malabar and Mangalore the cots are spread with seven mattresses or quilts, one above the other. This was also the case in South Malabar in the past but now not much attention is paid to the practice. At Quilandy and its surrounding area, the number of mattresses spread over the cots corresponds to the group status of the party. The higher the status the larger the number. Some groups spread three, some five and some seven mattresses. At Mangalore, a special function is held in the bride's house to inaugurate the decoration of the bridal chamber which may last for several days. On that day the bridegroom's maternal uncle or sister's husband has to place on the bridal cot a gold ornament which becomes the property of the bride. Although two cots are placed in the bridal chamber, only one is used by the couple.

In case *nikah* has not already been performed, the ceremony takes place a day or two prior to the *kalyanam* function. This ceremony takes place in the house of the groom. The bride herself is not present on the occasion but her consent has to be given on her behalf by her *wali,* or guardian, who is usually her father. In some places the *karanavar* of the bride's *tharavad* acts as the *wali.* In most cases the bride's consent is taken for granted, but sometimes it is ascertained by the assistant of the *gadi* who solemnizes the marriage contract. Just before the ceremony, the *wali* of the bride, together with a large party of men, come in procession to the groom's house. All the guests are first entertained to a dinner or at least light refreshments. After this the *gadi* solemnizes the *nikah* at which the groom and the bride's father clasp their hands.

On the eve of the *kalyanam* function there is a function called *mailanchi* in the bride's house. *Mailanchi* literally means henna and the ceremony consists of applying henna juice to the nails and toes, palms and feet, etc., of the bride. The juice has to be brought ceremonially from the *tharavad* house of the bride's father by a procession of women headed by female singers who belong to the group of Ossans. The sisters of the bride's father have the prerogative of applying the henna. This is purely a women's function. The inivited guests will come in their best attire. Particularly on this occasion it is customary for women to wear borrowed ornaments in addition to their own. But no clothes are borrowed. A large number of female guests are feasted on that night. Incidentally, on this occasion and even afterwards, the bride gives up the peculiar custom of observing *purdah* towards women.

On the same day, during daytime, there is a function in the bridegroom's house called *kanhudi* or *kanhikudi. Kanhikudi* literally means 'drinking of rice gruel' and it would appear that in the past only rice gruel was served to the invited guests who are only men. Nowadays, however, a full-scale dinner is served on the occasion.

Kalyanam may be regarded as the most important function of the Moplah marriage. In the evening, before the arrival of the bridegroom, the bride is ceremonially dressed in her own house in wedding clothes and adorned with ornaments. This ceremony is called *ponnoppikkal* (literally meaning 'putting on gold ornaments'). As in the case of the *mailanchi* ceremony the bride's father's sisters are required to assist at this function also. After this the bride is seated in a prominent place in full view of all the guests. This part of the function is called *oppana.* Presents are given to the bride at this time. The women singers will sing all the time. Only women are invited to this function.

About the same time in the bridegroom's house the groom has to undergo the ceremony of a shave called *monthala*. The actual shaving will have been done beforehand. The groom is clothed in his wedding dress and seated in the midst of young men who keep on clapping while the barber pretends to run the razor as though he is giving the groom a shave. Subsequently, the groom is seated in a prominent place when he is presented with wedding gifts and garlanded by the male guests.

Just before the bridegroom and the party are due to leave for the bride's house, a small party from the bride's side, headed by the *karanavar*, comes to extend an invitation. Before leaving, the bridegroom takes formal leave of his relatives and elders. His friends will extract from him a promise that later on he will throw them a party and, as security, take a ring. When the marriage procession is about to start, someone from the groom's side asks if the dowry called *kizhipanam* has been paid. The *karanavar* of the bride's side replies that he is ready to pay whenever demanded by the other *karanavars* present on the occasion. The amount—which is fixed at 300 *panams* at Ponnani, but is variable in other places—is enclosed in a small cloth bag or purse which also contains some rice and is handed over along with a knife to the chief *karanavars* present. These persons open the purse, count the money and hand it over to the bridegroom who gives it either to his *karanavar* or to his eldest sister's husband. After this, the wedding procession, which is the grandest of all processions connected with marriage functions, wends its way to the bride's house to the accompaniment of music and fireworks. At the entrance to the bride's house, on a raised platform, water is kept in a small copper vessel. One of the bride's brothers poses to wash the feet of the groom with this water when the latter drops an ornament, a gold sovereign or some coins, into the vessel as a present. At Mangalore the vessel contains milk instead of water. Next, the guests on both sides, consisting mainly of men, are entertained to a dinner. After the dinner, in the presence of the guests, the bridegroom is ceremonially taken to the bridal chamber. Most of the guests retire after having a look at the chamber. The bridegroom and his friends are then entertained to light refreshments in the bridal chamber after which they all, including the bridegroom, return to the groom's house. The bridegroom is now accompained by one of the bride's younger brothers who will thenceforward follow him like a shadow. It may be added that all this time the bridegroom has had no occasion to meet his wife. At Mangalore, however, a meeting between the bride and the groom is arranged during the *kalyanam* function at which the bridegroom ties a necklace called *bandi* around the bride's neck. But the bridegroom returns after the brief interview.

At Tellicherry and Cannanore, particularly in the higher sections, the functions of *kaniyath* (*nikah*) and *kalyanam* take place on the same day and in that case both the functions are held in the bride's house. When these functions are combined, the ceremony of *nikah* is performed first followed by the ceremony of leading the bridegroom into the bridal chamber. As at Mangalore, in these places also a meeting between the bride and the groom is arranged on the same day when the groom garlands the bride instead of tying a necklace. The bride offers betel to the groom and he gives her a present in cash. The amount varies according to the group status of the bride. At Tellicherry it is Rs. 101 in the case of Keyis, and for other sections Rs. 51, Rs. 41, Rs. 31 or Rs. 21 according to their status in that order. The consummation of the marriage, however, does not take place that night. But even in these places, particularly among the lower sections, in some cases the *kaniyath* and *kalyanam* ceremonies take place on separate days. When that is so, the *kaniyath* function is invariably held in the groom's house and *kalyanam* at the bride's place, as among the mother-right Moplahs in other places.

On the day following *kalyanam*, early in the morning, one of the bride's brothers arrives with a present of sweets and invites the groom to the bride's house. But the groom is reluctant to start and the brother-in-law stays on. At midday, another brother-in-law comes to invite the groom. The groom is still unwilling to go and his brother-in-law also stays on. This ritual is repeated in the evening by yet another brother-in-law. When the efforts of all the brothers-in-law to bring the groom over to the bride's place prove to be of no avail, the *karanavar* himself comes at night accompanied by four torch-bearers. A dinner is held at the groom's place and he is finally persuaded by the *karanavar* to go to his bride's house. At the bride's house the groom is entertained to a dinner or to light refreshments after which he is led by the *karanavar* into the *mandakam* (bridal chamber). When he is alone, the bride is brought to the door of the room by women to the accompaniment of music and the reluctant bride is pushed into the chamber. The door of the chamber is locked from outside. This ceremony is called *aravilakkal* (literally, 'pushing inside the room'). This is the night of the consummation of the marriage. If the bridegroom exercises his conjugal rights that night he is supposed to drop a coin in the vessel containing water intended for his bath. He also leaves some money under the pillow. The amount is called *koppinte kasu* and will be subsequently utilized by the bride in entertaining her friends to a party. The bridegroom is supposed to leave the chamber early in the morning before anyone can see him. The bride's people try to prevent him from leaving by locking the door from the outside, but the groom, with the connivance of the brother-in-law who is supposed to help him, often manages to escape. If he fails it is considered shameful. Whenever the groom leaves, the brother-in-law will accompany him.

Early next morning the bridegroom is sent sweets from the bride's house intended for his breakfast. A brother-in-law comes to invite him to lunch and again at night he is taken by his brothers-in-law for dinner and to spend the night with the bride. While going at night the bridegroom's path has to be lighted by four burning torches. Especially for the dinner a few friends of the bridegroom, but not relatives, will be invited along with him. While his friends depart soon after dinner the bridegroom stays on. This routine has to be repeated for forty days. Nowadays it is observed at least for seven days. During these days the bridegroom is required to take all his meals in the bride's house, where he is not to be served with fish which is the staple diet of the Mopiahs. There should be a wide variety of sweets and the bride's relatives also cooperate by sending to the bride's house sweets on different days.

In the meantime, various other functions take place. One day women guests from the groom's side go to the bride's house to invite the bride. The bride is ceremonially taken to the groom's house. This function is called *pudukkam* and only women are invited to it. In the case of rich families sometimes forty young women dressed as the bride accompany the bride to the groom's. The bride remains in the groom's house for a day or two. During these days the groom cannot sleep with his bride. Next, the bride is ceremonially taken back to her house, this function being called *marupudukkam*. After *kalyanam*, unless the bride has first visited the groom's house, she is not supposed to visit any of her relatives.

On another day a function called *mudiyum puvum* (literally, '*muras*[16] of rice and flowers') is observed. The bridegroom sends some *muras* of rice and flowers to the bride's house. The occasion is celebrated with a feast in the bride's house.

For seven days after *kalyanam*, and sometimes for forty days, there will be singing in the bride's house every night by hired women singers. The bride will be seated somewhere near the bridal chamber dressed in all her wedding apparel and ornaments. The women neighbours, friends and relatives, will come to see the newly wedded bride during these days. On the seventh day there will be a feast in the bride's house to which male guests on either side will be invited. Usually on this day, or sometimes on a later date, the bridegroom will send a trousseau called *mattaan* (literally 'to change clothes') and a present of money called *konthalakkasu*. Nowadays, only money is sent in lieu of the trousseau. Along with the present a bundle of tabacco is also sent and the size of the bundle will depend upon the value of *sthridhanam*. The bridegroom's close relatives have to be served a special dinner called *salkaram choru* in the bride's house without which they are not supposed to eat there on ordinary days.

The fortieth day after *kalyanam* marks the conclusions of the wedding festivities. On that day a grand feast is arranged for guests from either side in the bride's house. Nowadays, the marriage festivities are usually concluded on the seventh day itself. After this, no special attention is paid to the bridal couple. The bridegroom is required to take his meals in his own house and visit his wife at night. There will be neither any special invitations nor anyone to accompany him. His brother-

16. A *mura* is about 3 maunds of rice tied in a bundle covered with hay.

in-law, who until then accompanies him, will be sent back with a handsome present. It is supposed that after this the nightly visits of the husband to his wife's apartment should remain unnoticed. But nowadays it is usual for the husband to go to the wife's house early at night and return late in the morning.

Among the father-right Moplahs, such as the Malbaris of the interior of South Malabar, the marriage is celebrated on a lesser scale, the festivities being wound up within a week. They observe many of the salient features of the Moplah marriage ceremonies described above, but they modify these customs to suit their different type of kinship organization. For instance, among them the proposal of marriage has to come from the groom's side. The betrothal as well as *nishchayam* ceremonies take place in the bride's house. In the marriage negotiations the fathers of the bridal couple are the chief persons who exchange betel. The functions of *kaniyath* and *kalyanam* take place on the same day in the bride's house. After the ceremony, the bridegroom stays for a few days in the bride's house, but the marriage is not consummated there. A few days later, sometimes the very next day after the *kalyanam*, the bride and the groom are ceremonially taken to the groom's house and it is there that the marriage is consummated.

The marriage customs of the Thangals and Arabis are very different. Among them *kaniyath* (*nikah*) and *kalyanam* are celebrated on the same day and they take place in the house of the bride. Their *nikah* ceremony is performed on a carpet and hence it is called *padathil kaniyath* ('*nikah* on carpet'). All the guests present have to give presents in cash to *gadi* who officiates at the ceremony. Although all Moplahs carry decorated umbrellas, the Thangals, Arabis and members of certain *tharavads* of special esteem are allowed the use of specially decorated umbrellas. In their case, some of the local customs like *kanhikudi*, *monthala*, symbolical washing of the groom's feet by his brother-in-law, etc., are eschewed. The payment of *mahr*, which is ignored by all the other Moplahs, is strictly made at the time of the *nikah*. Their *nikah* ceremony is never performed much in advance of the *kalyanam* and only in their case does the consummation of the marriage takes place on the night of *nikah* itself. When a Thangal or an Arabi marries a wife from a lower group, the *nikah* ceremony takes place in the groom's house and *kalyanam* in the bride's, but the consummation takes place on the night of the *kalyanam* ceremony itself.

In general, invitations to the different marriage functions are restricted to different categories of guests. Only males are invited to some functions, only females to others and sometimes both males and females, but under no circumstances will men and women mix together. Some functions may be reserved only for children. On certain occasions, friends, relations and neighbours are invited, on certain others only close relatives, and there are also functions—as when the bridegroom is entertained to dinners in the bride's house every night—to which only friends, in this instance those of the bridegroom, are invited. If men and women are invited to the same function, the men will enter through the front entrance and will be entertained in the outer apartment, while the women will come in through the back entrance and will be attended to in the inner parts of the house.

For each function, a separate invitation has to be extended a few days earlier. This is done, in the case of males, either personally by the host or through hired persons or by printed cards. But close relatives, leading men, Thangals and Arabis have to be invited personally by the host himself. Especially at Quilandy, while going to invite the Thangals, the host has to be accompanied by an Arabis. The women have to be invited only by women and that too by the near relatives of the host in person. Hired persons or printed invitations cannot be sent in their case. Although invitations are sent a few days in advance of the function, a hired person will be sent on the day of the function to remind the invitees.

While there are two parties to a marriage, most of the marriage functions are celebrated in the house of one or the other party. Even then in most cases guests are invited on either side. The guests of each side will first assemble at the house of the respective party and then the guests from the side that does not celebrate, along with their host, will go in a procession to the house of the party that celebrates. For instance, guests will be invited on either side for the *nikah* ceremony which usually takes place in the bridegroom's house. In this case the guests on the bride's side will first assemble at the bride's house and after having some light refreshments there, and will go in a procession along with the *karanavar* to the groom's house where all the guests may be entertained to a dinner. Sometimes the guests of each side may be served dinner—the guests on the bride's side will take their dinner at the bride's place before leaving for the groom's and those on the groom's side will finish their dinner before the procession from the bride's side arrives. But when the guests on both the sides are to be entertained to dinner by one side, that side would naturally like to know how many persons the other side will invite. To ascertain this a few days before the function the side that celebrates will send to the other side a basketful of bundles of betel leaves. The number of invitees of the other side will be indicated by the number of bundles accepted from the basket, one bundle standing for twenty guests.

Conclusion

On the whole it will be seen that the Moplah marriage has two main aspects—one Islamic and the other local. From the Islamic point of view a Muslim marriage is a simple and unostentatious affair. The essential requirements of a Muslim marriage are that the marriage partner should not be chosen from among persons of certain degrees of relationship, that the partners to a marriage should give their full consent; that the husband should pay a contracted amount called *mahr* to the wife, and that the marriage contract or *nikah* should be solemnized in the presence of a witness, usually the *gadi*. The Moplahs, no doubt, satisfy all these requirements, but their local marriage customs almost overshadow the importance attached to Islamic practices.

In addition to the prohibited degree of relations for marriage prescribed by Islam, the Moplahs refrain from marrying within their clans. While the necessity of the full consent of the partners to a marriage is recognized, the consent of the bride is very often taken for granted. This may be attributed to the local practice of early marriages, particularly in the past. The payment of *mahr* to the wife is implicit in the marriage formula, but the Moplahs as a rule do not pay it. On the other hand, the payment of a dowry by the bride's side to the bridegroom, which is not an Islamic practice, is strictly enforced. Of the different types of dowries that are prevalent, that called *kizhipanam*, or *kashipanam*, has a ceremonial character and is paid on the day of *kalyanam*, and *sthridhanam* and *kadam-vaivippa* wherever they are in force, are settled informally. The *nikah* ceremony is performed as laid down by Islam, but the Moplah marriage is not regarded as complete without the function called *kalyanam*.

Apart from the essential Islamic requirements, there are also other practices which Muslims usually observe in general in connection with their marriage celebrations either because they were observed by the Prophet who is the founder of Islam or because they emanate from Arabia which is the fatherland of the Faith. The customs of giving a trousseau and other presents, together called *jihaz*, to the bride by her father and a dinner called *valima* given by the bridegroom in honour of the bride's relations are the most important of such practices. But these are not observed by the Moplahs. On the other hand, instead of the *jihaz*, among the Moplahs it is the husband who gives a present to the bride called *mattaan* and, instead of the *valima* dinner, it is the bride's side that gives a dinner called *salkaram choru* in honour of the bridegroom's relatives. These, and a host of other customs observed by the Moplahs, have nothing to do with the general Muslim practices.

Bibliography

Ali, Hamid (1938), '*Custom and Law in Anglo-Muslim Jurisprudence*, Calcutta.

D'Souza, Victor S. (1955), 'Sociological Significance of Systems of Names with special reference to Kerala', *Sociological Bulletin*, 4, pp. 28-44.

Iyer, C. Ramchandra (1883), *A Manual of Malabar Law*, Madras, Law Book House.

7

The Veil of Virtue: *Purdah* and the Muslim Family in the Bhopal Region of Central India

Doranne Jacobson

Among almost every people upon whom Islam has left its imprint there exists a conspicuous concern for feminine modesty, both of dress and demeanour. With but few exceptions, most Muslim women of the world are expected to avoid wearing scanty apparel and to limit their public activities. In some Islamic regions, a woman of good character is but seldom seen beyond the portals of her home, and in many areas women appear in lanes and streets only as silent veiled figures. In South Asia, the vast majority of Muslim women have always been veiled and sequestered to at least some extent, and ideally remain reticent in public. Such feminine veiling and seclusion are referred to as *parda*, from the Persian word for curtain (usually spelled as *purdah*).

Koranic proscriptions are often cited by devout Muslims as the basis for the observance of *purdah* by Muslim women, and certain of the Prophet's recorded words do seem to recommend some limitations on feminine activity and dress:

> Tell the believing men to lower their gaze and be modest. That is purer for them. Lo! Allah is aware of what they do.

And tell the believing women to lower their gaze and be modest, and to display of their adornment[1] only that which is apparent, and to draw their veils over their bosoms, and not to reveal their adornment save to their own husbands or fathers or husbands' fathers, or their sons, or their husbands' sons, or their brothers or their brothers' sons or sisters' sons, or their women, or their slaves, or male attendants who lack vigour,[2] or children who know naught of women's nakedness. And let them not stamp their feet so as to reveal what they hide of their adornment. (*Surah* XXIV, v. 30, 31).

As for women past childbearing, who have no hope of marriage, it is no sin for them if they discard their (outer) clothing in such a way as not to show adornment. But to refrain is better for them. (*Surah* XXIV, v. 60).

And when ye ask of them (the wives of the Prophet) anything, ask it of them from behind a curtain. That is purer for your hearts and for their hearts.
It is no sin for them (thy wives) (to converse freely) with their fathers, or their sons, or their brothers, or their brothers' sons, or the sons of their sister or of their own women, or their slaves. O women! Keep your duty to Allah. Lo! Allah is witness over all things.
O Prophet! Tell thy wives and thy daughters and the

1. According to a Muslim authority, there has been a difference of opinion as to what 'adornment' (*zinat*) means—the beauty of the body or only external ornaments and adornments. The use of the word in the concluding portion of the verse is taken by most to support the latter view, as only jewellery and the like could be revealed by the jingling caused by the stamping of feet. Most authorities appear to agree that the passage allows a woman to expose her hands and face—'only that which is apparent'—but not her neck, bosom, arms, ornaments, or decorated dress, which ought to be concealed beneath a plain cloak, except before the persons mentioned (Ali, 1935:701-2).
2. An early authority on the Koran includes under this term men who have no desire to enjoy women, such as decrepit old men, and 'deformed or silly persons, who follow people as hangers on, for their spare victuals, being too despicable to raise either a woman's passion or a man's jealousy.' Whether eunuchs are included in this category 'is a question among the learned' (Sale, 1843:291).

women of the believers to draw their cloaks close around them (when they go abroad). That will be better, that so they may be recognized and not annoyed. Allah is ever Forgiving, Merciful (*Surah* XXIV. v. 53, 55, 59).

(Pickthall, 1953: 255, 258, 305, 306)

The relevant Koranic passages, however, are somewhat ambiguous and do not prescribe in detail the ideal features of a woman's dress and behaviour. Indeed, Muslim women observe *purdah* in a wide variety of ways within South Asia and throughout the world, and some Muslim women do not obsever it at all (in the Laccadive Islands, for example [Dube, 1969: 24]). Furthermore, *purdah* and *purdah*-like behaviour are not restricted to Muslim women. There is evidence that women were veiled and secluded among various pre-Islamic Mediterranean, Arab, and Persian peoples,[3] and in recent centuries many Hindu, Christian, Buddhist, and other women of various regions of the globe have traditionally followed practices that closely resemble Muslim *purdah* observances in important respects. Therefore, on the basis of Islamic scriptures alone, it is difficult to explain or understand *purdah* in its many forms.

Clearly, any real comprehension of the functioning of the *purdah* system will come only from analyses of the practices associated with it within the framework of the cultural complexes in which they exist.

As a step in this direction, this paper examines *purdah* in the Bhopal area of Madhya Pradesh, Central India. An attempt is made here to relate women's veiling and seclusion to family, kinship, and inheritance among Pathan and non-Pathan Muslims of the region. It will be contended that, in the traditional setting, *purdah* served important functions in the family and

3. Royal seclusion of women in ancient Persia is mentioned in the Book of Esther of the Bible (*Esther*, 1:9-12;2:13). Altekar cites references to veiling and seclusion in ancient Greece and Assyria (1962:177).

In ancient Arabia, desert-dwelling women apparently went unveiled and associated freely with men, while city women were veiled. For the women of Mohammad's Quraysh tribe, veiling was probaby the general rule. In ancient Mecca, unmarried women and slaves paraded with unveiled faces around the Ka'aba to attract suitors and buyers, while married women wore veils (Levy; 1957:124,127).

the larger kin group. *Purdah* has played a vital role in the social integration of the groups whose women practise it and is important to the acquisition and consolidation of property and prestige by groups of kinsmen.

The data presented in this paper pertain primarily to the Muslims of Nimkhera, a village in Raisen District, about seventy kilometres east of Bhopal city, and to some of their relatives and associates residing in Bhopal and elsewhere. I have not attempted to obtain data from a systematically selected or large sample of Muslims of the Bhopal region, and there are several Muslim groups resident in Bhopal about which I have very little information and consequently do not mention. All of the data presented here were collected through extended participant observation of numerous facets of village and urban Muslim life, and from many lengthy interviews with informants.[4]

The Area

Bhopal city, the capital of Madhya Pradesh, and Nimkhera village both lay within the borders of former Bhopal State, the second-largest Muslim-ruled princely state in pre-independence India. While the population of the region now, as then, is predominantly Hindu, Islam has been an important cultural force in the area.

4. Field research, during which data for this paper were collected, was conducted in the Bhopal region for about three years, from 1965 to 1967, and in 1973-74. I am very grateful to the residents of Nimkhera and Bhopal for their generous hospitality and cooperation. I was assisted in the early period of my reaserch by Miss Sunalini Nayudu, whose help was extremely valuable. I am indebted to Dr Leela Dube of the University of Saugar and to numerous state government and district officers in Bhopal and Raisen for the many courtesies they extended. My husband, Jerome Jacobson, provided essential assistance, advice, and moral support. Nimkhera and the names of individuals in this paper are pseudonyms. The field research was supported by a fellowship and grant from the National Institute of Mental Health (United States Public Health Service), by the Ogden Mills Fellowship awarded by the American Museum of Natural History, and a Senior Fellowship from the American Institute of Indian Studies, for which I am most appreciative.

Both Bhopal and Nimkhera are situated on the easternmost segment of the Malwa plateau, where it meets the Vindhyan range, in an area of wooded hills and valleys, and generally fertile wheat fields. Bhopal's buildings cluster on hillsides and line the shores of large artificial lakes, said to have originally been constructed during the reign of the Hindu Paramara King Bhoja (1010-55). Although ancient in origin, the town remained small until the eighteenth century (Luard, 1908:95-96; Altekar, 1955:39).

Islamic incursions into the area began in the thirteenth century. From 1401 to 1531 independent Malwa Sultans ruled from Mandu, and one of their strongholds, Raisen Fort, is situated less than twenty-five kilometres from Nimkhera. During the sixteenth century, Rajputs, Gujarati Muslims, and Afghans fought bloody battles over Raisen Fort and nearby areas. The Moghuls controlled the region until the end of the seventeenth century, when Marathas and Afghans warred over it. Finally, an Afghan adventurer carved out a principality for himself by 1722 which came to be called Bhopal State and which later became a protectorate of the British. A unique feature of the history of the State was the succession of four female rulers (Begams), from 1819 to 1927, some of whom observed a modified *purdah* as they carried out affairs of state (Ganguly, 1957:71; Roy, 1960:29; Bool Chand, n.d.: 5; Majumdar, 1960:121; Luard, 1908:112,115).

Bhopal State merged with independent India in 1949, and in 1956 Bhopal city became the capital of Madhya Pradesh. Once a predominantly Muslim city of narrow lanes, crowded bazaars, and sandstone mosques, Bhopal is now expanding rapidly. Huge new factories, government buildings, and spacious residential areas have been built. With the influx of government servants and industrial workers from all over India, the metropolitan population of about 400,000 is now largely Hindu.

Raisen District, also once part of Bhopal State, is one of the smallest and least populous districts of Madhya Pradesh. It is relatively undeveloped agriculturally and educationally, despite its rich soil and consistent crop surpluses. The population of the district is 95 per cent rural and but 8 per cent

Muslim; however, over one-third of the district's town dwellers are Muslims (Tiwar, 1964; Pandya, 1974).

Nimkhera Village

The whitewashed houses of Nimkhera cluster on a wooded hillside and at the base of the hill beside a paved road. Just across the road, stretching north across fertile flatland, lie the village fields. The village is similar in many respects to hundreds of other settlements in Raisen District and the surrounding region. Most dwellings are unimposing, of stone and mud construction, roofed with country tiles. The spire of a new Hindu temple rises besides a small cement school building. Women in bright saris carry brimming water pots atop their heads from the village wells, while *pandits* chant their morning prayers and children cluster near a small mosque to read the *Koran Sharif.*

A few of the village men work at jobs outside the village, but most of the 630 villagers are farmers and agricultural workers supported by the abundant wheat and pulse crops grown on the village fields. Rice, vegetables, fruits, and various other crops are also produced locally.

The villagers are approximately 77 per cent Hindu and 23 per cent Muslim and belong to twenty-one Hindu castes and four Muslim groups. The Hindus include Bagheli Thakurs, the dominant caste, as well as land-owning Jijotiya Brahmans, Raojis and barbers, and landless carpenters, tailors, weavers, potters, goat butchers, washermen, leather workers, and sweepers. Dominant among the Muslims are a group of very prosperous Pathans. The other, poorer, Muslims include Fakirs, Sheikhs, probably descendants of local Hindus who were converted to Islam a few generations ago, and so-called Nau Muslims, very recent converts to Islam.

No written records indicate when the village was founded, but the presence of numerous old stone carvings of Hindu deities and carved temple pillars dating back to the eleventh or twelfth centuries suggest the presence of a large village here during that period. The village was apparently sacked at least once by Muslim invaders, since most of the ancient Hindu images have been broken. The Bagheli Thakurs and their accompanying service castes apparently came into the region from the north in the late seventeenth century and settled in areas previously occupied by Gonds.

In 1916, a family of Pathan Muslims migrated to Nimkhera and brought many changes to the village. Originally from Afghanistan, the family had emigrated to the Peshawar region (now in Pakistan) some years before. A poor Pathan, Hussein Khan, armed only with a letter of introduction to the Bhopal ruler, who was also a Pathan, brought his family to Bhopal to seek his fortune as a contractor and eventually settled in Nimkhera. The Bhopal Nawab favoured Hussein's son, Yusuf Khan, with important contracts, for roads and dams, and Yusuf Khan became a wealthy contractor. He is said to have purchased farm land in forty-eight villages, to have owned scores of trucks and other machines, and to have employed 5,000 labourers at a time. In Nimkhera he built several large earth and stone-walled houses for his family, the village mosque, and a guest house for his many eminent British and Indian guests. He is reputed to have been a stern man, but to have given money freely from his well-filled coffers to those who asked for it.

Yusuf Khan died prematurely in 1947, and most of his vast holdings were soon dissipated by his brothers. His sequestered wife and several children were left with a few thousand acres of land to divide and the slowly crumbling walls of their once impressive house to shelter them. Three of Yusuf Khan's sons and daughters married and moved to Bhopal and Indore, where their conjugal kin reside. Another son, Latif Khan, remained in Nimkhera with his wife and children to farm his lands and has become quite prosperous in recent years.

The road besides which the village is situated serves as an important link to the world beyond Nimkhera. The village Hindus travel the road by cart and bus primarily to visit kinsmen in other villages and to shop in the bazaars in Raisen and Vidisha, an ancient centre of Hindu culture. The village Muslims ride buses to Raisen and Bhopal, not only to market, but to visit their many town and city-dwelling kinsmen. For Latif Khan, the road, built by his father, is also important as an easy route for him to travel to government offices and so that his many sophisticated urban quests can visit him.

Economic Resources

There is a wide range in the economic levels of Nimkhera's Muslim residents.

The wealthiest man in the village is Latif Khan. Now about forty-five years old, he owns approximately 1,300 acres of land, which he tills largely with tractors. He also owns a bus, and operates a sandstone quarry, and a small flour mill. Within the past few years, through the intelligent utilization of modest resources and by dint of hard work, he has become a successful contractor, operating bulldozers and other earth-moving machinery to build roads and dams. He owns two automobiles and a truck; his village house has been replastered with cement, wired for electricity, and furnished with modern furniture, a large refrigerator, and electric fans. He recently purchased a sizeable old townhouse in Bhopal, where most of his ten children reside as they attend private schools there. In addition to the labourers engaged on his construction jobs, Latif Khan employs a large number of agricultural workers and overseers, household servants, and drivers. He offers generous and sometimes lavish hospitality to large numbers of urban guests, including many government officials and other friends. Clearly, Latif Khan's prosperity makes his family unique in the village, and his sphere of social activity is largely outside Nimkhera.[5]

None of the other Pathans in the village are as wealthy as Latif Khan. His relatives have sold most of their land. One of his cousins has recently enhanced his economic position by becoming Latif Khan's partner in the quarrying operation and has purchased a jeep and a house in Raisen. Another cousin owns a truck from which he derives a modest income. There is one poor Pathan couple who rent rice plots and do odd jobs.

A Fakir family, which used to live by begging and selling vegetables, has purchased a small plot of land and farms it. All of the other village Muslims are landless and live in small mud-

5. For a detailed account of the importance of Latif Khan's extra-village social and economic ties, see Jacobson (1975). The offering of hospitality is a vital component of Pathan life in the Peshawar region (Vreeland, 1957:120).

plastered houses or in rooms in out-buildings owned by Latif Khan. Some men work as tractor drivers for Latif Khan, and several men and women work as his household servants. One man works in his employ as the *Maulvi* of the village mosque, giving the call to prayer and providing religious instruction to the children. Several couples rent rice plots; some men are salaried agricultural workers; and several men and women do argicultural labour and other odd jobs. One couple runs a tiny sundries shop; another runs the teashop.

Many of these Muslims were originally poor Hindus who found it expedient to work for the Pathans and eat their food, thereby bringing themselves into the Islamic fold.

Muslim Groups

The Muslim groups found in the village are not strictly endogamous or ranked,[6] and, except for the Pathans and Fakirs, lines between the groups are blurred. The Pathans and the Fakirs usually, but not always, marry within their own groups, while Sheikh's and recent converts commonly marry each other. Children are usually regarded as members of their father's group, althouch in cases of inter-group marriage the wife is never formally taken into her husband's group.

The village Muslims regard themselves as outside the Hindu caste hierarchy and often state that all Muslims are equal before God. All Muslims can accept food from all other Muslims, and all men pray together in the mosque.

Despite these democratic ideals, status distinctions do exist among the Muslims, based upon group membership, wealth, character, and achievement. These distinctions resemble class more than caste distinctions (see Mines, 1972).

In Nimkhera, the well-to-do Pathans are considered superior to the other Muslim groups, who look to them for guidance in the proper performance of ritual and social activities, and for economic assistance. The Nimkhera Pathans are somewhat vague about the exact appellation of their group. The Pathans

6. The Muslim groups cannot, therefore, properly be called castes. Mines (1972) prefers the term 'subdivision' for such Muslim groups. In this region, the villagers do not use the terms 'Ashraf' or 'Ajlaf' (see Ahmad, 1966:269).

of Afghanistan are divided into a number of tribes and caste-like semi-endogamous groups, of which the Nimkhera Pathans seem ignorant. When pressed, the Pathans of Nimkhera say they belong to the Mirza Pathan group, but deny the existence of any lineages or clans among themselves.[7] One poor Pathan identifies himself as a Safi Pathan, different from the other Pathans of the village.

The wealthy Pathans say they can marry among any high-ranking Pathan groups, and within recent years they have also accepted as suitable matches with members of other relatively high-ranking and prosperous Muslim groups. There is, however, a certain ethnic pride in being 'strong Pathans' and, usually, matches made with other Pathans are regarded as most desirable.

The prosperous Pathans carefully distinguish themselves from the Fakirs and other poorer non-Pathans. These, and poor low-status Pathans, are considered 'low quality Mussalmans' by the elite Pathans. The possibility of marriage to people of this category is vigorously rejected. A proposed match between one of Latif Khan's cousins and the daughter of a poor Pathan overseer was quickly squashed. The fact that the young man's mother was of low-cast Hindu origin was what led to the proposal being made at all. He eventually married a cousin whose own mother was of similar Hindu background, but the cousin was nonetheless a member of his high status kin group.

Fakirs prefer to be endogamous and few outside their group desire to marry them. Even achieving noticeable prosperity, as one Fakir formerly resident in Nimkhera has done, is

7. Barth (1965) describes *khels,* which he translates as 'lineage' or 'tribe', among the Swat Pathan and notes the importance of patrilineal descent groups among landowners in particular. Vreeland observed partilineal *khels* ('large lineages') among the Pathans of the Peshawar Valley (1957:116). The Bhopal royal family has a *khel* affiliation according to Luard (1908). The Pathans who migrated to Nimkhera were almost certainly not landowners in Pakistan, and it is at least conceivable that they would rather forget their past, although their claim to high rank must have some truth to it since a close relative of the Nimkhera Pathans married a woman of the Bhopal Nawab's family.

unlikely to make them desirable marriage partners to those of other groups who know of their Fakir origin.

The other poor non-Pathans intermarry freely and are usually referred to simply as 'Mussalman'. The distinctions among them are seldom marked, except in fights, when references to low-caste Hindu origins are shouted as insults by those whose own ancestral origins have been obscured by a few generations. Occasionally, Pathans make disparaging comments about the recent converts, saying: 'They are Muslims in name only, just because they eat our food.'

Kinship Groups

Hindus of the Bhopal region recognize a kinship unit known as the *kutum* or *khandan*, an unnamed exogamous patrilineal group of four or five generations' depth, including patrilineally related males, their wives, and unmarried daughters. Muslims of the region sometimes use the word *khandan*, but not in reference to any carefully distinguished group of patrikin. Rather, in Muslim usage, the term most frequently refers to a non-exogamous bilateral kindred of blood relatives and their spouses. Other terms used by Muslims to refer to kindred are *azizdar* and *rishtedar*. Informants do not all agree on the groups to which these terms refer.

According to most informants, the *azizdar* and *khandan* are the same; they include all patrilineally related males and their wives, and also one's MoSi, MoSiHu, MoBr, MoBrWi, FaSiHu, Si, SiHu, Br, BrWi, Da, DaHu, and so on. Excluded from the *khandan* or *azizdar*, but counted as *rishtedar*, are consanguineal relatives or affines, e.g., MoBrWiSi, or SoWiFa.

One informant, expressing a minority opinion, agreed that *khandan* would include all blood relatives and their spouses, but stated that the *khas khandan* ('real' *khandan*) would include only patrikin (including, however, a married FaSi) and exclude mother's kinsmen. For this informant, *azizdar* was the same as *rishtedar*. 'Someone like my brother's wife's natal kin (*maikewale*) would be *rishtedar*,' she said.

Muslims frequently marry cross and parallel cousins, and a person related to ego through males may also be related through females. Further, given marriage between cousins, the kindred is often very nearly coterminous for several individuals.

While there is some emphasis on the patriline, maternal kin are very important. After marriage, a woman maintains contact with her natal kin, and she and her children visit them often, frequently for long periods of time. Adult sisters and sisters and brothers frequently help each other in various ways.

At marriage, the bride and groom acquire *nikai* parents who are usually, but not always, selected from among the relatives and friends of the bride. The *nikai* parents are supposed to act to resolve any difficulties that may arise for the newly-weds. The unity of kinsmen linked through a marriage bond is expressed in several aspects of Muslim marriage ritual (see Jacobson, 1971).

Close friends and associates are normally addressed by kinship terms rather than by name and are thus vaguely included in the circle of kinsmen.[8]

Household Composition

Household units vary greatly in size and range from one to fourteen individuals living together and sharing a common cooking fire and purse. The average household size in Nimkhera is 5.2 for all Muslims (6.85 for Pathans and 4.66

TABLE 1 : Muslims of Nimkhera Village, 1974

Group	*No. of Persons*	*No. of families*	*No. of Joint Families*	*Percentage of Joint Families*	*No. of Nuclear Families*	*No. of Landowning Families*
Pathans	48	7	4	57	3	5
Non-Pathans	98	21	3	14	18	1
Sheikh	17	3	0	0	3	0
Fakir	9	1	1	100	0	1
Recent Converts	72	17	2	12	15	0
Total Muslims	146	28	7	25	21	6

8. It is not unusual for friends and acquaintances not to know each other's names. This became apparent at one Pathan wedding, when several invitations had to be tentatively addressed to '*Mamu*' (MoBr), '*Chacha*' (FaBr), etc.

for non-Pathans). While 57 per cent of Pathan households are joint, only 14 per cent of non-Pathan households are joint. Patrilocality is considered ideal, although many couples do not live patrilocally.

Traditionally, the joint family has been considered desirable, and many urban and rural families of the Bhopal region are joint. Latif Khan and his wife, Birjis Jahan, however, say that joint living is bound to produce quarrels and that, further, they do not ever intend to depend on their children for support. They have said to their offspring: *'Shadi karo, alag raho!'* (When you get married, live separately!).

Latif Khan's family is joint only in that a recently-married son and daughter-in-law are living there temporarily, until they achieve enough financial security to set up an independent household. Latif Khan's mother and siblings all live separately. The very large size of the family lands contributed to the formation of nuclear families in this case; Latif Khan and his siblings inherited holdings in several villages, and it was necessary for each to establish a household near his own land. In the case of Fakir families, however, it is probable that land ownership holds the family together: father and married son cooperate in farming their small field.

Rules of Marriage

The Muslims have few rules restricting marriage beyond the nuclear family. The Koran prohibits a man from marrying his mother, daughters, sisters, FaSi, MoSi, BrDa, SiDa, SoWi, or WiDa. Further, a man may not be married to two sisters at the same time, nor may he wed a foster mother who has suckled him or others nursed by the woman who nursed him (Levy, 1957:104). The Pathans allow marriage to anyone not included within these proscribed relationships 'of blood and milk'.[9] Among Pathans, a sizeable percentage of marriages are contracted within the bilateral *azizdar* kindred. Cousin marriages are encouraged, and exchange marriages (marriage of a

9. Informants knew and spoke disapprovingly of a Bhopal Pathan who had married his sister's daughter, and a Fakir who had 'kept' his wife's sister as his second wife.

brother and sister to a sister and brother) are allowed by all the Muslims. The remarriage of divorcees and widows is allowed, although remarriage is not regarded highly unless the woman is fairly young.

For Muslims, marriage is a legal arrangement, although it is imbued with religious overtones. While it is desirable for all persons to be married, it is not a religious necessity (as it is among the Hindus of the region). Traditionally, marriages have been arranged by the parents of the principals. 'Love marriages', where the man and woman have expressed a preference for each other, are finding increasing favour among the prosperous Pathans. Even in such cases, parents or other relatives are expected to formally arrange the match.

Most high status Pathan girls are married some years after puberty: brides over twenty years of age are not uncommon, and Pathan grooms are almost always over twenty. Most lower-status Muslim girls are married by the age of about fifteen or sixteen to boys in their late teens or early twenties. There are two Muslim bachelors in the village who are over twenty-five years old. Although there are no unmarried adult females in the village, there are unmarried Pathan women in Bhopal.

Muslims consider it best that a previously unmarried girl marry a previously unmarried boy, but there are no rules restricting marriages between persons on the basis of their previous marital status. There is only one form of marriage, the *nikah*, and any two persons not prohibited from marrying each other by incest ruled may be united in a *nikah* marriage. Muslim men may have up to four legal wives at one time. However, plural marriages are not usual, though two recent residents of the village have had more than one wife.

The marriages arranged for high-status Pathans are quite commonly between cousins—both parallel cousins and other cousins—and other relatives. Unfortunately, the number of wealthy Muslims resident in Nimkhera is so small that the percentages of various types of their marriages must be evaluated with caution. Of the thirty-six marriages contracted by high-status Pathans about which I have information (involving residents of Nimkhera and their urban-resident kin), nineteen linked consanguineal and affinal relatives, while seventeen paired non-kinsmen (*gair*), as indicated in Table 2.

TABLE 2 : Marriages of High Status Pathans

	No.	*Exact Relationship*
Marriages to Relatives	19	
Consanguineal Kin	11	
patrilateral first parallel cousins	4	FaBrDa
patrilateral parallel cousins, more distant	2	FaFaBrDaSoDa
patrilateral first cross cousins	1	FaSiDa
patrilateral cross cousins, more distant	1	FaSiSoDa
matrilateral first parallel cousins	1	MoSiDa
matrilateral parallel cousins, more distant	1	MoMoSiDa
matrilateral first cross cousins	1	MoBrDa
Affinal Kin	8	
	2	FaBrWiSiDa
	1	BrWiSi
	1	SiHuSi
	1	(deceased) WiSi
	1	MoBrWiSi
	1	SiHuMoBrDa
	1	SiHuSiHuFaSiHu-SiDa
Marriages to Non-Relatives	17	
Pathans	13	
non-Pathan Sunni Muslim*	3	
Shia Muslim	1	
Total marriages	36	

*including two converted Hindus taken as second and third wives by a Nimkhera Pathan man.

This small sample and the statements of some informants suggest that marriage between cousins and other relatives is common and frequently preferred. Most Nimkhera Pathans state that marriage within the *azizdar* group is good, even if it involves matching a wealthy youth with a poorer girl. Informants state that there is no preference for marriage with any particular cousin or relative: whether or not a marriage is arranged with a particular relative depends on his 'suitability' as regards wealth, looks, and personality rather than on his particular kinship relationship to a possible spouse.

Some informants feel that thirty years ago it was more common for relatives to marry each other than it is now. However, of the nineteen marriages between relatives on which I have data, twelve occurred within the past twenty years. One of Latif Khan's children married a first cousin in 1974, and another of his children is likely to do the same.[10]

Marriage outside the circle of *azizdars* is usually approved only when the outsider is at least as wealthy as his prospective spouse. Marriages between Nimkhera Pathans and poor non-*azizdar* persons have taken place, but these have been strongly disapproved, even to the point of ostracism of the errant person by other *azizdar* members.

Pathans are concerned about the purity of the blood line, and they state that it is good for Pathans to marry other Pathans or non-Pathans of equal or higher status. Some Bhopal Pathans maintain a *shejra*, a written family genealogical record, which can be displayed to prove a prestigious pedigree. Even so, the son of a Nimkhera Pathan and his converted Hindu wife has married a 'pure' Pathan *azizdar* member. (The girl was poor, and for her the marriage meant an increase in wealth). Informants say that members of the present senior generation used to be much more concerned with the purity of the family blood line than are young adults today. Some older Pathans of the region insist on such high standards of pedigree that their daughters remain unmarried or marry very late.

The appearance of a prospective bride or groom is a matter of great concern. Among Pathans, fairness of skin and aquiline features are considered desirable. One informant, in fact, attributed *azizdar* endogamy to the desire of some families to ensure beautiful features for their offspring. 'I know a family who live near my relatives in Bombay', she remarked. 'They all look so beautiful; it's as if one is in fairyland. They marry among themselves so they'll have no fear of having any ugly

10. According to a study by Basu and Roy (1972), there has been a significant increase in marriages between consanguineal kin among Delhi Muslims since partition (38 per cent *vs.* 16 per cent in pre-partition years). Conversely, Korson's study in Karachi and Lahore indicates a decline in marriages between cousins and other relatives in the last generation (41.2 per cent *vs.* 23.3 per cent) (1971;148,152).

children. Look at my husband's cousin Istaq Khan; he married an outsider, and his children all look like their ugly flat-nosed mother's brother.'

This same informant remarked: 'Poor and ugly people don't care who they marry.' This, of course, is not true; everyone is interested in making a good match for his children, if possible.

For the poor Muslims, the financial prospects of a match are investigated, particularly in selecting a husband for a daughter and, as among the wealthy, the character and appearance of a bride or groom are important. For recent converts from low-status Hindu castes, concern with purity of family line is not emphasized, and kin group endogamy is not practicable except in a small number of cases. Sheikhs and recent converts arrange some marriages with non-relatives and virtual strangers living in not too distant villages and towns, but a large number of their marriages are arranged among close neighbours and associates in Nimkhera and a few nearby villages.

Mahr and Dowry

All Muslim marriages involves the signing of a marriage contract, the *nikahnama*, by both the bride and groom, indicating assent to the union. Included in the contract is a statement of the amount of *mahr* settled upon. *Mahr* is a payment to be given to the bride by the groom and his family whenever she demands it. If so agreed, some or all of the *mahr* may be paid at the wedding. *Mahr* is usually to be given in cash, but may also include real estate and jewellery. The pledge of *mahr* is said to be legally binding. Among wealthy Pathans, *mahr* can be a large sum, e.g., 50,000 rupees, 100,000 rupees, and so on, while among the poorer Muslims a *mahr* of 500 to 1,000 rupees or so is considered adequate. Informants stated that a good wife who feels her husband is devoted to her will never demand the *mahr* payment, but if a woman is divorced by her husband without just cause, she may demand immediate payment of her *mahr*. A widow may also demand *mahr* from her husband's kinsmen, although women who have enjoyed the love of their husbands are said to frequently 'excuse' the husband from *mahr* obligations when he is old or on his death-bed. In addition to the *mahr* pledge, the groom's kinsmen are expected to provide the bride with clothing and jewellery at the wedding.

Although divorce does occur, it is very infrequent and generally disapproved among high-status Pathans: consequently *mahr* is not often paid. Among low-status Muslims divorce is more common, but extracting *mahr* payments from disgruntled husbands is often quite difficult. If a woman does claim her *mahr*, the money is hers to do with as she wishes.

All Muslim brides are expected to bring dowries to their conjugal homes. These can range from a few cheap cooking pots to a grandly splendiferous array of household goods, clothing, milk-giving bovines, and even servants, donated by the parents of the bride. Detailed lists are kept of dowry items, and should a marriage end in divorce, a woman would ideally take her dowry things away with her. In practice, complete retrieval of a dowry is likely to be difficult.

There is no evidence that any Pathans of the region ask for or accept bride price payments, but one low status Muslim (a converted Hindu) in a nearby village was said to have 'sold' his divorced daughters to their second husbands.

Inheritance

The Muslims of Nimkhera, particularly the Pathans, attempt to follow Islamic rules of inheritance.[11] Both daughters and widows inherit shares of wealth, including land and houses, from their parents and husbands. Some women receive their property shares from their parents at the time of marriage. Muslim women, even if childless, remarried, or divorced, have complete rights to their inherited property, and may sell or give it to whomever they wish. Nevertheless, the power of most Muslim women in economic matters is

11. Interestingly, the Pathans of the Peshawar Valley exclude daughters from inheritance, but exchange dowry and bride wealth (Vreeland, 1957:116-117).

generally less than that of men. Women inherit smaller shares of wealth than men do (a son's share is twice that of a daughter's),[12] and *purdah* imposes limits on women's participation in money-earning activities.

Muslim Purdah[13]

Modesty and Female Conduct

The concept of modesty (*saram*) is central to the ideology of *purdah* as well as to all other rules governing women's dress and behaviour. Female modesty as it is conceived of in the Bhopal area is similar in many respects to that extant in much of North India and in some respects to that found in some parts of South India.

While small children are allowed to run about in various states of nakedness, all girls above the age of seven or eight wear clothing covering them from shoulder to ankle, even in the hottest weather. Most Muslim women wear pantaloons (*salwar*), a tunic (*kamiz*), and a scarf (*dupatta*) over the head and bosom, although a few Muslims sometimes wear saris. The classic Bhopali dress consists of a *kurta* pleated at the waist, tight *pyjamas*, and an extremely long *dupatta* looped from shoulder to knee. Other popular Muslim costumes are the *sharara*, a full skirt, and *gharara*, full flared pants, both worn with tunic and *dupatta*. The 'maxi' (floor-length dress) is worn by fashionable young women.

Women generally keep their heads covered with the *dupatta* or sari in public, in front of respected elders, and during prayers.

12. Informants seemed unsure of the relative size of shares due to inheritors and indicated that Islamic jural experts would be consulted should the need arise. Latif Khan and his wife state that they intend to give equal shares to all their sons and daughters. In any case, the exact monetary value of property to be divided may not be computed exactly, but particular items may be given or willed to each inheritor.
13. For further description and analysis of both Muslim and Hindu *purdah* and women's roles in this region, see Jacobson, 1970, 1974, 1975, n.d.a, n.d.b, n.d.c. A useful survey of some of the general characteristics of Muslim *purdah* in South Asia is provided by Papanek (1973).

Women exhibit modesty through demeanour as well as dress. From early childhood girls are taught to play with other girls rather than with boys, although siblings of different sexes may play together. The sexes are segregated to some extent in most adult activities. For example, at weddings women gather inside the host's house, while men are seated outside. At feasts, men and women are seated separately. It is unseemly for older girls or women to spend much time chatting with males other than close kinsmen. Women do not visit the Nimkhera teashop, where men sit for long hours. All women are expected to keep their eyes slightly downcast when they pass men in the village lanes or city streets, and open flirting is never proper. Illicit flirting or affairs are severely disapproved of. Girls and women are generally expected to show a certain amount of humility and reticence in the presence of groups of men.

It is generally regarded as improper for a girl or woman to stray very far from hearth and home, and when females do go on rare outings they are usually escorted by a male of the family. Women go on few trips 'just for fun'—only a few of the Pathan women of Nimkhera have ever visited a cinema, none without a male chaperon. By contrast, young men are allowed to roam about with their friends, visit Bhopal and go to the cinema, and go on other pleasure junkets, although they may be criticized for wasting money. Women say they would never wander about alone for fear of being molested or kidnapped by strange men. This fear of becoming the prey of evil men prompts most women to request a male escort, even if only a boy, on any foray into crowded city streets or deserted country roads. Women do not drive carts or cars and thus depend upon males to provide all such transportation.

Women and girls go on relatively few shopping trips; men make most of the purchases and run most shops. Traditionally, it has been generally regarded as unseemly for women to visit the bazaar, although it has been permissible for them to visit the collections of shops at religious fairs under certain circumstances. Women make some purchases from itinerant merchants who bring their wares to their homes (particularly bangle and cloth merchants). Ideally, women do not work outside the home, although poor women cannot adhere to this ideal.

Girls are not encouraged to participate in vigorous sports and games or to dance, although one Pathan girl learned swimming in a large well behind her home and another Pathan woman likes to dance at weddings. Otherwise, dancing before men or in public is the preserve of professional dancing girls and prostitutes. Women do not normally smoke cigarettes or *biris.*

The Practice of Purdah

The object of *purdah* as it is observed among Muslims is to prevent women from interacting with and being seen by certain men and, in some circumstances, certain women. Women observe *purdah* by remaining inside their houses, or in certain sections of their houses, by veiling their faces with their *dupattas,* and by wearing an all-covering garment whenever they do go outside of their homes. Proper observation of *purdah* requires certain architectural features, such as walled-in courtyards, private latrines, bathing facilities, and other secluded areas for women. The particular details of the manner in which *purdah* is observed vary among different families and socio-economic groups. The *purdah* practices of the high-status wealthier Pathan group are different in important respects from those of the lower socio-economic groups.

In this section, *purdah* is discussed as it generally existed in the Bhopal area prior to 1970 and still does today in some circles. More recent changes in the *purdah* practices of some people are discussed in the following section.

Purdah among Muslims of High Socio-Economic Status

Among wealthy Muslims of the Bhopal area, women in purdah (*pardawalis*) ideally do not allow themselves to be seen by men who are not their kinsmen. The wealthy Pathan women of Nimkhera and most of their Bhopal women associates appear before their fathers, brothers, husbands, uncles, and cousins, as well as before close male affines, such as sons-in-law, brothers-in-law and father-in-law. Close family friends sometimes come to be considered and treated as kinsmen, and a woman may meet society with such men as well as with her actual consanguineal and affinal relatives. These kinsmen are trusted—the men with whom a woman feels completely safe and for whom she has warm feelings, and they for her. With most men before whom she does not observe *purdah* a woman meets and talks with ease, subject to the normal restraints of feminine modesty. A young woman may feel shyness and reserve in the presence of her father-in-law (*sasur*) and husband's older brother (*jeth*), and she normally covers the top of her head with her scarf and refrains from garrulous conversation with these respected men. In cases of cousin marriage, a woman's father-in-law is also her mother's or father's brother, with whom she has probably had a warm relationship throughout her childhood. Pathans consider the idea of observing *purdah* before such a relative absurd and further feel that it is wrong for a woman to observe *purdah* before her father-in-law even if he is not related to her in any other way. In some households, all members of the family sit and eat together out of one platter.

A woman has a respect relationship with her son or daughter's *sasur* (her *samdhi*), but she can talk with him when occasion demands. She is also free to meet and converse with her son-in-law, who is 'like a son'. The element of trust is crucial again. As Latif Khan explained: 'How can my wife's mother observe *purdah* before me when she has given her own daughther to me?'

A Pathan woman should not observe *purdah* before a husband's younger brother (*devar*) of any age; the ideal relationship between the two is one of warmth and familiarity.

During her wedding, a Pathan bride shields her face from the view of her mother-in-law and other elder female affines. A secluded woman may decline to meet women who do not observe *purdah*, but this is very rare. Otherwise, women do not observe *purdah* before other women.

Among high status Muslims, it is essential that a girl remain a virgin until she is married. As soon as a girl reaches puberty or begins to show signs of physical maturity, her parents may insist that she begin to observe *purdah* and confine her social contacts to females and the circle of trusted male kinsmen.

Every care is taken to see that she does not become involved in a pre-marital affair. Some girls do manage to develop romantic attachments, but, according to informants, these rarely involve premarital sex, since a girl is taught to be wary and controlled and a Pathan youth of high status is reluctant to compromise the honour of his beloved. (Traditionally, virginity has been verified by inspection of the marital bedsheet.)

Since a girl does not normally seclude herself from males of her own household or from other close relatives, she usually has an open and friendly relationship with her cousins, some of whom may be resident with her in a joint family or frequent visitors to the household. Her husband, consequently, may be someone she knew well before her marriage.

Among high status Muslims it is quite permissible for a husband and wife to talk together in the presence of others, and even sitting together on a cot and engaging in mild physical demonstrations of affection are not disapproved.

Pathan informants state that in Bhopal a few old women maintain such strict *purdah* (*shakt parda*) that they appear only in the presence of their fathers, brothers, and husbands, and keep *purdah* from all possible marriage partners, including sisters' husbands, *samdhis*, and male cousins. But Pathan women said such stringency was very rare and that *purdah* should not be observed among such close relatives.

Pathan *purdawalis* often allow themselves to be seen by male family servants, although in the past this was disapproved in some families.

The element of trust is central to *purdah* as it is observed among the high status Muslims of Nimkhera and Bhopal. When a woman no longer trusts a kinsman, it is possible for her to begin secluding herself from him as a way of expressing her anger or distrust. Kinsmen who fight may also order their wives to observe *purdah* in front of the distrusted relative.

Ideally, Pathan women and girls past puberty do not appear before men who do not fall within the trusted circle. Women usually disappear into the back rooms of the house when casual male visitors enter their homes. In Bhopal, these rules are adhered to fairly strictly. But in Nimkhera, some of the Pathan women are rather lax and allow many village visitors to see them. Some of them feel that it does not matter if young or low-status Hindus or poor Muslim servants see them. However, one woman, married to a Pathan but herself a convert from a low-ranking Hindu caste, is most concerned that she not be seen by 'these poor farmer folk', as if her status would be lowered by the gaze of profane eyes. Latif Khan asks his wife to appear before certain visiting district officials, particularly those who are likely to think of *purdah* as a 'backward' custom. Another Pathan man never lets any visitors of high status see his wife.

Ideally, wealthy *pardawalis* do not leave their houses except to travel to and from the houses of relatives and very close friends, to attend weddings or other important ceremonies or make festival good-will or condolence calls. Women do not normally visit mosques, but pray and read the Koran at home. Some girls go out to attend schools and colleges, and girls and women occasionally attend special 'ladies nights' at Muslim religious fairs. Today, many high status veiled women of Bhopal occasionally visit the cinema with male escorts.

When these women make their infrequent forays outside, they wear over their clothing a garment (*burka*) which covers them from head to calf. The *burka* is usually made of black rayon and consists of a long shapeless loose cloak with sleaves topped by a cape extending from the head to the elbows, with a flap (*nakab*) covering the face. Another type of *burka* is of heavy dark or white cotton gathered at the crown of the head, with netted eyeholes. This style is currently popular in Afghanistan, but among women of the Bhopal area it is considered unfashionable. Young Bhopal women sometimes wear brilliant pastel *burkas*, and lace trimming is now common. Women in very strict *purdah*, when riding in a tonga through city streets, wear not only a *burka* but also hide behind a curtain tied across the open end of the carriage.

Pardawalis of high status seldom visit the Bhopal bazaars, even if thoroughly veiled and escorted, since it has been regarded as unseemly for a woman of good family to be seen in the bazaar, and veiling does not prevent recognition.

Prior to 1972, Latif Khan's wife, Birjis Jahan, observed strict *purdah* in Bhopal, but when she visited Indore and

Bombay she would visit the bazaar and dispense with her *burka*. She said there was no need to wear a veil in those sophisticated. places, since no one there took any notice of you. 'But in Bhopal, men go on staring at you, and when you wear a *burka* there's nothing for them to see.' Latif Khan felt very strongly that he did not want the leachers of Bhopal to have the privilege of seeing his pretty wife.

Purdah does not, of course, pertain only to feminine behaviour; it also requires certain actions of men. Men must work as intermediaries to the outside world for their sheltered womenfolk, conducting a thousand and one tasks on their behalf, and act as their protectors. One man, whose wife had been insulted, flew to battle with the offender, exclaiming: 'Did you think I had died and there was no one to defend her?' When entering a house or courtyard, a man must make his presence known, so that women can cover themselves properly with their headscarfs or disappear from view. Within his circle of kinsmen and close associates, a man must act decorously with women. Any improper sexual advance would be taken as an insult by a propositioned woman and her close male kinsmen. Conversely, outside the select circle, men frequently regard women as fair game, and even a veiled woman, if she is on the public thoroughfares of Bhopal, may be teased or molested. Such molestation can be turned aside if a fictive kinship relationship can be set up between strangers. For example, in dealing with a veiled woman customer, a shopkeeper might address her as 'sister', thus indicating a benign attitude toward her. In one case, a veiled woman who was being pestered by a youth on the street turned to him and boldly flipped back her veil. To her female companion she said: 'This poor chap probably doesn't have a sister, so I'll let him see my face.' The offender lowered his head ashamedly, muttered his apologies, and hurried away.

The women of Latif Khan's family do not wear *burkas* in the immediate environs of their village homes, but Latif Khan's mother sometimes goes to her fields in a *burka*, and she wears it for her frequent bus rides to her Bhopal home. One of his aunts moves only within a small radius of her house, and during more than fifty years of residence in Nimkhera has never entered the Hindu section of the settlement. Until the recent death of her husband, she had not left the village at all in over twenty years.

It is important to emphasize that the wealthy Muslim woman's observance of *purdah* is not affected by her age or whether she is in her natal home or her conjugal home. Whether or not she observes particular rules depends on a great variety of factors, such as whether or not she is in Bhopal city, whether or not her husband orders or encourages her to do certain things, and whether or not she must do certain kinds of work; but not on her age, or whether or not she is in her conjugal home (*susral*). These are important differences between the *purdah* observed by wealthy Muslim women and that observed by the poorer Muslim and Hindus.

Practising *purdah* does not completely prevent women from engaging in economic activities outside the home. Birjis Jahan, for example, is in charge of the family accounts, and controls various male servants who market produce and make purchases according to her instructions.

Until 1972, all of the high status Pathan women of Nimkhera observed some form of *purdah* and considered its observation to be a mark of prestige. Indeed, only women who could afford to pay servants to carry water and do agricultural labour for them could observe such seclusion. Yet some of Latif Khan's wealthy urban-dwelling female relatives did not observe *purdah* at all at that time. Latif's older brother is married to a well-educated city-bred woman who observed *purdah* for a few years after her marriage but gave it up many years ago. She resides in Indore and goes out without a veil on errands and for shopping. One of Latif's sisters, also an Indore resident, wears no *burka* as she attends to business matters in city offices and rides behind her husband on a motor scooter to their farm outside the city. Birjis Jahan's younger sister did not wear a *burka* when she walked to her college classes in Bhopal, although she was escorted by a servant boy. All of these women encountered a certain amount of opposition from their kinsmen for their daring, but finally they were allowed to give up *purdah*. Bombay relatives of Latif and his wife have never veiled themselves, although there are many *pardawalis* in Bombay. I once observed a young Bombay woman wearing gloves and socks with her *burka* so that not an inch of her skin was showing. Such stringency is said to have been once common in Bhopal.

A woman in *purdah* remains so even after her death. While all can see the face of a deceased man, a deceased woman's face can be viewed only by the close family members who saw her in life. Informants stated that at death the marital tie is severed and that a man should not see his deceased wife. After bathing and viewing, the body is covered with a shroud and carried to the cemetery for burial by a procession of men. As prayers are said, the body is placed in a grave dug waist-deep for a male, chest-deep for a female. Thus, a woman's body is shielded from the world for eternity by a foot more of earth than what covers the body of a man.

Purdah among Muslims of Low Socio-Economic Status

The *purdah* practised by Nimkhera Muslims of low socio-economic status is similar in many respects to that of high status Muslims and also to that of Hindus of the region.

Most of the recent converts and Sheikh Muslim women and girls barely observe any form of seclusion. These females do a great variety of agricultural and other labour outside of their homes and do not attempt to seclude themselves in the village. The women walk about the Muslim quarter of the village, fetch water and firewood, work in the wealthy Pathans' houses, and sit and work on their porches where they can easily be seen and spoken to by passersby.

Although they do not live in seclusion, most of these women do refrain from casual strolling about the village, and they leave the village only to visit relatives, to attend important functions such as weddings, or to visit the hospital. Those who own *burkas* wear them on such journeys, but several of the women do not possess one nor do they bother with tonga curtains.

High status Pathan girls begin to wear *burkas* before they are married, while the low status Muslim girls usually receive their first *burkas* at their weddings, and wear the veil for the first time as they depart for their conjugal homes. Among these Muslims, it is considered much more important to veil in the *susral* than in the natal home (*maika*). Although unveiled, engaged and post-pubescent girls living with their parents are usually closely supervised by their mothers and may be severely restricted in their movements.

Low status Muslims frequently veil their faces with their *dupattas* in the presence of older male affines, such as father-in-law, husband's older brother, child's father-in-law, and more distant affines. Veiling before such affines is a significant characteristic of Hindu *purdah*. Hindu women, however, veil before a much larger group of affines than do the poor Muslims. For example, a poor Muslims man and his wife's older sister may establish a warm relationship—he calles her "*apa*" ("big sister")—whereas among Hindus there is an avoidance relationship between two such affines. Unlike Hindus, poor Muslim women also usually refrain from veiling before a son-in-law. As among the high-status Muslims, low status Muslims do not disapprove of a husband and wife speaking to each other in the presence of others.

In some families, visiting married daughters are free to walk about with uncovered faces, while daughters-in-law remain secluded and closely veiled with a thick *dupatta*. In the opinion of Birjis Jahan, requiring such behaviour of a daughter-in-law but not a daughter is 'unjust oppression'.

One family of poor Pathans temporarily resident in Nimkhera paid lip service to an ideal of strict sequestration for women. For a few weeks after their arrival in the village, mother and nubile daughter slipped into their inner rooms whenever a strange male passed into view and did not leave the house even for fetching water. Before long, however, they began to sit and chat with men, and soon both women had established illicit liaisons with various men. Still, the mother loudly proclaimed that she and her daughter were observing strict *purdah* and that was why her overworked husband had to fetch the water.

The Fakir women of the area do not work outside of their homes, but they have much freedom of movement. Before her marriage, the teen-aged daughter of a prospering Fakir was 'in *purdah*' and stayed inside her fenced yard during the day. But at night she slipped out to meet a lover in the fields. The affair was common knowledge, and her *purdah* was regarded as a joke by the other Muslims. At her wedding to someone from a town, she received a *burka* which she proudly flaunted as a badge of supposed virtue and prestige.

The opposite situation existed in a Bhopal family temporarily resident in the village. The father of the family was a Saiyad, the mother a Pathan. Although relatively poor and not of high status, the parents regarded chastity in a daughter as very essential. Their fifteen-year old daughter behaved with perfect docorum, was married, and passed the test of her virginity. 'We may be poor, but we have our honour,' her mother remarked. She said it would have been a matter of great shame to her if it had been otherwise; she knew of a mother who committed suicide when her unchaste daughter was returned in disgrace to her natal home by her groom.

Changes in Purdah Observances

Among low status Muslims, *purdah* continues to be considered a mark of prestige and is not being abandoned. The little face-veiling and *burka*-wearing that women of this group do does not interfere with their work. If some of the poor Muslims were to become more prosperous, they would probably tend to observe more *purdah*, as in fact has happened in a few families. Certainly, none of the poor Muslims want to give up *purdah* because it is 'old-fashioned', quite the reverse is true. As the low status Muslims move further away from their Hindu pasts, and as they increase their contacts with Bhopal Muslims, they seem to be increasing their use of the *burka*. Older Sheikh women in neighbouring villages wore the full skirt (*ghaghra*) and sari of their Hindu neighbours until just a few years ago; now they wear *salwar-kamiz* like the Pathans and other Muslims do, and their newly-wed granddaughters wear *burkas* and remain secluded in their *susrals*.

In marked contrast, the observance of *purdah* by the wealthy Pathans of both Nimkhera and Bhopal is currently undergoing almost revolutionary changes. Much of the change in the village practices has been the result of immediate contact with sophisticated city dwellers who regard *purdah* as a slightly 'backward' or 'old-fashioned' custom. Among high status Muslims, *purdah* is being modified by individuals to suit their own concepts of what is convenient and proper for the modern age. Because of rapid changes, which are progressing at various rates in different families and among different women, there is no standard of *purdah* observance to which all wealthy Muslims adhere.

When Latif Khan's mother was a child in northern Pakistan more than fifty years ago, her father kept her secluded inside the house from babyhood. Once, when she was five years old, her father caught her peeping out through a tiny hole in the wall and severely punished her.[14] She and her sister were married to their first cousins, who had been resident with them in the same household, and from whom they were not sequestered. All later migrated to Nimkhera, where they remained in seclusion, never stepping outside their compounds, except on exceedingly rare occasions, and then only at night, veiled and under escort, as they stepped into a waiting vehicle. Latif Khan's grandmother was never seen even by male servants, but was known for her commanding voice,—emanating from an inner room. Once, when Latif Khan's mother had something wrong with her hand, a male doctor was called in. He was allowed to feel her wrist only through a piece of cloth, and he put the bandage on over the cloth without having seen any part of the patient.

When her husband suddenly died, Latif Khan's mother's world altered drastically. Her large well-staffed household broke up and she gradually began to come out of her strict seclusion so that she could supervise her property. She wears a *burka* as she goes about her work in the village and in Bhopal. She considers herself to be out of *purdah*, but says she derives no pleasure from it. 'What's the fun of coming out of *purdah* just so I can do work?' she asks. Thus, she still adheres to the idea that women should not go about freely

14. According to Vreeland, the Peshawar Valley has a reputation throughout Pakistan as a centre of conservatism with regard to *purdah* (1957:125).

enjoying themselves, but she has justified a certain amount of freedom for herself for purposes of work.

In the past there were special curtained sections in buses for women to ride in, but there are no hooks for hanging curtains in new buses. Further, today. some women who wear *burkas* lift up the face flap as soon as they get into the Bhopal city buses. Women now rarely curtain the tongas they ride in. Some modern Bhopal girls wear *burkas* of knee length, with sleeves short enough to reveal pretty wrists decorated with dozens of glittering bangles and bracelets. Conservative observers feel that these girls seem to be trying to attract attention and should not be surprised when youths purposely jostle them and flirt with them.

One Pathan man is encouraging his wife to give up *purdah*. He feels seclusion is bad for her physical and mental health and causes her to become helpless. This woman is so shy, however, after years of seclusion, that she rarely steps over her threshold and dislikes going out without a veil.

Latif Khan's wife spent a few childhood years in Bombay, but was reared primarily in Bhopal where she began wearing the *burka* at puberty. She seldom went out, even in the *burka*, but she went unveiled before her cousin, Latif Khan. The two fell in love, and sympathetic relatives arranged their marriage. She continued to observe *purdah* in most respects but, by 1965, Latif Khan had begun to take her out to tea parties at the homes of certain district officials in Raisen and to have her help him entertain such guests in their home. At first she was shy about these new social obligations, but she did object to some aspects of *purdah*. She resented not being able to shop in the Bhopal bazaars, and she objected to her husband's insistence that she wear a *burka* even in the most sweltering heat.

In 1972, over the mild protestations of her husband, Birjis Jahan decided she would no longer wear the *burka*. She and her teen-aged daughter Sultana now ride unveiled to Bhopal in a taxi or private car and shop in the bazaar and go to the cinema in the company of one of her teen-aged sons. Her *purdah* now consists of a modest demeanour and a pair of sunglasses. She recently declared, '*Purdah* has meant destruction to women. If you're closed up inside a room, how do you know what' going on outside?' She maintains that a woman's best *burka* is her downcast eyes.

It should be noted, however, that vestiges of the *purdah* ideal still remain. While Sultana wears no veil, she spends almost all of her time within her family circle, caring for her younger siblings and going nowhere alone. She wishes to attend college, but her parents encourage her to study privately, i.e., within her own courtyard with a private tutor. Having heard stories of immorality among college students, Sultana's parents are afraid to let her attend college, and she certainly would not be expected or allowed to seek employment outside her home. Sultana will probably marry a cousin who spends a lot of time in her home and with whom she has a pleasant easy-going relationship. In contrast, one of Sultana's male cousins hopes to marry a 'modern' girl he met at his school. The two 'fell in love', correspond, and occasionally meet.

Birjis Jahan still shrinks from being seen in the streets of Raisen. When she rides with her husband to Bhopal and should he have to stop *en route* in Raisen to conduct any business, he drops her off at the home of a friend and then picks her up on his way out of town. At a wedding in Bhopal which she attended *sans* veil, she hastened to the section of the house reserved for women, and when a group of men passed by, she held up a shawl to shield her face from their view. Sultana pulled the shawl down, saying, 'Mother, don't do that, I don't like it.'

Latif Khan's sister, Rafika, a woman of about thirty-five, now resident in Nimkhera, has completely given up the *burka* and has no qualms about visiting government offices in Raisen and elsewhere by herself. Clad in a sâri, which she says she wears so as not to be the object of possible anti-Muslim prejudice, she rides buses and makes purchases in the Bhopal bazaar alone. Considered something of a maverick by her family, she also drives a tractor on occasion. She enjoys dancing at village weddings, much to the annoyance of her prestige-conscious relatives.

Latif Khan's attitude toward *purdah* has changed too. While visiting a male friend whose wife had disappeared when he arrived, Latif Khan made friendly jokes with the invisible wife, urging her to step out of the inner room and sit with the two men. In Latif Khan's father's time, such remarks would hardly have been a laughing matter.

As the *burka* is increasing in popularity among the less prestigious socio-economic groups, for high status Muslims it is gradually taking on a slightly negative connotation. Nevertheless, in Bhopal many women of the middle and upper middle classes still wear the *burka*, thus still practising one aspect of *purdah* but moving about outside of their homes more than they would have done a few years ago. One Pathan woman, an affine of the Nimkhera Pathans, with an M.A. in English and unmarried at the age of forty, wears her *burka* to her job as the principal of a school. Two well-educated sisters veil themselves as they walk together to college and go shopping in the main bazaars of the city. Still others of the middle classes follow the old ways. A recent wedding in Bhopal featured a forty-five year old bride, never before married and reputed to be very chaste, who had been living in seclusion all her life and had scarcely ever ventured into the streets of the city. She married a widower whom she had never seen, and went to live under the aegis of a domineering, conservative mother-in-law who also observed strict *purdah*. One of the wedding guests, a well-educated and outgoing kinswoman of the bride, had never worn a *burka* and had just returned from a visit to the home of a successful relative living in the United States.

Purdah of the Begams of Bhopal

Interestingly, the earlier Begams (*queens*) of Bhopal seem to have observed no *purdah*, while those who ruled later practised it to varying degrees. The first ruling Begam of Bhopal, Kudsia Begam, took command of the government after the accidental death of her husband in 1819. Her only child, Sikandar Begam, and her granddaughter, Shah Jahan, ruled after her. According to a British political agent writing in 1854, when Shah Jahan was sixteen years old, all three Begams were out of *purdah*. 'The grandmother and mother ride, spear, and shoot grandly....The Regent (Sikandar Begam) is a wonderful woman in the way of government . . . talks exactly in her way like the fastest European woman you may happen to know, for example, mixing politics with her personalities . .' (Macpherson, 1865, quoted in Luard, 1908:30-1). Shah Jahan apparently adopted *purdah* later on, since she is said to have ceased observing *purdah* upon the death of her first husband in 1867 'which immensely facilitated her conduct of affairs' (Luard, 1908:33). Shah Jahan took a second husband, who was much disliked by her daughter, Sultan Jahan, who would succeed her. After this second marriage, Shah Jahan again began to observe *purdah*. According to Sultan Jahan, her mother retreated from public life so that her new husband could represent her and act on her behalf, thus adding to his power (Sultan Jahan, 1910:91-92). The details of these royal intrigues are too complicated to discuss here, but it is interesting to note that *purdah* was apparently used as a weapon of statecraft.

Begam Sultan Jahan was herself a great advocate of *purdah* and wrote a book outing its virtues (Sultan Jahan, 1921b). While ruling Bhopal State, she remained in seclusion as much as possible and always wore a veil in public.[15] Her veil was not the usual *burka*, but consisted of a long gown over which she wore a long white lace veil attached to a kind of headdress, which was plain or embroidered with silver and gold as the occasion demanded. She wore this costume when she gave necessary speeches, attended state affairs, and met Indian and foreign dignitaries. When conferring with her ministers (who were male) in her palace, she sat unseen behind a curtain. She saw to it that her daughters-in-law remained in *purdah* and supervised the education of her youngest daughter-in-law, Maimoona Sultan Begam, who was separated from her tutors by a screen.

Sultan Jahan Begam wished to demonstrate that it was possible for a woman to obtain an education and even to rule

15. Information about Sultan Jahan Begam is derived from her autobiography (Sultan Jahan, 1910, 1912, 1922a, 1927), and from her daughter-in-law, Her Highness Shahbano Maimoona Sultan, Senior Dowager Begam of Bhopal, wife of the last ruling Nawab of Bhopal, Hamidullah Khan (personal communication).

a state while observing strict *purdah*. The Begam and members of her family, including her veiled daughters-in-law, travelled to Europe several times. In 1911, she visited England to attend the coronation of King George V. She sent her sons to attend most official functions in her stead, and she appeared at a gala party at Buckingham Palace in her veil. When asked why she had not brought her daughters-in-law, she explained that it was only her position as a ruler that enabled her to move about with such freedom (Sultan Jahan, 1927:142-145). Sultan Jahan Begam abdicated in favour of her youngest son, who advised his wife to give up the veil while they were on a trip to England. Later, during the late 1920's, Sultan Jahan herself gave up *purdah*. She said, 'Well, now times have changed, and I must change with the times. I must set an example to the people of Bhopal to gradually come out of *purdah* and mix with people and educate their children' (Maimoona Sultan Begam, personal communication). Today, women of the former Bhopal royal family do not observe *purdah* of any kind. While the wife of the last ruling Nawab refrains from travelling in the narrowest alleyways of old Bhopal, she is driven about in an uncurtained car. Young women of the family wear blue jeans and drive in sportscars, as do elite women over much of the world.

The Functions of Purdah

The practice of *purdah* has been much criticised by foreign and Indian observers of Indian society, who feel that secluding and veiling women is detrimental to the well-being of women and their families (see, for example, Das, 1932; Caton, 1930; Newman, 1963; Vreede-de Stuers, 1968). However, it would not be unreasonable to suppose that such a long-standing and elaborate culture trait, as is the complex of behaviour involving the veiling and seclusion of women, would have some vital or important functions for the groups which practise it.

High Status Muslims

As we have seen, traditionally the Bhopal Muslim woman of high status revealed her face only within her own home in the presence of women and trusted males who were either close kinsmen or friends admitted into the family circle. Seclusion and wearing of the all-covering baggy black *burka* served to restrain girls and women from engaging in unsanctioned social contact, sexual activity, or marriage with strangers not approved by their relatives. Although many young women remained unmarried until young adulthood, and many owned property which might have given them the means for independent action, observing *purdah* tended to increase the chances that a woman would not involve herself in social contacts disapproved by her kinsmen, would remain chaste, and would marry only a relative or outsider carefully selected by kinsmen in accordance with the material and social standards of the family.

The Nimkhera Pathans certainly believe that *purdah* does restrict illicit sexual activity to some extent, although it does not completely prevent it. In the village, where gossip was rife about the illicit affairs of many villagers, informants stressed the chastity of high status Muslim women.

Through limiting the social contacts of marriageable women, even semi-'modern' girls who might feel they should have some voice in the choice of their husbands can be encouraged to 'fall in love' with an appropriate person, such as a cousin or close family friend. For young women who fail to select their own partners from their limited circles of approved social intimates, marriages arranged by their kinsmen are the only alternative to spinsterhood or loss of honour. If a young woman does manage to develop a romantic attachment to an outsider disapproved by her family, they can insist upon such strict *purdah* for her that the couple are physically prevented from ever meeting.

The *burka* is perceived as protecting women from the unwanted advances of lecherous men. Interestingly, although the baggy garment reduces the possibility of strange men being attracted by a woman's beauty, the very wearing of the *burka* suggests to some the special vulnerability of a woman and the possibility of a sexual relationship (a woman does not wear the veil in the presence of a brother, son, etc., with whom sexual relations are not a possibility). A printed calendar hung in many Bhopal teashops frequented by men depicts a young woman coquettishly lifting the face flap of her *burka*, as if to reveal forbidden fruits within. However, in addition to the physical barriers of seclusion and veiling, there exist further constraints on illicit romantic attachments: the ideology of self-control by women, and knowledge that lack of chastity is likely to result in disastrous dishonour for a woman and her family.

Why is preventing illicit sexual and matrimonial activity of such importance for high status Muslims that an elaborate code of restrictions on feminine activity has been enunciated and perpetuated among them?

Where *purdah* is practised and women's activities are severely restricted, in India, the Near East, and the Mediterranean, the chastity of women is associated with the honour of the family. Pathans sometimes remark that a man who would knowingly allow his wife to have an affair with a man is completely lacking in self-respect. In some parts of the Near East, an unchaste woman is considered so dishonourable to her family that she is sometimes killed by her natal kinsmen (see, for example, Antoun, 1968). Some writers have thus seen the prime function of *purdah* and feminine modesty prescriptions as a means of controlling women and thus maintaining family honour (e.g. Antoun, 1968; Peristiany, 1965). This is a circular argument, however, since an unchaste woman brings dishonour only where extra-marital sexual activity is severely dissapprov-ed.

Pathans are concerned with the purity of the blood line, and 'pure' Pathans are proud of their heritage. *Purdah* may function to ensure the purity of the blood line, but that this is its primary function among high status Muslims is doubtful. They do not emphasize purity, and in some cases Pathans are willing to accept the children of non-Pathan mothers as Pathans.

In the Bhopal royal family, as in ruling families throughout the world, kin group endogamy and other carefully arranged marriages were crucial to the working of statecraft (see, for instance, Sultan Jahan, 1910). Among the Swat Pathans of the mountains northeast of Peshawar, Barth has reported on the importance of affinal ties to politics and power (Barth, 1965: 11, 40, 107). The Nimkhera Pathans, however, are not involved in large-scale political activities at this time, and in fact consciously avoid enmeshing themselves in political affairs at the village and higher levels.

For the Nimkhera Pathans, the primary importance of kin group endogamy and other carefully arranged marriages outside of the kin group appears to lie in the consolidation and non-alienation of property. The role of *purdah* and feminine modesty in preventing unsanctioned alliances has been vital to Muslim kin groups most particularly because women inherit and control land and other wealth, and marriage to the wrong partner could drain the material resources of the kindred, affecting its prestige and material well-being.

Since there are few persons who are absolutely prohibited by Muslim law as marriage partners, within a small village or densely-populated town the chances of an unsequestered woman meeting and becoming involved with a socially inappropriate yet legally acceptable man are very high. But *purdah* restrictions ideally keep a marriageable female segregated from all possible husbands but those her kinsmen would accept as appropriate for her, someone who does not threaten the family estate.

The large extent of the wealthy Nimkhera Pathans' holdings is obviously crucial to the position of power and prestige, and to the high standard of living they enjoy.[16] There is strong feeling that the property of the family should not be allowed to fall into the hands of outsiders, particularly poor ones.

16. In other societies, *purdah*, feminine modesty, and kin group endogamy have been associated. In a Lebanese village, where women are veiled and secluded, kin group endogamy is vital to the consolidation of property and to the status system (Peters, 1963). Cousin marriage among Palestinian villagers has similarly been linked with retention of family property and family harmony (Grandqvist, 1931:68-9). Korson suggests that cousin marriage in Pakistan contributes to the successful adjustment of the bride, conservation of economic resources, and cooperation between relatives (1971:150-52).

The strength of this feeling can be judged by the fact that two Pathan women, despite practising *purdah* to some extent, managed to select for themselves relatively poor husbands of lower status Pathan families without the consent of their kinsmen, and were subjected to ostracism and severe criticism by members of their families. In contrast, a marriage sanctioned by all was arranged between Latif Khan's brother and a woman of a wealthy family, while Latif Khan's sister was married to the woman's brother. The family wealth taken out by the sister was in a sense returned by the brother's wife.

Among high status Muslims, the importance of *mahr* should not be overlooked. While *mahr* payments are seldom made, paying *mahr* to an unhappy wife could be financially disastrous to some families since *mahr* pledges are often much larger than what can actually be afforded by the groom's family. It is possible that a woman married to a member of her own *azizdar* is less likely to demand the pledge of a high *mahr* in the first place or its payment than a non-kinswoman is. Further, even if *mahr* is demanded and paid, payment to a kinswoman is less likely to be financially damaging to a kin group than payment to a non-kinswoman.

The *azizdar* groups of high status Pathans are often rent by dissension, and quarrels between siblings and cousins are far from uncommon. While to some extent *purdah* and kin group endogamy may exacerbate friction between kinsmen, they may also increase the strength of family ties and reduce or prevent tension within the kin group.[17] According to one informant, marriages between relatives may cause quarrels that result in divorce, unhappy marriages, or rifts between kinsmen, putting too much strain on pre-existing kinship

17. In the Pathan society of the Peshawar area whence the Nimkhera Pathans came, fights between kinsmen are common and extremely divisive, and involve bitter wranglings over land. There, cousin marriage tends to keep economic and social ties within a narrow range of currently compatible kinsmen (Vreeland, 1957:116). Perhaps quarrel between brothers and cousins may be averted or muted by the existence of strong affinal bonds between them and, as Barth has suggested for the Kurds, cousin marriage solidifies the minimal lineage as a corporate group in a factional struggle (1954:171).

relations in some cases. She admitted, however, that in the event of such quarrels the relatives of both spouses will work to end the fighting. When a woman marries her cousin, her husband's kinsmen are also her own and, in such cases, a woman may be less likely to be quarrelsome in her husband's home and her husband will be less likely to criticize her relatives. For the bride and her natal family, her marriage to a kinsman can be less harrowing than marriage to an outsider, particularly a stranger, would be. The bride is sent into a known situation and is likely to be treated with love and concern by her husband's family.

Certainly, the observance of *purdah* by women of a kin group tends to contribute to a sense of group identity and is a continual statement of the existence of special bonds between kin and the unity of the kindred *vis-a-vis* the outside world. Traditionally, each circle of kin has included women who appear unveiled to members of the trusted circle and do not appear before males outside the bounds of the group. Thus, veiling and unveiling of women act as continual reminders of kinship and obligation or the lack thereof between both men and women. Further, the importance of female virtue to the honour of the kindred provides a vital shared concern contributing to a sense of unity among kinsmen.[18] Thus, at least in theory, *purdah* should contribute to cooperation between kin. Such cooperation can be very important to economic prosperity and prestige. Kinsmen have reciprocal obligations to assist each other in times of need. Members of the same *azizdar* and close affines frequently cooperate in economic ventures, such as setting up a business together and working as partners. One prosperous Pathan in the Bhopal region has recorded some of his land under the name of an affine so as to escape land ceiling restrictions. He thus clearly trusts this affine not to steal his land. In other instances, friction between siblings and kinsmen has been so great that accusations of sorcery and threats of murder have

18. It has been suggested that the sanctity of virgins and chaste wives plays a critical role in holding together corporate groups of males in many traditional Mediterranean societies (Schneider, 1971:17-22).

been made, and quarrels have broken out in public. When this has happened, other Muslims of high status have been most critical. 'Fighting in public is crude; it's like the sweepers (lowest caste Hindus) or cats and dogs,' they remark. 'People of good family can hardly expect to keep the good opinion of others if they fight like that.'

Low Status Muslims

As we have seen, Muslims of low status in Nimkhera and the Bhopal area observe *purdah* somewhat differently than do the high status Muslims, particularly the Pathans. Accordingly, *purdah* functions somewhat differently among them.

For low status Muslims, *purdah* may restrict, but certainly does not prevent, illicit sexual activity nor does it ensure 'purity' of blood lines. Many of these women engage in extra-marital affairs, although some do not. Among these groups, brides are usually quite young and have little to say about their prospective marriage partners. Divorce is not uncommon. Except for a few pieces of jewellery, there is little permanent family property to consolidate or lose in most cases. Even so, a marriage arranged for a daughter with a youth whose family is financially solvent can bring increased prestige as well as economic benefits to the bride's family.

Beacuse of its previous association with the leisured and prosperious classes, the observance of *purdah*—or at least some of its more obvious features—adds to the prestige of many low and middle status Muslims in their own circles.

The extra-marital affairs of the women, when they occur, do not often include liaisons with older male affines, such as father-in-law, or elder brother-in-law, from whom the women usually veil their faces. Thus, veiling, in combination with respect for elders, among low status Muslims may to some extent prevent competition between men of the same household for the sexual favours of women, thus minimising tension within joint family households, within kin groups, and between neighbours.

Veiling within the family by a woman from her elder male affines and showing deference to these relatives also reduces the possibility that a daughter-in-law will openly argue or quarrel with elder men of her husband's family.

One important function of veiling by a daughter-in-law in her conjugal family is to provide a modicum of privacy for her in her new residence. At first she is likely to be ill at ease and unsure of herself, and a veil is her only protection from the large number of critically appraising eyes focused on her. As she gradually finds her place in her new home and becomes more at ease, she becomes more casual about veiling. Veiling by a high status Pathan bride at her wedding would seem to provide her the same kind of privacy at a critical and trying point of transition in her life.

Veiling from a child's father-in-law similarly prevents open expressions of hostility which might arise between affines, particularly when they are not otherwise related. For example, one Bhopal Muslim woman of low middle status disliked the treatment her newly married daughter was receiving at the hands of her new parents-in-law. The bride's mother cast aside the niceties of *purdah* and openly met the groom's father to make her feelings known. The discussion ended abruptly when the groom's father struck the bride's mother with his sandal (a gross insult), which led to a huge quarrel involving many relatives from both sides. The result was the division of the joint family, with the newlywed couple setting up their own household far from the officious in-laws, and an open break between the two groups of relatives. It is possible that had the bride's mother and the groom's father not been able to express their feelings so openly to each other, the dispute could have been resolved more amicably. On the other hand, her mother's intervention helped the bride in an unhappy situation and in the urban setting, with the groom earning his own salary, division of the joint family was perhaps advantageous to the young couple.

The Functions of Change

As we have seen, *purdah* and the *burka* remain prestigeful among most Muslims of relatively low status, and are finding increasing favour in some families, while well-to-do Pathans and other high status Muslims are abandoning and modifying their traditional practice of *purdah*.

Changes in *purdah* observances among the high status Muslims reflect changes in Bhopal as a city, and the relative importance to an individual of kinsmen and others far beyond the traditional trusted circle. While Yusuf Khan looked to the Nawab, a fellow Pathan, for contracts and to his brothers for important assistance and support, if his son Latif Khan is to maintain a position of prominence he must interact in a wider urban-oriented social network. Latif Khan finds it necessary to cultivate contacts among many government officials, most of whom are well-educated urban Hindus from outside the Bhopal region. Such contacts are necessary to ensure the smooth functioning of Latif Khan's many enterprises in agriculture, quarrying, and contracting, since official clearance is necessary for every phase of these operations. Latif Khan attends dinner parties given by these officials and invites many of them to his village home. At such functions, attended by people who consider *purdah* an anachronism, a mute or invisible wife would not be an asset. In fact, by refusing to bring his wife to a tea party given by an official and his wife, Latif Khan might insult his hostess by the implication that a decent woman does not appear before strangers, or his host by the suggestion that he does not trust him to behave properly with the wives of his guests. On the contrary, having his wife greet his important guests helps Latif Khan cement certain social ties.

Latif Khan's brother's daughter has married the son of a famous Bombay film personality. The wedding festivities, held in Indore and Bombay, were attended by large numbers of celebrities and elegant women. At such gatherings, Birjis Jahan would have felt foolish and old fashioned in her *burka*, and she was more inconspicous unveiled than she would have been veiled. Shortly after attending the wedding, Birjis Jahan gave her *burka* to her maidservant and her husband did not object too strenuously.

While *purdah* has traditionally been a way of ensuring the consolidation and expansion of family property through carefully controlled marriages within a relatively limited circle, today a Bhopal Muslim family might enhance their financial position and prestige through an alliance with a completely unrelated family from Bombay or elsewhere.[19] Needless to say, if Latif Khan were to seek spouses for his children within the elegant set who attended his niece's wedding, he would meet with little success if he and his family were known as old-fashioned and rustic.

Thus, in the past, it was socially and financially advantageous to a Bhopal family group if its women observed *purdah.* Today, as the old social circles of the high status Muslims of the Bhopal region alter and expand to include wider pan-Indian contacts, seclusion and the wearing of the *burka* become less desirable. Feminine modesty in dress and decorum remain important, but are modified as women are educated and encouraged to act outside the closed home environment Only by altering their actions, in accordance with the wide-ranging changes occurring throughout India can the high status Muslims of Bhopal hope to retain their position as an elite.

19. In fact, in at least one case of proposed cousin marriage, the match was seen as a potential danger to the young woman's parents' property in that the young man's wastrel father might try to seize control of the bride's inheritance.

Biliography

Ahmad, Imtiaz (1966), 'The Ashraf-Ajlaf Dichotomy in Muslim Social Structure in India', *Indian Economic and Social History Review*, 3, pp. 268-278.

Ali, Ameer (1935), *The Spirit of Islam*, London, Christopher's.

Altekar, A.S. (1955), 'The Rashtrakuta Empire', in R.C. Majumdar and A.D. Pusalker (eds.), *The Age of Imperial Kanauj*, The History and Culture of the Indian People, Vol. 4, Bombay, Bharatiya Vidya Bhavan.

——— (1962), *The Position af Women in Hindu Civilization*, Delhi, Motilal Banarsidass.

Antoun, Richard T. (1968), 'On the Modesty of Women in Arab Muslim Villages: A Study in the Accommodation of Traditions', *American Anthropologist*, 70, pp. 671-697.

Barth, Frederik (1954), 'Father's Brother's Daughter Marriage in Kurdistan', *Southwestern Journal of Anthropology*, 10, pp. 164-171.

———(1965), *Political Leadership among Swat Pathans*, London School of Economics Monographs on Social Anthropology, No. 19, University of London, London, The Athlone Press.

Basu, Salil Kumar, and Shibani Roy (1972), 'Change in the Frequency of Consanguineous Marriages among the Delhi Muslims after Partition', *The Eastern Anthropologist*, 25, pp. 21-28.

Bool Chand (n.d.—circa 1960), *Raisen Fort*, mimeographed manuscript at District Library, Raisen, Madhya Pradesh, bound 17-7-61.

Caton, A.R. (1930), *The Key of Progress: a Súrvey of the Status and Conditions of Women in India*, London, Oxford University Press.

Das, Frieda Hauswirth (1932), *Purdah: The Status of Indian Women*, New York, The Vanguard Press.

Dube, Leela, with Abdul Rahman Kutty (1969), *Matriliny and Islam: Religion and Society in the Laccadives*, University of Saugar Monographs in Anthropology and Sociology, Delhi, National Publishing House.

Ganguly, D.C. (1957), 'Northern India during the Eleventh and Twelfth Centuries', in R.C. Majumdar and A.D. Pusalker (eds.) *The Struggle for Empire*. The History and Culture of the Indian People, Vol. 5, Bombay, Bharatiya Vidya Bhavan.

Granqvist, Hilma (1931), *Marriage Conditions in a Palestinian Village*, I. Helsinki, Societas Scientiarum Fennica, Commentationes Humanarum Litterarum III. 8.

Jacobson, Doranne (1970), *Hidden Faces : Hindu and Muslim Purdah in a Central Indian Village*, Ph.D. dissertation, Columbia University, New York, University Microfilms, Ann Arbor, 73-16, 209.

——— (1971), 'Hindu and Muslim Wedding Ritual and Social Structure in Central India', Paper presented at the annual meeting of the American Anthropological Association, New York.

——— (1974), 'The Women of North and Central India: Goddesses and Wives', in Carolyn J. Matthiasson (ed.), *Many Sisters: Women in Cross-cultural Perspective*, New York, The Free Press.

——— (1975), 'Separate Spheres: Differential Modernization in Rural Central India' in Helen E. Ullrich (ed.), *Competition and Modernization in South Asia*, New Delhi, Abhinav Publications.

——— (n.d.a) (in press), 'You have Given Us a Goddess: Flexibility in Central Indian Kinship', in S. Devadas Pillai (ed.), *Changing India: Studies in Honour of G.S. Ghurye*, Bombay, Popular Prakashan.

———(n.d.b), (in press), 'Women and Jewellery in Rural India', in Giri Raj Gupta (ed.), *Main Currents in Indian Sociology*, Vol. 2, Family and Social Change in Modern India, Delhi, Vikas Publishing House.

——— (n.d.c), 'Purdah and the Hindu Family in Central India', in Hanna Papanek (ed.), *Parda: Systems of Sex Segregation in South Asia*, (in preparation).

Korson, J. Henry (1971), 'Endogamous Marriage in a Traditional Muslim Society: West Pakistan; A Study in intergenerational Change', *Journal of Comparative Family Studies*, 2, pp. 145-155.

Levy, Reuben (1957), *The Social Structure of Islam*, Cambridge, Cambridge University Press.

Luard, Charles Eckford (1908), *Bhopal States Gazetteer*, The Central India State Gazetteer Series, Vol. III, Calcutta, Superintendent, Government Printing, India.

Majumdar, R.C. (1960), 'The Invasion of Timur and the end of the Tughluq Dynasty', in R.C. Majumdar, A.D. Pusalkar, and A.K. Majumdar (eds.), *The Delhi Sultanate*, The History and Culture of the Indian People, Vol. 6, Bombay, Bharatiya Vidya Bhavan.

Mines, Mattison (1972), 'Muslim Social Stratification in India: The Basis for Variation', *Southwestern Journal of Anthropology*, 28, pp. 333-349.

Newman, Ruth E. (1963), *A Cross-Cultural Test of a Trait of Mental Process and its Categorical Correlates*, Ph.D. dissertation, New York, Columbia University.

Pandya, A.K. (1974), *Raisen District: District Census Handbook*, Census of India, 1971, Madhya Pradesh, Government of Madhya Pradesh.

Papanek, Hanna (1973), 'Purdah: Separate Worlds and Symbolic Shelter', *Comparative Studies in Society and History*, 15, pp. 289-325.

Peristiany, J.G., ed. (1965), '*Honour and Shame: the Values of Mediterranean Society*, London, Weidenfeld and Nicholson.

Peters, Emrys (1963), 'Aspects of Rank and Status among Muslims in a Lebanesc village, in Julien Pitt-Rivers (ed.), *Mediterranean Countrymen*, Paris, Mouton & Co.

Pickthall, Mohammed Marmaduke (1953), *The Meaning of the Glorious Koran*, New York, New American Library.

Roy, S. (1960), 'The Khalji Dynasty', in R.C. Majumdar, A.D. Pusalker, and A.K. Majumdar (eds.), *The Delhi Sultanate*, The History and Culture of the Indian People, Vol. 6, Bombay, Bharatiya Vidya Bhavan.

Sale, George (1843), *Selections from Kur-an, commonly called in England the Koran*, London, J. Madden and Co.

Schneider, Jane (1971), 'On Vigilance and Virgins: Honor, Shame, and Access to Resources in Mediterranean Societies', *Ethnology*, 10, pp. 1-24.

Sultan Jahan, Begam, Ruler of Bhopal (1910), *An Account of My Life*, translated by C.H. Payne, Vol. I, London, John Murray.

———(1912), *An Account of My Life*, translated by C.H. Payne. London, John Murray. (Part I is like the 1910 edition; Part II is an addition).

———(1922a), *An Account of My Life*, translated by A.S. Khan, Vol. II, Bombay, The Times Press.

———(1922b), *Al Hijab, or Why Purdah is Necessary*, Calcutta, Thacker Spink and Co.

———(1927), *An Account of My Life*, translated by C.H. Payne, Vol. III, Bombay, The Times Press.

Tiwari, G.N. (1964), 'Introducing the District', in G. Jagathpathi, *Raisen District: District Census Handbook*, Census of India, 1961, Madhya Pradesh, Government of Madhya Pradesh.

Vreede-de Stuers, Cora (1968), *Parda: A Study of Muslim Women's Life in Northern India*, New York, Humanities Press.

Vreeland, Herbert H., III (1957), 'Pathans of the Peshawar Valley', in Stanley Maron (ed.), *Pakistan: Society and Culture*, Behaviour Science Monographs, New Haven, Human Relations Area Files.

Muslim Kinship and Modernization: The Tyabji Clan of Bombay[1]

Theodore P. Wright, Jr.

Much of the literature on kinship in India looks rather static in character to a non-anthropologist.[2] It has not explored in any detailed way the effects of modernization on Hindu marriage patterns, let along among Muslims.[3] On the face of it, one might expect to find that individualism, as a key component of modernization, would undermine parentally arranged marriages and thereby the first cousin endogamy typical of Muslims.[4] But does this really happen among Indian Muslims,

1. The author wishes to acknowledge his indebtedness to the American Institute of Indian Studies and the State University of New York Research Foundation whose grants made possible field research in Bombay in 1969-70 during which he interviewed thirty-four members of the Tyabji clan. He is also indebted to the American Council of Learned Societies whose grant for 1974-75 gave him time to write this article.
2. A quick survey of articles in the *Social Sciences and Humanities Index* from 1968 to 1974 reveals only four titles under 'kinship' dealing with change and none of these are about India. Khare (1973) does, however, deal with kinship change in India.
3. For instance, Iravati Karve (1965) has nothing about Muslim kinship except a small section on the Moplahs. The need 'For a Sociology of India' including Muslims was first argued by Imtiaz Ahmad (see Ahmad, 1972).
4. See Murphy and Kasdan (1959) for the Arab Bedouin prototype; also see Granqvist (1931), Barth (1954), Ayoub (1959) and Khiri (1970).

or is this expectation another of the many normatively loaded confusions between modernization and westernization?

The Tyabji clan of Bombay, who were pioneers of both westernization and modernization in their community (see Chart I) illustrate within a relatively brief span of four or five generations the ways in which the change from close endogamy to exogamy may operate. This case study may foreshadow future trends for both minority and majority communities in India. It is significant for political scientists too because of the important all-India leadership role which the Tyabjis have played from time to time among Muslims.

The Tyabjis are descendants of Tyab Ali (ibn) Bhai Mian (1803-1863) and his younger brother, Feyzhyder (1805-1852). They were Sulaimani Bohras who migrated from Cambay in the present Gujarat state to Bombay early in the nineteenth century (Hollister, 1953: Chap. XVI). They rose from rags to riches in commerce. Like other Ismaili sects which had been persecuted intermittently by Sunni rulers, they did not share the increasingly dysfunctional feudal values of the North Indian and Deccani nobility, but exemplified the commercial skills and adaptability of the Weberian Protestant prototype. In short, they were early members of the new Indian middle class.

The question of how to justify including Feyzhyder's descendants, known by the surname of Fyzee, in an analysis of the clan is complicated by the fairly recent stabilization of family surnames among Bombay Muslims, although, as a group, they have done so far more readily than their North Indian co-religionists. Asaf A.A. Fyzee, in his translation of the autobiography of Tyabjee Bhoymeah quotes a family story of Abbas S. Tyabji that 'the name Tayyaballi was too long for his Parsi and Hindu friends, so they called him Tyabji and the name stuck' (Fyzee, 1962:10). But since the two sub-lineages, Tyabji and Fyzee, have been closely associated and have intermarried frequently, it seems logical to treat them as one in this study, as well as to include the descendants in the female lines of Tyab Ali's daughters and grand-daughters whose husbands later adopted the surname Abdul Ali, Ahmadi, Futehally, Hydari, Latifi, Lukmani and Mohammadi. As Hussain B. Tyabji wrote in his biography of his father, Badruddin, 'Tyab Ali was the founder of a great *qabeela* or clan which consists

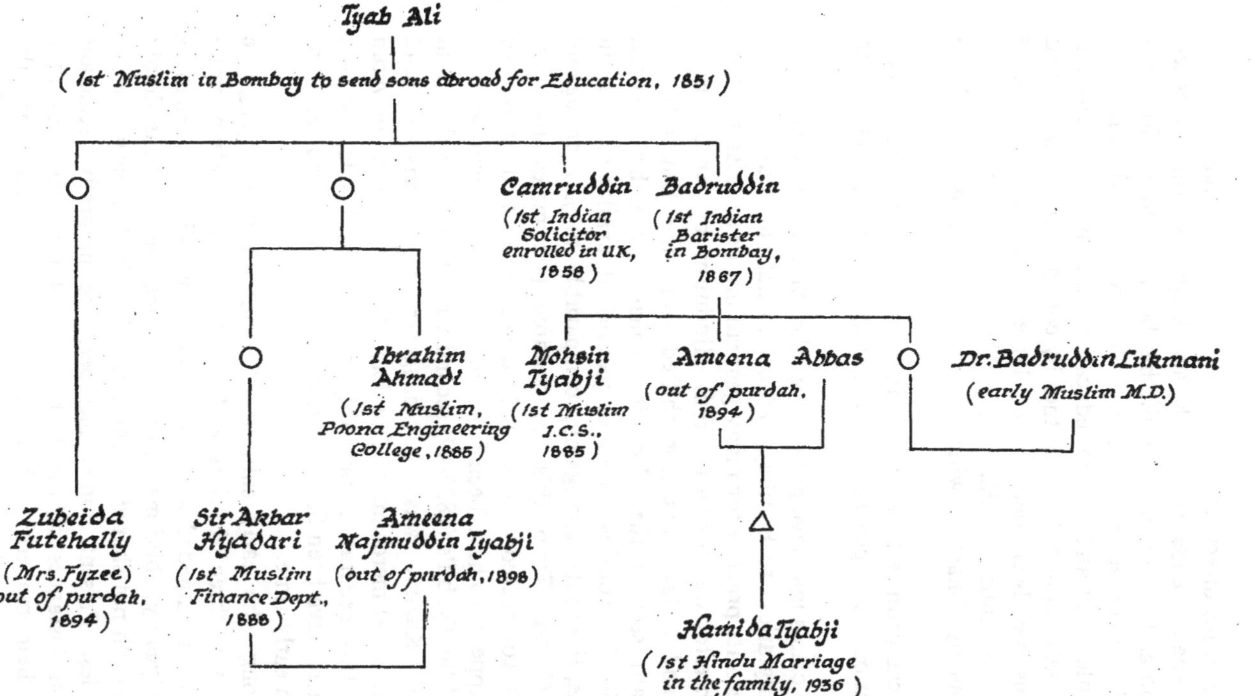

Chart 1: Pioneers of Modernization

not only of his direct male descendants . . . . bearing his name, but also the descendants through his daughters who inherited his blood and whose course of life has been guided by his own principles of character, courage, independence and enterprise, of enlightenment and love for education and broadmindedness. The *qabeela,* closely knit together by common institutions and traditions, has been one of the largest and most influential families in India.' (1952:10-11). The truth of this claim is borne out by Chart 2 which shows the membership of the clan.

We can count a total of 216 marriages in the clan. Their distribution by generation and sub-clan is presented in Table 1.

The clan's marriage pattern for the first three generations after migration to Bombay continued what one must presume had been its practice for many generations, or at least since an early ancestor was converted from Hinduism by Arab missionaries, and a later ancestor shifted from the Daudi to the Sulaimani sect of the Mustalian Ismailis or Bohras (Misra, 1962:150-53): cousins, cross or parallel if available, and, in any case, tight sect endogamy, comparable to *jati* endogamy among Hindus. Tyab Ali's ten children (six males and four females) contracted a total of thirteen marriages, only one of which appears to have been from outside the Sulaimani *jama'at.* Camruddin Tyabji's (1837-89) second wife, Khanar Sultan bint Mashadi Kazim, was the daughter of a Persian (and therefore Shia) merchant of Bombay. A Sindhi and an Arab wife in this generation probably came from inside the sect since there have been Sulaimanis in both Yemen and Karachi from an early time.

Among the early subjects of modernization among the Tyabjis were three Muslims, and, for that matter, Indian, practices which impeded social acceptance by Victorian englishmen: polygamy, child marriage and *purdah.* Perhaps one should add a fourth not shared by Muslims with Hindus: easy divorce for males. Present family members are naturally reluctant to reveal instances of the first two customs, proud as they are of their modernity, but one can infer cases in the second and third generations as long as contacts with

TABLE 1—Distribution of Clan Marriages by Generation and Lineage

	Tyabji	*Fyzee*	*Ahmadi*	*Lukmani*	*Latifi*	*Futehally*	*Mirza*	*Abdul Ali*	*Hydari*	*Mohammadi*	*Totals*
I.	1-(Bhai Mian)										1
II. Tyab	1-(Ali)2										3
III.	8	4	1	1	1	4	1	1	1		21
IV.	15(2)*	5(2)	2	2	4	2	1(2)	4	2	1	42
V.	18(5)	2(1)	2	5	7(1)	7	(6)	7	6	9	76
VI.	11(9)	(3)	(1)	2	(1)	9(4)	1	11(1)	(9)	10(1)	72
Total											216

† Figures in parenthesis show exogamous females.

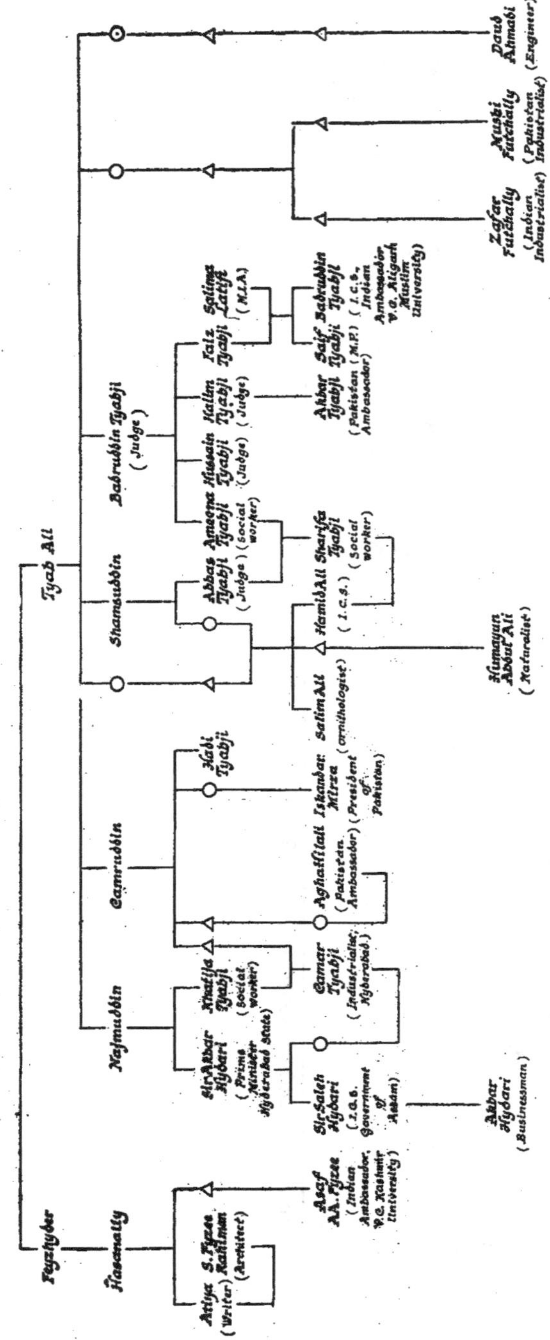

Chart 2: Clan Members in Who's Who in India and Pakistan

the British remained purely commercial, and before the requirements of higher education delayed marriage somewhat past puberty. The only acknowledged instance of polygamy was the Istambul marriages of Hasanally Feyzhyder (1838-1903) to two Turkish ladies when his Tyabji first wife refused to accompany him there on a prolonged business venture.

Regarding age at marriage, even Badruddin Tyabji (1844-1906), who followed his elder brother, Camruddin, to London for education in 1860, was engaged, as a precaution against European entanglements, at the age of fifteen to a girl of nine. He was married to her in 1865 when she was fourteen (Tyabji, 1952:22). The wives of his brothers appear, from their own and their eldest children's birthdates, to have been about thirteen at the time of marriage. Tyab Ali engaged two of his grandchildren when they were only two. Early marriage for the young men of this merchant community is not surprising when one considers how early they entered business. Tyab Ali himself was only ten when he had to abandon his education to work as a hawker.

A sharp rise in the age of females at marriage from about thirteen or fourteen to an average age of twenty-one coincided with their emergence from *purdah* in 1890s, a development of which the family is immensely proud. Badruddin, as the first Indian barrister in Bombay, mixed professionally almost entirely with Europeans. So he first encouraged his wife to introduce *zenana* parties made up of ladies of various communities. Then she learned some English and began meeting European women. In 1876, her husband sent three of his daughters to the first girls' school in Bombay which prolonged their education up to fifteen or sixteen. 'The circle of those before whom they appeared (unveiled) was constanly enlarged until it included practically all relatives and friends' (Tyabji, 1952: 79).[5] The distinction of first discarding the *burqa* altogether went, however, to one of the Judge's nieces, Mrs. Ali Akbar Fyzee, who went to England with Badruddin's daughter Ameena (Mrs. Abbas Tyabji 1866-1942) in 1894. Then in 1898

5. For Tyabji's spirited attack on *purdah* and early marriage at the Mohamedan Anglo-Oriental Educational Conference in 1903, see Noorani (1966:112).

another niece Mrs., afterward Lady, Hydari (Ameena Najmuddin 1878-1939) followed suit in Bombay itself at a party given by the Parsi, Jamsetji Tata. By 1904 Judge Tyabji's two youngest daughters were sent to boarding school in England.

The rising age of marriage and the prolongation of education also led to a sharp decline in the number of children per couple from 5.4 in couples married before 1898 to 2.3 for couples married after that date. Tyab Ali, as we have seen, had ten children and Badruddin had seventeen. By the fourth generation, a two-child family was practically the norm. One can speculate that contraception may have been introduced about this time. By way of comparison, great-grand-father the author of this study, who lived from 1804 to 1885, had eighteen children by one wife; the next generation (who lived from 1832 to 1888) produced only three. In both cases there is a lag of at least one generation between urbanization and decline of the birth rate. These cases would seem to indicate that religion may have little to do with this phenomenon.

Although Judge Badruddin Tyabji is reported to have 'contemplated with favour not only intermarriages between different sects of Mussalmans, but also between good and broad-minded Hindus and Mussalmans' (Tyabji, 1952:77), endogamy remained the norm in the Tyabji clan for another generation. Of the thirty-one marriages in the fourth generations, no less than twenty-four were clan-endogamous, thirteen being parallel cousin and eight cross cousin unions, the others more distant. It was at this stage that the other Sulaimani families mentioned above were incorporated by the children of Tyabji females of the third generation marrying back into the main line. Which fortunate families of the *jama'at* were so favoured seems to have depended upon longstanding business connections (Abdul Ali, Ahmadi, Futehally, Latifi), modern educational achievement (Hydari, Mohammadi), and reward for conversion from the rival Daudi sect (Lukmani). A sample of the complexity of the inter-marriage network and incorporation of other sub-clans is shown in Chart 3.

The gap between a theoretical acceptance of exogamy and its actual occurrence may be partly explicable by the continuation of the joint family until well into the twentieth century. Various dates—from the death of the Judge in 1906 down to

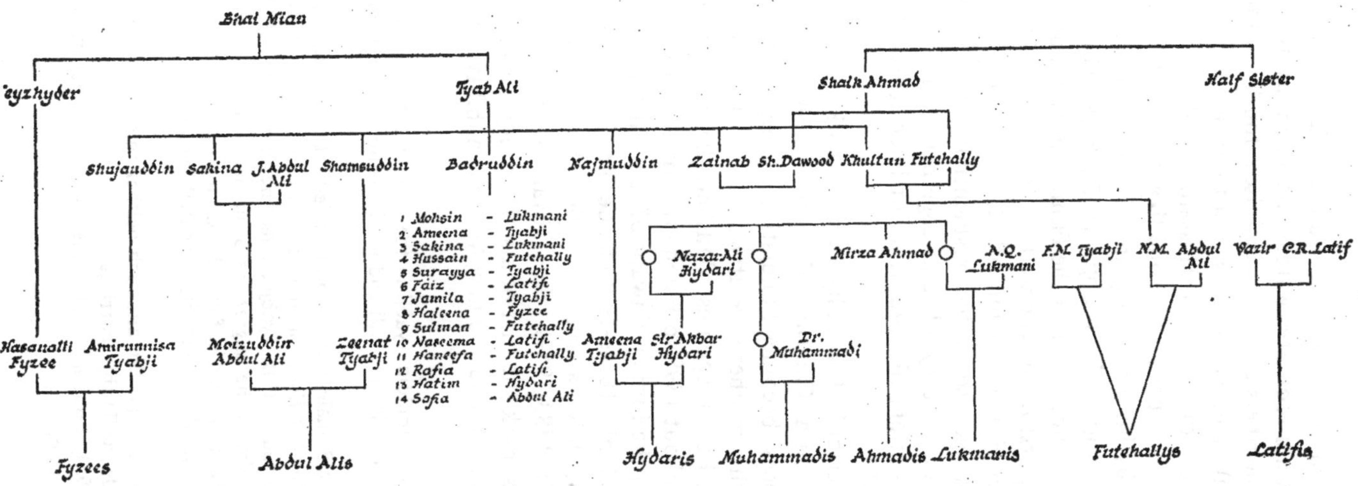

Chart 3: Clan Intermarriages in Generation III and IV

the partition of his estate in 1918 and the sale of the family houses in Khetwadi soon afterwards—are cited as the termination. Older members can still reminisce fondly about the rotation of family meals according to a fixed pattern of days of the week. Badruddin's son Hussain recalled that 'Badruddin's house was a patriarchal one like his father Tyab Ali's . . . surrounded by his sons living in adjoining houses to his, all taking meals together' (Tyabji, 1952:329).[6] This pattern was actually little affected when the family moved out of the Mu·lim *mohalla*, first from Khetwadi to Byculla in 1871 and then to Somerset House on Cumballa Hill in 1881. Even after the various lineages separated residentially, some moving further out to Bandra, they all came together again for summer holidays at hill stations like Matheran or later at Fyzee's property in Kihim.[7]

If we can overlook Hassanally Fyzee's Turkish wives, sect exogamy began with Camruddin's second, Shia wife. Once started, this process becomes cumulative through marriage of the issue with the mother's relatives. Two of Camruddin's children acquired Shia spouses. Dilshad Begum (1879-1925) was married in about 1898 'o Fateh Ali Mirza of the Murshidabad house of the former Nawabs of Bengal.[8] Her brother Kazim, 'Mirza Jan' (1876c-1926) made an equally brilliant, if more modern, match about 1917 with the sister-in-law of Sir Mirza Ismail (1883-1959), the Diwan of Mysore State.[9] These marriages mark the first of a series of hypergamous connections with the old and the new Muslim nobility of North

6. The papers of Badruddin Tyabji in the National Archives of India, New Delhi, contain his will and an indenture of partition deed dated 1918.
7. Tambimuttu, a Sinhalese poet who married into the family, wrote a play, *The Land of Kim*, which gently satirized these family get-togethers. Badruddin F.B. Tyabji likens 'the annual "tribal" holiday exodus to Kihim to the migrations of nomadic ancestors in which the Chiefs, the grey beards, formed a Council of Elders which gave the tribe its solidarity and its essential character' (see Tyabji, 1962:114).
8. See P.C. Majumdar (1905), although neither this book, nor Walsh (1902), records the Tyabji marriage.
9. See Ismail (1954), although again, this book does not mention the Tyabji connection.

India and Hyderabad. After Sir Akbar Hydari became Prime Minister of the latter state, there were intermarriages with the influential Shia Bilgrami family of UP and Hyderabad. Not to be outdone by the senior branch, the Fyzees soon married Nazli Begum (1874-1968) to Sidi Ahmed Khan, the Sunni Nawab of Janjira, a small state on the coast south of Bombay (see Vadivelu, 1915:324).[10] With hypergamy set in a degree of, what Cora Vreede-de-Steurs calls, 'ashrafization'—'the attempt to rise in the Muslim social scale through . . . emulation of the life style of a higher class' (Vreede-de-Steurs, 1968:6).[11] Since the values of the old Mughal ruling class of North India were essentially feudal, a potential conflict was created between modernization and ashrafization as expressed in different kinds of exogamy.

Along with ashrafization went 'Urduization', the replacement of the clan's original Gujarati tongue by the North Indian, and largely Muslim, lingua franca of Urdu (Dittmer, 1972). This shift was already accomplished by Tyabji by family fiat in 1959.[12] His decision stemmed from family aspirations for all-India Muslim leadership. Badruddin is quoted as asking, 'How could a Mussalman be worthy of being a leader of Mussalmans if he did not know Urdu?' In his competition later with Sir Syed Ahmed Khan for Muslim leadership he was taunted by the *Times of India* as being a 'Sulaimani Bohra, a small sect . . . who have little in common with the war-like Mohamedan people of upper India'. There are certain parallels in the career of his grandson and namesake, Badruddin F.B. Tyabji (b.1907), ICS, who accepted the Vice-Chancellorship of Sir Syed Ahmed Khan's Aligarh Muslim University (1962-65) and later retired to Hyderabad where he ran unsuc-

10. The *Times of India* (1948) mentions Lady Kulsum Begum Dowager Begum of Janjira (b. 1897) so apparently Sidi Ahmed Khan remarried to get an heir when Nazli Begum bore him no son.
11. The manuscript letters of Camruddin Tyabji in the Bombay University Library include one dated 20 March, 1876, addressed to Sir Salar Jung of Hyderabad in which he recommended his brother, Amiruddin, for appointment to the state service, 'an aspiration which most of our family have always felt of serving a Muslim prince.'
12. Tyabji (1952:14) attributes this act to Badruddin, but the date is too early.

cessfully for Parliament in 1971. Since all members of the clan have known English too for over a century, knowledge of Urdu has not cut them off from Western influences and experiences.

One might suppose that the degree of ease or resistance to exogamy with other sects and religions would depend upon a sort of theological social distance scale. If this were true, then marriage outside the clan and the *jama'at* would be easiest with (a) the Daudi Bohras, from whom they split in the late sixteenth century; (b) the Khoja Ismailis, from whom the Bohras split in the twelfth century; and (c) with other Shias. Fourth (d) would be Sunni Muslims. Beyond the confines of Islam would come the 'ahl-e-kitab', the tolerated 'people of the book': (e) Christians, (f) Jews and (g) Parsis. Lastly (h) would come polytheists, which in the Indian context would mean Hindus and Buddhists.

Actually, the stages of exogamy have occurred in a different serial order and magnitude: (1) Shia (1860, 1898, 1917), 13 cases; (2) Sunni (1905, 1927), 23 cases; (3) European Christians (1919, 1929, 1930, 1937 ff), 15 cases; (4) Indian Christians or Anglo-Indians (1919-2, 1940s), 7 cases (total Christians, 22); (5) Hindus (1936, 1962 ff), 5 cases; (6) Khojas (1960s), 4 cases; (7) Jews (c.1927, 1960), 2 cases; (8) Daudi Bohras (1946, 1966), 2 cases; (9) Buddhist (1950?), 1 case?; (10) Parsi (c.1953), 1 case.

European, particularly British Christian, marriages are readily understandable once visits to and education in the metropolitan centre became the custom. It was against this very eventuality that Tyab Ali sought to guard by engaging his sons to girls of their own sect and religion before their departure from Bombay. Early and prolonged residence in England without this precaution is said by some to have been the cause of the marriage of three of Sir Akbar Hydari's (1869-1941) sons to Europeans (Swedish, French and English). Beginning with this family, we can generalize that exogamy began with the males and spread only much later to the more sheltered females, at

13. For Badruddin F.B. Tyabji's Vice-Chancellorship at Aligarh, see Wright (1966:53). For his candidacy in Hyderabad in 1971, see Bernstorff (1971:292) and Kundmiri (1972:23 ff).

least as far as extra-Islamic marriages are concerned. Islam, like most religions, is more resistant to females marrying out of the faith than males (Levy, 1965:103, 138). After Indian independence and the replacement of the Indian Civil Service (ICS) with its youthful maximum age for taking the entrance examination, another reason for sending youth to England for their undergraduate education disappeared and present family policy is to send them abroad only at the post-graduate level.

To a stranger it might appear odd that there have been more marriages with European Christians than with Indian Christians or Anglo-Indians. The answer probably lies in the lower status which both of these groups had in the eyes of the British rulers and therefore of Indians themselves. After Independence, Indian Christians were somewhat suspect in nationalist circles for their loyalty to the foreign rulers. It may be surmized, therefore, that these marriages in the Tyabji clan are unlikely to have been arranged by the parents and to be among the earliest examples of unarranged marriages.

The breakthrough in North Indian Sunni Muslim marriages came in the mid 1920s for a very modern reason. It is said that Abbas S. Tyabji (1866-1936) read a book about genetics which dwelt upon the danger of increasing the incidence of undesirable and inheritable physical traits in a family as a result of too much inbreeding.[14] Cases of bad eyesight and 'nervous disposition' in some branches of the clan were then attributed to the practice of repeated cousin marriages. Two existing engagements between cousins were consequently broken and one of the girls was then married to a Sunni from the United Provinces.[15] Respondents emphasize more the regional

14. Actually, an earlier North Indian marriage was that of Munira Begum (1885-c. 1972), daughter of Najmuddin Tyabji, to Mazhar-ul-Haque (1866-1930), a Gandhian leader in Bihar in 1917 (see Ayde 1970:3).

15. Dr. Sewall Wright, a geneticist, offers the following observation on the question of the genetic effects of close endogamy: 'With respect to cousin marriages, there is undoubtedly a considerably increased risk of the segregation of unfavourable homozygotes. Unfavourable genes tend for various reasons to be recessive or of little effect unless inherited from both parents . . . which they might if the parents are closely related' (Personal communication dated March 7, 1975).

than the sectarian character of this broadening of the marriage network. Several such Sunni marriages are said to have ended later in separation or divorce which restored somewhat the preference for regional endogamy.

The first Tyabji wedding to a Hindu came in 1936 as a concommitant of the family's long participation in the Indian nationalist movement. Judge Badruddin had been the third president of the Congress in 1888 (Zakaria, 1970:52, 103)[16] and his nephew, Abbas, joined Gandhi in 1920 and was one of his chief lieutenants in Gujarat during the second non-co-operation movement in 1931. Hussain Tyabji, in an appendix to his biography of his father, claims that seven family members went to jail during the struggle for Independence. The principal Indian nationalists in the clan and their relationship are shown in Chart 4.

Nevertheless, the marriage of Abbas's grand-daughter, Hamida (1910-65), to Prabodh Mehta is said to have occasioned quite a controversy in some family circles, especially as it was a female who was marrying out. It must be remembered, of course, that exogamy is a matter of reciprocal group attraction and repulsion on both sides. Those communities and sects which, like Hindu castes and like the Daudi Bohras and Khojas, exert strong pressures on their members to preserve group purity will be more resistant to intermarriage even if the attitude of the other partner's community or family is favourable. The Syedna of the Daudi Bohras has thus far successfully resisted efforts by some of his sect to curb his control over marriages, but the Tyabji clan was such an important component both in numbers and influence of the smaller Sulaimani Bohra sect that they were able to overcome their religious leaders' objections to exogamy (Wright, 1975).

Another factor inhibiting marriage alliances with Hindus is the subtle strain of 'Islamization' which runs parallel to, but is not identical with, 'ashrafization' and 'Urduization'. The Tyabjis, like other West-coast Muslims (D'Souza, 1955 and 1973), are proud of their partly Arabic ancestry as reflected in

16. The diary of Abbas Tyabji which he kept during his participation in the 1932 non-cooperation movement is in the possession of his son, Salahuddin Tyabji, Shamsabad, Andhra Pradesh.

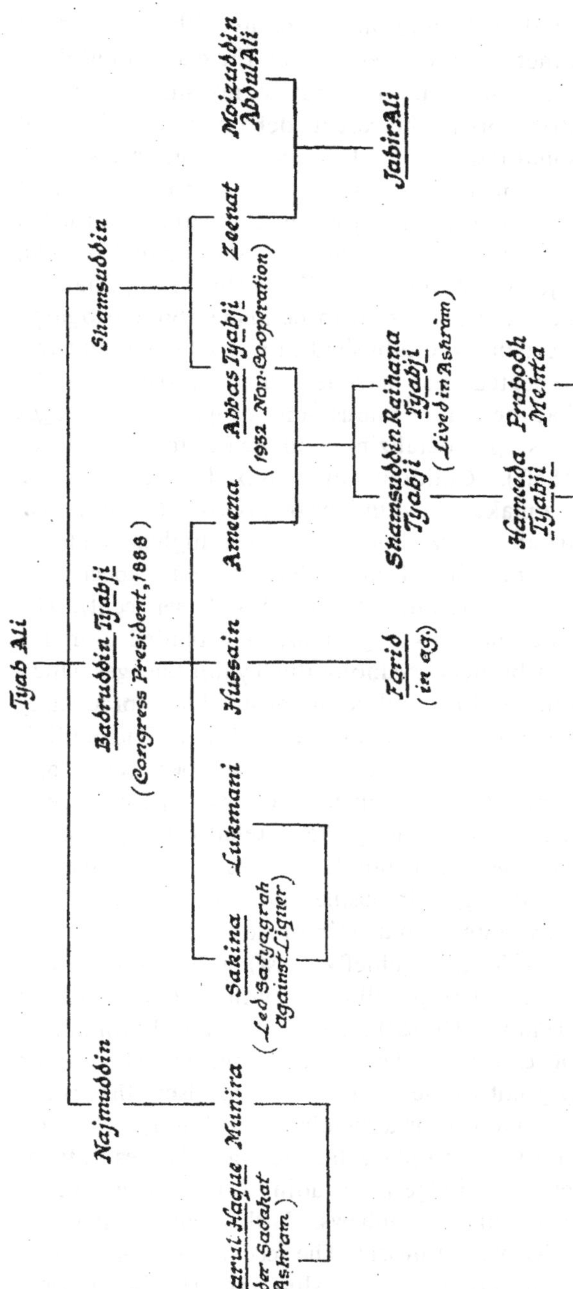

Chart 4: Participation of Clan Members in the National Movement

Arabic names, scholarship and physiognomy. While modernist in belief and practice, few members of the clan would deny their Islamic identity outright. It is really no surprise that so many of the contributors to the recent debate over reform of the Muslim personal law in the English-language press have been Tyabji clan members: Asaf A.A. Fyzee, Zafar and Laeeq Futehally, Danial Latifi, Yasmeen Lukmani, Badruddin Tyabji and his sister, Kamila, and, on the orthodox side, Salahuddin Tyabji (See Wright 1970:72) as shown in Chart 5.

An obvious but necessary point to be made about exogamy is that once a precedent is established in a particular lineage, it tends to be repeated and becomes cummulative, with the eventual result that the endogamous and exogamous lineages may drift apart, stop socializing and cease to intermarry (Ahmad, 1973:185ff). Children of a mixed marriage have little reason not to make mixed unions themselves. For instance, the Fyzee, Hydari and Mirza lineages show a higher incidence of exogamy of all types (60, 64 and 100 per cent respectively) than those with the surname of Tyabji (43 per cent). The Mirza lineage, the most hypergamous, has tended to marry back into the Shi'a branches. Among the Tyabji lineages which have survived (Shujauddin's and Najmuddin's have practically died out in the male line) the main line of Judge Badruddin's descendants is the least exogamous (40 per cent) and Camruddin's the most (67 per cent). The lowest percentage of outmarriage, however, is shown by the Futehally (24 per cent) and Abdul Ali (17 per cent) families. These are the lineages which have remained largely in business and one can speculate that the same advantages that reinforced endogamy in the earlier generations of Tyabjis (chiefly trust) are still operative here. A few recent marriage alliances with Memon or Khoja business families (Parpia, Dossal) may indicate the beginning of a new direction of exogamy. Those clan members who oppose further endogamy point to the ill-effects of nepotism that is apt to result. It is quite natural for a member of a family who has achieved distinction to try to place his young relatives advantageously. The letters of Judge Badruddin Tyabji include many such efforts on behalf of his nephews. Is this really as harmful as an ultra-rationalist would insist? The recent work of Hanna Papanek and Thomas Timberg on Muslim and Hindu business

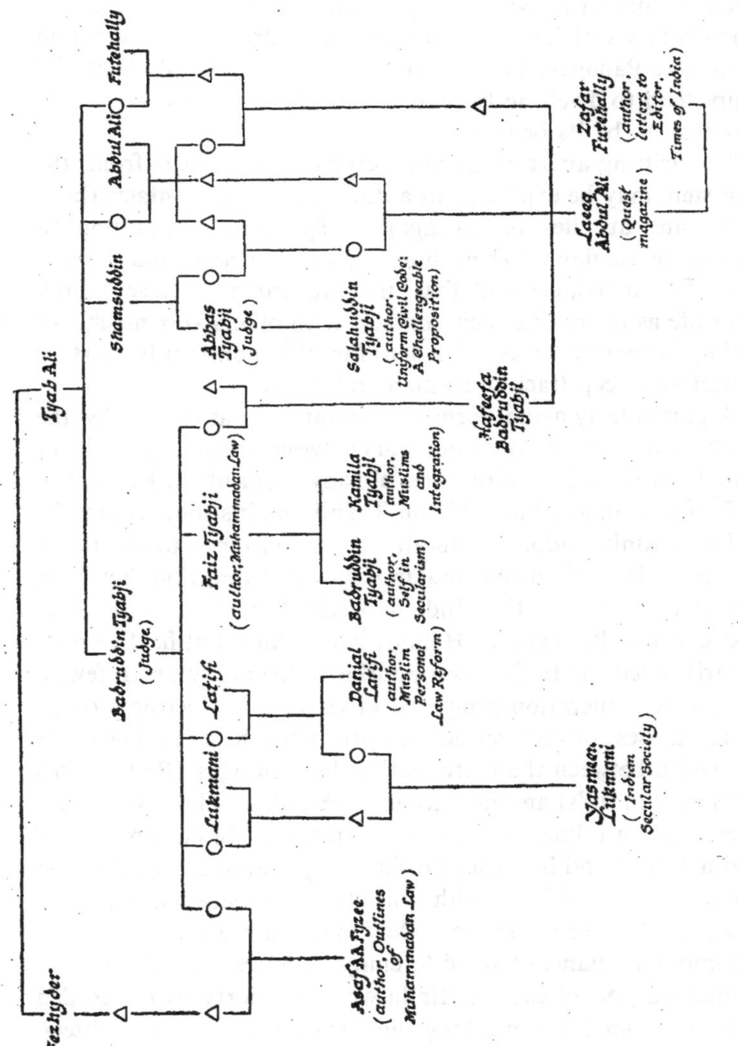

Chart 5: Participation of Clan Members in the Muslim Personal Law Debate

castes show that nepotism can be economically functional (and therefore modern) where it generates a level of trust and responsibility which cannot be expected of strangers recruited on 'merit' (see Pananek, 1973; Timberg, 1969 and 1973). Minority groups tend to dwell on the evils of ascription until they are in a position to be its beneficiaries.

The drifting apart of the more exogamous lineages from the main stem may be expressed in a decline of social contacts (both routine and at rites of passage) or by actual emigration to Pakistan or England. When interviewed, partners and descendants of outmarriages said that they regarded a close family social life as restricting their contacts with others too much, or lacking in variety, or as a burden for the non-family partner to meet and keep track of so many relatives.

A particularly acute form of separation was caused by the partition of 1947 and the three wars between India and Pakistan. Some members of the clan were already resident in Karachi in 1947—for instance, Judge Hatim Tyabji and his son, Akbar, the Pakistani Ambassador. Naturally they continued to live there. Due to the family's strong Indian nationalist tradition, however, those who were in the Indian Civil Service at that time (Badruddin F.B. Tyabji, Hamid Ali, Alma Latifi, Salah A. Hydari) opted for India. During the following years a few of the younger generation emigrated in search of career opportunities in business or civil service. Surprisingly, there is no negative correlation between the more nationalist lineages (Badruddin's and Shamsuddin's) and migration to Pakistan. Those who went came from all lineages about equally. The Shi'a progeny of Kazim Tyabji and his sister Dilshad migrated and provided the new country of Pakistan with one of its Presidents, Iskandar Mirza (1899-1969). Those who made ashrafi hypergamous matrimonial alliances tended to emigrate more than those with endogamous, or, of course, Hindu wives. Of forty-two recorded emigrants from India and long time residents abroad, eighteen (43 per cent) were children of exogamous parents and thirty-one (74 per cent) had themselves made marriages outside the clan. Thus exogamy seems to be a much more important cause of emigration than ideology.

Unlike the poorer and middle class Muslims of Delhi whom Basu and Ray (1972) studied, the Tyabji clan is somewhat more mobile and has not limited its marriages to one province. Partition and emigration did, therefore, render more difficult a pre-existing endogamous exchange. More easily ascertainable is the fact that those women from the Indian side who did marry Pakistanis experienced a high divorce rate. As one family member commented, 'coming from a Nationalist family, they couldn't stand the anti-Indian atmosphere on the other side.' It seems likely, therefore, that completely separate lineages are developing on either side of the frontier, with the Pakistani segment choosing the path of ashrafization/Urduization/Islamization in its marriage patterns and style of living, and the Indian part pursuing a double course of close endogamy on the one hand and extra-Islamic exogamy and emigration to the West on the other hand. Some lineages will display more of the former and others more of the latter, but neither are likely to practise endogamy or exogamy exclusively because continued modernization loosens parental control and replaces arranged marriages with individual choice.

So far, despite the high degree of Westernization and modernization in the clan, it appears that most matches still involve a larger amount of parental initiative, or at least participation, than in the West. But it should not be assumed that this is necessarily resented by the young people, or that it is less 'modern', in the sense of rational, than the emotional and romantic bases upon which Westerners choose their partners which produce such a horrendous divorce rate. The Tyabji clan's divorce rate—10 per cent of marriages (and 68 per cent of these 22 broken marriages are exogamous unions)—is lower than in the West although higher than the overall Indian divorce rate because of the continuing disapproval of divorce and remarriage by the Hindus majority.

Since the 1940s, Tyabji women have been prolonging their education to the B.A. level and a few (Yasmeen Lukmani and Salima Tyabji) beyond that to the M.A. This implies further strains on endogamy and marital stability, to judge by Western experience. It is possible for Westerners and modernists to conceive, however, as argued by Papanek (1971) in a paper on joint family and women's education, that women's 'liberation' in India may actually be facilitated by relatively early, endogamous marriage and the joint family which will allow talented women to pursue their advanced education and careers, undiverted by the individualistic search for a mate in the American-style 'dating game' and enjoying built-in babysitters from among the older women and younger sisters in the extended family? Out of the turmoil of the late 1960s in America has come a greater appreciation of the disadvantages of the nuclear family for child-rearing and of the advantages of larger group living. What the communes of the period failed to provide, however, was stability and I would argue that the long historic experience of human kind demonstrates that this can be provided only by multi-generational groups tied together by blood relationship.

Bibliography

Ahmad, Imtiaz (1972), 'For a Sociology of India', *Contributions to Indian Sociology*, New Series, 6, pp. 172-77.

———(1973), 'Endogamy and Status Mobility among the Siddique Sheikhs of Allahabad, Uttar Pradesh', in Imtiaz Ahmad (ed.), *Caste and Social Stratification Among the Muslims*, Delhi, Manohar Book Service.

Ayde, S.R. (1970) *Mazharul Haque*, New Delhi, Sampradyikta Virodhi Committee.

Ayoub, Millı ent (1959), 'Parallel Cousin Marriage and Endogamy: a S:udy in Sociometry', *Southwestern Journal of Anthropology*, 15, pp. 266-75.

Basu, Salil Kumar and Shibani Roy (1972), 'Change in the Frequency of Consanguinous Marriages among the Delhi Muslims after Partition', *Eastern Anthropologist*. 25, pp. 21-28.

Barth, Fredrik (1954), 'Father's Brother's Daughter marriage in Kurdistan', *Southwestern Journal of Anthropology*, 10, pp. 864-71.

Bernstorff, Dagmar (1971), *Wahlkamf in Indien*, Duesseldorf, Bertelsmann Universitae Tsveslag.

Dittmer, Kerrin (1972), *Die Indischen Muslims Die Hindi-Urdu Kontnoverse in der United Provinces*, Weisbaden, Otto Harrassowitz.

D'Souza, Victor S. (1955), *The Navayats of Kanara*, Dharwar, Kannara Research Centre.

———(1973), 'Status Groups among the Moplah Muslims on the Southwest Coast of India', in Imtiaz Ahmad (ed.), *Caste and Social Stratification Among the Muslims*, Delhi, Manohar Book Service.

Fyzee, A.A.A. (1962), 'Tyabjee Bhoymeah', *Journal of the Asiatic Society of Bombay*, (New Series) Vols. 36-37, Supplement, pp. 1-24.

Granqvist, Hilma (1931), *Marriage Conditions in a Palestinian Village*, Commentationes Humanarum Litterarum III-8, Helsinki, Societas Scientiarum Fennica.

Hollister, John (1953), *The Shias of India*, London, Luzac & Co.

Ismail, Sir Mirza (1954), *My Public Life*, London, George Allen and Unwin.

Karve, Iravati (1965), *Kinship Organization in India*, 2nd ed., Bombay, Asia Publishing House.

Khare, R.S. (1973), 'One Hundred Years of Occupational Modernization among Kanyakubja Brahmans: A Geneological Reconstruction of Social Dynamics', in Milton Singer (ed.), *Enterpreneurship and Modernization of Occupational Cultures in South Asia*, Durham, Duke University Press.

Khuri, Faud I. (1970), 'Parallel Cousin Marriage Reconsidered: A Middle Eastern Practice that Nullifies the Effects of Marriage on the Intensity of Family Relations', *Man*, New Series, 4, pp. 597-618.

Kundmiri, S. Alam (1972), '1971 Elections and Communalism in Hyderabad', *Secular Democracy*, 5, pp. 19-23.

Levy, Reuben (1965), *The Social Structure of Islam*, 2nd ed., Cambridge, Cambridge University Press.

Majumdar, P.C. (1905), *The Masnud of Murshidabad*, Omraoganj, Saroda Roy.

Misra, Satish C. (1964), *Muslim Communities in Gujarat*, Bombay, Asia Publishing House.

Murphy, Robert F., and Leonard Kasdan (1959), 'The Structure of Parallel Cousin Marriage', *American Anthropologist*, 61, pp. 17-30.

Noorani, A.G. (1969), *Badruddin Tyabji*, New Delhi, Publications Division, Ministry of Information and Broadcasting, Government of India.

Papanek, Hanna (1971), 'Purdah in Pakistan: Seclusion and Modern Occupations for Women,' *Journal of Marriage and the Family*, 33, pp. 517-50.

———(1973), 'Pakistan's New Industrialists and Businessmen: Focus on the Memons', in Milton Singer (ed.), *Enterpreneurship and Modernization of Occupational Cultures in South Asia*, Durham, Duke University Press.

Timberg, Thomas A. (1969), 'The Origins of Marwari Industrialists', in Robert Beech and Mary Beech (eds.), *Bengal: Change and Continuity*, Occasional Paper No. 16, East Lansing, Asian Studies Center of the Michigan State University.

———(1973), 'Three Types of the Marwari Firm,' *Indian Economic and Social History Review*, 10, pp. 1-36.

Times of India (1948), *India and Pakistan Yearbook and Who's Who*, Bombay, Bennet Coleman and Co.

Tyabji, Badruddin, F.B. (1962), *Chaff and Grain*, Bombay, Asia Publishing House.

Tyabji, Hussain B. (1952), *Badruddin Tyabji: A Biography*, Bombay, Tacker and Co.

Vadivelu, A. (1915), *Ruling Chiefs, Nobles and Zamindars of India*, Madras, G.C. Loganadhan Bros.

Vreede-de-Steurs, Cora (1968), *Parda: A Study of Muslim Women's Life in Northern India*, Essen, Van Gokum and Co.

Walsh, J.H. Tull (1902), *The History of Muradabad District*, London, Tarrold and Sons.

Wright, Theodore P., Jr. (1966), 'Muslim Education in India at the Crossroads: The Case of Aligarh', *Pacific Affairs*, 39, pp. 50-63.

———(1970), 'The Muslim Personal Law Issue in India: An Outsider's View', *Indian Journal of Politics*, 4, pp. 69-77.

———(1975), 'Competitive Modernization Within the Daudi Bohra Sect of Muslims and its Significance for Indian Political Development', in Hellen Ullrich (ed.), *Competition and Modernization in South Asia*, New Delhi, Abhinav Publications.

Purdah, Family Structure and the Status of Woman: A Note on a Deviant Case[1]

A.R. Saiyed

Assisted by Pathan Mirkhan

While there is a general paucity of sociological studies dealing with Indian Muslims, studies of their family life—especially those concerning the position of woman—are particularly scarce.[2] A major reason for the absence of the latter category

1. The data on which the present paper is based formed a part of a large study entitled, 'Muslims of Konkan: An Explorative Study'. It was conducted under the auspices of the Dr. Zakir Husain Institute of Islamic Studies and was funded by the University Grants Commission. The senior author was the Director of the Study, and the junior author served as the Principal Investigator. The study was in the nature of a survey that extended over three districts of Maharashtra state and covered sixteen villages and four towns. The main aim of the study was to construct a cultural profile of the community known as 'Kokni Muslims'. Given the nature of this study, the present paper's orientation is towards generalizations based on our survey. Thus, the findings reported here are not those of a 'village study' of the usual anthropological type. The data presented here covers six villages. Unfortunately, due to circumstances beyond our control, we are not in a position to reveal the names of the villages concerned.
2. One of the rare works which deserves mention here is that of Vreede-de-Steurs (1968).

of studies is the prevalence of *purdah*[3] among Muslim women, which has rendered the task of systematic observation and empirical data collection very difficult, if not impossible. Seclusion and isolation have rendered her inaccessible both intellectually and socially to research and researchers, The difficulties of fact finding in this area have either compelled social scientists to desist from dealing with the actual situation concerning the position of the Muslim woman, or, alternatively, to remain contended with the textbook view concerning her.[4]

In the present paper we shall be concerned—somewhat briefly[5]—with the position of Muslim women as observed in a group of villages in the north-central part of Ratnagiri district in Maharashtra. These women belong to a regional-cum-linguistic community of Muslims known as 'Kokni Muslims'. The paper will seek to establish that the position of these women is sharply different from the one that generally prevails—or, at least, is believed to prevail—among Indian Muslims taken as a whole.[6] It is the contention of this paper that this deviance

3. In the present paper, by '*purdah*' we shall connote the seclusion, isolation and segregation of women; in the present context we shall be concerned with Muslim women only.
4. For a good illustration of the lack of any discussion of the Muslim women see M.N. Srinivas (1975). As an inveterate empiricist Srinivas has obviously been handicapped by the lack of factual information, and has accordingly limited himself to just one sentence on the position of Muslim women in India. As regards limiting the discussion to the textbook view, one may refer to Kapadia (1959). It is intersting to note that while Kapadia's book is interspersed with empirical data on Hindu family life, there is no such data concerning Muslims.
5. Our brief treatment is necessitated by the fact that our original study was not limited to the observation of family life alone but covered a wide range of topics. Further, for purposes of the present paper we have selected only that part of our data on family as concerned the illustration of deviation from *purdah*.
6. The difficulties and limitations of making any generalizations regarding the Indian Muslims, given their heterogeneity as well as the complexity of the Indian society, are fully recognized. Nevertheless, the attempt to generalize cannot, and should not, be altogether given up or else the sociological enterprise will be reduced to futility. Of course, the greater the scantiness of data—as in the case concerning Muslim studies in India—the greater is the problem besetting generalizations. But, while realizing all this, we have

is largely due to the non-observance of *purdah*. Certain existential factors, and traditions, too, have a role to play in this situation, but it appears that their role would have been muted if the women of this region had been in seclusion.

Before presenting the data, we propose to briefly discuss the ideal-typical position of the *purdah*-bound Muslim woman,[7] so that the deviation between the 'ideal' or stereotyped view and our empirical data can be more vividly seen.

Purdah and Muslim Women

Most major religions of the world have taken a keen interest in the position of women, and have made various pronouncements concerning them. Coincidentally, practically all of them have created a confusing picture of what they have wanted

proceeded here on the basis of some broad personal observations which would seem to indicate that, barring the lowest classes, Muslims, in all regions of India, have traditionally considered *purdah* both as an ideal and as a practical desideratum. As individuals and groups have moved up in the social ladder, their commitment to *purdah* has become stronger as a part of their 'Islamization'. A few westernized women have managed to escape *purdah* but these have not met with the approval of the orthodox, and not all the wealthy families have allowed their women to emulate the westernized non-*purdah* observing families. The exigencies of recent changes—especially in metropolitan areas—has led to some dilution in the rigours of *purdah*. Thus, young school and college girls leave their homes in the Muslim *mohallas* clad in *burqas* which are either removed on reaching a sufficiently safe distance from one's *mohalla* or upon reaching one's institution or place of work. However, this concession has not yet led to the females gaining enough confidence to interact on a hetero-sexual basis with some freedom. Thus, the social and psychological restrictions associated with *purdah* continue to operate, and, as of now, changes in form have not yet been accompanied by changes in content. But even the changes that we have just referred to are not universally observed for, under the influence of the fundamentalist Muslim groups, individuals and groups who were not very strict about the seclusion of their women are now seeing the merits of *purdah*.

7. Actually, the remarks that follow would be true of any group in which women are secluded and isolated. In support of this point see the report of a speech by Rama Mehta (1975) on *purdah* among the Oswal women of the erstwhile Mewar State.

their actual position to be. Islam is no exception to this generalization. Two sayings attributed to the Prophet Mohammed will illustrate the point in question. The first of these is: 'I have not left any calamity more detrimental to mankind than women'; and the second: 'The world and all things in it are valuable, but more valuable than all is a virtuous woman' (Hobhouse, 1951:202).

Such contradictory statements have given both critics and sympathizers enough material to keep 'proving' their respective cases and 'disproving' those of their opponents. But, in any case, there has been little concern for empirical facts. For the apologists of Islam what has mattered most is that the Prophet of Islam gave to the Muslim woman rights which were unknown in contemporary Arab society.[8] Thus, under Islam woman came to inherit property along with her male relatives and to hold this property in her own right. Kapadia has, in this connection, gone to the extent of observing: 'But the greatest contribution of Islam to the cause of woman was to invest her with property rights' (1959:198). Another fundamental change in favour of women was that their consent to a marriage was made obligatory. Thus, no Muslim marriage can be solemnized on the basis of a consent given by the girl's parents or guardians alone. Islam also gave the Muslim woman the freedom to seek divorce on her own initiative, albeit it is much more easy for the male to obtain a divorce. However, as a protection against whimsical divorces the Muslim woman has been provided security by the *mahr* (the dower) which she can claim from her husband if she is divorced without good cause. Even the much maligned phenomenon of 'four wives' is hedged with the qualification that all the wives should be treated alike. (This impossible condition, apologists point out, has virtually prohibited polygyny). Finally, one other little known privilege is the right to hold public positions: indeed, a Muslim woman can even act as a judge except where retaliation is involved (Hobhouse, 1951:202).

These rights and privileges, which even in the context of

8. For a useful discussion of the position of Muslim women in the initial period of Islamic society, and with particular reference to the Arab context, see Levy (1957).

modern developments appear to be quite impressive, were indeed remarkable in the context of the socio-economic conditions prevailing in pre-Islamic Arab society. Indeed, they have led Ameer Ali—a very sympathetic commentator and interpreter of Islam—to wax eloquent in the following words: 'The Teacher who, in an age when no country, no system, no community gave any right to woman, maiden or married, mother or wife, who secured to the sex rights which are only unwillingly and under pressure being conceded to them by the civilized nations in the twentieth century, deserves the gratitude of humanity. . . .'[9] In actuality, however, the Muslim woman in India, and, indeed, in most other countries where Muslims are to be found in significant numbers, have not made the progress that they should have made as a natural corollary to the privileges and rights conferred upon them by their religion. Indeed, judged by modern values, the emancipation of Muslim women is a major problem even in Muslim states[10] where legislation and social reforms do not bristle with the socio-political problems that afflict similar attempts in a state where the Muslims constitute a minority and are, therefore, suspicious of any change through legislation. Why, then, should there exist this chasm between

9. This quotation is taken from Kapadia (1959:202). It may, however, be added that there is some basis for Ameer Ali's bold statement. Thus, for example, commenting on the position of the English women in Victorian times, O.R. McGregor writes: 'Outside the family, married women had the same legal status as children and lunatics; within it they were their husband's inferiors. By marriage they moved from dependence on fathers or male relatives to dependence on husbands . . . ' (Fletcher, 1962:95). In recent decades, the rough passage experienced by the Hindu Code Bill in the Indian Parliament is too well-known to need any recapitulation here.

10. In this connection, it is interesting to note that, according to Khushwant Singh's report on the United Nations' Conference on women held at Mexico in June 1975 as part of the International Women's Year, there was no delegation from Saudi Arabia. The same report also points out that whereas the Kuwait Government grants scholarships to its young men to study abroad, similar scholarships are denied to young girls of that country. The existence of segregated banks in Pakistan where only female patrons can bank, and where they are exclusively served by a famale staff, are all indicators of the Muslim woman's lack of emancipation in Muslim majority states.

the Muslim women's privileges on the one hand, and their actual condition on the other? If our observations have indicated anything, then the answer would seem to lie in the phenomenon of *purdah*. Her seclusion, isolation, and segregation have in one stroke, as it were, nullified the rights that have been granted to her.[11] Indeed, in the face of the disabilities that *purdah* has bestowed upon the Muslim woman, her rights and privileges have virtually remained unsung and unapplauded. And, in evaluating her status, the general tendency has been to focus attention upon the fact of seclusion and isolation and their consequences, rather than upon her rights and privileges.

While the various arguments in support of or against *purdah* are not of concern to us, yet it would be relevant here to discuss some of its sociological and psychological implications for the individual, the family and the community. Accordingly, following a perceptive analysis by Blitsten (1963, Chap. IX), we shall briefly present some of the dysfunctional aspects of *purdah*. This emphasis, it will eventually become clear, is necessary for providing a frame of reference for the fuller appreciation of the data, concerned as it is with a deviation from the usual observance of *purdah*.

Seclusion, isolation and segregation are known to characterize several non-industrial societies, yet none has practised these in as extreme a form as the Muslim societies, especially of the Arab world.[12] Indian Muslims too have traditionally been staunch supporters of *purdah*—especially the Muslims of Delhi and UP who have been the reference models for most

11. By emphasizing the role of *purdah* in the Muslim woman's lack of emancipation, we are not oblivious of the fact that there exist negative statements concerning her even in the Koran (see Blitsten 1963:197). However, it is our opinion that in real life it is not so much the favourable or unfavourable statements that matter as much as cultural traditions and social mechanisms. Most men who consider the woman to be inferior to man have not read a word about her inferiority anywhere. For this reason, the endless discussions based on scriptural or text-book views are for purposes of real consequences, largely of no consequence.
12. It is of some interest to note in this connection that when one looks to the Muslim countries east and southeast of India, *purdah* is not seen to be enjoying the rigour and respectability that it does in India and in the countries west of India.

Indian Muslims. The prevalence of *purdah* has invested Muslim family life and the Muslim woman with some interesting and unique characteristics.

In terms of familial relationships, the most obvious impact of seclusion has been an extreme segregation of sex-roles. This has caused a sharp differentiation in the husband-wife relationship. Accordingly, the complementarity between the partners is reduced to a minimum in the Muslim family. This, in turn, has thwarted the rise of equalitarianism in husband-wife relations.[13] Further, the rigid restriction of familial roles has led to minimal mutual expectations on the part of the partners and this has, in fact, reinforced the males' negative evaluation of the capabilities of the females. Traditionally, nothing has been expected of her outside of the domestic sphere and, as has already been indicated, even in this sphere certain very specific roles are assigned to her. The narrow concept of the daughter and wife roles led to the de-emphasizing of any ormal education among females. One latent effect of the denial of education to women has been the perpetuation of the lowly position of the Muslim woman—and her acceptance of it.

Further, seclusion and isolation have forced the Muslim woman into a limited circle of interaction, which has denied her the opportunity of learning to function as a mature and confident individual who is aware of her rights and privileges, and can struggle to prevent their violation. Consequently, the safeguards provided for her by Islam against plural marriages or unfair and undeserved divorce often get reduced to nought.

Purdah has also rendered the Muslim woman incapable of contributing to, and participating in, a host of activities which are eminently suited to her interests and talents. Thus, few

13. A Muslim lady social worker of Bombay, with considerable experience of working among Muslim women, sums up her observations concerning husband-wife relationship as follows: 'She (the Muslim woman) enters marriage with the idea that her husband is God, and firmly believes, since it has been dinned into her, that *sajdah* (the Muslim act of prostration in worship), if it is allowed to anyone after God, is to be done to her husband' (Personal communication).

Muslim women—especially in India—are to be found in the field of music[14] or fine arts. Similarly, the Muslim women's participation in welfare, and other community work, is negligible.[15] Unfortunately, in present day India this negligence has recoiled upon the Muslims themselves and they have not been able to effectively tackle their social problems or provide much needed community services. Both these failures have hindered the social progress of the Indian Muslims, but, as yet, there is little recognition of the link between women's emancipation and the community's progress.

Finally, seclusion—and its corollary, lack of education—have had economic ramifications too. *Purdah* and its attendant disabilities have incapacitated the Muslim woman from making any significant economic contribution either towards her own independence or towards the economic viability of the family. (This is especially true of the lower middle class Muslims.) The former failure has led to her exploitation, and the latter has hurt the family's economy. Deprived of the contribution of half their potential contributors, Muslim families have found it difficult to face straitened circumstances and improve their economic conditions which are generally backward. Especially in the event of the untimely demise of the male bread-winner, the family is forced to sink into poverty since the woman is incapable of meeting the crisis. The *purdah*-

14. The case of Indian classical music is particularly interesting. As is well-known, the field of north Indian classical music has been traditionally dominated by Muslim *ustaads*. However, the various *gharanas* have produced hardly any women singers. On the other hand, the Muslim *ustaads* have trained a large number of prominent Hindu female musicians.
15. In quantitative terms the contribution of Muslim women to this field is negligible, and it is a fact of some significance that even today the School of Social Work run by the Jamia Millia Islamia is unable to attract any Muslim female students. Interestingly, some of the westernized Muslim families of Bombay have produced a number of Muslim women who have been pioneers in the field of social welfare. Thus, one can mention such names as Kulsum Sayani, Fatema Ismail, Zulie Nakhuda, Wahabuddin Ahmed, and Zarina Currimbhoy. Incidentally, none of these women have been prominent specifically in the sphere of Muslim reform, or the amelioration of the position of Muslim women.

bound mother is also a poor educator of her children, and generally fails to motivate them towards higher levels of educational aspirations and achievements. This failure also prevents the upward mobility of the family. Indeed, one may go to the extent of suggesting that a major factor in the generally backward economic condition of mostI ndian Muslims is *purdah*.

It is perhaps worth pointing out here that it would be a gross mistake to imagine that the lives of men remain unaffected in a situation where women suffer from such disabilities. In the general context of woman's emancipation, Rossi has observed: 'Social and personal life is impoverished for some part of many men's lives because so many of their wives live in a perpetual state of intellectual and social impoverishment' (1964). It would be difficult to deny the pertinence of these remarks.

But to return to the generalizations made above, lest we may be misunderstood and subjected to the charge that they are not only too sweeping but also without any factual base, let it be clarified here that they are not meant to be dogmatic assertions, but, rather, comprise an attempt to construct an 'ideal-type'.[16] The relevance and utility of this tool of sociological analysis is too well-known to need any elaboration here. At the same time, it is admitted that these generalizations can also be viewed as hypotheses. In either case, there is no denying the need for a careful and critical empirical scrutiny. In what follows the relevance of our generalizations will become clear in as much as we are dealing with a deviant case.

With this clarification, we now turn to our field data wherein it will be seen that the non-existence of *purdah* has helped a group of Muslim women to take advantage of certain existential conditions, and enjoy a freedom which is somewhat unique among Indian Muslims. It should be pointed out here that we are not seeking to establish a cause-effect relationship in the present paper. Rather, the discussion will emphasize how an association between the absence of seclusion and isolation and

16. Explicating Weber's concept, Timasheff observes: 'The ideal or pure type is a mental construct. It is formed by exaggeration or accentuation of one or more traits or points of view observable in reality' (1967:179).

the existence of certain socio-economic conditions has helped the community of women under consideration to remain free from the traditional social disabilities of their Muslim sisters. But let us first describe the setting of the study.

The Setting

Our data pertain to a group of villages located in the northern and central part of Ratnagiri district of Maharashtra state. Along with Kolaba district, Ratnagiri constitutes what is known as the Konkan or Kikan region; the inhabitants of the region are called Koknis. Both the Hindus and Muslims of the region have a distinct sub-culture of their own which distinguishes them from the Hindus and other Muslims of Maharashtra. Between Kokni Hindus and Kokni Muslims there is a certain cultural affinity, a notable feature of which is the widespread use of Hindu surnames by Muslim families. In fact, it is often impossible to identify a Muslim on the basis of his surname alone.

Geographically, Ratnagiri is generally hilly and coastal, with several creeks. The hilly terrain does not give much scope for cultivation, yet rice is grown wherever possible. There is some forest wealth also. Ratnagiri is the home of the famous Alphonso mango, and the harvesting and marketing of mangoes is a lucrative seasonal business. Finally, there is plenty of marine wealth in the form of fish, shrimps and other sea-food. In recent decades, the mechanization of fishing operations has helped the region's economy. However, taken as a whole, Ratnagiri district is economically very backward. Its natural resources have not been fully exploited. There is practically no industrialization, and the total absence of rail transportation has hampered the development of the entire district.

As a result of the grossly undeveloped conditions of the region, the population has resorted to large-scale migration. Both Hindus and Muslims seek employment in Bombay in large numbers. The latter even go beyond the country's shores in significant numbers. Several Kokni Muslims have taken up jobs or have established business in the Muslim countries of Arabia, Africa, and South-east Asia. The merchant navy—both Indian and foreign—also absorbs many Koknis. As a result of this pattern of employment, many Ratnagiri villages are populated mostly by women, children and the aged. These individuals are supported by funds that are remitted by male relatives from wherever they are. A number of male members of several Kokni Muslim (Jamaati) families are working abroad. They remit their savings home which are invested in houses, rice fields, jungles and mango *wadis*.

In contrast to the general trend of urban residence among Indian Muslims, Ratnagiri district has a fairly large rural Muslim population, and one can find a number of villages where the Muslims are numerically dominant. In fact, due to their employment and business establishments abroad, the Kokni Muslims also enjoy economic dominance in quite a few of these villages. Indeed, in the course of our study we found two villages which had topped the Maharashtra state's small-savings campaign thanks to the affluence of their Kokni Muslim population.

Unlike northern India where Muslim settlement is associated with military conquests, the Muslim settlement of Konkan took place under peaceful conditions. This has prevented the rise of the usual communal friction, and in Ratnagiri, especially, communal harmony and economic security have given the Muslims a sense of confidence in themselves. This confidence, in its turn, has prevented an excessive concern for Islamization, and the efforts of the various Muslim fundamentalist groups have not met with any remarkable success in this region. This failure of the fundamentalist groups[17] has thwarted the acceptance of orthodox Islamic practices, including the acceptance of *purdah*; as such, the well-known symbol of female seclusion, the *burqa* is conspicious by its absence among the Muslims of this particular region.

It has already been mentioned that the Muslim settlement of Konkan occurred under non-violent conditions. Ironically

17. According to our information such fundamentalist groups as the Tablighi Jammat, and the Jamaat-e-Islami have been successful in spreading their influence in some other parts of Konkan. Another similar group whose influence has been felt in some villages is that of the Wahabis. The present paper, however, is not the proper place to analyze the reasons behind the failure of these groups in that part of Ratnagiri district with which we are concerned.

enough, the first Arab settlers of this region were refugees from their homeland in Iraq, who had fled from the tyranny of Hajaj bin Yusuf As-Saqafi, the then Governor of that place. The absence of a confrontation between the local population and the Arab emigrants perhaps facilitated inter-communal marriages with the local women. There is reason to believe that these occurred on quite a significant scale, especially with women of the Hindu agricultural castes. In addition, the usual voluntary conversions from the depressed Hindu castes have also taken place. These two differing origins have created two separate groups of Kokni Muslims, namely, those who are the products of inter-marriages, and those who are converts. The former are known as the Jamaatis, and the latter as Daldis; the latter, however, resent this term and prefer being called Mahigirs. The Jamaatis are conscious and proud of their Arab ancestry and constitute the elite group. The Mahigirs are the descendants of the Hindu Koli caste of fishermen. Even today they continue their traditional occupation. Their preoccupation with fishing necessitates their staying in villages which are by the side of creeks. The Jamaatis, on the other hand, tend to avoid living in the fishing villages partly because of the foul stench which pervades these villages, and partly because their interest in agriculture, forests, and mango groves are better served in the villages that lie away from the creeks. Thus, there is a virtual segregation of residence with the interior villages having no Mahigirs, and the creek villages having mostly Mahigirs. (In terms of Hindu-Muslim composition, the villages of Ratnagiri reveal more joint residence, than in terms of Jamaati-Mahigirs.) This residential segregation in turn restricts the interaction between the two groups to a bare minimum and, therefore, the observation and study of a caste-like situation between the two groups is not easily possible. The Jamaatis and the Mahigirs share certain socio-cultural traits, speak the same dialect, and belong to the Shafi sect of Sunni Muslims. Nevertheless, there is considerable social distance between the two and endogamy is strictly practised.

Apart from these two groups, who constitute the Kokni Muslim category, there are two other groups of Muslims who are to be found in this region, namely, the Dakhnis and the Khojas and Memons. Neither of these are native to Konkan, nor do they share the sub-cultural patterns of the Kokni Muslims. The Dakhnis are an Urdu-speaking group who have come into Konkan mostly from Bijapur. They belong to the Hanafi sect (as do most Indian Sunni Muslims). The Khojas and Memons are trading communities, originally from Gujarat, and their number is almost insignificant in the region.

Of the groups identified above, our interest is primarily in the Jamaatis. The peculiar occupational structure of the men in this group plus the non-observance of *purdah* by the Jamaati women have had an interesting repercussion on the status of women in this group. We now proceed to an examination of this situation.

The Jamaati Women

It should first of all be noted that the Jamaati households in the villages under reference tend to consist largely of old and retired men, women and children. Adult males who are of an employable age are, usually, away from their homes. In fact, at least two of the villages we surveyed appeared to be almost bereft of men. The pattern of residence is somewhat fluid in nature and matri-patrilocal residence[18] is to be frequently found, especially in cases of intra-village marriage.

Due to the frequent absence of the males, the *de facto* control over the affairs of the nuclear family is in the hands of women. In families where there happen to be two, three or more adult brothers, efforts are made to schedule vacations so that at any given time one of the brothers is present in the village. However, it is not possible for this individual to singly manage all the affairs of the extended family. Moreover, the recurring substitution of brothers prevents not only continuity but also the assumption of power and authority to any great extent by the males. Such a situation has provided the women an opportunity to take charge of the affairs of the family, and their non-observance of *purdah* has become a facilitating condition.

18. This term has been suggested by Murdock (1966:17) to indicate a residential pattern in which there is matrilocal residence until the birth of the first child; thereafter, there is permanent patrilocal residence. Matri-patrilocal residence is thus a form of transitional residence.

In practical terms, the Jamaati women, in this region, have been saddled with multifarious roles which are well beyond the sphere of the conventional roles normally fulfilled by *purdah*-observing Muslim women. Thus, to begin with, there are the traditional intra-familial roles. In addition, there are such non-conventional roles as marketing and shopping, attending to the out-of-home needs of children, supervising their schooling, social visits, etc., which are generally male responsibilities in traditional Muslim families. But that is not all. Due to the fact that many individuals remit savings from abroad to be invested at home, several Jamaati women have to fulfil some significant non-familial roles. These extend to the supervision of rice fields—especially the supervision of the various farm operations and of the labourers working in these fields. One often sees well-to-do Jamaati women in the fields, in charge of the situation, in these villages. Apart from the rice fields, there is also the investment in jungles and mango *wadis*. Their purchases and sales, as well as the arrangement of contracting the yields of the jungles and the mango groves to interested parties, are also supervised by women. All these responsibilities are discharged with confidence and competence, and, obviously, have to be based upon a good knowledge of market conditions and other business expertise. To facilitate these operations, the concerned women have titles to property and independent bank accounts.

Clearly, all these operations are conducted with sufficient success for the men-folk to have the confidence to trust their women to manage their hard-earned savings. These important economic functions performed by the Jamaati women, help the upward mobility of the Jamaati families. Moreover, the success of some women acts as an incentive for the men to earn more and send their savings back home for further investments. Obviously, the observance of the normative seclusion and isolation would, in the first place, have made it difficult (in the absence of men) to carry on normal activities, and, in the second place, would also have threatened the economic stability and prosperity of several families.

The assumption of so many extra-familial roles has pushed these women into a situation where they cannot relinquish their responsibilities even when their menfolk return home on vacation, for, such husbands, or brothers, are only transients in the village; often, they tend to be in a relaxed mood and are not much inclined to interfere, especially when things are proceeding smoothly. This observation will indicate to an extent that the role structure of these families continues to be of the segregated type, and that there is neither much mutuality nor joint endeavour in the performance of the various roles. But, sociologically, it is significant to note that this segregation operates in favour of the women, in as much as the inequality of weightage in the role structure is not in favour of the males. It is also of interest to note that, notwithstanding the dominance secured by the woman in terms of some very important responsibilities, the Jamaati family continues to remain, in the ultimate analysis, patrilocal, patrilineal and patriarchal—though of course, the last of these components, in contrast to the usual *purdah*-observing family, is considerably diluted. To that extent the Jamaati women enjoy a higher status than do most Muslim women in India.

The foregoing description will have indicated that the capacity to fulfil the multifarious roles could have been possible only through an appropriate process of socialization, which allows adequate freedom to young and adolescent girls to grow up in relatively unrestricted and uninhibited psycho-social and socio-cultural environments. Accordingly, it was observed that the usual Muslim practice of excessive protection and sheltering of young and teenage girls was not in force to any noticeable extent. Unlike the situation in traditional Muslim communities, hetero-sexual interaction is not taboo among adolescents of school-going age. Girls were found to attend co-educational institutions and study along with boys till the stage of high school graduation. Where Urdu medium high schools are non-existent, the Muslim girls attend Marathi medium schools. In tune with the general atmosphere, female students even in the upper classes study under teachers of both sexes. Moreover, at least one instance was found where Muslim girls were found to be participating in dances and other bisexual stage performances in the school. In one of the high schools a large sized photo of a woman donor was prominently displayed on the wall of the school's office. (Even though they are located in villages, the Muslim schools are distinguished by the lack of the *madrassah* atmosphere and, instead, exhibit distinct signs of a modernistic educational approach).[19] Thus, the puritanical flavour of orthodox Muslim cultural life is not visible in the socialization of young and adolescent girls. To those familiar with the socialization of females in a *purdah* set-up, the facts just stated will seem to suggest an almost revolutionary situation.

Thanks to their hetrosexual experiences in their formative years these girls eventually grow into women who are quite confident of themselves in their relations with males, even if they happen to be strangers. Much to our surprise, our data collection was facilitated rather than hindered by the women—many of whom showed a great deal of co-operation. Some female respondents even went to the extent of inviting the junior author to their homes (when he approached them for some time to reply to his queries), though there were no male members present in the house at that time. It need hardly be mentioned here that generally in a Muslim set-up it would be impossible for a male investigator—and difficult, perhaps, even for a female investigator—to have access to women for an interview under such circumstances.[20] Indeed, so complete is the lack of their inhibition that these women even get themselves medically examined by male doctors. Seen in the context of Muslim conservatism, this departure from traditional mores is indeed unique. Relevant in this connection are Hanna Papanek's observations: 'In Pakistan, most women who use Western-trained doctors at all expect to go to 'lady-doctor', and if none is available, social pressure may force women to forego medical care' (1964:162).

It may be added that these women interact freely not only in their homes or their villages but they are quite confident of themselves even outside their villages. Thus, they move freely from one village to another and go shopping and marketing, as well as to restaurants and movies, in the nearby towns without the protective mantle of their menfolk. In fact, whenever

19. To our great surprise, in one of the village schools we came across, a mosque had been converted into a laboratory.

20. For an interesting and insightful account of data-collection in a *purdah* society see Papanek (1964).

necessary they stay overnight in hotels (in the towns) even though they are unaccompanied by men. (To be sure, this is also a favourable comment upon the conditions existing in Ratnagiri district.) Much of this style of life, it will be realized, is possible due to the flow of funds from their generous husbands and/or other male relatives. These surplus funds, and their free mobility, enable the Jamaati women to forget the dullness of their village life in the cinemas and theatres located in the towns and so they patronize them frequently. In addition to the Hindi films, Marathi dramas are also liked. One of our visits to a popular Marathi stage-play revealed that it was Muslim women who constituted the majority in the audience. The idols of the Hindi screen are a popular topic of evening gossip (which can easily be overheard by casual passers-by because the women sit outside their homes on the door-steps, and exchange pleasantries with neighbours). Freedom and money to spare have also made the Jamaati women conscious of the latest fashions as well as personal beautification. By village standard, their level of sophistication is somewhat unusual. Gold ornaments too are immensely popular.

The non-observance of *purdah* obviously facilitated the observations we have just made. But what needs to be mentioned here is that in traditional Muslim communities one sees no such public display of fashions and personal adornments since the woman is encased in a *burqa*. It is unthinkable for her to open herself to public gaze even in the plainest of clothing. All her adornment and beautification is for the private pleasure of her husband and lord only. In the context of this conservatism, the Jamaati woman has achieved tremendous emancipation.

Let us now relate how the non-observance of *purdah* has helped these women to forge a unity and function as a pressure group. It is a truism that individuals and groups who are unprivileged and exploited are unable to ameliorate their condition through joint action, since such action is prohibited by their seclusion and isolation. Seclusion and isolation deny unprivileged individuals and groups the opportunity to forge a unity, as well as the opportunity to protest. It is not surprising, therefore, that one never hears of any feminist movements among *purdah* women. Since they cannot come together, they cannot struggle together. In the course of our fieldwork, however, we were informed of an incident which illustrates how the absence of *purdah* can make a dramatic difference to 'woman power'.

The women of village K, which is a very affluent Jamaati village, frequently go to a nearby town for their shopping and recreational needs. The town's shopkeepers are much benefited by this clientele. Sometime prior to our visit to K, it appears that some eve-teasers of the town harassed some of the K women when they had gone to see a movie there. The women of K retaliated by completely boycotting the cinemas and other commercial establishments of the town. The impact of this withdrawal of patronage was so great that within a short period a delegation of businessmen from the town came to the village to apologize, and gave an undertaking that such untoward actions would not occur in the future. Since the tendering of this apology and guarantee no further trouble, we were informed, has taken place.[21]

It may be pointed out here that the Jamaati women do not utilize their freedom merely for their personal enjoyment. In some villages they were found to be active in Mahila Mandals, and other women organizations. Often the initiative for forming such organizations has come from the women themselves. We encountered at least one instance where a Muslim woman was the *pradhan* of the village, and in quite a few cases they were office-bearers in the Mahila Mandals (Incidentally, Muslim women were found to be active in these organizations even in those villages where Hindus were in a majority).

Such participation obviously brings the Hindus and Muslims together in these villages. It is perhaps worth remarking here that stronger bonds between members of a village community are established when the women get to know one another, and co-operate and participate in common activities, than when only men interact with one another. Thus, in a latent way the absence of seclusion can be highly functional for the integration of those village communities where both Hindus and Muslims live.

We now turn towards a very crucial aspect concerning the status of woman, namely, the nature of husband-wife relation-

21. This story was verified by the inhabitants of the town concerned.

ships. *Purdah* has been a deterrent in the emergence of egalitarianism in this relationship, and thanks to it the traditional Muslim husband has been a strongly authoritarian figure. Among the Jamaatis, however, there is an absence of authoritarianism and harshness in the relationships between the spouses. Indeed, these were obseved to be both democratic as well as cordial. There exists a spirit of companionship between the spouses, and one cannot but note the tendency of Jammati couples to walk side by side rather than for the husband to keep himself a few steps ahead of the wife. (Indeed, such equality is not to be found in many couples even in an urban centre like Delhi). Unlike the segregated recreational patterns that are chearacteristic of *purdah* families, the Jamaati women tend to withdraw themselves from their peer-groups when their husbands are at home and spend their recreation time in the company of their spouses. The couple frequent movies and restaurants and appear to enjoy each other's company. In these outings children may or may not accompany the parents.

In the light of what has been said earlier concerning the absence of many males from their homes, it is not difficult to realize that equalitarianism and cordiality between the Jamaati husbands and wives are facilitated by the fact that many couples are together only for a short and transitory period which leaves the two with little time or inclination to stress their respective rights and privileges, or points of difference. It is in the nature of this transitoriness for the partners—when they get the opportunity to come together—to be in a holiday (if not a honeymoon) mood; in this mood each is keen to be nice and pleasant to the other. There is also the knowledge that separation is round the corner. Sometime is, of course, also spent in discussing pragmatic matters concerning various family affairs. These have eventually to be looked after by the wife, hence her opinions and views have to be given due respect and attention. All these factors, then, have made male authoritarianism incongruent in this particular setting. Of course, not each and every Jamaati husband is away from the family. Thus, in these families, atleast, the potential for the domination of females by males is present. However, what must be realized is that the Jamaatis have developed a sub-culture which stresses norms of male-female equality and the tender treatment of the weaker sex. As a result, therefore, even the husbands who stay back are not very different from those who do not.

Since both the existential conditions as well as the norms of family life are such as to minimize marital tensions and conflicts, there is an exceedingly low incidence of divorce and polygyny. (Some of our female respondents good-humourdly pointed out that their menfolk had little use for an additional wife under the circumstances.) Even the barrenness of a wife seldom leads to remarriage, and, according to one informant, a second wife is taken only where the barren wife herself initiates proceedings for the second marriage. Should this information be correct, then, this condition implies a very favourable position for the women. (Incidentally, it was also observed that parents of unmarried girls were not unduly worried over the marriage prospects of their daughters; they seemed to be remarkably relaxed about the whole matter. But the girls themselves were quite anxious and even upset.)

The marriage customs observed also indicate the favourable position of women. For example, in some of the villages of this region the groom's family is required to pay a specific amount of money, known as the *haq-dana*[22] to the *jamaat*[23] of the girl's village. Then, again, in a number of villages the marriage occurs not at the girl's house or village but at the boy's place. Accordingly, when the two parties belong to different villages, it is the girl's party that goes in a *baraat* to the boy's village. The *baraatis* are lodged in a house, the

22. The *haq-dana* is a specified amount of money which the groom's father has to pay to his *jamaat* at the time of marriage—a sort of matrimony tax. However, in certain villages custom requires that the groom's father should pay this amount to the girl's *jamaat* also.

23. The '*jamaat*' may be translated as the council or *panchayat* to which the Kokni families belong. The word 'Jamaati', however, has nothing to do with the word "*jamaat*"—even though there appears to be an etymological affinity between the two. The Mahigirs too have their own *jamaats*. Where a village is small, there is only one *jamaat* for all the residents, but where the population is large, *jamaats* are organised on a locality basis. Mahigirs and Jamaatis never have a common *jamaat*. Like a *panchayat*, the *jamaat* is the organ for exercising social control. But it is not concerned with mere social control, and performs several welfare functions as well. Its president is held in great respect by all the people.

janosa, which is specially reserved for them, and are given a right royal treatment. In at least one village it was observed that immediately after the *nikah*, the groom rushed towards his female relatives and warmly shook hands with them. Finally, mention must be made of the *Paanch Maang, Das Maang* custom. According to this custom, immediately after the marriage the bride's party brings the groom to their village where he stays for five days. On the fifth day some of his relatives come to take the couple back to the groom's village. After a few days there, the couple again returns to the girl's house and on this occasion stays there for ten days. Again the *mangaari* come and take the couple back. Thereafter, patrilocal residence is finally established. (These days, of course, some modifications have arisen; thus, the periods of stay at the bride's village have been curtailed.) While a fuller analysis of these, and other customs, must wait another opportunity, it would be adequate to simply point out here that these customs are indicators of the fact that the women of this region enjoy a good position.

Having described the freedom and the favourable position enjoyed by the jamaati women in the villages of this region, we must now clarify that given all these privileges and independence life is not completely idyllic for them. Our discussion, thus far, may perhaps have already indicated that linked with their somewhat unique position is a certain amount of loneliness. This causes both physical and psychological strains. It has already been seen that, in addition to the conventional responsibilities, there are several extra-familial roles which these women have to discharge all by themselves. Obviously this is physically taxing. But physical strain is only a part of their problem; the prolonged absence of their menfolk affects them psychologically as well. The behavioural manifestation of this is seen in the fact that Jamaati women exhibit an excessive concern for health. They go rushing to doctors even for minor complaints. This widespread hypochondria, it may reasonably be hypothesized, is due to the psychological insecurities generated by their loneliness. Also, the long absences of the menfolk are a source of concern, for, in moments of crises, help can neither be received nor rendered. A certain amount of frustration must also be caused by the unfulfilment of normal sex urges and other emotional needs. One adjustment mechanism against insecurities and frustrations, which is popular among traditional Indian women, is that of *mannats*. In view of the freedom and independence enjoyed by the Jamaati women, it would, logically, appear that they should have been relatively free from dependence upon *mannats*. But such is not the case. Visits to *dargahs* and reverence for *taziyas* are an important part of their life. Thus, while enjoying a great deal of freedom from male dominance, these women have not been able to achieve complete tranquility of the mind. The ironical fact that strikes the observer here is that, whereas women who are unhappy are generally so due to the presence of their dominating husbands, these women are victims of mental strain because of the absence of their men.

One latent effect of absentee husbands is that the Jamaati women do not enjoy the right of inheritance as daughters, even though this privilege has been granted to them by their religion. The reason for this anomaly is that in several cases (due to the absence of their husbands) the parents continue to look after their daughters even after they have been married. As a compensation for this prolonged support, daughters are denied a share in parental property. But while women lose property rights in their family of orientation, they often become property owners in their family of procreation. One of our interesting discoveries in this connection was that most of our respondents (many of whom were educated) were unaware of the religious prescription in this matter. (There was, unfortunately, no way in which we could find out whether they were truly ignorant or feigned ignorance.) When these individuals were drawn into a discussion on the issue, they stoutly defended the non-granting of inheritance rights to daughters.[24] To these people, the pragmatic aspects of the matter outweighed

24. The observations of Sterling (1966:123) in a Turkish village are of relevance here. According to Sterling, the inheritance claims of daughters are generally admitted to be formally valid, *but are by no means always accepted or enforced* (emphasis added). He adds: 'The fact that their sisters are either married and out of the household, or else very young, puts the adult brothers in a strong position. They can and do frequently ignore their sister's rights.'

religious injunction. This situation has two important implications. First, that notwithstanding religious laws, Muslim communities which have landed wealth will tend to deny inheritance to daughters, and, second, existential conditions may force Muslim communities to give more importance to certain pragmatic considerations even if this involves a violation of religious laws or principles. This need not always be true, but nor will it be true that religious laws and injunctions are always invoilable as some apologists and opponents of Islam would have us believe.

Two final comments. While it has been shown that Jamaati women enjoy considerable independence, yet there is one notable restriction on their freedom, namely, the restriction of endogamy. Jamaati girls are not free to marry young men belonging to the other Muslim groups that live in these villages. In the course of our fieldwork, our respondents and informants could recall just one case where a Jamaati girl had married a Mahigir boy. The alliance, however, had been stoutly opposed by parents and relatives on both sides, and the young couple had to flee to Poona in order to get married and could never return to their village. It may, however, be mentioned here that the Mahigiri youths whom we questioned also revealed no desire to marry Jamaati girls. This resistance on the part of the latter has automatically solved what might otherwise have become a matter of great tension and conflict between the two groups. Nevertheless, at a purely theoretical level of abstraction, it may be said that the endogamy restriction is a social fetter that restricts the Jamaati woman's freedom. The other limitation pertains to higher education. Notwithstanding the non-observance of *purdah* and freedom of movement enjoyed by the Jamaati girls, higher education, that is, college level education, is not much in vogue. Indeed, even teacher education, which is becoming quite popular among Muslim girls in India, is not much in evidence in this region. One reason for this negligence is that Ratnagiri district has no more than a couple of colleges, and these are located in far-flung towns. And the Jamaati girls do not make the effort to go some distance or to take up residence in hostels. In fact, if a high school is not easily accessible, high school education too is not considered worth the trouble. This lack of emphasis on education, let it be noted, is actually due to the low priority given to education in general rather than to any strictures on female education as such. This is indicated by the fact that the Jamaatis do not even place much importance on educating their boys. However, the denial of higher education to these women appears to be doubly unfortunate in as much as the Jamaati women are favourably placed to benefit from it. But by neglecting higher education these women have not achieved their potential, both at the personal as well as the group level.

Conclusion

With the above description of the position of the Jamaati women in a particular region of Konkan,[25] we have accomplished the basic purpose of the paper. Also, we indicated how their non-observance of *purdah* has assisted this group of Muslim women to gain independence and a generally favourable status. We have not maintained, as was pointed out at the very outset of the paper, the absence of *purdah* to be a causative factor. The social phenomena are far too complex to allow the establishment of causal links. Moreover, our study had limitations which precluded the search for any causal connections; nor was such a search included in our aims.

All the same, one intriguing question that does suggest itself in the present context is whether the favourable position of the Jamaati women is due to their non-observance of *purdah* or whether it is the result of a peculiar set of regional existential circumstances. We feel that this is not an either-or situation; rather, both factors, in association with each other, have helped the women concerned.

At the same time, however, it would be worth mentioning that the women of another Muslim group, namely, the Dakhnis, observe *purdah* even though they live in these very villages. Why should this be so? One possible answer is that the Dakhni men

25. It may be pointed out here that the Jamaatis are not confined to the region with which we have been concerned in this paper. They are to be found all over Konkan, but it is only in one part of Ratnagiri district that their women are non-observers of *purdah*. Mahigir women, incidentally, also do not observe *purdah*.

generally stay home and do not migrate from their villages in search of a livelihood, as a result of which it is not necessary for the Dakhni women to be out of *purdah*. This answer, however, does not appear to be entirely satisfactory in as much as the harshness of economic conditions impinges equally upon both the Jamaatis and the Dakhnis. Why then should the latter group continue to tolerate these conditions and not try to improve its position in the way in which the Jamaatis have done? May it not be postulated, then, that the Jamaati men have been encouraged to go out precisely because they could depend on their women to manage the various intra- and extra-familial matters? In any case, it is clear that those groups and communities whose women are not disabled by seclusion and isolation are more favourably placed to improve their condition than groups whose women are in a *purdah*.

Finally, it is hoped that the fact has not escaped attention that the non-observance of *purdah* and the independence of the Jamaati women is not a case of lower class behaviour. Elsewhere in this paper it has been pointed out that lower class Muslim women, due to the exigencies of their improverished condition, tend to be non-*purdah* observing. Our Jamaati women are evidently not in this situation. Nor have they shown any inclination to secure respectability in the orthodox Islamic framework by resorting to seclusion; indeed, these Jamaatis have resisted the Islamization efforts of fundamentalist groups. At the same time, however, the non-observance of *purdah* in this case has not been the result of either Westernization or modern higher education. Thus, seen from various perspectives, the women we have considered in this paper represent a truely deviant case among Indian Muslims.

Bibliography

Blitsten, D.R. (1963), *The World of Family*, New York, Random House.

Fletcher, R. (1962), *Britain in the Sixties: The Family and Marriage*, London, Penguin.

Hobhouse, L.T. (1951), *Morals in Evolution: A Study in Comparative Ethics*, London, Chapman & Hall.

Kapadia, K.M. (1959), *Marriage and Family in India*, London, Oxford University Press.

Levy, R.(1957), *The Social Structure of Islam*, Cambridge, Cambridge University Press.

Mehta, R. (1975), 'From Purdah to Modernity' report of speech in *Times of India*, Delhi, August 23.

Murdock, G.P. (1966), *Social Structure*, New York, The Free Press.

Papanek, H. (1964), 'The Woman Field Worker in a Purdah Society', *Human Organisation*, 23, 160-163.

Rossi, A.S. (1964), 'Equality Between the Sexes: An Immodest Proposal', *Daedalus*, 93.

Singh, K. (1975), 'My India, My Mexico', Bombay, *The Illustrated Weekly of India*, Bombay. August 3.

Srinivas, M.N. (1975) 'Status of Women in India', *Times of India*, Bombay, April 18 & 19.

Sterling, P. (1966), *A Turkish Village*, New York, John Wiley & Sons.

Timasheff, N. (1967), *Sociological Theory*, New York, Random House.

Vreede-de-steurs, C. (1968), *Parda: A Study of Muslim Women's Life in Northern India*, Essen, Van Gorkum & Co.

10

Kinship and Marriage among the Meos of Rajasthan

Partap C. Aggarwal

The Meos are a Muslim caste[1] who occupy an area popularly known as Mewat straddling the border of Rajasthan and Haryana. Computations based on the 1961 Census reveal their total number to be about 350,000. The 1901 Census, which lists the Meos separately, puts their population at 335,164. The smallness of the increase in their number over sixty years can be explained by some loss in 1947 through migration to Pakistan.

The name Mewat is believed by the inhabitants of the area to have been derived from the Meos who constitute the largest single ethnic group in the area, and who are economically and

1. Many British officers claim that the Meos are a tribal group. Bannerman observes, for instance, that '. . . Colonel Porolett in his Gazetteer of Alwar 'writes, 'the similarity between the word Meo and Mina suggests that the former may be a contraction of the latter. Several of the respective clans are identical in name (Senegal, Nai, Dulot, Pundlot, Dingal, Balot); and a story told of Daria Meo and his lady-love Sisbadani Mini seems to show that they formerly inter-married. In Bullanshar a caste called Meo-Minas is spoken of in the Settlement Report, which would seem further to connect the two." However, it is possible that apostate Rajputs and bastard sons of Rajputs founded many of the clans as the legend tells' (1902:156). Risley, on the other hand, characterizes the Meos as an 'example of a tribe turned caste' (1915:76). The Meos refer to themselves as a *jati*, observe the prevailing rules governing inter-caste conduct, and jealously guard their high rank (see Aggarwal, 1973:73-88).

politically dominant. Mewat is not a recognized administrative unit; consequently, it does not appear on any of the available maps. It includes parts of the Gurgaon district of Haryana and two neighbouring districts of Rajasthan (Alwar & Bharatpur). The total area of Mewat is roughly 3,090 square miles. It is a rugged area with the main range of the Aravalli hills lying across the middle. Arable land suitable for agriculture is to be found in narrow valleys which are dotted with more than 2,000 Mewati villages ranging in population from 250 to 5,000.

The Meos have lived in Mewat for a long time, for thousand of years according to popular legends. Historical evidence, however, goes back only to the middle of the thirteenth century A.D. when a Mewati king named Rana Ranpal ruled from his capital called Hindwari-Indwar. The ruins of this city can still be seen in the heart of Mewat. Around 1398, mention is made of a Mewati prince by the name of Bahadur Nahar, who also ruled from the same capital. Finally, in the beginning of the sixteenth century we hear of Hasan Khan Mewati who fought against Babur on the side of Rana Sanga in the famous battle of Sikri.

The Meos claim Rajput ancestry but this claim is largely unsubstantiated. The Meos have been economically and politically dominant in Mewat, being, in fact, the rulers for a long time. Dominant ruling groups are known to have elevated themselves in the caste hierarchy (see Sinha, 1962; Shah, 1964: 95; and Srinivas, 1968:190). Given their position in Mewat, the Meos would undoubtedly have had a good chance of success. In any case, the Meo claim to Rajput descent is rarely, if ever, disputed by non-Meos. It was only on a few occasions that I heard some Thakurs violently contesting the Meo claim. I was told by my Meo informants that these types of protests have begun to be made only in the last fifteen years. Apparently, and quite understandably, they coincide with the decline in the power of the Meos. It, however, seems reasonably safe to assume that the Meos were converted to Islam from Hinduism—the predominance of Hindu rituals in their ceremonies, their Hindu names, the magnitude of their inter-dependence with the Hindu caste structure, and some historical evidence, all tend to support this belief. The fact that a vast majority of Indian Muslims are converts from Hinduism further strengthens the plausibility of this assumption.

It is widely alleged in Mewat that the Meos used to be cattle raiders. The Meos themselves take pride in this allegation because it indicates their strength and prowess as a group. However, nowadays the Meos are predominantly agriculturists. There is some evidence in the form of abandoned police stations which indicates that the British had to make extra efforts to subdue the Meos. But the available evidence does not provide a clear picture of the past avocations of the Meos and we can be sure that for several centuries, whatever else they may have done in their spare time, the major occupation of the Meos has been agriculture.

At the time of India's partition, the Meos had the traumatic experience of being identified as Muslims and were pressured into leaving for Pakistan. It is alleged that three major factors led to a polarization between the Hindus and the Muslims in Mewat. First, at least two important Meo leaders, Sardar Muhammad of Gurgaon and Sapat Khan of Bharatpur, joined the Mulsim League and favoured the formation of Pakistan. Sapat Khan openly agitated for the inclusion of Mewat in Pakistan. A second factor was the communalist stance of the Maharajas of Alwar and Bharatpur, both of whom were Hindus. They were influenced by the RSS and the idea of a Hindu state. Thirdly, the influx of Hindu refugees from Pakistan, some with visible injuries on their bodies, incited the local Hindu population. As a result of all these factors, riots broke out in Mewat and were made worse by the support provided by the police and the militia of the states. Recognizing that the Meos were only partially Muslim in view of their cultural practices, some attempts were made to reconvert them to Hinduism *en masse*. *Shuddhi* camps were organized and a number of Meos were hurriedly processed. Although the Meos did not oppose this, their passivity did not help. Almost all the Meos of Alwar and Bharatpur were forced to migrate to Gurgaon. There they waited for a few months for the return of normalcy. At this time, some Meos decided to migrate to Pakistan. It is estimated that about twenty per cent of the Meo population emigrated. A few months later peace was restored and the Meos of Alwar and Bharatpur returned to their villages and were resettled. As far as can be ascertained, the Meos are living a normal life today in their original homes. Those who were converted to Hinduism have again become Muslims and they now live more or less the life they lived before partition. The emigrants have been replaced by refugees from Pakistan. It must be pointed out that the Meos have shown a tendency to abandon their Hindu customs and replace them by corresponding Muslim practices since 1947 (see Aggarwal, 1969, 1971).

This essay is concerned with a discussion of kinship and marriage among the Meos. This discussion is based on data drawn from a detailed study of a single Meo village[2] called Chavandi Kalan in the Alwar district of Rajasthan, situated in the geographical heart of Mewat.

The Pals, Gotras and Pattis

The entire Meo caste is subdivided into a large number of exogamous groups. Members of each of these groups claim common ancestry and therefore have a close genetic relationship. Consequently, marriage between a man and a woman belonging to the same group is considered incestuous. These groups are of two types: the *pals* and the *gotras*. In all there are thirteen *pals* and over sixty-seven *gotras*.

The Pals

In addition to being exogamous social divisions, the *pals* are also territorial units. The entire territory of Mewat is divided into twelve *pals* and one *pallakra*. In fact, there is no real difference between the *pals* on the one hand and the *pallakra* on the other. Nevertheless, the distinctive name of the latter with the suffix 'ra' connotes a slightly inferior status. Indeed, members of the *pallakra* are often teased about the fact that their territory is not called a *pal*. There is no record as to when and why Mewat was divided into *pals*. According to legend, however, the various *pals* were demarcated in Akbar's time (A.D. 1556-1605) in order to quell feuds between various Meo

2. All Meos live in villages. A few individuals who migrate to the cities in search of employment or for other reasons tend to maintain contact with their families in the village and eventually retire there. Meo lawyers and politicians usually live in towns within Mewat and their families rarely accompany them there. Hence, it is meaningful to discuss Meo kinship and marriage by reference to a single village.

clans. It seems more likely that the *pals* correspond to the administrative divisions which existed at the time when Mewat was politically autonomous. In fact, even today each *pal* has a hereditary leader known as the *Chaudhari*. He is usually an influential and wealthy man who presides over the *pal* council and is given a tribute when he attends social functions such as important festivals and marriages. However, the *pal* divisions are no longer significant in any sense. After the establishment of British rule in the latter part of the nineteenth century, new administrative divisions were created which completely ignored the *pal* boundaries. In fact, Mewat itself was divided and merged into two princely states and a British Indian province.

Yet, knowledgeable Meos remember the *pal* boundries today, several decades after they were erased. By consulting a few old men I was able to draw the *pal* lines on a map of Mewat. Although it cannot be said that these lines are accurate, the agreement between various informants is quite remarkable. Many Meos claim even to know the number of villages in each *pal* but the figures are legendary and unreliable. However, these figures are still frequently used by the Meos. For instance, at an elaborate funeral feast a person may invite all the '757 villages' of his *pal*.

Pals, including the *pallakra*, are clustered into four groups, each of which bears the name of a Rajput *vamsh* (clan). It is claimed that the members of the *pals* have descended from the Rajput clans with whose names they are associated. Each *pal* is subdivided into *thamas*. In most cases the *thama* divisions are associated with the sons of the founder of the *pal* to which they belong.

The Gotras

In each *pal* its own members predominate, but often due to migration there are members of other *pals* living within its territory. Also, in each *pal* there live a number of other Meos who are called the *nepalia*, i.e., those who have no *pal*. The *nepalia* belong to one of the sixty-seven or more *gotra* divisions. The exact number of *gotras* is not known. During the course of my research, I was able to collect names of eighty *gotras*, but only sixty-seven of them could be verified.

The *gotras* are distinguished from the *pals* not only by their lack of territorial association, but also by their smaller size. In other words, the *gotras* are, as a rule, smaller than the *pals*, except perhaps for the three very small *pals*. The function of the *gotras* and the *pals* is almost identical. Both are exogamous divisions and help to regulate marriage among the Meos.

The Pattis

The *pals* and *gotras* are larger groupings, based on territorial association and the fiction of common descent. Each Meo village also reveals the presence of smaller kinship groups called *pattis*. Thus, Çhavandi Kalan, the studied village, is divided into six *pattis*. According to legend, the members of each *patti* are descended from one of the six sons of the founder of the village. Each *patti* is, therefore, known by the name of its ancestor who, of course, was a Meo. Apparently the dominant position of the Meos in the village is emphasized. Members of non-Meo castes living in each *patti* do recognize their special bond with the Meos of the *patti*, but they also admit their subordinate position.

The myth of the origin of the *pattis* implies a patrilineal relationship between the members. But this is not true, for all members of a *patti* are not always related through the male line. Some families are descendants of female relatives who had set up a matrilocal residence in a *patti* because of special circumstances. Although the kinship bond between the members of a *patti* is not always close, a large number of families in each *patti* do tend to be related quite closely. Furthermore, there has always been a political bond between the members of a *patti* which was recognized by the government even before Independence. For instance, a prominent Meo male of each *patti* was recognized as the *Namberdar*. This position was hereditary and it changed very rarely, only when the family lost its economic and political influence. The *Namberdar* was responsible for tax collection on behalf of the government and was paid a small commission as a reward for his services.

The number of households in each *patti* varies widely. The biggest *patti* has 108 members and the smallest only nine. All the households are not always situated close to each other. It is believed that originally they were located in the same vicinity but individual households later shifted to new sites. For example, a majority of the members of a large *patti* recently shifted to a hamlet outside the village. In any case, the importance of the *patti* divisions is now diminishing. The Indian government no longer recognizes them nor are the services of the *Namberdars* as tax collectors in demand. The *patti* affiliation of families and individuals is still remembered, however. Nowadays, *patti* solidarity is often invoked in political contests during elections.

Family and Kinship

The basic corporate unit among the Meos is referred to as a *ghar*, which is best translated into English as 'household'. It consists of relatives who live in one house, cook on a common *choolah* (hearth), and own property jointly. Most households are small, consisting of four to eight members—but their membership can be as large as twenty-five, or as small as one. One person living alone, particularly when he owns property, is considered to constitute a household. However, if that member happens to be a woman it is not recognized as a household. In recent years, because of the fear of loss of land, there has been a tendency for the larger households to break up into small nuclear family units.

Patrilocal residence is preferred by the Meos for all newly married couples. The bride comes to live in the groom's parental home where she is given a separate room for privacy but shares the hearth with her mother-in-law. She is regarded as a new member of the family and is expected to participate in the family activities and to share the corporate property and resources. A bride who tries to establish a special claim to things belonging to the household is considered brash.

Exceptions to the rule of patrilocal residence are rare, but they do occur. For example, matrilocal residence may be arranged in a very special set of circumstances. A man lacking male heirs may invite a daughter and her conjugal family to establish residence in his home. In such cases a son of the daughter is usually adopted by the grandfather and is made the legal heir to his property. Normally, the adoption of a daughter's son requires the consent of one's brothers and patrilineal ocusins, something that is difficult to obtain. Hence, matrilocal residence is attempted only when there is little danger of a conflict over inheritance. In any case, even if a daughter's son is adopted by the grandfather, the former retains the *gotra* of his father.

The joint (or extended) family is the ideal type among the Meos. In other words, it is considered desirable and prestigious for a man to have his sons and their families living in his household. This prevents a division of land and enhances the economic and political influence of the family in the village. Most Meo joint families are lineal in structure, i.e., a man and his wife living with their sons and their families. Collateral joints families, i.e., several brothers and their families living together, also occur, but they are less common. Married brothers without the unifying presence of their father are usually unable to stick together. A mother does not seem to have the same uniting influence over her sons as the father.

Decent is traced among Meos through the male line, i.e., through one's father, father's father, and so on. Only the males occupy positions of a permanent nature in the family. The place of women in their families of procreation is at best tenuous. The terms of reference—and often even the term of address—used for women is that of their native village and their parent's *gotra* or *pal*, such as 'the one belonging to such-and-such a *gotra* or village'. In other words, a woman retains her parental *gotra* even after marriage. Her affiliation with her husband's family is enhanced if and when she bears sons. Then she is referred to as 'the mother of so-and-so'. Unless a widow marries one of her husband's brothers, or has had sons, she often must return to her parents' home. Throughout her life a married Meo woman frequently visits her natal family and retains close contact with her brothers and nephews. Whenever she visits her parents, she utters conventional complaints in a patterned, singsong style and weeps on her mother's shoulder. The words of these stylized laments remind the parents that they are neglecting their daughter by not inviting her frequently enough. A daughter visiting her parents, or a sister her brothers, is supposed to express these mock complaints even though she may have visited them quite often.

Like descent, property is inherited through the male line among the Meos. A man inherits his father's property and bequeathes it to his sons. Brothers have an equal claim to their father's property regardless of their order of birth. Also, a father is believed to be an equal partner with his sons. Therefore, if family property has to be divided between a father and his sons, each gets an equal share. When a division occurs in a large joint family with three generations of relatives, the senior most male and his sons share the property equally. Each of the sons would when divide his share with his sons. This kind of division is very rare indeed, but, if it does occur, the head of the family is free to bequeath his share to one or more of his sons and grandsons. Meo females do not have any claim to their fathers' property. They have the right of maintenance in their families both before and after marriage. Even if a man has no male heirs his daughters do not have the right of inheritance—his brothers and their male descendants can claim his property. Theoretically, a man can make a specific will to transfer his property to his daughter or daughters, but this is considered improper. A woman who tries to press a claim to her father's property, even on the basis of his will, invites the hostility of her consanguineal relatives. In recent years there have been cases of married women claiming inheritance rights to their father's property. In each case the prevailing opinion among the villagers was against them. However, the statutory law in India (the Hindu Code) now recognizes that women have equal rights with their brothers in their father's property. The Muslim cannon law makes a similar provision. Recently, a Meo woman involved in a dispute over inheritance had to take the matter to a court, an act that generated a great deal of hostility against her in the village. Hence, even today Meos avoid such disputes. The only property that a woman has sole claim to is the gifts which she may have received from her father or brothers.

Children are highly valued by both men and women. Although more outward happiness in expressed at the birth of a son, female children are valued more highly for the labour they can contribute to the family. Even when quite young they help in the household work and look after younger siblings, while the mothers go out to work in the fields. As they grow older their participation in the house and farmwork increases. Finally, when they marry, their parents receive a bride-price which, in many cases, is quite substantial.

There is a fairly clear division of labour among the members of a household. The women are responsible for all the housework, including cooking, bringing water from the village well, cleaning, and other domestic tasks. Children are entirely their responsibility, although older female children help in looking after their younger siblings. Women also take complete care of the domestic animals, except for grazing them which is done by adolescent boys. Men may sometimes help with the chopping of fodder which women bring from the fields, but they do this on a voluntary basis. Agricultural work, especially ploughing and operating the *charas* (a device for lifting water out of a well), is considered the domain of the males. However, women help with the planting, weeding, harvesting, and other operations which require a great deal of labour. Men have sole charge of transport work involving the use of bullock carts and camels. They cart manure to the fields, harvested crops to the threshing ground, and grain to the market town.

Unlike both the Muslim and Hindu high castes, Meo women do not observe *purdah* (seclusion). According to the Meos, *purdah* is not practical for their women because they have to work in the fields. In recent years some non-Meo Muslim families living in Mewat have adopted *purdah* and have tried to influence the Meos. But the Meos never responded favourably to the practice of seclusion. A Meo informant said: 'We cannot afford *purdah*. Our women do a great deal of work outside the house. We could hardly survive if our women were to be restricted to the house.' Meo women, however, do avoid certain relatives in their families, especially male affinals who are older than their husbands. In the presence of these relatives Meo women cover their faces and avoid any kind of contact with them.

Marriage and Rules of Exogamy

Marriage is considered essential by the Meos for both males and females. There is no Meo female above fifteen in Chavandi Kalan who has not been married at least once. There are a few adult males, however, who are bachelors, but most of them are fairly young and still hope to obtain wives. Those males who get married late do so largely because they cannot afford the bride-price or they suffer from some physical defect such as blindness, a deaf-mute condition, etc. There is only one Meo male in Chavandi Kalan above thirty who is still unmarried and is unlikely to marry. This person was orphaned during partition in 1947, and was unable to obtain any help in obtaining a bride.

Most marriages take place fairly early. Out of 200 married Meos in Chavandi Kalan, 108 were married before they were fifteen years old, and 181 before they attained the age of twenty. It is considered proper for wives to be younger than their husbands; consequently, girls marry at a younger age than boys. Most girls marry between the ages of eight and fifteen, and boys when they are twelve to eighteen years old. Occasionally, however, Meo men do marry women who are older; especially in levirate when a widow is wedded to a child brother of her deceased husband.

The majority of marriages among the Meos are monogamous but polygyny is permissible. There is only one polygynous family in Chavandi Kalan. When I interviewed the head of this family, he did not mention the fact that he had two wives. But later on he admitted that he had married his brother's widow as his second wife. This hesitation to admit having two wives indicates that polygyny is not preferred. Normally, if the first wife is barren, a man may take a second wife; but this is not the only reason for polygyny. Sometimes, although very rarely, rich Meos take two or more wives for reasons of prestige. Occasionally, a Meo may marry his brother's widow as his second wife if it is considered advantageous for the family. In any case, since the prestige attached to polygyny is not very great and since bride-price is high, such marriages are rare in Mewat.

There is no prohibition on widow or widower remarriage among the Meos. As a matter of fact, all widows, unless they have many children, continue to remarry till they are too old to do so. Widowers also remarry provided, of course, that they can afford the bride-price.

Because of the high economic value of women, Meo men rarely divorce their wives. According to local custom, women cannot divorce their husbands. A common way of leaving a husband is by eloping. This is possible because of the indulgent environment of their natal village which they visit frequently.

However, if a woman abandons her husband and wishes to marry another man, the first husband must be paid *jhagra* (compensation) by the man who wants to marry her. Unless the amount of *jhagra* is amicably settled, elopement can lead to serious feuds which sometimes last for generations.

Both the levirate and sororate are practised by the Meos. As a matter of fact, levirate, which involves a man marrying his elder brother's widow, is quite common in Mewat. Marrying a younger brother's widow is not considered proper because the two are supposed to stay strictly away from each other. But such a marriage is permissible in special circumstances. Occasionally, levirate marriage is polygynous. When a family is keen on retaining a young widow and lacks an unmarried male, a polygynous marriage is permitted as the only alternative. Women play a very important economic role in Meo households and are not very easy to obtain in marriage. Hence, a widow is encouraged to marry a brother of her husband; and if she is not very young and, especially if she has children, she is likely to accept this arrangement. A Meo woman of Chavandi Kalan who has married her first husband's younger brother said: 'When my first husband died, I decided to marry his younger brother. I had two sons and was quite attached to my husband's family. So it was better to stay. Who knows what kind of family I would have gone into if I were to marry someone in another village.'

Since marriage is considered to be a matter that concerns the entire family and not just the individuals to be wedded, the decision for the levirate arrangement is made by the older male members of the household. However, the elders cannot impose their decision on the widow. They make the offer, but it is her prerogative to accept or reject it. Sometimes, if the widow is reluctant and the family wants her to stay, pressure may be put on her through other relatives. But, in any case, the final decision rests with her. If the levirate arrangement is not suggested for lack of suitable males in the family, or because of the family's unwillingness to keep her, a widow has no other choice but to return to her natal family. If she has adult sons she can, however, continue to live with their families if she chooses to do so, regardless of whether they are still living in the joint household or whether they have established separate households. Usually, she would live with her youngest son.

Sororate is quite permissible among the Meos, but it is much less common than levirate. This is so because of the complexities arising from the settlement of the bride-price. A girl's parents are expected to treat their son-in-law and his family with a great deal of deference and caution, and this practice is commonly observed by Meos. Hence, when a girl dies, it is very difficult for her parents to bargain the bride-price with the widower's family for a second time. Consequently even if they have another daughter, they try to avoid the sororate arrangement.

Multiple weddings are quite common in Mewat. Attracted by the economics of such an arrangement, parents often marry two daughters to two different men at the same time. A single series of ceremonies and rituals then suffice for the two couples. The bridegrooms in such marriages are often unrelated and belong to different villages. However, in some instances the bridegrooms are brothers.

Village Exogamy

The Meos throughout Mewat practise strict village exogamy. In Chavandi Kalan no one could recall any violation of this rule. There is a strong feeling that all the Meos of a village have a common ancestry. This makes them so closely related that marriage among them would be incestuous. Actually, a majority of the Meos in a village belong to one exogamous *pal* or *gotra*. But several such groups may be represented in each village. Members of intermarrying *gotra* groups must also obey the rule of village exogamy. In addition to the feeling that the members of each caste in a village are closely related there exists the practice of referring to fellow villagers in fictive kin terms. For example, all the daughters of the village, regardless of caste, are addressed by village men as 'sister' or 'daughter', depending on their relative ages. The entire community is visualized as an extended family, and members of each generation born in the village are believed to be like siblings, unless, of course, they are actually closely related in a different way.

The Meos believe that in the past people avoided marrying in any of the villages in their *thama* or even *pal*, but this restriction is now limited to one's own village. However, several men of a village may bring brides from another specific village, or several women of a village may marry into a village other than their own. As a matter of fact, both are common practices. The exchange of brides between two villages, though rare, is permissible if the other rules of exogamy are observed. The only restriction is that a father and a son are not allowed to marry women of the same village. In other words, a man may not marry a woman from his mother's or stepmother's village. The Meos put it like this: 'Father and son cannot go to the same village as bridegrooms.' But a man and his grandson may marry women from the same village.

Avoidance of Cousin Marriage

Both cross-cousin and parallel cousin marriages are avoided by the Meos. Their kinship terminology is of the Hawaiian type, i.e., the same kin terms are used for siblings and cousins. There is no definite rule regarding the degree of removal of the cousin whom one must avoid marrying. Any person with whom a cousin relationship can be traced cannot be married. In recent years, attempts were made in Mewat by some individuals to break this rule. I was informed that a Meo in Gurgaon district arranged the marriage of his son to his brother's daughter, asserting that such a marriage was allowed by Islam. The Meos in that village became so infuriated at this attempted 'incest' that they beat the culprit and turned him out of the village.

Gotra Exogamy

As has been mentioned earlier, the entire Meo caste is divided into thirteen exogamous *pals* and sixty-seven or more *gotras*. A Meo informant told me that, in the old days, the practice was to avoid marrying into one's own, one's mother's, one's mother's mother's, and one's daughter's or sister's *gotra*. But this practice has been modified greatly in recent years and now one has to avoid marrying into one's own *gotra* only.

In actual practice, there is a preference for obtaining brides from certain *gotras* and *pals* and similarly a tendency 'to give' daughters to certain others. In Chavandi Kalan three *pals* (Landavat, Demrot, and Dehngal) and one *gotra* (Bilavat) are represented. Of these, only the Landavats and the Demrots have lived in the village long enough to have contracted marriages for their members. The Bilavat *gotra* is represented by only one individual, who came to live in the village recently. The Dehngals also are recent immigrants.

The Landavats and the Demrots of Chavandi Kalan have intermarrying relations with ten *pals* and six *gotras*. The frequency of inter-*gotra* marriages contracted by the Landavats and the Demrots of Chavandi Kalan, as of June 1964, is shown in Table I. The Landavats of Chavandi Kalan exchange brides with six *pals* and three *gotras* and they have no reciprocal relationship with the other *pals* and *gotras*. In the case of the latter, they only give daughters to two *pals* and one *gotra* and obtain brides only from two *pals* and two *gotras*. The Demrots have marriage relations with three *pals*—from two of them they receive brides and to one of them they give daughters. However, these frequencies of marriage alliances are not based on any fixed rule. It is also quite possible for the Meos of Chavandi Kalan

TABLE 1: Number of Marriages Contracted by the Landavats and Demrots of Chavandi Kalan with other Palsand Gotras.

Pals and Gotras	*Brides obtained by Landavats*	*Daughters given in marriage by Landavats*	*Brides Obtained by Demrots*	*Daughters given in marriage by Demrots*
Pals				
Balot	0	2	0	0
Chhirakdot	4	8	0	1
Dairval	1	3	0	0
Demorat	3	0	0	0
Dehngal	10	35	3	0
Duhlot	2	3	0	0
Nai	17	10	2	0
Pahat	0	5	0	0
Pundlot	2	1	0	0
Singhal	39	0	0	10
Gotras				
Besar	0	1	0	0
Bilavat	2	1	0	0
Gorvat	1	3	0	0
Kamalia	4	1	0	0
Saugam	2	0	0	0
Siroiya	2	0	0	0

to marry Meos of *pals* and *gotras* other than the sixteen listed in Table 1.

Although it is not clear why the Meos of Chavandi Kalan prefer to arrange marriage alliances with particular *pals* and *gotras*, there are three possible reasons for this. First of all, it is evident from the figures in Table 1 that preference is given to marriages with members of other *pals* rather than those of other *gotras*. This preference is due to the larger size and greater political importance of the *pals*. A second factor that seems to influence the decisions of the Meos with regard to marriage is the tendency to give daughters to *pals* located in the north-east and to receive brides from those situated in the south-east. Lastly, convenience and economy seem to be important considerations in arranging marriages. Since most of the travelling is done on foot or by bullock cart and camel over dirt paths, it is understandable that marriages are seldom contracted with families living at a great distance from Chavandi Kalan. This is illustrated by the figures in Table 2, which indicate that over sixty per cent of Meo marriage alliances were contracted within a radius of twenty miles and over ninety per cent within a radius of thirty miles.

TABLE 2: Distance of Marriage Alliances of the Meos of Chavandi Kalan.

Distance of village of Bride or Groom from Chavandi Kalan (miles)	*Brides obtained in marriage*		*Daughters given in marriage*	
	No.	*Per cent*	*No.*	*Per cent*
1 to 10	5	5.3	17	21.0
11 to 20	56	59.6	33	40.8
21 to 30	26	27.7	26	32.1
31 to 33	5	5.3	1	1.2
34 to 40	2	2.1	2	2.5
41 to 50	0	0	1	1.2
51 to 60	0	0	1	1.2
Total	94	100.0	81	100.0

Bride-Price and Dowry

Late one evening in 1964 in Chavandi Kalan, women in a Meo house suddenly began to sing loudly—an occurrence which indicated that a son had been born. In another part of the village a woman remarked: 'Too many boys are being born this year. It means there will be a famine.' A Bania woman who overheard this comment said : 'This is very true. Too many boys does mean famine for the Meos. After all, they will have to pay a high bride-price for their marriages.' The first woman, who was a Meo, did not like this allusion to bride-price and said: 'Well, not all Meos pay bride-price. Some give dowry. There are all kinds of people.' The Bania woman answered: 'That may be so, but I have yet to see a Meo family of Chavandi Kalan that gave dowry to a daughter's husband's family.'

This conversation points to a very important change in a Meo custom which generates a great deal of ambivalence and anxiety. According to most of my informants, the Meo practice used to be that the bride's family gave a dowry to the groom's family at the time of marriage. This custom still persists to some extent. Some families in Chavandi Kalan give huge dowries to their daughter's affinal families. One family even borrowed large sums of money for this purpose in 1963 because they wanted to outdo one of their relatives.

Another custom which existed together with this was that a girl's parents and all her consanguinal relatives neither accepted gifts from her affinal family nor ate food at her husband's home. The father of two young men who were married to two sisters from Chavandi Kalan told me: 'My sons' father-in-law came to our village a few months before their marriage. He met me and my sons. In the evening when we offered him hospitality, he refused to eat any food. Instead, he gave one rupee each to the boys. That to us was an indication that he had decided to betroth his daughters to my sons.' There are several old men and women in Chavandi Kalan who would hestitate to eat at their daughters' husbands' homes.

Accepting a bride-price or any kind of gift from a daughter's husband's family is considered sinful by most Meos. A man of Chavandi Kalan was suffering from a chronic sore on his knee. Several Meos believed that his suffering was due to his accepting a bride-price for his daughters. One Meo said: 'He is suffering because of his own *pap* (sins). He has been taking large amounts of money as bride-price for his daughters. This is bad. One can never "digest" the money gained from the sale of daughters.' In a more conservative part of Mewat, Lachmangarh, an old Meo boasted: 'We don't sell our daughters in this area like the Meos of Landavat *pal.* We give a dowry to our daughters, which is the proper thing to do.'

While the feeling against bride-price is still strong, the actual practice has changed considerably. The former Meo custom of not accepting food and other hospitality from a daughter's affinal relatives has become almost extinct. Except for some very old people, hospitality is readily accepted by people at their daughter's husband's home. There is a custom amongst the Meos to send for the newly married daughter after she has spent two or three days in her husband's village. In the past a *kamin,* such as a Nai, was sent with a younger brother or cousin of the bride to bring her back for a visit. But now the bride's father, her uncles, brothers, and several other relatives and friends may go to the groom's village for this purpose. Sometimes ten or more people go and stay in the daughter's husband's village for three days before returning with her and they accept hospitality without hesitation. Although feeling against bride-price is still strong, the custom has become quite prevalent. A bride-price was paid in nearly all the marriages that have taken place in Chavandi Kalan in the last five years. An unmarried young Meo complained to me: 'Things are going from bad to worse these days. People are demanding three to four thousand rupees for child brides four to five years old.' Another Meo said: 'With the custom of bride-price becoming more common, the incidence of cheating has increased. People take bride-price for a child bride and before *gauna* marry her again to some other person and charge a price for the second time.'

The bride-price is settled between the families of the prospective bride and groom. Part of the amount is paid at the time of the engagement, and the rest at marriage and *gauna.* If the girl is very young, the major portion of the bride-price is paid at the time of the *gauna*. The amount varies from three to five thousand rupees. As a rule it tends to be lower for younger brides. A good part of it is in the form of cash, but farm animals and silver ornaments are also given. Sometimes a girl's father may cancel a debt entirely by means of bride-price or a debt may be partially repaid through an adjustment with the bride-price.

In north India, the prevailing practice among high caste Hindus is to give dowry to the daughter's husband's family at the time of her marriage. Some educated Hindus have decried this custom, but the practice has increased rather than decreased in recent years. Even some of the lower castes have adopted the practice of giving a dowry in an attempt to raise their status. But, among the Meos, the trend is in the opposite direction.

There are two probable explanations for the increase in the popularity of bride-price in Mewat. The first and most important reason is the increasing economic value of women. In the past, the Meos depended on the labour of low-caste men and derived their income by raising cattle. But now cattle raising has diminished in importance and low-caste labour is scarce. The burden of additional agricultural work has fallen on the Meo women. Consequently, successful farming depends on the presence of women in a household. There are cases where families had to abandon normal agriculture because of the lack of women. From all this it is fairly clear that the economic value of Meo women has increased and, as a consequence, there is a tendency toward the custom of bride-price.

Secondly, the adoption of the practice of bride-price by the Meos is facilitated by the fact that they are becoming more Islamized and are relatively less concerned about their status in the Hindu caste hierarchy. Although the Meos resent the lowering of their status in Hindu eyes, they realize that their customs make little difference to their social position. They are now looked upon as Muslims by the Hindus, and their social and ritual status coincides with that of their co-religionists.

Meo Kin Terms—Their Extensions and Implications

The Meos have a repertoire of more than sixty terms of reference in their kinship system, each of which refers to one or more types of relative. In addition, there are a few terms of address which do not coincide with these. Among the criteria used in these terms, sex is the most important; no term denotes two relatives of opposite sex. Generation is second in importance; relatives of different generations are rarely subsumed by the same term. Other considerations—age difference, consanguinity and affinity, lineality, laterality, sex of the speaker, etc.—are used to distinguish between some relatives but not others.

Table 3 lists all the kin terms of the Meos. For convenience of discussion, the terms are divided into four groups. Group A includes the terms for relatives in ego's generation, and Group B those for ego's parent's generation. The terms for relatives in the second and third ascending generations are grouped under C. The fourth group, D, consists of terms referring to relatives in the generations descending from ego's.

Group A

There are twenty-three terms of reference in this group. The criteria of consanguinity and affinity are taken into account in all of them, and relatives of each kind are always referred to by separate kin terms. However, within each of these categories relatives are distinguished in a variety of ways. Among one's consanguinal relatives, considerations of lineality, age and laterality are completely ignored. Ego's male siblings and male cousins through either parent are referred to by the same term-*bhai*. Similarly, all of one's female siblings and cousins are called *bahin*. Relatives who refer to each other as *bhai* are considered to share the family 'honour'. Even if they do not get along well together—which is especially common among brothers—they help one another in case of feuds with kin and non-kin. If a person needs financial help, he is likely to turn first to his *bhai*. The degree of closeness of relationship is important in regard to expectations of support, but in emergencies the *bhais*, however remotely related, stand together. A Meo saying goes: 'when going to fight in a battle, one remembers one's *bhai*.' Two *bhais* who have a very affectionate relationship refer to each other as *bhair*.

The females who refer to each other as *bahin* have very affectionate ties. Virilocality scatters the *bahins* after marriage,

TABLE 3 : Meo Kinship Terms

No.	*Term of reference*	*Genealagical relationship*	*Term of address*	*Remarks*
GROUP A				
1	bhāī aff. m.s. bhaiṛ	Br, FaBrSo, FaSiSo, MoBrSo, MoSiSo, MaSo, FaSo	b.n., lālā	Bhaiṛ used very rarely
2	bhābī	EBrWi	bhābī	Joking permitted
3	bahū	YBrWi, SoWi	b.n., bahū	Strict avoidance
4	bahin aff. w.s. bhāeli	Si, FaBrDa, FaSiDa, MoBrDa, MoSiDa, MoDa, FaDa	b.n., lālī	
5	behnoī	SiHu, cousin's Hu	b.n., jījā	Jījā for formal address
6	samadhī	SoWiFa, DaHuFa	b.n.	
7	samdhan	SoWiMo, DaHuMo	none	Joking permitted but not called by name
8	berbānī	Wi	are, teknonymy	
9	sālā	WiBr or wife's male cousin, BrWiBr	b.n.	Also used as a term of abuse
10	sālāhelī	WiBrWi	b.n.	Joking permitted
11	sālī	WiYSi	b.n.	Joking permitted
12	barsās	WiESi	none	Strict avoidance
13	sāḍhū	WiSiHu	b.n.	
14	gharvālā	Hu	taknonymy	
15	sauk	HuWi	b.n., bahin	Sauk is a term of abuse

• *Explanation of abbreviations* : Br, brother; EBr, elder brother; YB., younger brother, Si, sister; ESi elder sister; YSi, younger sister; Hu, husband; Wi, wife; Fa., father; Mo, mother; So, son; Da, daughter; b.n. by name; aff., affectionate; m.s., man speaking, w.s., woman speaking: (speaker's sex indicated only where significant).

TABLE 3 (*Contd.*)

No.	*Term of reference*	*Genealogical relationship*	*Term af address*	*Remarks*
16	devar	HuYBr or husband's younger male cousin	b.n.	Joking permitted
17	devrānī	HuYBrWi	b.n.	
18	jeṭh	HuEBr or husband's elder male cousin	none	Strict avoidance
19	jeṭhānī	HuEBrWi	b.n.	
20	nanad	HuSi or husband's female cousin	b.n.	
21	nandeū	HuSiHu	b.n.	Joking permitted
GROUP B				
22	bāp	Fa, MoHu	bābo; kāko or tāū for MoHu; aff, buḍḍhā	
23	mā	Mo, FaWi	māī; māī or māosī for FaWi	
24	tāū	FaEBr or father's elder male cousin	tāū	
25	tāī	FaEBrWi	tāī	
26	kākā	FaYBr or father's younger male cousin	kākā	
27	kākī	FaYBrWi	kāki	
28	phuphī	FaSi HuFaSi	phuphī	
29	phuphā	FaSiHu, HuFaSiHu	phuphā	
30	māmā	MoBr or mother's male cousin	māmā	

TABLE 3 (*Contd.*)

No.	*Term of reference*	*Genealogical relationship*	*Term of address*	*Remarks*
31	māmī	MoBrWi	māmī	
32	māosī,	MoSi or mother's female cousin FaWi	māosī, mā	
33	māosā	MoSiHu, SiHuFa	māosā	
34	susrā, ḍokrā	WiFa, WiFaBr, HuFa HuFaBr	chaudbrī, w.s. buḍḍhā bāp	Dokrā has a slightly less derogatory connotation than susrā
35	sās, ḍokrī	WiMo, WiMoSi, HuMo, HuMoSi	m.s. none, w.s. buā	m.s. strict avoidance. Dokrī has a slightly less derogatory connotation than sās
GROUP C				
36	dādā	FaFa, FaFaBr, FaMoBr	dādo aff. buḍḍā bāp	
37	dādī	FaMo, FaFaSi, FaMoSi	dādī aff buḍḍbī mā	
38	nānā	MoFa, MoFaBr or mother's father's male cousin	nāno	
39	nānī	MoMo, MoFaBrWi, MoMoSi	nānī	
40	dadsusrā	WiFaFa, WiFaFaBr. HuFaFa	m.s. chaudhrī w.s. buḍḍhā bāp	
41	dadsās	WiFaMo, HuFaMo	w.s. bua	
42	paṛdādā	FaFaFa	dādā, buḍḍhā bāp	
43	paṛdādī	FaFaMo	dādī, buḍḍhi mā	
44	paṛnānā	MoFaFa, MoFaFaBr	nāno	
45	paṛnānī	MoFaMo, MoFaFaBrWi	nānī	

TABLE 3 (*Contd.*)

No.	*Term of reference*	*Genealogical relationship*	*Term of address*	*Remarks*
GROUP D				
46	beṭā	So, spouse's So, WiBrSo. WiSiSo, SoWiBr	b.n., chhorā, lālā	
47	betī	Da, spouse's Da, DaHuSi, WiBrDa, WiSiDa	b.n., chhorī, lālī	
48	bhatījā	BrSo	b.n., chhorā, lālā	
49	bhatījā-bahū	BrSoWi, HuBrSoWi	b.n.	
50	bhatījī	BrDa	b.n., chhorī, lālī	
51	bhānjā	SiSo, HuSiSo	b.n. lālā	
52	bhānjā-bahu	SiSoWi, HuSiSoWi	b.n.	
53	bhānjī	SiDa, HuSiDa	b.n. lālī	
54	asnāo	DaHu, DaHuBr, SoDaHu SoSoDaHu	b.n.	
55	navāsā, dheotā	DaSo	b.n., lālā	Dheotā is more commonly used by educated people
56	navāsī, dheotī	DaDa	b.n., lālī	Dheoti is more commonly used by educated people
57	potā	SoSo	b.n. lalī	
58	potī	SoDa	b.n. lālī	
59	pot-bahū	SoSoWi	b.n.	
60	parpotā	SoSoSo	b.n., lālā	
61	parpotī	SoSoDa	b.n., lālī	

but they look forward eagerly to re-unions when the family news will be exchanged. This is especially valuable because there is no person among a woman's affinal family to whom she can freely express her feelings. On the other hand, there is considerable friendly rivalry between *bahins.* When a Meo woman asks her husband to buy her an ornament, she cites the example of her *bhaeli* (affectionate term for sister or female cousin) who has one. The *bhai* and the *bahin* have a very special relationship. The *bhai* has to help and protect his *bahin* all her life. He listens to her complaints about her husband's family and tries his best to intercede on her behalf. If the *bahin* becomes a widow or is abandoned by her husband, she can always return to live with her *bhai.* In order to insure help in an emergency, she keeps in close touch with her *bhai* and his family. He, in turn, is expected to be indulgent to her and her children.

While age distinction is ignored with regard to cousins and siblings, it does enter into the terms for their spouses because of the differences in the expected behaviour. A male ego refers to his elder brother's wife as *bhabi* and to his younger brother's wife as *bahu*; the term *babu* also refers to his son's wife, and strict mutual avoidance is required in relation to both his son's wife and his younger brother's wife. *Bhabi,* on the other hand, refers to a class of relatives with whom one can joke. Furthermore, one can marry one's widowed *bhabi* but not a widowed *bahu.* An exception is sometimes made regarding one's younger brother's widow when marriage with her is considered beneficial for the family, but one may never marry one's son's widow. A female ego refers to her elder and younger brothers' wives as *bhabi* and to her son's wife as *bahu*; her brothers' wives refer to her as *nanad,* and there is always rivalry between them. A woman makes sure that her *bhabi* does not dampen her brother's affection for her.

An age distinction is made concerning one's affinal relatives. A male ego distinguishes between his wife's elder and younger sisters (or female cousins) and refers to them as *barsas* and *sali* respectively. Strict avoidance is expected in relation to a *barsas,* whereas joking is permitted with one's *sali.* Also a widower may marry his *sali,* but he can marry a *barsas* only in very special circumstances. No age distinction is made between one's wife's brothers (or male cousins). They are referred to as *sala* and no special deference is shown to them. One can joke with one's *sala* and his wife, called *salaheli.* The term *sala* is also used as an abuse: if a man calls another man *sala*, it implies sexual intercourse with the latter's sister. I noticed many times that whenever two Meos, one of whom was a *sala* of the other, introduced themselves to me, the *sala* always quickly added jokingly that the other individual was his *sala*. This is done by the *sala* to save himself from the embarrassment of being referred to by a word of abuse. The *behnoi* (sister's husband) is expected not to protest against this statement, but a person familiar with the system can judge the correct relationship. One traditionally owes a great deal of deference to a sister's husband, but this is changing. A man came to Chavandi Kalan for the fourth time to take his wife back to his village. He felt quite irritated when his *sala* refused to send her on a certain day, and left the village in anger. When I asked the *sala* if he was worried about his sister's husband's anger, he replied, 'No, not at all. *Sala* refused to wait even for a couple of more days. If he cares, he will come back for the fifth time for my sister. We must treat the *behnoi* strictly. Otherwise they become too proud and lose respect for their wives. Now he will treat my sister better because he knows that we will brook no nonsense.' One refers to one's brother's *sala* as *sala* and can joke with him as with one's own. A joking relationship also exists between a man and his wife's sister's husband, known as *sadhu.*

The term for 'wife' is *berbani*, which is also the term for a 'woman'. This is significant in that it indicates the tenuous position of a woman in her affinal home. Her function is to bear children for her husband's family, and her status grows with the birth of her children, especially males. A husband never calls his wife by name, and he often hesitates to mention her name even in her absence. He refers to her by her parent's *gotra* or by her natal village, e.g., 'Chavandi-Ki', which literally means 'woman of Chavandi'. The term of address for a wife is *aray*, a common expletive similar to the English 'hey' when used to attract someone's attention. The husband is referred to as *gharvala,* which literally means 'one who owns or belongs to the household.' In a polygynous household, the co-wives refer to each other as *sauk*, and the term implies constant quarrelling.

It is also used as a term of abuse for women who quarrel with other women, including their own daughters.

A female ego must distinguish between her husband's elder and younger *bhais*. The younger brothers of the husband are *devar*, and joking is permitted with them. A woman's husband's elder brother is *jeth*, and mutual avoidance is mandatory. A distinction is also made between the terms used for the wives of her husband's older and younger brothers. A woman has to show more respect to her husband's elder brother's wife, *jethani*, than she does to his younger brother's wife, *devrani*. No distinction is made between her *nanads*, her husband's sisters and female cousins, with regard to age. She has a joking relationship with the husbands of these women, *nandeu*.

The parents of one's son's or daughter's spouse are referred to as *samdhi* (male) and *samdhan* (female). Here, although no terminological distinction is made, a male ego is expected to treat his daughter's husband's parents with a considerably greater amount of deference than that used towards his son's in-laws, but the difference has narrowed in recent years. A female ego, however, has always been allowed to joke with the *samdhi* related to her through her daughter.

Group B

The sixteen terms of reference in this group refer to relatives in the first ascending generation in relation to ego. The criterion of laterality is of consequence, and matrilateral relatives are distinguished from those related through one's father. One has different rights and duties with regard to one's patrilateral and matrilateral uncles. All the matrilateral uncles are *mamas* and their spouses *mamis*, regardless of their age in relation to one's mother. The relationship with one's *mama* is emotionally very close, and young children especially value their indulgent attention. Thanks to patrilocal residence, one visits the *mama* only occasionally; and the *mama* does not have to discipline his sister's children. A Meo child returning from a visit to its mother's brothers is often very unhappy for some time. The child notices the difference in the treatment it gets and it wants to return to its *mama*. As a child grows older and assumes family responsibilities, its relationship with the mother's brother become weaker, but the tenor of indulgence continues in their relationship. One's mother's sisters, *maosis*, also are very indulgent, but patrilocality makes one's contact with them even less frequent than with the *mama*. The relationship with one's mother's sister's husband, *maosa*, tends to be less close.

Ego's patrilateral uncles have a rather formal relationship with him. They do have the right to discipline him, but only in exceptional circumstances would they do so. However, one shares the family honour with one's partilateral uncles and can count on their support in feuds and in elections. Age distinction is important, and one's father's elder brother, *tau*, and his wife, *tai*, are terminologically distinguished from his younger brother, *kaka*, and his wife, *kaki*. In a collateral joint family household, the oldest among the brothers becomes the head of the family; and, because of his greater authority, this *tau* is owed more deference. The deference one owes to one's *kaka* is a great deal less. Their wives are treated very much like mothers.

One's father's sisters are *phuphis* and their husbands *phuphas*, regardless of their age in relation to one's father. A *phuphi* is expected to indulge her nephews and nieces and so she establishes a warm relationship with them. After she is married, she maintains this relationship by frequent visits and by performing certain ritual services at the life cycle rites of her nephews and later by bringing gifts when children are born to them. A *phupha* often accompanies his wife on these visits but he has no close relationship with his wife's brother's children.

Since descent is traced through the male line among the Meos, lineality is important, and one's father (*bap*) is distinguished from his brothers. The father represents the major authority figure in the nuclear family unit among the Meos. Even in a joint family household he has the prerogative of disciplining his children, who are always identified in relation to him as, for example, 'son of Ghotu.' If a mother or an uncle discovers that a child has been disobedient, the father is informed about it, and it is up to him to punish the child. A mother (*ma*) is often very indulgent towards her children. A Meo saying which expresses this relationship, runs thus: 'When sick (i.e., helpless) one remembers one's mother.'

The affinal relatives in this group are referred to as *susra* (male) and *sas* (female) regardless of the speaker's sex. These terms of reference are not very respectful and are, therefore, never used in address. For reference, the alternate set of terms, *dokra* and *dokri*, are somewhat more respectful. A male ego addresses his wife's father as *chaudhri*, a rather formal term of respect used for prominent non-kin and strangers. There is no term of address for one's wife's mother, since mutual avoidance is the prevailing rule and one is not expected to converse with her. Women used to cover their faces in the presence of their son-in-law, but this practice is becoming less common now.

A female ego addresses her husband's mother, his father's sister, and his father's brother's wives as *bua*, and his father as *buddha bap*. However, since she must avoid her father-in-law, she seldom talks directly to him but whenever she needs to she will address him through a child. She will loudly ask the child to convey a message to the *buddha bap* so that the old man could hear her. He, in turn, replies to her queries in a similar manner through the child. A female ego does not distinguish between her husband's father and his uncles on the basis of age.

Group C

For the members of the second and third ascending generations there are only ten terms of reference. In these generations one distinguishes between the father's and the mother's parents and grand-parents. One's father's parents and their cousins are *dada* (male) and *dadi* (female), and those of the mother *nana* (male) and *nani* (female.) *Nana* and *nani* are one's indulgent grandparents. Children are always nostalgic about their *nana's* house. One has a fairly pleasant relationship with one's father's parents and grandparents, but their authority rather dampens the warmth. Nevertheless, a child turns to its *dada* for companionship and spends many a memorable hour listening to his bed-time stories. Especially, when a person is very old, he devotes a great deal of attention to his grandchildren. The relatives in one's great-grandparental generation are *pardada* and *pardadi* on the father's side and *parnana* and *parnani* on the mother's side. One's relationship with these kin is very similar to that with one's grandparents. One's affinals in Group C are referred to by the same terms as one's affinals in the parental generation (Group B), and no behavioural distinctions are made between these two groups.

Group D

The kin terms for the various descending generations are shown in Group D. In the first descending generation, lineality is important. One's sons (*betas*) and daughters (*betis*) are distinguished from one's brother's and sister's children, who are further differentiated from each other. These distintions are crucial with regard to inheritance as well as mutual rights and duties. A son has the first claim to his father's propery; then come the brother's sons, and last the sister's sons. A father is almost solely responsible to discipline his sons and only in special circumstance his brother's sons (*bhatijas*) and daughters (*bhatijis*). But one's sister's sons (*bhanjas*) and daughters (*bhanjis*) must always be indulged and helped in case of need. One's wife's sister's sons and daughters are terminologically merged with one's own offspring; this relationship is relatively unimportant, and the terms *beta* and *beti* are used for them in a rather generic sense. These terms are also used in this sense for non-relatives of the appropriate generation

The term *bahu*, which appears in Group A, is also used to refer to one's son's wife. One's brother's and sister's son's wives are also one's *bahus* as far as the behaviour expectations are concerned; but, in order to distinguish between them, the term *bhatija* or *bhanja* is prefixed to the term *bahu.* These distinctions are more important for a woman speaker because she has a far greater authority over her *bahu* (son's wife) than over her *bhanja-bahu* or *bhatija-bahu.*

The husbands of one's daughter, brother's daughter, sister's daughter, son's son's daughter, etc., are referred to by a single-kin term, *asnao*. An *asnao*, in whatever way related, has to be treated with particular attention. Special food has to be prepared for him when he visits, and one must avoid offending him. However, as the importance of women is increasing, people tend to treat the *asnao* more casually. The relationship with one's daughter's son (*navasa* or *dheota*) and with one's daughter's daughter (*navasi* or *dheoti*) is always more indulgent than with one's son's son (*pota*) and daughter (*poti*)). One's son's son's wife (*pot-bahu*) is treated in the same way as one's son's wife. Exceptional affection is shown towards one's son's son's son (*parpota*) and daughter (*parpoti*). The following Meo saying highlights this relationship: 'The interest is more dear than the principal.'

Summary

In this essay we have briefly analysed the complex kinship relationships which regulate the social life of the Meos. We have also described the rules and customs relating to marriage. Meo kinship and marriage rules closely resemble those of the high caste Hindus in North India. A major change is with regard to the exchange of gifts at the time of marriage. The old custom of dowry is replaced by bride-price. Although this change has become well established in practice, it has not yet been given the social and moral approval.

As Muslims, the Meos feel under pressure to conform to the prevailing Muslim customs. For instance, the non-Meo Muslims, particularly the religious practitioners, wish that the Meos should accept the custom of cousin marriage. But the Meos have strongly resisted it thus far. Their relative isolation from the wider Muslim community, and close contact with the local Hindus, account for this resistance. The Meos are also under pressure to adopt *purdah*, i.e., seclusion of women. This they resist because Meo women have to work in the fields. Also, since women in modern Indian society are struggling to improve their status vis-a-vis men, it is unlikely that the Meo women will accept *purdah*.

Caste solidarity and kin loyalty appear to have been strengthened in Mewat in recent decades due to the adoption of democratic form of government based on adult franchise in India. This is because traditional loyalties are invoked during elections by the contestants, not only in Mewat but elsewhere as well.

Bibliography

Aggarwal, Partap C.(1968) 'Changing Religious Practices: Their Relationship to Secular Power in a Rajasthan Village', *The Economic and Political Weekly*, 6, pp. 547-551.

Aggarwal, Partap C. (1971), *Caste, Religion and Power; An Indian Case Study*. New Delhi, Shri Ram Centre for Industrial Relations and Human Resources.

——— (1973), 'Caste Hierarchy in a Meo Village in Rajasthan', in Imtiaz Ahmad (ed.), *Caste and Social Stratification among the Muslims*, Delhi, Manohar Book Service.

Bannerman, Captain A.D. (1902), *Census of India. 1901 Vol. XXV, Part I*, Lucknow, Nawal Kishore Press.

Risley, H.H. (1915), *The People of India*, London, W. Thacker & Co.

Shah, A.M. (1964), 'Political System in Eighteenth Century Gujarat', *Enquiry*, 1, pp. 33-95.

Sinha, S. (1962), 'State Formation and Rajput Myth in Tribal Central India', *Man in India*, 42, pp. 75-77.

Srinivas, M.N. (1968), 'Mobility in the Caste System', in M. Singer and B.S. Cohn (eds.), *Structure and Change in Indian Society*, Chicago, Aldine Publishing Company.

11

Urbanization, Family Structure and the Muslim Merchants of Tamilnadu

Mattison Mines

There are two distinct views of Indian urbanism and of the relationship of urban society to rural social organization. The first sees Indian urban society as fundamentally indigenous, as organized around the same principles as the rural sector, and India's rural and urban social structures are seen as the same. It is from this viewpoint that Pocock (1960; see also Lynch, 1967) argues that caste and kinship are the fundamental ingredients of the Indian social order, and that their organizational importance is the same in the city as well as in the village.

The second view holds that urban and rural societies are different and that social organization reflects this difference (Hardgrave, 1970).[1] In this view urban social organization is not simply the outcome of rural forms adapted to the urban environment. It consists of new forms. True, caste and kinship are important in the city, but they are of a form different from that found in the village. Urban society involves a different kind of order, an order in which people come together self-consciously to form new units, voluntary associations. The new order has a contractual basis which contrasts it with the natural order of the rural, caste and kinship dominated, status society.

1. Barnett (M.S., n.d.) calls attention to this distinction in viewpoints.

Both these positions represent simplifications of India's urban social order. The first view overstresses the similarities between rural and urban social orders, and the second overstresses the differences. For example, the significant roles of caste and kinship in rural and urban settings have already been ably demonstrated (see Lynch, 1967; Rowe, 1964; Woodruff, 1960). Similarly, the basic differences in urban and rural social orders have been recognized and described (see Hardgrave, 1969, 1970; Marriott, 1968; Rowe, 1964).

An eclectic synthesis is called for, one which contrasts rural and urban social structures, while demonstrating the relative significance of the forms of social organization. Several questions have to be answered. Are family and kinship organizations fundamentally different in cities compared to villages? What are the areas of life that kinship organizes in urban contexts? Do voluntary associations replace kinship as the basis of social organization? Answers to these questions will help resolve the antithetical positions noted above.

Among rural migrants to Indian cities, caste and kinship continue to be important determinants of social order. Migrants are poor and ignorant, and lack knowledge of urban life and jobs. For them a move to the city, even on a temporary basis, involves a journey into a 'foreign land' (Rowe, 1964:14). Under these circumstances, migrants settle in areas where their relatives have preceded them and in this manner create the urban residence patterns of the migratory sections of Indian cities. The organization of these sections reveals that people clearly choose where to live in cities on the basis of kinship, village of origin and caste (Rowe, 1964:13-14). Rowe writes that this preference is so pervasive in Bombay that the city's residence pattern is suggestive of a map of the North Indian countryside. Bombay is not unique; other studies of migrants and of urban slum-dwellers indicate similar findings (see Lynch 1967; Woodruff, 1960), and I have observed a similar patterning among Muslim and Hindu migrants in Madras City.

Among migrants, kinship and caste organize basically the same aspects of life in cities that they do in villages. True, some differences are to be observed. For example, in North India migrants usually travel alone, without their families, so that their normal relationships are truncated. But migrants are still sociologically oriented toward rural life and the village remains the focus of their family lives. Eventually, Indian villagers hope to return to their rural homes and there take up normal life.

But what about permanent urban dwellers? Are their lives organized similarly to those of migrants? Are they also basically rural oriented?

The Tamil Muslims of Pallavaram City provide an example of a population with a long urban history which is suitable for purposes of an examination of urban social adaptation. Pallavaram's Tamil Muslims are a segment of Tamilnadu's Muslim Tamil minority, who have a proportionately large urban population, even outnumbering Hindus in some towns (India, 1902:13). The Tamil Muslims' urbanism is associated with their occupational propensity for business and through history they have earned a reputation as shrewd, hard working merchants. According to the 1961 Census (India, 1962), more than 55 per cent of Tamilnadu's Muslim population lives in urban centres. By comparison, the state's urban population as a whole is 26.7 per cent urban.

Pallavaram is a town of over 50,000.[2] Located just south of Madras City, it is an urban satellite of the metropolis. Since it is within easy commuting distance of Madras and has a rapidly developing industrial sector of its own, Pallavaram's size has mushroomed during the last twenty years. The town's bazaar has expanded too. It is in the bazaar that the Muslim merchants work, and most of them live and conduct their social affairs around it. The Muslims are one of the most successful groups of merchants[3] in the bazaar, although they are not as numerous as the Hindus. Concomitant with Pallavaram's growth, there has been an influx of Muslim and Hindu merchants into the bazaar.

Pallavaram's merchants have come from throughout Tamil-

2. Data on Pallavaram and its Muslims are based on research conducted between September 1967 and February 1969. I wish to express my appreciation to the Foreign Area Fellowship Program which supported this research.

3. It is important to note that Muslims are divided into fourteen recognized subdivisions in Pallavaram and so do not constitute a single social body (see Mines, 1972b:338).

nadu state—a few from as far afield as Kashmir and Rajasthan. Sixty-six per cent of all merchants claimed to have migrated to Pallavaram; seventy-four per cent of the Muslim merchants have. Merchants come from a wide variety of places and represent a wide variety of castes and religious communities. The merchant population does not form a uniform community (see also Fox, 1967:301) similar to those found in the urban slums studied by Woodruff (1960), Rowe (1964) and Lynch (1967). In the merchants' residential areas surrounding the bazaar there is no clear residence pattern based on caste or religion. The merchant castes—of which, including the Muslim subdivisions, there are thirty-eight—live intermingled among one another. The competitive nature of the merchants' occupation explains their diverse backgrounds. Successful competition requires the merchant to deal with persons of all castes. Merchants, regardless of caste or community, are attracted to wherever there are economic opportunities so that the chances of a single community or caste monopolizing a bazaar are extremely limited.

The residence pattern of the bazaar is determined by the desire of the proprietors to live as close as possible to their shops. Merchants want the convenience of returning home for lunch and the customary afternoon nap. Living nearby their shops also enables them to keep a close eye on their business. Commuting from outside Pallavaram is uncommon.

Despite the migratory origins of a large percentage of Pallavaram's merchants, fifty-three per cent of the merchants surveyed[4] indicated that they had kins engaged in business in the town. Sixty-one per cent of the Muslims merchants have relations of this sort. If one counts relations engaged in business in the Madras metropolitan area the percentage increases greatly. Quite simply, Muslim merchants choose where to migrate in

4. These and subsequent figures were collected in a comprehensive survey of all shop merchants within the bazaar. The survey was made by the author and his research assistant using a formal questionnaire. The total number of respondents was 197. However, not all merchants who were surveyed answered all the questions asked. One of the main reasons for this was that proprietors were not always available for interviews and their shop assistants often did not know answers to some questions. Thus, percentages are not always based on the total sample of 197.

terms of where they have kinsmen and where they expect to find economic opportunities. Merchants are quite explicit about this.

They migrate to where they have relations in business because these kins know the nature of local consumer demands and can give advice about the kinds of business which are likely to prove successful. Similarly, since they are established in the area they can support the incoming kins in the face of other established merchants. If the newcomer needs a loan, his kinsman may provide the loan or can help procure one by vouching for the latter's reliability. Social-concessional credit loans of the type described by Hazlehurst (1966:96ff) are sometimes 'underwritten' in this fashion. And relatives are usually the first source of loans to which merchants turn. Relatives cooprate closely with each other mainly because it is socially and economically profitable. Cloth merchants, for instance, will share the cost of cloth which must be bought in larger quantities than is convenient for them to buy separately and will share the cloth.

Tamil Muslim merchants migrate as family units. This is the prevailing pattern throughout much of South India (see Gist, 1955; Woodruff, 1960) in contrast to North India (Rowe, 1964). Migration of single males is associated largely with poverty and with merchants who originate in Kerala or in the North. The practical value of a merchant migrating with his family is readily apparent when we examine the structure of business management.

Bazaar enterprises are family businesses, and family organization forms the basis of business management. This pattern of organization is widespread in South Asia and is as characteristic of large-scale enterprises (Singer, 1968; Papanek, 1973) as it is of small-scale endeavours (Fox, 1969; Hazlehurst, 1966; Berna, 1960). Typically, the head of the household is also the manager of the business. His sons act as his assistants and oversee cash transactions in his absence. If a merchant has no sons, then a son-in-law or a poor relation substitutes. The point is that a close kinsman, preferably someone whose fortune is tied to the proprietor's family fortunes, acts as manager and overseer at all times. Such assistants are necessary to enable the merchant to have the freedom of movement necessary to replenish stocks and handle personal needs without fear of theft by a disloyal employee whose interests do not coincide with his own. It is for this reason that partnerships between unrelated persons are a very rare business practice in Pallavaram as they are in small-scale industry in Tamilnadu as a whole (Berna, 1960:48). The self-interests of men who are not members of the same corporate household do not coincide. Often for good reason, suspicion and mistrust loom larger in partnerships and soon lead to their dissolution.

Given this kind of mistrust, it is little wonder that, as businesses grow in size, family organization continues to dominate the structure of business management. The pattern of business expansion in the Pallavaram bazaar is to multiply the number of enterprises one has following the rule of not placing all one's eggs in one basket. As the merchant's fortunes wax he divides his investment and sets up new shops of different kinds meeting a different set of consumer demands. Abdullah provides an example. His first shop dealt in sundries. Subsequently, he opened a firewood shop, a provision store dealing in foodstuffs, a bakery and a general merchandise store selling everything from soda pop to chillies.

The joint family structure is well suited to the management needs of this type of business expansion. The household head occupies the apex of authority and oversees all the family enterprises. His sons individually manage the separate shops, while their sons or other relations act as their respective assistants. There seem to be no real limits to which this type of family business management structure can be expanded. Milton Singer, for example, found it prevalent among large-scale industrialists in Madras (1968:426). If the demand for management personnel is greater than the supply of family members, then Muslim merchants introduce new members into their household. Commonly, poorer relations are brought into the household, often while quite young. Sometimes a son-in-law is recruited. In any case, the effort is always to see that the management is in the hands of persons whose interests coincide with the proprietor's.

The incidence of joint family organization in the bazaar falls within the range of what has been found elsewhere in urban India (Kapadia, 1966:273-308). Forty-three per cent of the businesses are operated by joint families which usually consist of a man and his sons, less frequently his sons-in-law. All of the larger enterprises, many of which consist of multiple businesses, are operated by joint families. It is among the larger merchants that the economic advantages[5] of joint family management and the organizational advantages coincide.

What other areas of the merchant's social life does kinship organize? It is evident from the foregoing discussion that the household is *the* corporate economic unit of Pallavaram's Muslim Tamils. Accordingly, all economic activities fall within its jurisdiction. For a household member to conduct a business on the side, clandestinely, is intolerable. Such behaviour is nevertheless not unusual. When discovered, such transgressions are dealt with harshly, often with the expulsion of the guilty party from the household.

Not everyone within the household has an equal share in its economic assets. According to the Tamil Muslims, only agnates are shareholders. They may include a man, his sisters if they have not already separated from the household, his sons and daughters, and any children his sons may have. A female agnate is said to have a share equal to one-third that of her male counterpart, but the custom varies among families. Commonly, a woman is said to receive her share of wealth in the form of dowry (*siirtanam*). Tamil Muslim women may also receive at marriage valuable gifts (*parisam*) from the groom's family, largely in the form of jewellery and other presents not including cash. Such wealth belongs personally to her. Persons who are not agnates have no right to household wealth except as dependants. This is why poor relations who have been brought into the household often become self-seeking. There is no other way for them to gain financially unless the household head is generous and launches them into business or marries them to his daughters. Both practices occur, but often enough disputes arise before this happens.

Among Tamil Hindus, the *pangaali* is a unit ot agnatically related coparceners, all of whom share certain ritual obligatic

5. Fox (1969:171 fn) notes that joint families receive a significantly greater tax exemption than do single-earner families. Hence the economic advantages of joint family management are multiple.

(e.g., observance of death pollution). Most Tamil Muslims also recognize this kin grouping which is an agnatic sublineage. Among Muslims, however, its significance is modified, since the unit has no ritual significance and death pollution is theoretically not recognized. Among Muslims, the *pangaali* corresponds to the corporate household and coparcenary rights are terminated by partitioning. Among Hindus, partitioning may occur but the *pangaali* persists as a ritual unit.

The patrilineage in Tamilnadu is known as the *vamsam*. Tamil Muslims recognize such a unit, but it has little importance in Pallavaram. However, in the extreme south of Tamilnadu *vamsams* are significant social units among certain Muslim groups. A Rawther from Ramanadapuram District indicated that there *vamsams* are named, exogamous and ranked groups. Certain Muslim *vamsams* in Ramanadapuram have titles which include Hindu caste names, a clear sign that the Muslims belonging to them are converts to Islam to whom caste distinctions still have some relevance. The occurrence of Hindu caste names among Tamil Muslims is extremely rare. Except for the Ramanadapuram Muslims, I never encountered such usage. Unlike the Christian population of the state, Muslim converts forget their former caste affiliations.

Muslims living in Pallavaram who come from Dindigal and its hinterland in Madurai District distinguish a kin unit which is similar to the *vamsam*. They call it the *vakayyaraa*, the Tamil equivalent of 'etcetera', or *kudambam peer* (family name). Typically, the family name designates a place of origin, an incident in the life of an ancestor or the former occupation of an ancestor. *Aattumiiran vakayyarra*, *Paalapattiyaan vakayyarra* and *Seemartaa vakayyarra* represent examples of such names. *Aattumiiran* refers to the founder of a *vakayyaraa* who, people say, once ate a whole goat single-handed. The name reflects the legend. *Paalapattiyaan* refers to a village, and so on. Some names are humorous; some are straightforward and descriptive. The *vakayyaraa* name is a common means of identification. When one seeks to establish a person's identity, knowledge of his *vakayyaraa* name reveals his family connections and his identity as a representative of his kin group becomes apparent.

The *vakayyaraa* differs from the *vamsam* and the patrilineal *pangaali* kin units. It is not a corporate group as the *pangaali* is, and it is not patrilineal. Every person belongs both to his mother's and to his father's *vakayyaraa.* It is not uncommon for individuals who know a woman's *vakayyaraa* to refer to her children in terms of her family name rather than the father's. Most often, however, when a person is asked who he is, the question is meant to elicit the father's *vakayyaraa,* not the mother's. Greater emphasis is placed on the father's name than on the mother's. As a result, the family name usually refers to an agnatically related grouping incorporating the *pangaali*—but not always. *Vakayyaraas* may be bilateral. One Labbai family from Vellore, North Arcot, uses the family name of household head's wife's father, who was in his day a very important man in the Muslim community of Tamilnadu state. The *vakayyaraa,* therefore, is a cognatic grouping with a patrilineal emphasis simliar to the bilateral kin units of the Sinhalese described by Leach (1960:116-126) and classified as quasi-unilineal by Murdock (1960:7-9).

The economic relevance of the *pangaali, vamsam* and *vakayyaraa* is that they define the property-owning units among Muslim and Hindu Tamilian merchants. The *vakayyaraa* group usually refers to the extended joint family, *pangaali* to a ritually related group of coparceners among Hindus—to coparceners among Muslims. Unlike the *pangaali,* the *vakayyaraa* is not an exogamous group.

In Pallavaram caste distinctions are not significant among the Tamil Muslims (Mines, 1972b, 1973a), but subdivisional ethnic distinctions are. Subdivisional ethnicity is based on place of origin and differences in customs including language. There are four Tamil Muslim subdivisions—Rawther, Marakayar, Kayalar and Labbai. In Pallavaram, none of the subdivisions stand in a subordinate or superordinate relationship to one another. They are not economically or socially interdependent groups. On the contrary, they fiercely defend their equality and independence. All except the Marakayars, who are few in number, share in the management of the local Big Mosque. Local Muslims take this as a sign of their equality, as they do also their commensality, joint prayer and joint use of the graveyard and Koranic school. It is important to note here that Tamil Muslims are not internally divided by caste but that caste is important to them when they interact with Hindus. In their native villages Muslims relate to others as a caste with many of the characteristic features of interdependence, but caste is absent amongst themselves.

In Pallavaram the stress of intergroup relations is on equality. The presence of intergroup marriages among the Tamil Muslims clearly reveals this (Mines, 1972b). In no instance does anyone express the feeling that such marriages are improper. No social ostracism takes place, and the children of such marriages suffer no social stigma. Intergroup marriages often do raise some eyebrows because they are unusual (I recorded ten among Tamil Muslims) and it is common to hear speculation that such marriages are love-matches. Some are, some are not.

Intergroup marriages and the popular acceptance of them reveals two features about Tamil Muslim ethnic divisions. First, in Pallavaram the divisions are not corporate groups; and, second, blood purity does not greatly affect social status. Usually membership in a group is determined by one's parentage. In the case of intergroup marriages, children may align themselves with the division of either their mother or their father. The example given above of a Labbai family which identified with a maternal family name is illustrative. Their Labbai designation, like their family name, is traced maternally. Paternally they are Rawthers. Hence, shifting ethnic identity occurs fairly readily, at least in the cities.

For Hindu castes, blood purity is considered essential to caste membership, and purity is an important component of their ideology of caste ranking. The offspring of mixed, intercaste marriages are stigmatized and are not accepted as equal to their parents. Among Muslims, children of mixed marriages are accepted and are treated as equal to their parents. In fact, they can choose to emphasize the more prestigious side of their family. The following case provides an example of intermarriage among Tamil Muslims.

There is a core of Muslim merchants in the bazaar area, all of whom have fairly large businesses and all of whom are distantly related to one another. These merchants form a leadership clique among the Muslims. One of their members is the most powerful political figure in the town; he is associated with the popular ruling DMK Party and is president of one of the Pallavaram governing councils (*panchayats*). These merchants are among the leaders of the Pallavaram Merchants' Association which is composed of a majority of the Hindu and Muslim merchants in the bazaar. And several belong to the governing board of the Pallavaram Big Mosque. The Mosque is frequented by the largest *jama'at* (membership) and all the members of this kin-related clique are Labbais except for a Rawther family which married into the group three years ago after twenty years of residence in the town. For a number of years the head of this Rawther household has been on the governing boards of the Big Mosque and the Koranic school and has held a position of respect in the community as a successful businessman and as a religious leader.

When I enquired into the reasons for arranging the marriage which give this merchant's family kin ties with the Labbai members of the clique, I found that they were twofold. The first was that by becoming kinsmen to numerous wealthy businessmen the family cemented ties which emphasized their social prestige. Second, although this Rawther merchant and his family had been living in Pallavaram for twenty years, the town had not become their home, their 'native place'. Shortly after the marriage they sold their house in their native village, an act which symbolized their family's gradual social reorientation toward Pallavaram and away from their village of origin. Until this intergroup marriage the Rawther family had arranged most of its marriages with families from or nearby its native village. The children of the marriage are still too young to indicate what subdivision they will identify with, but, given the patrilineal emphasis of Tamil Muslim kinship and the relative prestige of the Rawther family, they will probably identify with the Rawthers.

It becomes clear that ethnic identity is closely related to kinship identity, and that the two overlap in some contexts. In cities, ethnic identity provides clues to social and cultural heritage. It provides Tamil Muslims with an identity which lies beyond the realm of kinship, which in the context of the city often does not extend much beyond the joint family. It identifies a person with a group which is general enough to be meaningful in cities, where kinship structures family and business organization but little else. In the village, subdivisional distinctions are of little relevance, since everyone is of the same group. There kinship's influences is more pervasive, organizing not just family and the distribution of wealth but local organization, political allegiance and much else (see Lewis, 1965; Mandelbaum, 1970). The size of cities and the limited nature of kin ties among urban residents weakens the role of kinship in organizing urban social life.

Tamil Muslim shopkeepers are interested in joining, through marriage, families following similar types of professions and occupying similar economic positions. An examination of six genealogies of Tamil Muslim merchants revealed that in 70 per cent of the marriages the grooms were engaged in business. It was found that a high percentage (61 per cent) of the marriages occurred between relatives, although the exact nature of the relationship involved in all cases was not always known by the informant. Cross-cousin marriage among first cousins was not common; but classificatory cross-cousin marriage was much more common. Patrilateral parallel-cousin marriage, although it is allowed among Muslims, was also not common. Tamil Muslims are ambivalent about the propriety of this type of marriage, because patrilateral parallel-cousins are classed by Tamilians as brothers and sisters.

A survey of Pallavaram's shopkeepers indicates that 70 per cent had fathers who were businessmen before them. Obviously, shopkeepers breed shopkeepers. Shopkeepers do show flexibility in the kinds of businesses they run. Slightly less than half of these merchants are engaged in enterprises which are different from those of their fathers'.

Kinship does not determine the nature of social integration in the bazaar; business does that. Kinship's web, however, ties Tamil Muslims to relations living in numerous urban centres and villages. Most merchants maintain regular contacts with their native places. Sixty-six per cent of Pallavaram bazaar's merchants originate from elsewhere, 74 per cent of these from urban areas. Merchants are, thus, a highly urbanized stratum of society.

Most merchants return annually to their native places or to places where close relatives live. In addition, two-thirds own, or have close relatives who own, a house, if only a hut, or a small amount of land in their place of origin. Property and kinship tie people to their native places. Merchants have many reasons for visiting their homes. The most common reasons are to see relatives, to attend life-crises ceremonies, to attend festivals, to visit an ailing relative, to arrange a marriage, to attend to business, and to go just to get away from it all—to take a vacation.

Tamilians prefer to marry kinsmen and 61 per cent of Pallavaram's Tamil Muslims do. There is no restriction on marrying locally—village exogamy is absent. But among Muslims marriages do not occur predominantly among persons of the same native place. Analysing 138 marriages gleaned from the genealogies of three Tamil Muslim merchants, it was found that 38 per cent of the marriages occurred between people from the same place. This data obscures the influence of urbanization on marriage. As a highly urban population, the mobility of Tamil Muslims is high. Genealogies indicate that Tamil Muslim merchants have relations scattered in an average of seven different towns. The range is between three and thirteen. Distances between kinsmen range from just a few miles to the distance between Rangoon and Pallavaram. The result of urbanization is the regional dispersal of kinsmen. This means that Muslims often have relations concentrated in more than one locality, or kin-centre (see Mines, 1972:85ff). Taking this urban dispersal of kinsmen into account, it was found that most marriages were between persons who are related and whose relations share at least one common kin-centre.

It sometimes happens that neither the family of the groom nor of the bride reside in the kin-centre. However, the bride and the groom may both consider the centre to be their native place. What happens is that at yearly festivals or such occasions as life-crisis ceremonies men and their wives return to their kin-centres, meet kinsmen and friends, sometimes for the first time in years, hear news about their relatives and fellow villagers, display their successes in conspicuous consumption, learn about who is marriageable, and make arrangements for the marriage of their children. It is not uncommon for the bride's family to hold the wedding at the kin-centre where a maximum number of kinsmen can attend, even though the bride's family is not in full-time residence there.

I visited some Rawther villages in Madurai District near Dindigal where most of the houses were deserted for much of the year except during an important annual festival. At that festival a large number of the Muslims who were merchants in towns all over Tamilnadu returned to the village to arrange marriages, to observe the first hair-cutting ceremony of their children, to perform *khatna* (circumcision), to give feasts, or for other events. People renewed friendships, old disputes were revived, factional divisions continued, and newly successful individuals made efforts to raise the social status of their families. Class consciousness was high. The native village of these merchants, many of whom had been living elsewhere for generations, was a focus of social interaction among kinsmen normally living in separate localities. It also gave Muslims a sense of their subdivisional ethnic identity when they returned to the city. The village in this fashion formed, once a year, a nexus in the network of social interaction for its absentee natives. Muslims who had no special reason for returning to the village might stay away for years or until they had some purpose for returning.

Most of the year Muslim merchants live in the town or city where they are conducting business. During the year, in addition to maintaining ties with relatives in the kin-centres, merchants retain close social contacts with relatives living in surrounding towns. If a death or some other event of importance to kinsmen occurs, messages are sent to relatives. If the relatives live close enough they come with their families to the house where the occurrence has taken place or, minimally, they send a family member to represent them. A number of ceremonies are performed throughout the year by various families, as the occasions for them arise, and relatives are invited to these also. Ceremonies like *puu poodutal*, a girls' maturation ceremony, or *maktab*, a boy's first Koran lesson, are times for close relatives to gather. At such occasions relatives will travel from their own town to another town in order to participate, although the feeling of obligation to attend simple ceremonies is not very strong.

It is apparent from the foregoing discussion that kinship

is of fundamental importance to merchants in the urban setting. But kinship is not what brings all the merchants together within the bazaar area. Other factors link them, particularly shared business interests, politics and religion. The Pallavaram Merchants' Association is an expression of the merchants' common interests. Its main purpose is to regulate holidays within the bazaar so that no unfair competition can occur when shops close to replenish their stocks. The Association has set aside Tuesday as a day when all shops should close enabling merchants time to restock their stores. Members who do not cooperate in this manner are fined. Similarly, the Association puts pressure on non-members to observe the holidays recognized by it. The Association, which is about ten years old, used to perform other functions, including the annual feast and settlement of disputes.

In terms of the active involvement of their members, the political party organizations and religious organizations are much more important than the Merchants' Association. Both of the major political parties, the Congress and DMK, have organizations centered in Pallavaram to which merchants of several different castes as well as different religions belong. Hindu and Muslim merchants are prominent in both party organizations, and members of both communities hold offices in them.

The Hindus and Muslims have religious associations in Pallavaram. The Muslims, for example, operate three mosques and several shrines within the town. Merchants are prominent religious leaders among the Muslims and are the leaders of the largest mosque in town. They control the board of directors of the Big Mosque as well as the *Madrassah* (Koranic school) Board. Hindus have temple associations which manage temple affairs. And Jains are closely coorperative in their religious pursuits, although they do not have an association in Pallavaram proper.

In addition to the three associations discussed so far, there are several others which have merchant members both within the town and in Madras. Among the more formal of these are the *Jamaat-e-Islam-i-Hind*—an Islamic, ideologically-oriented, political association regionally based in Madras City; and various caste associations—such as the Achari (goldsmith) caste association, known as the *Visvakarma Sangam*, and the jewellers' association. The *Jamaat-e-Islam-i-Hind* is a national organization. The others are part of statewide organizations. Despite the prominence of some of these groups, it would be incorrect to think that they displace caste or kinship in bazaar society. Although numerous Hindus belong to caste associations, very few of them actively participate in the affairs of these associations. This is similarly true of those Muslims who very occasionally attend *Jamaat-e-Islam-i-Hind* meetings.

Of the associations, the Big Mosque *Jama'at* and the local political organizations are the most important to the merchants of the bazaar. This is because the activities of these organizations are concerned with problems crucial to most merchants, and consequently they delineate the most important social areas for leadership among the merchants of the bazaar area.

Associations do not form as important a factor structuring social relations within the town as Kenneth Little (1965) has found in West Africa or as Rowe (1964) contends for Bombay. This may well be the result of two things—the size of Pallavaram and the merchant occupation. Pallavaram is not a large town. It is small enough so that face-to-face relationships prevail within the bazaar. Beyond the simple functions of the Merchants' Association, merchants feel that they can most effectively handle their business affairs individually or in a small cooperating group usually composed of relatives, friends or close associates such as neighbours. This is in part a function of the merchant occupation which is by its nature, competitive and, as we have seen, based on the family structure. I was told several times when enquiring about leadership in the bazaar that each merchant thinks of himself as king.

In Pallavaram, merchants join associations when they feel that there is some personal gain to be obtained. This is why the Merchants' Association was initially so successful in attracting members. Each merchant stood to benefit from a uniform weekly closing day. But so many kings make for weak cooperation. The Association has not developed beyond the management of this minimal cooperation. Merchants feel that the Associations' value to them is limited to achieving what they cannot obtain separately. They see no gain in making the Association into something more. Similarly, the jeweller's association experienced a brief period of vigorous activity before a hiatus set in when the Indian Government tried to ban the use of twenty-two carat gold. When the crisis to the jewellers passed, the involvement of the Pallavaram merchants in the Association dropped. The Association lies dormant pending another crisis which threatens its members' well being.

Much more important than associations in structuring links among people in the bazaar are the cooperative bonds formed by neighbours and friends. Despite their highly competitive orientation, merchants within the bazaar feel that a certain degree of cooperation is necessary. Neighbouring shopkeepers often help one another at times when they are in financial or domestic need. Such cooperation is common between established., successful merchants and their poorer neighbours. In this case the wealthier merchant's help may be the key to the smaller merchant's survival. In return, the larger merchant receives the loyalty and support of the person he has helped.

The bases of friendship are, of course, numerous. Friendships are limited to persons of approximately the same age. Cliques of three to four merchants who gossip together, grumble about their troubles and assist one another are common and long-standing. Friendships are not limited by caste or religion. Friendships occur which may seem superficially unlikely, such as one between a Jain and a Muslim. Jains and Muslims are almost proverbially antagonistic due to the association of Jains with money-lending and vegetarianism and Muslims with meat-eating and an abhorrence of money-lending. Yet bonds such as this one are formed often while the persons involved are in school. Friendships form the basis for very strong cooperative links between merchants. It is often through such ties that needed finances are raised, new credit is arranged and other business contacts are made.

Taking into account the presence of ties of caste, of small cooperative groups of merchants, of friendship, and of associations, kinship must be viewed as just one mechanism by which the urban social organization of the bazaar is formed. Yet urban life does not involve a complete transformation to a contractual, voluntary order either. Voluntary associations are not nearly as pervasive as these other phenomena in structuring links among people of the bazaar. It does not appear, therefore, that the development of associations indicates a transformation of Indian social structure or that they herald a shift from kinship to contract as the structural basis linking social relationships in the urban setting. Their existence, however, does indicate that with urbanization the basis of Indian social organization diversifies.

It has been commonly felt that when the rural dweller moved to the city he moved into an arena in which his old social structure based on village patterns was no longer adequate to maintain social unity. Alice Dewey's analysis is fairly typical of this kind of thinking, although she writes about Java:

> Village organization is based on interdependence among the inhabitants. Good relations with one's neighbours give access to land and to labour, and without the cooperation of others neither rich nor poor could farm successfully. However, when people leave the village they leave the social and economic basis for the organization and its sanctions, the demands of trade and wage labour do not furnish a new basis for group formation, since in most instances, it is economically preferable to work independently. The old social structure therefore loses its force .... In the future, trade unions, political parties, or other organizations may create structured groups (1962: 41-2).

This kind of transformation has not occurred in the Pallavaram bazaar. The Muslim merchant's adjustment to urban life has been one which has relied heavily on the maintenance and utilization of existing kin ties to assist his entry into the city and into business and then to bolster his social niche once he is there. Kinship forms the basis of business organization. It has not lost its force because it still has a valid economic basis. Merchants say that without the help of their kinsmen and the cooperation of their neighbours they could not operate a successful business. From time to time, every merchant is in need of support, sometimes financial, sometimes social. Kinship lies at the crux. Businesses are family concerns, merchants migrate where they have relatives, and business credit as well as loans frequently involve social-concessional ties. These are just a few of the important ways in which kinship influences business behaviour. Similarly, kinship is naturally important in the formation of social alliances, since it is one's kinsmen whom one relies on as potential allies in times of need. Friendships and neighbourly cooperation likewise are important. At the same time, kinship's influence in the city is not as all-encompassing as it is in the countryside. Kin units above the joint family are not significiant, and kinship's influence is negligible in politics and residential organization.

Associations do not replace kinship as Little (1965) has found in West Africa or as Dewey (1962) had predicted for the poor Javanese trader. In Pallavaram, associations are primarily important for achieving particular social ends such as the establishment of uniform holidays or the fighting of the imposition of gold restrictions. Once such goals are achieved the associations become dormant. This is why political and religious associations are the most active in Pallavaram. Politics and religion embrace an unending series of problems: their goals are never completely achieved.

Bibliography

Barnett, S.A. (n.d.), 'Urban is as Urban Does', M.S.

Berna, James J. (1960), *Industrial Entrepreneurship in Madras State*, Bombay, Asia Publishing House.

Dewey, Alice (1962), *Peasant Marketing in Java*, New York, The Free Press.

Fox, Richard (1967), 'Family, Caste, and Commerce in a North Indian Market Town', *Economic Development and Culture Change*, 15, pp. 297-314.

———(1969), *From Zamindar to Ballot Box*, Ithaca, Cornell University Press.

Gist, Noel P. (1955), 'Selective Migration in South India' *Sociological Bulletin*, 4, pp. 147-160.

Hardgrave, Robert L., Jr. (1969), *The Nadars of Tamilnad: The Political Culture of a Community in Change*, Berkeley and Los Angeles, University of California Press.

Hardgrave, Robert L., Jr. (1970), 'Urbanization and the Structure of Caste', in Richard E. Fox (ed.), *Urban India: Society, Space and Image*, Comparative Studies on Southern Asia, Monograph No. 10, Durham, Duke University Press.

Hazlehurst, Leighton W. (1960), *Entrepreneurship and the Merchant Castes in a Punjabi City*, Comparative Studies on Southern Asia, Monograph No. 1, Durham, Duke University Press.

———(1968), 'The Middle-Range City in India,' *Asian Survey*, 8, pp. 539-552.

India, Government of (1902), *Census of India, 1901, Vol. XV, Madras, Part I*, Madras, Government Press.

———(1962), *Census of India, 1961, Vol. IX, Madras District Census Handbooks, Part X, i-xii*, Madras, Government Press.

Kapadia, K.M. (1966), *Marriage and Family in India*, Calcutta, Oxford University Press.

Lambert, Richard D. (1962), 'The Impact of Urban Society Upon Village Life' in Roy Turner (ed.), *India's Urban Future*, Los Angeles and Berkeley, University of California Press.

Leach, Edmund R. (1960), 'The Sinhalese of the Dry Zone of Northern Ceylon', in George P. Murdock (ed.), *Social Structure in Southeast Asia*, Chicago, Quadrangle Books.

Lewis, Oscar (1965), *Village Life in Northern India*, New York, Vintage Books.

Little, Kenneth (1965), *West African Urbanization*, Cambridge, Cambridge University Press.

Lynch, Owen (1967), 'Rural Cities in India: Continuities and Discontinuities', in Philip Mason (ed.), *India and Ceylon: Unity and Diversity*, London, Oxford University Press.

Mandelbaum, David G. (1970), *Society in India*, Vol. I, Berkeley and Los Angeles, University of California Press.

Marriott, McKim (1968) 'Multiple Reference in Indian Caste System', in James Silverberg (ed), *Social Mobility in the Caste System in India*, Comparative Studies in Society and History, Supplement III, The Hague, Mouton.

Mines, Mattison, (1972a), *Muslim Merchants: The Economic Behaviour of an Indian Muslim Community*, New Delhi, Shri Ram Centre for Industrial Relations and Human Resources.

———(1972b), 'Muslim Social Stratification in India: The

Basis for Variation', *South-Western Journal of Anthropology*, 28, pp. 333-339.

———(1973a), 'Social Stratification among the Muslim Tamils in Tamilnadu, South India', in Imtiaz Ahmad (ed.), *Caste and Social Stratification among the Muslims*, Delhi, Manohar Book Service.

———(1973b) 'Tamil Muslim Merchants in India's Industrial Development', in Milton Singer (ed.), *Entrepreneurship and Modernization of Occupational Cultures in South Asia*; Comparative Studies on Southern Asia, Monograph No. 12, Durham, Duke University Press.

Murdock, Geogre P. (1960), 'Cognatic Forms of Social Organization', in G.P. Murdock (ed.), *Social Structure in Southeast Asia*, Chicago, Quadrangle Books.

Papanek, Hanna (1973), 'Pakistan's New Industrialists and Businessmen: Focus on the Memons', in Milton Singer (ed.), *Entrepreneurship and Modernization of Occupational Cultures in South Asia*, Comparative Studies on Southern Asia, Monograph No. 12, Durham, Duke University Press.

Pocock, David F (1960), 'Sociologies: Urban and Rural', *Contributions to Indian Sociology*, 4, pp. 63-81.

Rowe, William L. (1964), 'Caste, Kinship and Association in Urban India', Wenner-Gren Foundation for Anthropological Research, Burg Wartenstein Symposium.

Singer, Milton (1968), 'The Indian Joint Family in Modern Industry', in Milton Singer and Bernard S. Cohn (eds.) *Structure and Change in Indian Society*, Chicago, Aldine Publishing Company.

Woodruff, Gertrude M. (1960), 'Family Migration in Bangalore', *Economic Weekly*, 12, pp. 163-172.

Caste and Kinship in a Muslim Village of Eastern Uttar Pradesh[1]

Imtiaz Ahmad

This essay has been prompted by two recent comments on the significance of kinship in Muslim communities in South Asian countries. The first is the comment made by Hamza Alavi at the beginning of his perceptive analysis of kinship in West Pakistan villages. 'Underlying much of the literature on South Asian rural societies', writes Alavi, 'is the assumption that these societies are structurally similar, if not identical in every detail, and that the distinguishing feature of the structure of social institutions in those societies is their focus

1. The fieldwork on which this paper is based was carried out between 1960 and 1962. I subsequently returned to the village for brief visits in 1967 and 1972, but my discussion is based primarily on the data collected during the first phase of fieldwork. I am grateful to the Delhi School of Economics and Ministry of Education, Government of India, for awarding me a Research Fellowship of the Department of Sociology, University of Delhi, and the Humanities Scholarship for undertaking fieldwork in the village between 1960 and 1962 and to the University Grants Commission and the Jawaharlal Nehru University for Research Grants to revisit it in 1967 and 1972 respectively. I am also thankful to Professors M.N. Srinivas and M.S.A. Rao who, as my research supervisors at that time, offered me their valuable advice. However, I am alone to blame for the many deficiencies from which this paper obviously suffers.

on caste and the related *jajmani* system as bases of social organization. The kinship system, which is generally accorded a central place in social anthropological analysis, is in this case relegated to the background. In the Muslim rural society of West Punjab, however, the contrary is true. There it is the kinship system rather than caste which embodies the primordial loyalties which structure its social organization' (Alavi, 1972:1). The second is Hardy's comment calling in question 'the operational usefulness of the "caste" model for the understanding not only of distinctions of wealth, status, and power, but also of the primal area of caste functioning, namely, of marriage relationships' (Hardy, 1975:392).

These comments rest on two distinct sets of assumptions which, while they are not explicitly stated by their authors, are nevertheless implied by their statements. The first assumption is that caste does not exist among the Muslims and any attempt to apply the 'caste' model to the study of the social structure of Muslim communities in South Asian countries is likely to distort the nature of social reality and thereby obstruct the understanding of the basic features of Muslim social organization in South Asia.[2] Hardy does not adduce any

2. This assumption is not limited to these two authors, but is more widely held. If the literature on social stratification among Muslims in South Asia is carefully examined, it will be found that there is a strong association between the nationality of the authors and their preference for the caste or class framework of analysis. Generally speaking, scholars working on Muslim groups in India (see Ahmad, 1973) Ceylon (see Mauroof, 1972) and Nepal (see Gaboreau, 1972) have employed the concept of caste in the analysis of social stratification in Muslim communities. On the other hand, Pakistani scholars have usually tended to use the class framework to the exclusion of the caste framework (see, for instance, Inayatullah, 1958; Khan, 1968; Ahmad, 1970 and Alavi, 1972). Pakistani scholars seem to maintain that their own society stands in contrast to the characteristic pattern of caste-based groupings, and they deny altogether the relevance of caste as a feature of the social structure of their society. Even where they concede the presence of a caste-like social stratification among Muslims, they argue that it owes itself to some Islamic tenets and is not due to the acculturative impact of Hinduism (see Khan, 1968). I am personally unable to see the validity of these formulations, but comparative studies focussing on the distinguishing features of the

empirical evidence to support this assumption by the very limited scope of his contribution, but Alavi tries to substantiate it by providing empirical data from his field area. 'Groups bearing the same *zat* names are not, by that token, brought together to constitute societal units nor does the concept of *zat* imply any rules of social interaction', asserts Alavi. 'The endogamous system has the effect of constituting compact, tightly organized and self-contained but, at the same time, small and localized *biradari* groups. It creates a social organization which is locally cohesive but spatially fragmented. All *biradaris* in the endogamous system have *zat* names. Such names are used locally, as surnames, to identify the *biradaris*, but the existence of *zat* names does not signify the existence of caste in the contemporary society' (Alavi, 1972:26).

The second assumption underlying both the comments is that caste and kinship are mutually exclusive principles of social organization and the presence of one automatically rules out the existence of the other. This assumption is again implied by both Alavi and Hardy. Indeed, Alavi comes very near to stating it explicitly when he seeks to draw a distinction between those South Asian rural societies which are organized on the basis of caste and the related *jajmani* system and those structured on the principle of kinship and when he decries the almost total lack of interest in the study of kinship on the part of those who have looked at the structure of South Asian societies in terms of the caste system.[3]

structure of social stratification in the different South Asian countries could be fruitfully explored. Such studies would go a long way in delineating the unity and diversity among Muslim communities in South Asian countries (see Ahmad, 1975).

3. It is not altogether correct that studies of the kinship system have been neglected by sociologists and social anthropologists who have focussed their attention on societies wherein the existence of caste is an established fact. Quite to the contrary, the study of kinship has been a central concern even of those scholars who have been primarily interested in the study of caste and its related *jajmani* system (see, for instance, Dumont, 1957; Karve, 1953; Mayer, 1960; and Madan, 1965). Furthermore, there has been a resurgence of this interest in kinship in these societies and a number of extremely refreshing studies have appeared on the subject recently (see, for

Unfortunately, neither Alavi nor Hardy state explicitly whether their assertion, that caste and kinship are mutually exclusive organizing principles of social organization, applies generally or holds good only for Muslim communities. The former, their assumption could be refuted easily. More than a decade ago, Mayer's excellent analysis (Mayer, 1960) of Ramkheri had shown that caste and kinship existed as principles of social organization simultaneously, each serving a different function in different social contexts. Clearly, therefore, Alavi and Hardy are positing the mutual exclusiveness between caste and kinship as being a particular feature of Muslim communities in South Asian countries rather than maintaining that it holds true for all communities. This conclusion is buttressed by the fact that Alavi refers approvingly to Mayer's analysis and adopts his terminology for his particular purposes.

My aim in this paper is to examine the assumption implied by both Alavi and Hardy that caste and kinship constitute mutually exclusive organizational principles of social structure. I realize that this assumption on their part is largely a product of the assumption that there is no caste among the Muslims, but I shall skip the examination of that question almost entirely. For one thing, I have already dealt with this question at some length elsewhere (see Ahmad, 1973a) and nothing much would be gained by going over the arguments presented there again. Furthermore, the question of the presence of caste among the Muslims has been shrouded in a controversy wherein arguments have ranged, as Alavi rightly notes, from purely ideologically charged refutations (see Inayatullah, 1958 and Khan, 1968) to attempts to show that the ideological-religious justification as well as the formal cultural attributes of caste are not to be found among the Muslims[4] so that the final settlement of this question could

instance, Van der Veen, 1972; Pocock, 1972; Vatuk 1972; and Shah, 1974). Among the two most detailed analyses of kinship among Muslim communities of the region are the studies by Dube (1969) and Kutty (1972).

4. Alavi himself tends to lean toward this position towards the end of his paper. 'The central criteria of caste-oriented behaviour, namely, that of ritual pollution and associated purificatory rites,

best be left to wider empirical evidence.[5]

I propose to base my examination on data drawn from a village called Rasulpur (which is a pseudonym) in eastern Uttar Pradesh. Included in Rasulpur's population are four Hindu service or occupational and two middle castes, represented by a total of twenty-five households. However, I have still chosen to call Rasulpur a Muslim village because the large majority of its residents are Muslims and the dominant group in it is also Muslim. Located in the Ramsanehighat sub-division (*tehsil*) of Barabanki district at a distance of approximately forty-nine miles from Lucknow, the former seat of Oudh rulers and the present capital of Uttar Pradesh, the village is well-connected both by road and railway, and about one-third of its inhabitants have travelled out of the village at some time or the other.[6] Some residents of the village are, in fact, employed in Bombay in the textile mills and handloom industries, one of which happens to be owned by a local member of the Julaha (weaver) caste.[7] Even so, Rasulpur is

do not exist', he writes. 'No dietary restrictions differentiate people with different *zat* names; such dietary restrictions as do exist are those which are enjoined by Islamic law and are observed in equal measure by all groups. Nor are there any restrictions on commensality. There is no hierarchy of castes. High status is accorded to Syeds who claim descent from the sons of Fatima, the daughter of Prophet Muhammad. But such a status is accorded to them in Arab society also; but that society is not organized on the basis of caste' (1972:26).

5. Some empirical evidence on this question is found in Ahmad (1973). However, as I had noted there, 'we would need a larger number of individual studies of particular communities in different parts of India (and I would now say other countries as well) than are included here before we can hope to reach anywhere close to a comprehensive and complete understanding of this complex social institution' (Ahmad, 1973a).
6. Some residents of the village were in the army and had been as far away as Burma during the second World War. One old-time resident of the village had settled down in Burma and started his own business there after the War. He returned to the village when the Indian settlers started facing difficulties following the establishment of military government there almost at the time I was preparing to leave the village after my first visit.
7. The fact that one of the members of their village owns a flourishing handloom industry in Bombay has been an incentive for the villagers

not an urbanized village. Its economy continues to remain predominantly agricultural, and its social structure remains traditional.[8] Since Alavi's central argument in positing the absence of caste and the mutual exclusiveness of caste and kinship among the Muslims is that they lack a formal framework of social interaction in terms of caste (*zat*) identification,[9] I shall first briefly outline the caste stratification of

to migrate to Bombay. Some of them stay on and work there, but most return after some months. One barber boy who had run away to Bombay told me that he found urban life and working conditions too tiresome and difficult. Those villagers who have travelled outside the village have stayed away for periods ranging from a few days to three or more years. It is worth noting that while the local Julaha who runs the handloom industry has permanently settled in Bombay, he maintains his house in the village and periodically sends his children there (and sometimes comes himself) for their vacations.

8. When I was trying to select a suitable village for undertaking fieldwork, I visited approximately twenty-five villages. One of my chief requirements was that the village should be a traditional one. Surprisingly, Rasulpur was about the only village which met this requirement fully. It was located in a Scheduled Development Block and the Community Development Programme had not reached it then. Nor was there a school in the village. The large majority of the villagers were illiterate. They lived by agriculture or their specialized crafts. Furthermore, social and economic differences had remained intact. Even though the abolition of zamindari had been effected and holdings were being consolidated, the predominant position of the landowning caste was clearly evident. So also was the rigid observance of social rules of interaction among the different social groups. I found the village greatly changed in all these respects in 1972, but I have omitted a discussion of those changes here. They will be discussed in a forthcoming full-length study of the village's social structure.

9. Since Hardy's comment was based on Alavi's work, and Alavi alone presents ethnographic evidence in support of his contention, I am obliged to refer to Alavi's study alone. I believe that Alavi's contention—'that in the Muslim rural society of West Punjab it is the kinship system rather than caste which embodies loyalties and which structures its social organization' (Alavi, 1971:1)—could easily be accepted as a fairly accurate description of Muslim social structure in rural West Punjab. If I have chosen to dispute his contention, it is only because his opening and concluding observations suggest that he is trying to proffer a general point about Muslims which is not borne out by my own data.

the village[10] and shall then go on to examine the kinship correlates of the social groups found in the village, both within and outside it.

Caste Stratification

The entire population of Rasulpur, comprising 1434 persons, is divided into eleven social groups which are referred to by the villagers as *zats*. I translate the word '*zat*' here as caste and my reasons for doing so shall become evident as we proceed. I should like to point out, nevertheless, that the precise referent of this local term often varies according to the context as also the level of general information the villager assumes the person talking to him possesses about the social composition and structure of the village. Depending on the context, the term is used to refer to broad religious communities as well as smaller social groupings. I remember that when I first visited the village in order to collect some preliminary information so that I could select a suitable village for my fieldwork, I was told by the villagers in response to my query regarding the number of castes (*zats*) in the village that there were only two *zats*. Again, I was told the same thing by other villagers during the first few weeks of my settling down in the village for fieldwork. The reference on both occasions seemed to be to the two religious communities whose representatives resided in the village. However, after I had stayed in the village long enough for the villagers to assume a general understanding of the broad communal division of the village on my part, the term '*zat*' was invariably used to refer to smaller social groupings whom I designate here as castes. I am inclined to think that the correct and precise referents of the term '*zat*' are the local social groupings, and the villagers extend it to describe religious communities only when they are talking to outsiders.

10. I shall confine myself to presenting only the broad features of this stratification system here as I propose to present a detailed discussion on the subject in a separate paper in the revised edition of *Caste and Social Stratification among the Muslims* to be published shortly.

The castes (*zats*) are broadly similar groups, possessing a set of attributes which are closely identical to the ones commonly associated with caste in India.[11] The first characteristic of these groups is that they bear distinct names which are used to identify all those belonging to the group. The castes are, in other words, named groupings. These names are either derived from the occupations which their members are traditionally associated with or denote their source of origin. Thus, names like Julaha, Teli and Faqir, which refer respectively to the castes of weavers, oil-pressers, and religious mendicants and beggars, are derivations from the traditional occupations which members of these groups either pursued in the past or are engaged in today. On the other hand, names like Khanzada, Sheikh, etc., indicate the source from which the members of those castes claim their origin and descent. The Khanzadas claim to be Pathans and the Sheikhs claim to be descendants of those who followed the Prophet Muhammad during his historic flight from Meeca to Medina.[12]

The second attribute of *zats* in the village is their association with a traditional occupation which, as we indicated above, is implied by the name of some of the castes. This association applies in the case of all castes in Rasulpur, though

11. For a detailed discussion of these attributes see Hutton (1946). Ghurye (1950), Srinivas (1952) and Beteille (1966). For a discussion of these attributes among Muslims see Ahmad (1973a),

12. Sheikh is a generic term and groups with a wide variety of social and economic backgrounds have been found to lay claim to the generic category represented by it. They usually distinguish themselves from one another by adding prefixes such as Siddiqui, Qureshi or Ansari to indicate their descent from one or the other of the associates of Prophet Muhammad. Surprisingly, the Sheikhs of Rasulpur, of whom there are only two households in the village, do not use such prefixes. There is a large population of Sheikhs distributed in approximatety 24 villages lying east of Rasulpur over an area collectively referred to as 'Sheikhana' who too do not use any prefix before their caste name. However, the Sheikhs of Rasulpur deny that they belong to the same Sheikh category and claim to be members of a different caste (*zat*). Clearly, the division of a group bearing the same generic name and living closeby into distinct caste owes itself to the territorial restriction of the caste, reinforced by endogamy (for a detailed discussion of this point, see Ahmad (1973c).)

there exists a rather important distinction in the nature and exclusiveness of the occupations associated with those castes whose traditional calling is implied by their caste name and those whose caste names are indicative of origin or descent. The occupations of the former group of *zats* are closed in the sense that those belonging to other castes would not like to take them up.[13] The occupations traditionally associated with the latter group of castes are, on the other hand, open.[14] Members of castes whose names generally reflect their origin are commonly concentrated in them, but these occupations are not specifically reserved for them. As a matter of fact, wherever the circumstances of a person belonging to a caste whose calling is a closed occupation, in the sense indicated above, allow his taking to what have been called open occupations, he does often engage in them even if his involvement is only marginal or supplementary. Such involvement usually results in raising the person's economic and social status among his caste fellows.

It should not be thought from the above that everyone in the village engages in his traditional calling and that no

13. It is easy to see why this is so. Occupations are usually ranked and the status assigned to them is a prime determinant of whether a person wanting to change his occupation would adopt a lower occupation. All occupations associated with castes whose names imply their occupation are treated as low, and this may be one of the reasons for the reluctance of the villagers to adopt these occupations in preference to their own traditional calling. I realized that for a Nai (barber) a shift from his own traditional calling to weaving or butchery might still be a step upward, and I repeatedly queried the villagers whether such change would be possible. I was again and again told that, while there was no theoretical bar to such a change, there was no instance of such change having occurred within the village context.

14. Principal among these occupations is agriculture, which is the predominant occupation of the landowning caste of Khanzadas. The Sheikhs, who represent the only other group belonging to the category of castes whose name does not specifically imply an occupation, are not associated with any particular traditional occupation. Of the two Sheikh households in the village, the head of one works as a mason while the other was, until recently, doing business in Burma. Since his return from Burma, he has been contemplating setting up a small-scale industry for manufacturing aluminium utensils. None of the Sheikh households owns any land.

occupational change has taken place in the village. Several Weavers and Butchers, who have succeeded in accumulating some capital, have taken to trading in foodgrains. Some of them have also invested in land and engage in agriculture. At the same time, those members of the Khanzada caste who go to Bombay often work in the handloom industry owned by the local Julaha businessman.[15] The essential point worth remembering in this connection is that each caste in the village, and especially the castes whose names themselves imply association with a traditional occupation, are deemed to have a special occupation associated with them. Furthermore, while occupational changes do occur, a person's caste as a whole is identified with the occupation which is considered traditional for that caste.

Since the division of castes entails a degree of occupational specialization amongst them, the relationship among the different castes tends toward economic interdependence. Not all castes are engaged in this system on the same plane or in a similar capacity. The different castes participate in the system in different capacities according to their place in the productive organization revolving around land. The Khanzadas, who are predominantly landowners and whose principal occupation in the village is cultivation, form the nucleus of the system of economic interdependence among the castes. They are referred to as the *jajmans*. Castes whose names imply a traditional occupation,[16] while they do not

15. It is worth noting here that attitudes and ideas about occupations change with a change in context and place. No Khanzada would think of engaging in weaving within the village. If he did, his status would suffer greatly. On the other hand, Khanzadas who go to Bombay in search of employment often work as weavers in the textile mills This is largely because working as a weaver in Bombay is not considered as leading to any lowering of their status in the village.

16. I have all along drawn a distinction in this paper between castes whose names imply a traditional occupation and those whose names indicate their origin, but this distinction is not equivalent to the one drawn by several scholars between *ashraf* and *ajlaf* castes. The term *ashraf* is usually used to denote castes whose members claim foreign ancestry. While it is true that castes whose names indicate their source of origin usually claim foreign ancestry, claims

have any particular collective designation, render specialized and traditional economic and ritual services for their *jajmans*.[17]

Of course, the fact that the Khanzadas are the nucleus of the system of economic interdependence prevalent among castes does not mean that they alone are entitled to receive services in the village. It would be evident that the pre-eminent position of the Khanzadas as service receivers owes itself to their position as landowners and cultivators. In other words, if they are the major services receivers, this is because they alone are in the favourable situation to fulfil the conditions which the status of a *jajman* entails. Others too are entitled to receive services under the system if they can meet those conditions, and this does happen sometimes. Whenever members of other castes in the local community come to possess the elements that give the Khanzadas their pre-eminent position in the social system, they too can receive services. Thus, landowning Julahas in the village do employ and receive services of some castes as part of the traditional arrangement of the system. However, this does not mean that this is possible all along the scale or for all castes. It is impossible for castes below a certain level, especially if they are serving castes, to become service receivers even if they come to possess the means required to sustain such traditional arrangements. Such persons tend in the normal course to discard practising their traditional occupations and

of foreign ancestry are also preferred by some members of castes whose names imply a traditional occupation. Thus, the Julahas in Rasulpur call themselves Ansari Sheikh and claim to be descendants of Abu Ansar, a close associate of Prophet Muhammad. Or, again, the Butchers call themselves Qureshi Sheikhs. Furthermore, the distinction made here between castes whose names imply a traditional occupation and those whose names indicate social origin is not made by the villagers themselves. They look upon all castes as social groupings sharing common attributes and the interaction among them is determined by their relative position in the social and economic structure rather than the pecularities of their names.

17. For a detailed discussion of this system of economic interdependence in Hindu villages, see Wiser (1936), Also see Pocock (1962), Beidelman (1959) and the recent case studies of predominantly Hindu villages by sociologists and social anthropologists.

stop rendering their services to others once they start owning land or other means of independent subsistence in view of the enhanced prestige which their exclusive dependence on land brings to them. However, they are barred both by custom and the reluctance of those who continue to engage in traditional callings from capitalizing on this enhanced prestige to become service-receivers. Such a person would indeed be considered an upstart if he were to try to engage the services of other serving castes along the same lines as the relationship that exists between them and the Khanzadas.[18]

Each caste within the village is not only identified with a distinct name and traditional occupation, but is also associated with a distinctive life-style. The distinctions of life-style among the castes in Rasulpur are certainly not as elaborate as have been reported by scholars for other regions (see, for instance, Beteille, 1966:50-58), but these differences nevertheless exist and, what is more, the villagers themselves believe that there are differences. These distinctions relate either to religiosity, pattern and degree of interaction with non-Muslim castes, and dining habits.

Perhaps, the incident which occurred in the village shortly after I settled down there would serve to illustrate the differences of life-style among castes. Just prior to my taking residence, the village had gone through a cholera epidemic. After the epidemic had passed, which coincided with the time that I took up residence in the village, the villagers organized a collective village feast. Since this was a ritual feast organized as an act of thanksgiving, the Faquirs (religious mendicants) and Bhats (bards) were the guests of honour at it and they were fed first. However, the Faquirs got up and refused to take their meal. Enquiries on my part at the time did not elicit a satisfactory answer to this strange behaviour, but, subse-

18. I have not so far introduced the concept of hierarchy in this discussion. Anticipating the introduction of this concept below, it can be stated that the standard rule is that a person can be a service receiver only from castes who rank lower than his own. Where the castes are roughly of equal status, they exchange their services but their relationship is one of equality rather than one of superordination and subordination that exists between service-receivers and service-givers traditionally.

quently, I learnt that the cause of the fracas was the insistence of the Bhats that they sit in the same row as the Faquirs. The Faquirs argued that, unlike the Bhats who accepted alms from both Hindus and Muslims, they accepted alms only from Muslim households. Being superior in status, thus, they could not sit in the same row with the Bhats and dine with them. The dispute was eventually settled through the intervention of the Khanzadas who prevailed upon the Bhats to move a little distance to one side and thus create a gap in the row.

This incident serves to illustrate the differences of life-style among the castes and highlights their critical significance in ordering social interaction among them. The interaction among the different castes is based on a principle of hierarchy expressed through well-defined forms of behaviour. Appropriate forms of behaviour are prescribed for members of the different castes, and a person who engages in behaviour which is considered inappropriate for his caste is supposed to be violating the customary norms of behaviour as well as the established rank order of castes. If such violations are of an insignificant nature or relatively harmless, they may be dismissed or ignored with a passing comment. However, if they are of a serious nature, the person engaging in them is ostracized both by his own caste fellows as well as by those of the locally dominant caste who, by virtue of their control over land, are in a pre-eminent position *vis-a-vis* the erring members.

This should not be taken to mean that disputes as to relative ranking do not arise or that the ranks assigned to castes are universally accepted. To be exact, disputes over the rank assigned to castes often arise, especially where a caste or castes are able to stake claims to mobility through acquisition of material wealth. The Julahas provide excellent examples of such disputes. Previously, the Julahas of this village, as indeed of the whole region, were a depressed group and were assigned a status considerably below the Khanzadas. Since Independence, the rapid rise in the demand for their products and the enterprise shown by some of them in entering other open occupations, such as trading in foodgrains, have combined to raise their economic prospects and they have been claiming a status equal to that of the Khanzadas. Their claim is not accepted widely, but this has not prevented them from challenging the superiority of the Khanzadas and from engaging in behaviour which would be considered a violation of the established hierarchical norms.

The establishment of a separate mosque by the Julahas provides a good example of their bid to challenge Khanzada superiority. Originally, there was only one mosque in the village. The Khanzadas stood in the front rows while saying their prayers in that mosque and the Julahas and other castes were required to stand behind them. Furthermore, the Imam of the mosque was also a Khanzada. Since several Julahas had succeeded in performing the pilgrimage because of their economic prosperity, they were unwilling to stand behind the Khanzadas, whom they considered less pious,[19] especially as they also wanted to lead the prayers themselves. When the Khanzadas persistently refused them these privileges, they established their own mosque. They quickly raised funds and converted it into a *pukka* structure. For a long time, I was told, the Khanzadas used to say their prayers in the old mosque and the Julahas said theirs in the new mosque, but currently some Khanzadas also say their prayers in the new mosque.

The criteria used in ranking the castes are not universally agreed upon among the villagers, which is possibly why disputes over rank are common, but the villagers do conceive of the different castes as occupying different hierarchical positions. Using a removable card ranking technique, first outlined by Marriott (1957), I was able to obtain a broad hierarchy of the different castes in the village. Surprisingly, the rank assigned to the different castes by the respondents showed a broad degree of consensus, except that each respondent tended to place his own caste a little higher than the rank conceded to it by others. The hierarchy emerging from the replies of the respondents is set out in Fig. 1.

19. I must add that the Khanzadas are not a particularly religious caste and their style of life today is much less Islamized than that of the Julahas.

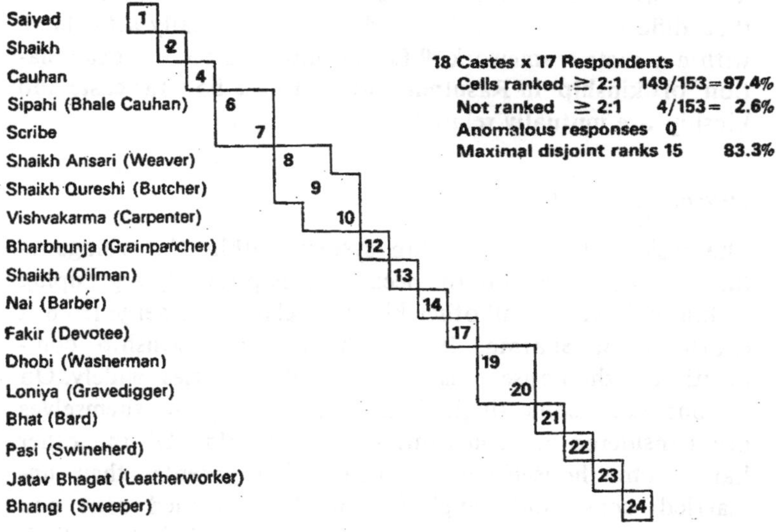
Saiyad
Shaikh
Cauhan
Sipahi (Bhale Cauhan)
Scribe
Shaikh Ansari (Weaver)
Shaikh Qureshi (Butcher)
Vishvakarma (Carpenter)
Bharbhunja (Grainparcher)
Shaikh (Oilman)
Nai (Barber)
Fakir (Devotee)
Dhobi (Washerman)
Loniya (Gravedigger)
Bhat (Bard)
Pasi (Swineherd)
Jatav Bhagat (Leatherworker)
Bhangi (Sweeper)
1
2
4
6
7
8
9
10
12
13
14
17
19
20
21
22
23
24
18 Castes x 17 Respondents
Cells ranked ≥ 2:1 149/153=97.4%
Not ranked ≥ 2:1 4/153= 2.6%
Anomalous responses 0
Maximal disjoint ranks 15 83.3%

Fig. 1.

The Kinship System

Since the starting point of this paper was the view put forward by Alavi and Hardy recently positing the absence of caste among Muslims, I presented the foregoing discussion on caste stratification in Rasulpur to show that a formal framework of social interaction among the different castes does exist within the village. Of course, I have not dealt with the interplay between wealth or power and caste in as much detail as Hardy's comment cited earlier would seem to call for. However, the evidence I have presented above indicates that differences of wealth and power are usually articulated within a caste framework.[20] Let us now turn to an examination of kinship in Rasulpur and try to see how far caste and kinship are mutually related.

Structure of Kinship

The basic unit of the kinship system within the village is the household (*ghar*) both because it is primarily a grouping of kin and because all other kinship relations emerge from it (Fortes 1958: Sharma, 1973). The size and kinship composition of the households in the village varies widely. On the one hand, some single individuals living by themselves are considered as constituting a household. On the other hand, some households comprise either parents, their unmarried sons and daughters, or their married sons and their spouses and children, or siblings, and, in turn, their spouses and unmarried children. The villagers consider large households to be desirable, but recognize the inevitability of the break-up of large and complex households over time. As

20. This is best reflected in the contrasting atttiude shown by the Khanzadas towards Sulaiman, the prosperous Julaha textile mill owner, in their dealings with him in Bombay and within the village. When they work in his mills in Bombay, they show him the respect which is due to him as an employer. However, when Sulaiman or his children come to the village during vacations, the Khanzadas expect him to show the deference due to them by virtue of their status in the village. Surprisingly, both the Khanzadas as well as Sulaiman accept this duality and act according to the norms appropriate to the situation.

a matter of fact, there are specific social norms regarding the distribution of property between various households according to which such a break-up is expected to take place. These norms relate to the share to be distributed among the separating households, and the position of unmarried children and parents in relation to the separating households.

Since the existing social norms favour complex households, the large majority of the villagers try to continue to maintain complex households until the tensions and conflicts within the household make joint living difficult if not quite impossible. If the tensions cannot be contained, the household is then broken up and each separating household sets up its own hearth and keeps its income to itself. Further, if the household owns any land, it is divided equally among all the sons or brothers and each son or brother is given the share to which he is entitled. If the separation of a complex household takes place during the life-time of the father, then he too keeps a share for himself. Sometimes parents are unwilling to divide their property among the separating sons, but this usually leads to considerable conflict between them and their separating son or sons. The son or sons usually engineer pressure from relatives and friends to prevail upon the father to divide the property in the interest of family harmony and peace.

Upon the break-up of a father-centered complex household, the separating sons set up their separate households, leaving the father either to go on living in a separate household or to live with one of the sons. Where parents wish to join one of the sons, they prefer to live with the youngest son, and this preference is buttressed by the prevalent norms. However, it is not altogether unknown for them to want to live with the eldest or one of the middle sons. Similarly, while the village norms require that a widowed mother should live with the eldest son, it is not unknown for her to prefer to live with the younger sons. On the whole, the prescribed norms are quite flexible and actual social practice regarding the residence pattern of parents after the break-up of a father-centered complex household varies widely.

Even though the household is primarily a kinship group, consisting as it does of either siblings or parents and children and other equally close consanguines, the significance of this unit does not lie only in kinship relations. It is equally important in defining the structure and size of the castes within the village. This is demonstrated both by the fact that the size of a caste is usually enumerated in terms of the number of households belonging to it and by the tendency of the villagers to collectively describe the households belonging to each caste as a *bhai-band* or *biradari*. This latter fact is of considerable significance in that it shows that the households belonging to each caste in the village conceive of themselves as a collectivity and designate themselves as such.

The *bhai-band* or *biradari* group is a kinship group, but in order to understand its linkage with caste it seems necessary to briefly elaborate the usage of the terms *bhai-band* and *biradari*. The connotation of both the terms is roughly the same and they refer to structurally similar groups. Their differential use for different castes seems to be determined by the status and certain other attributes associated with the castes. The term *biradari* is usually employed for those castes which have an occupational name and generally possess a formal caste organization in the form of a caste *panchayat* (council). Thus, the villagers usually describe the households belonging to the Julahas (weavers), Telis (oil pressers) and Nais (barbers), etc., as *biradaris*. On the other hand, the term *bhai-band* is normally used to designate the households belonging to castes which lack a formal caste organization centering round a caste *panchayat* and whose names indicate social origin rather than occupation. The Khanzada and Sheikh are the only two castes of this kind in Rasulpur and the term *bhai-band* is restricted to the households belonging to them.

Furthermore, the terms *bhai-band* or *biradari* and *zat* are employed differently. The former is used by a person while referring to the households belonging to his own caste. While referring to the households belonging to a caste other than his own, he uses the term *zat*. Thus, when a Khanzada or Julaha informant wanted to tell me that a particular event concerned the households belonging to his caste, he usually said that this happened amongst his *bhai-band* or *biradari*. On the other hand, when he was narrating something concerning the households of another caste, he usually simply said that that thing happened among the Julahas.

Perhaps, on the face of it, this differential usage of the terms *zat* and *bhai-band* or *biradari* does not seem so significant, but to my mind it is crucial. It serves to indicate that there is absolute congruence or overlap between caste (*zat*) and *bhai-band* or *biradari* at the level of the village, and whether the term *zat* or *bhai-band* or *biradari* is used by a person depends largely upon the context of the conversation and his referent.

The term *bhai-band* and *biradari*, as Alavi rightly notes, are difficult to translate easily into English. However, it is quite clear that the accent in both terms is on a sense of solidarity, amity and equality.[21] This sense of solidarity and amity is not merely a fictional notion, but rests on demonstrable kinship linkages. Since all the households belonging to each caste are descendants of one common ancestor, or a few related common ancestors, who had settled in the village at the time it was established or subsequently, they are related by ties of common descent. On account of the custom of preferential cousin marriage prevalent among some *bhai-bands* or *biradaris* (not all *biradaris* practise it and some explicitly prohibit it), these ties of descent may sometimes be cut across by ties of affinity between two or more households, but the ties of descent almost always exist amongst them. Since the primary purpose of my research in Rasulpur was not kinship,

21. The solidarity and amity existing among members of a *bhai-band* or *biradari* is widely recognized, but there is no obvious demonstration of it amongst members of the *bhai-band*. Among the *biradaris*, on the other hand, the fraternal solidarity and amity supposed to prevail among their members and anticipated by their kinship links is expressed through appropriate social rituals. The practice among the Julahas of the village represents the most elaborate form of this ritual, though similar practices exist in other *biradaris*. Each year, on the occasion of *Idul-Fitr*, all Julaha household heads in the village form themselves into a party and go from house to house eating vermicelli (*siwayan*). The vermicelli are served at each house in a common plate and every member of the party partakes of the dish from the same plate. Participation in this ritual, which is supposed to symbolize the amity and equality amongst the Julaha households within the village, is unfailingly regular. It breaks only when a household is excommunicated from the *biradari*.

I did not collect detailed genealogies for all *bhai-band* or *biradaris*, but for the ones that I did collect genealogical data I was able to map their kinship inter-connections through descent. The extent and complexity of these inter-connections tended to vary, however, according to the size of the *bhai-band* or *biradari* and the depth of the memory of the respondents regarding genealogical linkages among the constituent households. Even where a respondent was unable to recall the exact linkage between two households, and this usually happened where the linkage went back several generations, he seemed sure of their common descent. The linkages existing, or presumed to be existing where they are not empirically demonstrable, among all the households of a *bhai-band* or *biradari* suggests that the *bhai-band* or *biradari* is essentially a collection of related households in the context of the village.

However, the *bhai-band* or *biradari* is not a territorially limited group. While these terms are used to designate a collection of related households of a caste within the village, they are equally applied to designate other groups whose membership extends beyond the territorial boundaries of Rasulpur. Thus, as Alavi rightly notes in the context of West Punjab villages, the term *bhai-band* or *biradari* may be seen as a term with a sliding semantic structure. However, unlike as in West Punjab, it does not denote a progressively restricted group of kin in Rasulpur. Corresponding with the shift in the connotation of the term, a progressively larger group of either actual or potential kin are denoted by it.

Outside the village, the term *bhai-band* or *biradari* denotes two distinct groups of kin. Firstly, it denotes a group of kin related to the households of the *bhai-band* or *biradari* in Rasulpur by ties of affinity. The actual size of this group tends to vary for each *bhai-band* or *biradari* according to its numerical size and demographic composition within Rasulpur, the extent of its geographical spread in the region and the attitude of the *bhai-band* or *biradari* towards marriage among close kins. Of the two *bhai-bands* in Rasulpur, the Khanzadas are restricted in their distribution to just this village and thus the *bhai-band*, in this sense, does not exist in their case, since their affinal links are largely confined within Rasulpur. A few Khanzada marriages have taken place in other villages, but this is a recent trend and I shall return to a discussion of this presently. Previously, the Khanzada affinal links were confined within Rasulpur.

Practising different forms of preferential marriages and close *bhai-band* endogamy, they tended to limit the marriages of both daughters and sons within the *bhai-band* in the village. The *bhai-band* of the Sheikhs, of whom there are two households in the village, is distributed over the villages from which they have brought wives or to which their mothers belonged. However, since the Sheikhs too allow preferential marriages, their *bhai-band* of affines is relatively narrow and does not extend widely over the region adjoining the village.

Of the *biradaris*, the Julahas are a fairly numerous caste in Rasulpur, but they practise village exogamy and prohibit close family endogamy and preferential cousin marriages. The *biradari* of the Julahas in this second sense, consequently, extends widely over the region. The same is true of the Faquirs, though they allow preferential cousin marriages. Among other *biradaris*, the *biradari* in this second sense extends narrowly outside the village. People prefer to contract marriages within known circles where they can be sure of the pedigree of the concerned families. Consequently, the *bhai-band* or *biradari* in this second sense, which may be distinguished from the *bhai-band* or *biradari* of the village by being called the *biradari* of affines, tends generally to be larger than the *bhai-band* or *biradari* of the village. Furthermore, the composition of the *biradari* of affines varies from one household in the village to another though, as already indicated, the possibility of such dispersal and variation is greatly restricted by the strong preference for contracting marriages within known circles.

Since my argument in this paper is that caste and kinship as understood in the sense of *bhai-band* and *biradari* are co-terminus, it would be useful to ask how far the *bhai-band* or *biradari* of affines is contained within the caste. Caste as a group has relevance only in a local context where it serves to order relations among strata within a village or *mohalla* (ward of a town or city), and where its boundaries are defined by the fact that each caste has a name and its members are believed, as, indeed, they believe themselves to share certain characteristics in terms of occupational specialization, life-style and behaviour patterns. Outside the local context, caste can be understood as a named category of persons sharing a common occupation, life-style and behaviour pattern. Following the contention put forth elsewhere (Ahmad, 1973b), I shall argue that this broad conception of the term caste (*zat*) is misleading, but for the present I tentatively accept this definition in order to answer the query posed above.

As indicated earlier, the different *bhai-bands* or *biradaris*, which can also be denoted as castes in view of the overlap which we noted above between caste and *bhai-band* or *biradari* at the village level, differ as to their marriage patterns. We noted that the Khanzadas, Sheikhs and some occupational castes practise preferential cousin marriage and allow close endogamous marriages, while others prohibit such marriages, and extend the prohibition to marriage within the village. However, despite this difference in their marriage patterns, the different *bhai-bands* or *biradaris* (or castes) cannot clearly be divided into 'endogamous' and 'exogamous' systems (see Alavi, 1972:25-26). Looked at as a category bearing a common caste (*zat*) name, the *bhai-bands* or *biradari* of both types are endogamous in that their marriages are restricted to the group and do not extend beyond it. Or, to put the same point differently, all *bhai-bands* or *biradaris* or affines are limited to households whose members share the collective name of the caste, irrespective of whether they practise preferential cousin marriages or not. Thus, the *bhai-band* or *biradari* of affines is in both cases endogamous. It comes into existence within the framework of the caste (*zat*) rule requiring a person to marry within the caste by endogamy. Once again, therefore, the correspondence between caste and *bhai-band* or *biradari* is maintained.

One point where this correspondence seems to break down is with respect to the marriages of the Khanzadas outside Rasulpur. There are three such marriages, and these would seem to provide an exception to the rule of endogamous marriages encountered in the case of other *bhai-bands* or *biradaris* in the village. However, I would contend that this is not so at all. The three instances where Khanzada marriages have taken place outside the village and, since they are confined to just Rasulpur, exogamously, two are marriages of Khanzada boys and one of a Khanzada girl. The boys have been married to a Pathan girl in one case and in the other to a Khankhar girl whom the Khanzadas consider equal to themselves. The girl has been married into the Sheikh caste. This Sheikh caste is not the same Sheikh group whose representatives reside in the village. Even though sharing the same generic name, the local Sheikhs are a different caste. Somewhat interestingly, the Khanzadas consider the local Sheikh caste to be roughly equal, or perhaps a little lower, to themselves, but they consider the Sheikhs among whom the Khanzada girl has been married as superior to themselves. If the status of the castes among whom Khanzadas have married exogamously is borne in mind, it would be clear that these exogamous marriages are still within the approved degrees of marriage to outside castes. The marriage of the two Khanzada boys has taken place in castes of about the same status, while the Khanzada girl has been married hypergamously.

A second kin group denoted by the term *bhai-band* or *biradari* outside the village is the total population of households bearing the same *zat* name as the *bhai-band* or *biradari* of the village. The *bhai-band* or *biradari* at this level does not comprise actual kin and no kin links between persons falling under the *bhai-band* or *biradari* can be demonstrated. Nor need they exist. However, the group denoted by the term *bhai-band* or *biradari* at this level is still a group of potential kin in the sense that a person can negotiate and seal a marriage in a household of the *bhai-band* or *biradari* at this level without in any way infringing the rule of *bhai-band* or *biradari* endogamy. This group is sometimes called the entire *bhai-band* or *biradari* of all the households of a caste in the village.

The entire *bhai-band* or *biradari* is co-terminus with the entire population of a caste within the region. Either the caste does not exist outside of the region, or, if a population bearing the same caste name exists, it is regarded as a distinct caste. The members of the entire *bhai-band* or *biradari* do not regard the members of the population outside the region as belonging to their caste. Nor are they prepared to form marriage alliances with them. As a matter of fact, such alliances would be considered as constituting an infringement of the rule of caste endogamy and, in the case of the *biradaris* organized into *panchayats*, would invite sanctions usually imposed against erring members for violating the principle of caste endogamy.

Conclusion

The starting point of this paper was the formulation put forth by Alavi and Hardy that kinship rather than caste is the salient basis of social organization in Muslim communities in South Asian societies and it is kinship which structures their social organization. Using data drawn from a Muslim village in eastern Uttar Pradesh, this paper has tried to show that the mutual exclusiveness between caste and kinship implied by the formulation of those authors does not conform to the reality of the social situation in Rasulpur. There, caste and kinship co-exist and overlap. Neither is more real than the other. I suspect that the question as to whether caste or kinship is really the basic principle of social organization among Muslims has emanated from the fact that analysis of Muslim communities have so far either limited themselves to the study of caste (see Ansari, 1959; Gupta, 1956; and Ahmad, 1973) or kinship without taking the two dimensions of social life together. Perhaps, as Mayer (1960) has indeed noted, it is only a simultaneous focus on caste and kinship that can help us to understand the ways in which they co-relate in real settings.

Bibliography

Ahmad, Imtiaz (ed), (1973), *Caste and Social Stratification among the Muslims*, Delhi, Manohar Book Service.

Ahmad, Imtiaz (1973a), 'Introduction', in Imtiaz Ahmad (ed), *Caste and Social Stratification among the Muslims*, Delhi, Manohar Book Service.

——— (1973b), 'Endogamy and Status Mobility among the Siddiqui Sheikhs of Allahabad, Uttar Pradesh', in Imtiaz Ahmad (ed), *Caste and Social Stratification among the Muslims*, Delhi, Manonar Book Service.

——— (1975) 'The Social Structure of Muslim Communities in South Asia', in Dietmar Rothermund (ed), *Islam in Southern Asia*, Wiesbaden, Franz Steiner.

Ahmad, Saghir (1970) 'Social Stratification in a Punjabi Village', *Contributions to Indian Sociology*, NS 4, pp. 105-125.

Alavi, Hamza (1972), 'Kinship in West Punjab Villages', *Contributions to Indian Sociology*, NS 6, pp. 1-27.

Ansari, Ghaus (1959), *Muslim Caste in Uttar Pradesh: A Study in Culture Contact*, Lucknow, Ethnographic and Folk Culture Society.

Beidelman, T.O. (1959), *A Comparative Analysis of the Jajmani System*, New York, J.J. Augustin. (Monograph of the Association for Asian Studies, No 8).

Beteille, A. (1966), *Caste, Class and Power: Changing Patterns of Stratification in a Tanjore Village*. Berkeley and Los Angeles, University of California Press.

Dube, Leela (1969), *Matriliny and Islam*, Delhi, National Publishing House.

Dumont, Louis (1957), *Hierarchy and Marriage Alliance in South India Kinship*, London, Royal Anthropological Institute (Occasional Papers No 12.)

Fortes, Meyer (1958), 'Introduction', in Jack Goody (ed.), *The Developmental Cycle in Domestic Groups*, Cambridge, Cambridge University Press.

Gaborieau, Marc (1972), 'Muslims in the Hindu Kingdom of Nepal', *Contributions to Indian Sociology*, NS 6, pp. 83-103.

Ghurye, G.S. (1950), *Caste and Class in India*, Bombay, Popular Prakashan.

Gupta, Raghuraj (1956), 'Caste Ranking and Inter-Caste Relations among the Muslims of a Village in North-Western India', *Eastern Anthropologist*, 10, 2, pp. 30-42.

Hardy, Peter (1975), Review of Imtiaz Ahmad (ed.), Caste and Social Stratification among the Muslims, *Bulletin of the School of Oriental and African Studies*.

Hutton, J.H. (1946), *Caste in India*, Cambridge, Cambridge University Press.

Inayatullah, I (1958), 'Caste, Patti and Faction in the Life of a Punjab village', *Sociologus*, 8, 2, pp. 36-46.

Karve, Iravati (1953), *Kinship Organization in India*, Poona, Deccan College.

Khan, Zillur R. (1968), 'Caste and Muslim Peasantry in India and Pakistan', *Man in India*, 21, 2, pp. 133-148.

Kutty, A.R. (1972), *Marriage and Kinship in an Island Society*, Delhi, National Publishing House.

Madan, T.N. (1965), *Family and Kinship: A Study of the Pandits of Rural Kashmir*, Bombay, Asia Publishing House.

Mauroof, M. (1972), 'Aspects of Religion, Economy and Society among the Muslims of Ceylon', *Contributions to Indian Sociology*, NS 6, pp. 66-83.

Mayer, A.C (1960), *Caste and Kinship in Central India*, London, Routledge and Kegan Paul.

Marriott, McKim (1957), 'A Technique for the Study of Caste Ranking in South Asia', Paper presented at the 56th annual meeting of the American Anthropological Association, Chicago.

Pocock, D.F. (1962), 'Notes on *Jajmani* Relationships', *Contributions to Indian Sociology*.

——— (1972), *Kanbi and Pattidar: A Study of the Pattidar Community of Gujarat*, Oxford, Clarendon Press.

Shah, A.M. (1974) *Household Dimension of the Family in India*. New Delhi, Orient Longman.

Sharma, S.P. (1973), 'Marriage, Family and Kinship among the Jats and Thakurs: Some Comparisons'. *Contributions to Indian Sociology*, NS 7, pp. 81-103.

Srinivas, M.N. (1952), *Religion and Society among the Coorgs of South India*, Oxford, Oxford University Press.

Van der Veen, Klass W. (1972), *I Give Thee My Daughter: Marriage and Hierarchy among the Anavil Brahmins of South Gujarat*, Assen, Royal Van Gorcum Ltd.

Vatuk, S. (1972), *Kinship and Urbanization: White-Collar Migrants in North India*, Berkeley and Los Angeles, University of California Press.

Wiser, W.H. (1936) *The Hindu Jajmani System*, Lucknow, Lucknow Publishing House.

Glossary

achari— Tamil Muslim word for the goldsmith.

ajri— Gujari word for shepherd.

angathi pindhua— Ring ceremony among the Assamese Muslims.

Anna— Ceremony of fetching the bride from her natal home.

apa— Honorific term of address for elder sister.

Ararilokkal— Malayalam word for the night of consummation.

Ashrafization— Process of culture change involving raising of social status through claiming descent from Muslims of any of the four groups of foreign extraction.

asnao— Meo term for a man's daughter, brother's daughter, sister's daughter and great grand daughter.

Aughar— Literally 'grapes', the word denotes a sweet dish prepared out of crushed wheat.

ath mangola— Assamese Muslim custom requiring parents of a bride to invite the bridegroom for a ceremonial feast on the eighth day after marriage.

azizdar— Literally 'relations', the term denotes non-exogamous bilateral kindred of blood relatives and their spouses.

bad nazar— Evil eye.

bahu— Term of reference as well as address for a man's daughter-in-law or younger brother's wife.

bahin— Sister.

baksish— Gujarati term for gifts presented by distant relatives and friends to the bride or bridegroom.

bakri— goat.

ban— forest.

bandi— A part of *Kalyanam* function among the Moplahs at which the bridegroom ties a necklace round the bride's neck.

bangsha— Assamese Muslim word for a kinship grouping similar to lineage.

bap— Father.

baraat, barat— Marriage party.

barsas— Meo kin term for the elder sister of a man's spouse.

bedai— Literally, 'farewell', the word denotes the ceremony of sending the girl to her conjugal home.

behnoi— Meo kin term for a man's sister's husband.

beta— Son.

beti— Daughter.

bhade— The fifth month of the Assamese calendar, usually falling between August-September.

bhai— Brother.

bhair— Meo term used by two or more brothers to refer to one another, especially when the relationship among them is a close and affectionate one.

bhabi— Elder brother's wife.

bhangi— scavenger.

bhanja— Sister's son.

bhanji— Sister's daughter.

bhatija— Brother's son.

bhatiji— Brother's daughter.

Bhatija-bahu, bhatij bahu— Brother's son's wife.

bheer— sheep.

bianam— Folk songs sung by Assamese Muslim women during marriage celebrations; the act of singing folk songs at marriage.

biri— Country made cigarettes prepared out of *tendu* leaves.

biradari— Caste brotherhood.

bohag— First month of the Assamese calendar, usually falling between April-May.

bua— Meo term of address for a female ego's husband's mother, his father's sisters and his father's brother's wife.

buddha bap— Honorific term used by a Meo female ego to address her husband's father.

burka, burqa— a long loose dress worn by Muslim women to observe *purdah*.

bustee— Slum.

chacha— Paternal uncle.

chaddar— Literally 'sheet of cloth', the word denotes a ceremony whereby a man can enter into a leviratic union with his deceased brother's widow.

chait— The twelfth month of the Assamese calendar, usually falling between March-April.

Chaudhari— Hereditary leader of a *pal* among the Meos; leader of a clan or caste; head of a caste *panchayat* or council.

charas— Large leather bags used for drawing water from a well for irrigational purposes.

chuba— Literally 'a sector of a village', 'a cluster of houses; the term also denotes a patrilineal grouping functioning more or less as a sub-lineage among the Assamese Muslims.

choolah— hearth.

daaj— Gujari word for dowry.

dada— Paternal grandmother.

dada potre— Gujar Bakarwal maximal lineage; a grouping comprising all descendants of an actual ancestor sharing common grazing rights in pasture lands.

Dakhni— A Southerner; pertaining or belonging to south India.

Daldis— The section of Kokni Muslims supposed to be descendants of converts from depressed caste Hindus.

dara dhara— Assamese word for the best man, usually a close friend of the bridegroom who sits near him during the marriage ceremony.

dastarband— Gujar Bakarwal succession ceremony.

dera— Gujar Bakarwal term for household or family.

devar— Kin term for woman's husband's younger brother; the term usually implies a joking relationship.

devrani— A woman's husband's younger brother's wife.

dheota— Meo term for one's daughter's son.

dheoti— Meo term for one's daughter's daughter.

dokra— Meo term for father-in-law; the term is considered more respectful than *sasur*.

dokri— Meo term of reference for mother-in-law; this term being considered more respectable than *sass*.

dudh— milk.

dupatta— Scarf; piece of cloth used for covering the head and bosom.

Ekada— A formal arrangement among a set of villagers to contract marriage among themselves.

fatiha— An offering to God, the Prophet or a Muslim saint, so-called because the first chapter of the Koran, called Sura fatiha is usually read as part of the ritual.

gair— Non-kinsman.

garmiyan— The summer season.

gauna— Ceremony of sending the girl to the groom's house after she attains pubetry; the ceremony usually takes place in communities which still practise child marriage and among whom the girl goes to her husband long after her wedding.

geet— folk songs sung by women on ceremonial occasions.

ghar— Literally, 'house', the word is used throughout north India to refer to a household.

gharana— Literally, 'family line', the word denotes the groups of musicians who sing or play in a particular style supposed to be characterstic of the group's teacher.

gharara— Long flaring lower garment, usually worn by high caste Muslim women in north India.

ghar jamai— Son-in-law who lives in the house of his father-in-law.

gharwala—Term of reference for husband; head of the household.

gotra— A Hindu clan tracing its paternal linkage from a common ancestor, usually a saint or sage.

haq dana— A specified sum payable by a Jamaati Kokni Muslim to his Jamaat at the time of marriage of his son.

Id— A major Muslim festival of joy and celebration.

Imam— A prayer leader in the mosque; in the plural, frequently applied to the founders of the schools of Muslim religious law.

ijma— Consensus, either of the whole Islamic community or of the learned regarding what is truly Islamic.

Islamization— Cultural process whereby groups and individuals distinguish themselves from non-Muslims by purifying themselves of the so-called un-Islamic customs and practices.

jajman— Patron, the recipient of ritual and economic services under the *jajmani* system.

jajmani— System of exchange of services and goods among castes in rural India.

jamaat— A group or party, the total membership of a community.

jan— Gujarati word for marriage party.

janj— Gujari term for marriage party.

jeejaron ka-har— Necklace of beads.

jeth— Kin term denoting a woman's husband's elder brother.

Jamaatis— A section of the Kokni Muslims supposed to be descendants of inter marriages between Arab settlers and local women.

Jamaat-e-Islammi-Hind— A communal Muslim organisation, recently banned.

jethani— Kin term for a woman's husband's elder brother's wife.

jhagra— Meo term for the sum payable as compensation by a man who elopes with another man's wife to her former husband.

jihaz— Moplah word for dowry.

joran— Assamese word for the ceremony of presentation of gifts to a bride from the groom's side.

kaka— Meo term for father's younger brother.

kaki— Meo term for father's brother's wife.

kalghub— Gujarati word for a bouquet of flowers.

kafila— Caravan, a collection of families who move together with their cattle during their seasonal migrations.

kamiz— shirt, tunic.

kanhudi, kanhikudi— Moplah term for serving of rice gruel to men for drinking in the marriage in the past, now a full scale dinner.

kaniyath— Moplah term for the *nikah* ceremony.

karkhana— Small scale factory.

karanavar— Head of a *tharavad* or one of its segments, usually the oldest male.

karkhanedar— Owner of a small-scale factory.

karigar— Craftman; worker in a small-scale industry.

kati— Seventh month of the Assamese Calendar.

khatna—Circumcision

khandan— A group of families bearing a common name and

enjoying more or less similar social status; a non-exogamous kin grouping of four to five generation's depth.

khel— A patri-kin unit among the Assamese Muslims.

Kizhipanam, Kazhipanam,. Kashipanam— Money paid outright to the groom by bride's father.

konthalakkasu— Moplah word for the presentation of money to the bride by the groom.

koppinte kasu— Amount of money left by the bridegroom under his pillow after consummation of marriage.

kotha— Gujar Bakarwal term for mud-stone houses.

kurta— Tunic, pleated at the waist.

ɣuutu— An unnamed exogamous patrilineal group of four to five generation's depth, including patrilineally related males, their wives, and unmarried children.

ma, amma— Mother.

Madrassa— Islamic or Koranic school for younger children, intended for the teaching of the Koran, Arabic and Islam.

magni— Literally, 'asking', the word refers to the ceremony of betrothal.

Mahigir— Title used by Kokni Muslims of indigenous origin to describe themselves.

Mahr— Dower.

maikewale— A woman's natal kin.

mailanchi— ceremony of applying henna juice to the nails, eyes, palms and feet, etc., of the bride.

Maktab— School for elementary religious instruction.

mama— Meo kin term for mother's brother.

mami— Meo kin term for mother's brother's wife.

mamu— Maternal uncle.

mandakam— Moplah term for the bridal chamber.

mangaari— Kokni term for those sent to the bride's house to fetch the bride and groom back to the groom's house or *vice versa*.

mangni— The ceremony of betrothal.

manji— Messenger; the person carrying invitation to a social function.

maosa— Meo kin term for mother's sister's husband.

maosi— Meo kin term for mother's sister's husband.

marumakkathayam— Law relating to succession to the office of the *Karanavar*.

marupudukkam— Moplah term for the ceremony of taking bride to her house.

mattaan— Moplah term for the presentation of trousseau to the bride by the groom.

mazar— Tomb of a Muslim saint.

mannat— Wish.

maulavi— Literally, 'tutor', the word is used as a title of respect for a Muslim religious teacher.

mena— Assamese term for leader of a *chuba*.

mendhi— Henna paste, the ceremony at which henna paste is applied to the bride and bridegroom.

mirasi— Professional musician.

mohalla— Section or ward of a village, town or city.

monthala— Moplah word for shaving of the bridegroom before the wedding.

Mosalu— Gujarati word for gifts brought by groom's and bride's mother's brothers for their respective sisters and sister's husbands.

Motowalli— see *Murrabbi*.

mudal-sambandham— Moplah term for common property relations.

mudium puvum— Moplah term for the ceremony of sending rice and flowers to the bride's house by the groom's side, usually followed by a feast at bride's house.

murrabbi— Arabic word meaning head; Informal leader of a *Khel* among Assamese Muslims.

nakab— the flap of a *burka* covering the face.

namghar— Assamese word for Hindu temple.

Namberdar— Hereditary leader or head of a *patti* among the Meos; person responsible for collecting revenue on behalf of the government in British India.

nana— Maternal grandfather.

nanad— Kin term referring to a woman's husband's sisters.

nandeu-nandoi— Term of reference for a woman's husband's sister's husband.

nani— Maternal grandmother.

navasa— Daughter's son.

navasi— Daughter's daughter.

nepalia— A derogatory Meo term denoting a person not belonging to any *pal*.

neuta— Invitation to a wedding or any other social ceremony.

nikah— Ceremony of marriage contract.

Nikahnama— Legal document listing the details of the marriage contract.

nishchayam— Moplah word for the ceremony of fixing the date of a wedding.

Noor Nama— A religious poem in Gujari language.

Okanni— A rite among Sunni Surati Vohras at which small denomination coins are circled over the head of a bride and then given away to the poor.

oppana— Moplah term for the ceremony of seating the bride before the guests.

pagri— A lump sum of money paid by a tenant at the time of renting accommodation and is in addition to monthly rent; also turban worn by the groom at the time of wedding.

Paanch maang— A custom among the Jamaati Kokni Muslims requiring the bride's party to bring the groom to their village for a five day stay.

pal— An exogamous territorial group among the Meos, supposed to be originally co-terminus with the administrative divisions of the territory of Mewat.

pallakra— An exogamous territorial division among the Meos similar to the *pal* usually inferior to a *pal*.

pandit— Hindu priest.

pangaali— A unit of agnatically related coparceners among Tamil Hindus; the corporate households among Muslims.

panjika—Almanac.

Parisam— Tamil term for valuable gifts sent to the bride by the groom's family.

patti— Neighbourhood or ward of a village; a social group based on fiction of descent from a common ancestor among the Meos.

Panchayat— Literally, 'council of elders', the term denotes caste council.

noani— Assamese Muslim term for the ceremony of giving ritual baths to the bride and bridegroom before marriage.

pardada— Paternal great grandfather.

Pardadi— Paternal great grandmother.

Parnana— Maternal great grandfather.

parnani— Maternal great grandmother.
parpota— Paternal great grandson.
parpoti— Paternal great granddaughter.
phagun— Eleventh month of the Assamese Calendar.
phupha— Father's sister's husband.
phuphi— Father's sister,
pithi— Gujarati word for turmeric; the ceremony at which turmeric paste is applied to the bride and groom.
ponnoppikkal— Moplah term for the ceremonial wedding dress and ornaments of the bride.
pota— Paternal grandson.
poti— Paternal grand daughter.
potbahu— Meo term for paternal grandson's wife.
Pradhan— Village headman.
pudukkam— Tamil word for the ceremony of taking the bride back to the groom's house by women.
puh— Ninth month of the Assamese Calendar.
pula-sambandham— Moplah term for relationship by pollution.
purdah— Veiling of women.
purdawali— A woman in *purdah*.
pun poodutal— Moplah term for a girl's maturation ceremony.
qabeela— Clan.
qarz— Interest free loan obtained from relatives or friends.
qarza— Loan obtained from a bank or a government agency, usually with interest payable on it.
qawwali— Muslim devotional music.
Quran Sharif— Honorific word of reference for the Koran.
qurbani— Sacrifice.
rishta— Literally 'relationship', the term denotes an offer of marriage.
rishtedar— Literally 'relations', the term denotes consanguineal relatives of affines.
rukhsati— The ceremony of sending the bride to her husband's house.
salkaram choru— Dinner meant for bridegroom and his close relatives hosted by the bride's side.
samdhi— Term of reference for the father of one's son's or daughter's spouse.
salwar— Pantaloons.

saram— Corrupt form of the Urdu word 'sharm', meaning 'modesty'.

sas, sass— Gujari word for mother-in-law.

sasur, susra— father-in-law.

sadhu— a man's wife's sister's husband.

sajdah— The Muslim act of prostration in worship.

sali— kin term for one's wife's sisters, especially younger sisters.

sala— Term for one's wife's younger brother; also an abuse.

salaheli— Meo kin term for one's wife's younger brother's spouse.

sarik— Meo kin term used by co-wives to refer to each another.

samdhan—Kin term for the mother of one' son's or daughter's spouse.

satma— Literally 'seventh day', the word denotes the custom requiring the bride's father, brothers and other male relatives to go to her conjugal home and fetch her back.

shadi— Marriage.

shahwala— Gujari corruption of Urdu 'shehbala', meaning bridegroom.

shakt parda— strict observance of *purdah*.

shar, sharia, Shari'at— The law of Islam.

sharara— A full skirt.

shastric— Pertaining to the *shastras*.

shijra— Family tree.

shuddhi— The process of conversion of non-Hindus to Hinduism and reconversion of those already converted to other religions.

sopari— betlenut.

sthridhanam— Moplah word for a woman's property; property made over to bride by her *tharavad*.

sunna— practices and precepts of the Prophet.

surah— any of the 114 chapters of the Koran.

susral— conjugal home.

talaq— Divorce.

tai— Meo kin term for father's elder brother's wife.

tau—kin term for father's elder brother.

tamuli— Assamese Muslim term for the bestman.

taziya— A model or representation of tne Shrines of Hassan and Husain, sons of Ali, cousin and son-in-law of Prophet Muhammad.

tehsil— An administrative sub-division of a district.

temorchi— Uzbeck word for blacksmiths.

tharavads— A matrilineal residence group, usually characteristic of the Nayars and Moplahs.

thama— A sub-division of a Meo *pal*, usually associated with the son of the founder of a *pal*.

urduization— Process of spread or increased use of Urdu as the *lingua franca*.

ustaad— Literally 'teacher', the word refers particularly to a teacher of music.

vadhao— Gift of grain and sugar brought by relatives at the time of wedding for the family of the bride or the groom; the ceremony of presentation of this gift.

valima— dinner given by bridegroom in honour of the bride's relatives.

vamsom— Tamil word for a patrilineage.

vamsh— clan, a social group comprising descendants of a common ancestor.

vakkukodukkal— Literally 'word-giving', the word denotes the formal bethrothal ceremony among Tamil Muslims.

visvakarma Sangam— jewellers' association named after Hindu God of machine and tools.

wadi— Orchard.

wali— guardian.

zat— Urdu equivalent of the word, '*jati*', meaning the effective, endogamous unit of the caste system.

zinat— adornment.

zirga— Gujar Bakarwal tribal council.

Index